URBAN SOCIOLOGY

URBAN SOCIOLOGY

Contemporary Readings

Edited by

Fuad Baali
Western Kentucky University

Joseph S. Vandiver
University of Florida

New York

APPLETON-CENTURY-CROFTS
Educational Division
MEREDITH CORPORATION

CONTENTS

PREFACE

The need to use all relevant knowledge and all relevant skills in meeting the problems of contemporary cities is sufficiently self-evident that the point need not be labored. Sociology is one—perhaps the most basic one—of the academic disciplines which emphasizes both theory and research focused upon the city. Particularly in the United States, urban sociology has developed as an important specialization within the broader discipline of sociology itself. The emergence of urban sociology as a counterpart to the emphasis on rural sociology, and the impetus given to urban sociology by the remarkable men at the University of Chicago who, during the 1920's and 1930's, converted that great city into their sociological laboratory, are among the factors contributing to the distinctiveness of sociology in America.

It is our hope as editors that we have assembled within this volume a series of readings that will introduce the student to the sweep of contemporary urban sociology. The selections should acquaint the reader with the sociologist's way of looking at urbanization as a process and the large city as a community. Although, as it happens, both editors are very interested in the ecological approach which has contributed so much to the development of urban sociology, they agreed that, in this book, ecological perspectives will be introduced as they relate to other topics, rather than being organized into a distinct section. By so doing, it is hoped that the tendency to present urban ecology as a subdiscipline, more or less apart from other sociological orientations, will be avoided.

We have made an effort to include a wide selection of materials which incorporate writings of many widely known urban sociologists. The goal has been to avoid articles by experts upon urban affairs, however stimulating their writings might be, unless those articles seemed specifically sociological in outlook.

Each chapter, organized on a thematic basis, is introduced by a few pages of commentary. As editors we have tried to provide enough linking materials on each topic so that this book may serve as a text in college courses in urban sociology. For those who utilize another volume as a text, this collection of readings will provide useful supplementary materials on almost all themes covered by most texts.

The editors wish to express their deep appreciation to those who assisted in making this book possible. Shari W. Schneider helped with the chores involved in locating and reproducing materials from disparate sources. Assistance by the Office of Sponsored Research of the University of Florida greatly facilitated the fulfillment of our work. We wish especially to mention Mrs. Steven Derr, who took upon herself much of the responsibility for the correspondence concerning permissions, and Richard Galenes, who contributed far more time than his job as an assistant demanded. His counsel was as valuable as his labor. Finally we wish to acknowledge our wives, Linda Baali and Marylee Vandiver, who merit more than customary gratitude for helping to make this book a reality.

F.B. and J.S.V.

INTRODUCTION

Concern with the problems of contemporary man and his adaptation to the urban world of the twentieth century is universal, and the sociologist is one of the professional specialists whose skills are needed in the search for solutions to metropolitan dilemmas. This book, accordingly, presents sociological interpretations which touch upon a broad range of urban problems. To be sure, a few selections were written by social scientists other than sociologists. Robert C. Weaver, to cite an example, is an economist; Oscar Lewis is an anthropologist. The academic discipline with which an author is affiliated was not the definitive criterion, but care was taken to include in this work only those offerings which seemed distinctly relevant from the sociological viewpoint.

In the United States today, the phrase, "the urban crisis," has become a popular designation embracing the entire range of problems which beset the cities, in which, or near which, most Americans reside. Moreover, short of thermonuclear suicide on the part of human societies, it is difficult to imagine an end to the interest in urban and metropolitan affairs. The growth of cities, and the growth of large cities, has become worldwide.

To be sure, the different portions of the world vary in the fractions of their populations which are urban, in rates of urban growth, in impetus to such growth, and in many other respects. The problems perceived in connection with urbanization accordingly differ widely among societies. There are, of course, common problems which inescapably arise wherever large human aggregations develop, but even these are met in a wide variety of ways and with varying degrees of adequacy.

At the risk of oversimplification, two contrasting patterns of metropolitanization in the world today may be identified. In those nations in which industrialization is advanced and in which, generally, the level of living is high, additional migration to the city presumably results for the most part from the attraction—the "pull"—of expanding employment opportunities in the industrial and distributive activities of the large city. Because most such societies already are predominantly urban, additional increments to the metropolitan population tend to be relatively small on a proportional basis.

The contrasting pattern of urban growth today is character-istic of much of the world, including most of Latin America, Africa, and the vast stretch of Asia (except for Japan). In these countries, some of which have enormous rural populations and virtually all of which are now experiencing rapid rates of natural increase, urban-ization is occurring less because the city offers industrial or other opportunities than because of the lack of opportunity—the "push" —in the countryside. The surplus population drifts to the city for lack of any real alternative. In many nations today, such cities are growing with great rapidity. The rural overflow, crowding into the existing city or creating jerry-built slums on the outskirts, in either case forms an enormous *lumpenproletariat*.

One would not suppose that a nation so highly industrialized as the United States would show similarities in its metropolitan growth patterns to the type of growth just described for the devel-oping nations. Such similarities do exist, however. The sheer mas-siveness of the modern migration from American farms has created a vast displacement of former rural residents. The technological revolution on American farms has occurred on so sweeping a scale that the resultant depopulation comprises one of the greatest mass migrations of all times.

In 1935, the farm population of the nation was estimated at more than 32,000,000 people while, in 1967, the comparable figure was only 10,800,000. Although a changed definition of farm resi-dence accounted for a small part of this reduction, the flight from the farms of the bulk of the agricultural population has approached literal depopulation in some areas. When one considers, along with the magnitude of the actual loss of people, the high rates of natural increase which characterized the rural-farm population, one begins to see the scale of the total movement. In the span of one genera-tion, between the mid-1930's and the mid-1960's, a net migration of nearly 30,000,000 persons left American farms.

Migration on this scale takes persons of all kinds—all ages, all educational levels, all economic levels—but of particular impor-tance, as one views the urban crisis in metropolitan America, is the likelihood that the migration has siphoned from the countryside the bulk of its least established, least independent, inhabitants. Because agricultural labor had required little in the way of training, the laborers and sharecroppers and inefficient small farmers who were displaced typically had little to offer a society undergoing automa-tion. All too often, the migrants from the countryside were low in educational level, in economic reserves, and in marketable skills.

A generation ago, most of the very poor residents of America's great cities were the foreign-born, struggling to adjust to a strange

way of life. In those days, the rural poor in the nation were principally of old American stock, white and black. Today, the farm population of the nation has become much more heavily middle-class
than it has ever been before, partly because of the relative prosperity of those farmers who, being technologically efficient, have survived in agriculture, and partly because of the transfer into cities
of a large proportion of the rural poor.

Smith has suggested that not only the technological transformation of American agriculture, but also institutionalization of
public assistance, has contributed to the urbanward shift of the
poor.[1] Before the assumption of governmental responsibility for
aiding the indigent—that is, before the 1930's—the very poor in
America tended to eke out an existence based on whatever resources
were available from relatives and from such public and private
sources of poor relief as existed. The lower costs of rural living, and
the possibility of supplementing food supplies through patch farming and perhaps a few chickens and a cow, led such people to
remain in or drift toward the country. During the early 1930's,
there was a definite back-to-the-farm movement of this type. With
the establishment of governmental responsibility for public assistance, subsistence agricultural areas ceased to be a haven for the
poor. Indeed, the greater access in the city to the specialized personnel and services provided through welfare programs has presumably had quite the opposite effect.

The majority of migrants from American agricultural areas
during the 1940's, 1950's, and 1960's were white, but many, very
many, of them were black. Negro migrants, maintaining the great
movement from the plantation areas which started during World
War I, continued to move from farms into the cities, South and
North. Many of these migrants moved not merely to the cities, but
to the big cities, and not merely to the big cities, but to the inner
cities. Many of these migrants were among the least prepared of all
farm residents for effective incorporation into the metropolitan
economy. Compounding their difficulties of adaptation, great in any
event, have been the additional disadvantages of discrimination in
employment, in housing, and in other aspects of American life. The
cities of the nation have therefore become the action centers of the
struggle of black Americans for a sense of identity, for recognition,
and for achievement.

The rates of crime have always been high in urban America,
whether the basis of comparison is with less urbanized parts of our
own society or with cities of other Western nations. The influx of
millions of ill-prepared migrants from rural America has intensi-

[1] Suggested by T. Lynn Smith in conversation with one of the editors.

fied the problems of law enforcement in the crowded low-income areas, white or Negro. Racial tensions have exacerbated the difficulties. Riots in the ghettos, disorders on campuses, protests against American war policy, indeed, all the forms of civil disturbance, added to the chronic and apparently increasing hazard of crime, have led to much of the contemporary concern over the "urban crisis." In a report in 1968 on "the urban unease," Wilson noted that a poll of residents in one of our large metropolitan centers showed that the traditional urban problems of housing, transportation, pollution, etc., were far overshadowed by concern over the disorderliness and hazards which they perceived as characterizing the city of today. "The common theme," he reports, "seemed to be a concern for improper behavior in public places."[2]

Modern forms of rapid transit have eliminated the former necessity for most persons to live relatively close to their work. The move toward the suburbs, long established as a trend, became greatly accelerated in the United States and other Western nations following the end of World War II. In the United States, as many metropolitan residents now live outside the central cities as reside within them, and current patterns of growth suggest that this movement toward the metropolitan periphery will continue. Such expansion in the future may occur in the largely uncoordinated manner of most suburbanization in the past. It may, on the other hand, increasingly occur in "new towns," such as Reston, Virginia; or Columbia, Maryland. The one safe assumption appears to be that growth will continue around the urban perimeter.

The chapters that follow will present topics ranging from the origin and development of cities through urbanization as a process, urbanism as a way of life, suburbanization, social organization in the urban setting, the neighborhood in the city, and urban pathology, to conclude with a consideration of the importance of planning for the urban life of the future.

---

[2] James Q. Wilson, "The Urban Unease: Community vs. City," *The Public Interest* (No. 12, Summer, 1968), 25–39.

URBAN SOCIOLOGY

Chapter 1

THE ORIGIN AND DEVELOPMENT
OF CITIES

To contemporary man, the city is a "natural" and expected place to
live. In many Western and industrialized nations, the majority of
all the population lives in urban communities, and throughout the
world, cities are growing rapidly. It is true that urban residents
preserve many traditions and many values which indicate the persistence of rural thought patterns in the city. It is equally or even
more important, however, that the urban impact upon rural communities has diffused urban orientations far beyond the limits of
the cities. Man's life today in many parts of the globe is an urbanized life, and the prospect for tomorrow is that this will become
characteristic of more and more of the world.

It is only within the past 100 or 150 years that societies, truly
urbanized in the modern sense, began to appear. Cities themselves,
in their preindustrial form, emerged only after advanced Neolithic
cultures were well established. It is now rather widely held that the
very earliest cities emerged about 4000 B.C., probably in what is
now Iraq.

Accustomed as we are to the prevalence of cities, and of big
cities, we may fail to realize how basic a step the emergence of the
earliest cities represented in the development of human societies.
The first cities, small as they might seem from our own viewpoint,
were differentiated from previously existing communities by two
basic criteria: they were larger in total population; they contained

1

within their population large numbers of workers who were not directly involved in the food quest.

The very existence of such a community necessarily demonstrated that certain rather complex cultural achievements had been made. Obviously, and basically, no society could support an urban community unless the food producers—the farmers, the herdsmen—had reached a level of efficiency that yielded surplus production. It was necessary that the average farmer or herdsman not only feed himself, his family, and have something left over, but that he be able to do this dependably, permitting communities to develop in which there lived many people who were not compelled themselves to produce the actual necessities of existence.

The very existence of the city required, further, a regular flow of transport of the agricultural surplus into the city. Whether by boat, in wagons, on the backs of animals, or by human portage, there inevitably existed routes for such transport, and the regular use of such routes.

The existence of the city demonstrated the emergence of specialization. There is no reason to suppose that food producers ever relinquished the surplus created by their labor out of sheer love of urban brethren; something was received in return. Specialized religious activities, military protection, planning and coordination of irrigation systems, the handiwork of artisans and craftsmen, these and other urban activities provided the countryman with services and goods which compensated him for the materials which he contributed to the town.

The existence of a city, depending upon the flow of surplus production into the community and the return flow of services or goods to the rural producers, inevitably involved a fairly complex system of distribution and/or exchange. A market, more fixed and more continuous than the periodic open markets of the countryside, was the typical, although not the only possible, setting in which such exchange occurred. Fixed, continuing markets ultimately led to shops, to stores.

The administrative complexity of the priestly, military, political, and market functions of the emerging city created relationships and obligations too involved to be kept in mind by all. Some form of record keeping, some form of writing, developed with urbanization. There are exceptions; in pre-Columbian Peru and in sub-Saharan Africa, sizable cities developed with no system of writing. Even with exceptions duly noted, the general concurrence of urban development and the need to maintain permanent records seems quite clear.

The emergence of cities, in short, marked the transition of societies from primitive to civilized. Man moved from the Neolithic into the age of written history.

Cities of the ancient world, of necessity, lived in close symbiotic linkage with their hinterlands. The potential size of the city was limited by the resources of the area from which it could draw its sustenance. As imperial centers emerged, the area of this hinterland became greatly magnified, although very often much of the area tributary to the large city was despoiled in the process.

Until relatively recent times, other factors as well limited the development and growth of cities. Important among these limitations was the unhealthfulness of the congested community. Cities offered man the opportunity to be in the center of activity, but they also subjected him to a particularly high risk of contagion. Deaths outnumbered births in most cities of the past, even during fairly normal conditions. Plague, siege, famine, flood periodically cut heavily into the base population of the cities. Throughout most of the past, migration from the countryside to the city was necessary, not only if the city were to grow but even if it were to be maintained.

The technological transformations of the past two centuries have altered the conditions of urban life. No longer is any city so completely dependent upon a given hinterland for its subsistence as was earlier true. The intricate functional specialization, which enables the contemporary city to operate, creates its own problems and its own threats of chaos when essential elements in the web of mutual dependence cease to operate, but these are problems of a different order. Despite such problems, despite growing problems of pollution, of crime, of racial tensions, and despite the sheer inconveniences and annoyances so often ascribed to metropolitan existence—despite all of these things, contemporary cities are not unhealthful locations. Their populations do grow through natural increase; the most highly urbanized nations of the earth are among those of greatest longevity.

The selection from Robert C. Cook gives an overview of the development of cities. Cook traces the emergence and growth of cities in the past, describes their magnitude today, and offers a warning of the threat to the future inherent in uncontrolled population growth.

In the second selection presented here, Smith makes no effort to discuss the origin of cities or their development throughout time. His approach is to interpret changes from colonial times to the present in terms of the functions served by cities in Latin America.

Smith's insistence that adequate study of cities requires that urban functions be analyzed is a principle capable of generalization. More specifically, his interpretation of the emerging functions of Latin American cities can also be considered meaningfully in connection with the selection in the next chapter by Harroy, which also deals with urbanization in the developing countries of the world.

The World's Great Cities:
Evolution or Devolution

ROBERT C. COOK

Editor, *Population Bulletin*

A major side-effect of the unprecedented speed-up in world population growth today is the ever-increasing concentration of people in cities the world over.

The rate of city growth will continue to vary in different areas of the world, decelerating in the older, industrial countries and accelerating in the agrarian, underdeveloped countries which hold two thirds of the world's people.

Urbanization is a vastly different process in those countries than it was in the West where the Industrial Revolution generated the capital needed to build the economies which could provide for the growing populations. Jobs were plentiful in the industrial cities of the West, and this provided the "pull" for the countless millions who migrated, and still do, from country to city.

The situation is often the reverse in the underdeveloped countries today. There, the "push" is the gross overcrowding of the rural population living at or near the bare subsistence level. More often than not, the migrant goes to an even more precarious urban situation where he cannot find work readily and must spend his limited savings. From the socio-economic and humanitarian points of view, the trek to the cities in the underdeveloped countries will continue to be more of a curse than a blessing as it absorbs limited capital and generates tension.

Today, there are 61 cities with a million people or more in the world, compared with only ten in 1900.

Condensed from the *Population Bulletin*, September, 1960. Published by the Population Reference Bureau, Inc., 1755 Massachusetts Avenue, N.W., Washington, D.C., 20036. Reprinted by publisher's permission. (The research report for this *Bulletin* was prepared by Selma R. Rein. The *Bulletin* was written by Annabelle Desmond.)

Now, two people out of every ten live in cities of 20,000 or more population. If the present trend continues—and there is every indication that it will for some time—almost half the world's population will live in cities that size by 2000; and by 2050, nine people out of every ten.

The giant of all time, the New York-northeastern New Jersey metropolitan agglomeration, has a population of over 14.5 million, according to preliminary tabulations from the 1960 census. That is more than the combined population of Australia and New Zealand; and it is almost half the entire population of Mexico!

New York's borough of Manhattan shows a 15 percent decline in population since the 1950 census. But with 1.7 million people Manhattan's population density is 75,900 per square mile.

On the other side of the world, Calcutta's population of 5.7 million is small in comparison. But projections based on current trends would give Calcutta a population of between 35 and 66 million by the year 2000! At Manhattan's density, Calcutta would sprawl over an area about as large as Rhode Island.

Obviously, such a projection is merely a *reductio ad absurdum*. The problems of food distribution and sanitation in the absence of very rapid economic development, are only two of many factors which would cause death rates to rise and check such multiplication of people long before standing-room-only develops.

Few people seem to understand that the pattern of tomorrow's city is being formed by today's rapid population growth. Will the city remain the traditional center of culture or will it degenerate into a socio-economic sinkhole for mankind?

Can the sprawling shantytowns which make up the cities of Asia, Africa and Latin America evolve into habitable places which provide adequate services so necessary to urban life?

Will the shabby, decaying, smog-ridden central cities of the industrial West be cleansed of the blight which has been accumulating since the Industrial Revolution began? Or, will the deteriorating central cities continue to sprawl out at an even faster rate, consuming untold acres of prime farm land with their insatiable appetite for space? Will these cities be able to win back the fleeing, more prosperous residents and the industries whose tax revenue is essential to their financial stability?

As man increasingly becomes a city-born and city-bred creature, the problems of city living and city organization will intensify in complexity and embrace the planet. Drift and improvisation cannot solve them. Dynamic global action is essential now if the cities of tomorrow are to have a true, not imagined, relationship to the needs and enduring values of the people who will live in them.

FROM THE BEGINNING

Today's cities trace their origin to the villages of pre-history where a few hundred people lived and walked each day to their fields to produce the food necessary for survival. As animal domestication and the development of agriculture increased the efficiency of food production, those people who were no longer needed to tend the land became potters, spinners, weavers and other artisans.

The great cities of ancient time rose in India's rich alluvial Indus valley, in the lands adjacent to the Mediterranean, the Red Sea, and the Persian Gulf and in China. They were relatively small places covering a few square miles. Little is known about the size of the population of these ancient cities. Obviously, that was controlled by the agricultural economies which supported them, and the agricultural surpluses which made urban societies possible were never very large. Until about 1000 B.C., it is believed that no more than 1 or 2 percent of the world's population were city dwellers, and that these pre-historic metropolises did not exceed 100,000 people. Until very recently, urban communities have been dangerous places to live because, with primitive amenities, and no knowledge of the cause and control of disease, even low degrees of congestion invited epidemics. Brutally high death rates appear to have held life expectancy at birth to no more than about 20 years.

With the growth of population, the city grew in size. As its population pressed ever-more severely on the food supply, the city had to absorb more land. According to Harrison Brown, Professor of Geochemistry, California Institute of Technology, land seizure and the right to water were frequent causes of war; and many wars were started by "half-starved barbarians who cast envious eyes upon urban wealth and decided to attempt to take it for their own." Often they succeeded. Discussing the rise and fall of those early cities, Dr. Brown states:

The populations of the ancient oriental empires were eventually limited by deaths resulting from starvation, disease, and war, and, to a lesser extent, by conscious control of conception, by abortion, and by infanticide. Sanitation measures were seldom taken, except in the homes of the higher classes. Famine surged over the ancient lands at frequent intervals. As the crowded conditions, the filth, and the food situation in the ancient cities worsened, contagious diseases, and with them high rates of infant mortality, prevailed.

* * *

Thus increased mortality and, to a lesser extent, conscious family limitation continuously lowered the rate of population growth in the ancient oriental empires. But in the new regions where urban culture was surging upward, populations grew rapidly. The changes resulted in the destruction of old civilizations and the creation of new ones.

The fascinating history of the world's great cities cannot be told in limited space. Only the briefest discussion of the urbanization of Europe is possible here.

Many of the world's ancient cities were already in ruins by the time the Greco-Roman civilization (600 B.C. to 400 A.D.) arose and created the first great cities of the west. New civilizations in the Orient were also building proud and beautiful new cities, and many of these flourished along the great trade routes of Europe and Asia.

Athens and Rome were among the first great cities on the European continent. Rome, Alexandria and Byzantium (Constantinople, and now called Istanbul) became the giants of the period, with estimated peak populations of 350,000, 216,000 and 190,000, respectively. Some historians allege that Rome had over a million people at her zenith. Athens, Syracuse and Carthage had populations of 120,000 to 200,000.

During the early days of the Greek and Roman Empires, population growth remained in balance with the food supply. But the rapid growth of the cities soon put heavy pressure on the productive capacity of the land. Unfortunately, Greek civilization evolved in a region where only 20 percent of the land area could be cultivated, and this placed severe limits on food production. As the cities grew, their populations became increasingly dependent upon imports of grain from outlying districts and provinces. As the demand for food grew, hills and mountains were laid bare of their forests. Few of those areas have recovered from the exploitative land practices prevalent during the golden years of the Greek Empire.

The Roman Empire repeated this pattern but destruction extended over a vastly greater area. The insatiable appetite of the rapidly growing population denuded Italy's hills and mountains and made deserts of untold millions of acres along the Mediterranean. Again, as the population of the Italian peninsula grew rapidly, grain imports from adjacent regions and then from Africa became necessary to feed the multitudes. As the center of the empire continued to pile up population, the desperate need for food spurred Roman conquest. According to the historian, V. G. Simkovitch:

Province after province was turned by Rome into a desert, for Rome's exactions naturally compelled greater exploitation of the conquered soil and its more rapid exhaustion. Province after province was conquered by Rome to feed the growing proletariat with its corn and enrich the prosperous with its loot. The only exception was Egypt, because of the overflow of the Nile . . . Latium, Campania, Sardinia, Sicily, Spain, Northern Africa, as Roman granaries, were successively reduced to exhaustion. Abandoned land in Latium and Campania turned into swamps, in Northern Africa into a desert. The forest-clad hills were denuded.

With the fall of the Roman Empire, Europe entered a period of population ebb which lasted from about 450 to 950 A.D. Italy, Gaul, Iberia, North Africa, Greece and Egypt were especially affected, and so were their cities. It has been estimated that Rome had about 350,000 people at the time of Augustus, 241,000 around 200 A.D., 172,600 about 350 A.D., 36,000—48,000 about 500 A.D., and only 30,000 in the 10th century. Cities of fairly considerable size had grown up elsewhere. Baghdad with an estimated population of 300,000 was the capital of the Caliphate Empire. Cordoba with 90,000, and Seville with 52,000 had risen in Moorish Spain. Constantinople with its 160,000 to 200,000 inhabitants was the pride of the Byzantine Empire.

Usually new cities of the period arose around an old Roman armed camp, at a crossing of a river, around a church, an abbey or a fortified chateau. Frequent wars made high places desirable locations for cities of the Middle Ages because they were easily defended. Many of these cities had two settlements, one on the heights and another nearby on a plain which provided water and fields for cultivation. A relatively small population lived within a walled area, and as population grew the walls were extended.

When Europe's population began to increase again during the 10th century, cities began to grow and the number of villages also increased. This period of growth came to an abrupt halt in 1348 when the bubonic plague swept across Europe. It has been estimated that 20 to 25 percent of the people died in two disastrous years, and that by 1400 this and other epidemics had reduced the continent's population to about 60 percent of the pre-plague level.

FROM THE RENAISSANCE TO THE INDUSTRIAL REVOLUTION, 1400-1800

Population grew slowly during the first part of the Renaissance and accelerated toward the end of the period. City population followed the general pattern. In Italy, the cradle of the Renaissance, the population of Florence shifted up and down while that of Venice and Rome about doubled.

Two of the giants of modern times, London and Paris, were testing their growth during this period. Estimates of the population of Paris by 1550 range from 130,000 to 500,000.

The impact of technology on population growth was even more

abundantly demonstrated during the period 1600-1800. Technological advances in transportation gave great impetus to commerce and exploration. The people of northern Europe began the colonization of the New World, and this siphoned off some of the surplus population. Cities were established along the Atlantic coast of North America and many maritime cities of Europe grew rapidly. As the empty lands of America were filled up by the descendants of immigrants from Europe, the frontier pushed westward.

The vast breadbaskets of North America made food more plentiful in Europe. Prior to the American Revolution, Edmund Burke noted that England's annual import of grain from America exceeded a million pounds in value. The population of the North American continent grew at a rate of from 20 to 30 percent a decade after the initial settlement, but not all of this growth was due to natural increase. Immigration had been an important factor in the population growth of the United States from 1620 until World War I.

During the 17th and 18th centuries, the foundations were laid for many of the great European fortunes which later supplied the capital needed to spark the Industrial Revolution. In England, technological advances in mining, manufacturing and agriculture were setting the stage for that revolution which ushered in the most rapid population growth the world and many of its cities had ever known. The conversion of two million acres of waste land and forest to farming during the 18th century greatly increased agricultural productivity and the food surplus available for the urban population.

The discovery which possibly had a greater impact on population growth than any other was made by the British physician, Edward Jenner, whose vaccination against smallpox was introduced in 1792. This initial step in man's ability to defer death opened the way for controlling the diseases and epidemics which had flourished in villages and cities since the beginning of time. To Pasteur and an army of microbe and virus hunters who have followed Jenner goes the credit for making the city a relatively safe place in which to live.

THE INDUSTRIAL-URBAN REVOLUTION, 1800-1900

Throughout history, cities have often experienced rapid spurts of growth, but the tremendous growth potential they now display could not have developed without the techniques of modern medicine, public health and sanitation. These made cities safe havens for the rapidly increasing working class of the Industrial Revolution. In England, the death rate began to fall about 1730 and it continued a leisurely downward trend for more than two centuries. The slow pace of that decline allowed another important phenomenon to develop—a slow decline in the birth rate. This appears to have occurred first in France about the middle of the 17th century, in Ireland during the 1820's, in the United States after 1830 and in England during the 1870's.

In 1798, Thomas Robert Malthus, a 32-year-old curate who was astounded by the rabbit-like proliferation of the working people living in misery and squalor, published his famous critical analysis on the problem of poverty in England. He insisted that to effect a cure of the "unspeakable ills of society" it would be necessary to get to the root of the matter. As Malthus viewed the problem, "the poverty and misery arising from a too rapid increase of population had been distinctly seen, and the most violent remedies proposed, so long ago as the times of Plato and Aristotle." Malthus defined the problem in these terms: *How to provide for those who are in want in such a manner as to prevent a continual increase in their numbers and of the proportion which they bear to the whole society.*

Malthus was followed by a succession of "pamphleteers"—one was Francis Place, a working man himself—who denounced the congestion and miserable living conditions and urged the working people to have fewer children. Finally, in 1876, the right to discuss fertility control was established in the British Isles when the government lost the case of "Regina *vs* Charles Bradlaugh and Annie Besant." This decision established the right to distribute a pamphlet concerning birth control which had been widely circulated throughout England for 40 years and it opened the way to free dissemination of fertility control information.

Kingsley Davis, one of this country's leading students of urbanization, points to several factors which helped the cities of western Europe achieve a much higher degree of urbanization than the ancient cities:

Yet it was precisely in western Europe, where cities and urbanization had reached a nadir during the Dark Ages, that the limitations that had characterized the ancient world were finally to be overcome. The cities of Mesopotamia, India, and Egypt, of Persia, Greece, and Rome, had all been tied to an economy that was primarily agricultural, where handicraft played at best a secondary role and where the city was still attempting to supplement its economic weakness with military strength, to command its sustenance rather than to buy it honestly. In western Europe, starting at the zero point, the development of cities not only reached the stage that the ancient world had achieved but kept going after that. It kept going on the basis of improvements in agriculture and

12   Urban Sociology

TABLE 1-1. TOTAL WORLD POPULATION AND WORLD URBAN POPULATION:
1800-1950

		Population (in millions) living in localities of:			Percent of world population living in localities of:		
Year	World population	20,000 to 100,000	100,000 and over	Total	20,000 to 100,000	100,000 and over	Total
1800	906	6.1	15.6	21.7	0.7	1.7	2.4
1850	1,171	22.9	27.5	50.4	2.0	2.3	4.3
1900	1,608	59.3	88.6	147.9	3.7	5.5	9.2
1950	2,400	188.5	313.7	502.2	7.8	13.1	20.9

Source: United Nations, *Report on the World Social Situation*, New York, 1957, p. 114. (Based on data from Kingsley Davis and Hilda Hertz.)

transport, the opening of new lands and new trade routes, and, above all, the rise in productive activity, first in highly organized handicraft and eventually in a revolutionary new form of production—the factory run by machinery and fossil fuel. The transformation thus achieved in the nineteenth century was the true urban revolution, for it meant not only the rise of a few scattered towns and cities but the appearance of genuine urbanization, in the sense that a substantial portion of the population lived in towns and cities.

England, the world's most highly urbanized country today, is the classical example of the processes of industrialization and urbanization because she led the world in both. By 1801, 26 percent of the population of England and Wales lived in cities of 5,000 or more; and 21 percent in cities of 10,000 or more. The United States did not reach this degree of urbanization until 1880 when 25 percent of the population lived in cities of 5,000 or more. In contrast, only about 20 percent of India's population live in cities of that size today.

By 1861, 55 percent of the total population of England lived in urban areas; and by 1891, 72 percent, with only 1.3 percent of the population living in urban districts smaller than 3,000 population. Until 1861, the rural population suffered a relative decline in numbers as cities grew more rapidly. The numerical peak of the rural population, 9.1 million, was reached in 1861. It declined 11 percent, to 8.1 million by 1891.

London, a mud flat on the banks of the Thames when Caesar arrived, grew from 864,800 to 4,232,000 between 1801 and 1891—an increase of almost 400 percent. In 1891, Greater London with 5.6 million people, three fourths of whom lived in the city proper and the remainder in the "outer-ring," had the distinction of being the world's largest city. It covered an area of 690 square miles and included every parish of which any part was within 12 miles of

Charing Cross. Today, it has an area of 722 square miles, and includes the Administrative County of London (London AC) also Middlesex County, and parts of Surrey, Hertfordshire, Essex and Kent Counties. The population of Greater London is slightly over 8.2 million. London AC which includes the City of London and 28 metropolitan boroughs is identical with the 1891 area. It comprises 117 square miles and has a population of 3.2 million that represents a 28 percent decline from its 1901 peak.

Between 1811 and 1891, England's large cities with 100,000 population increased from 1.2 million to more than 9.2 million. Although London absorbed a lesser share of this growth, 14.6 percent of Britain's population lived in the capital city of 1891 and 17.3 percent lived in the other large cities. In terms of the aggregate urban population, 44 percent resided in London and the 23 large cities.

USA DURING THE 1800's

The first census was taken in 1790, soon after the Republic was born. It reported a population of 3,929,214. Only 5 percent lived in the 24 "urban" places of 2,500 population or more. Obviously, the rural-urban distinction was not clear-cut, and most of the people lived under essentially rural conditions. The largest cities were port cities: Philadelphia, New York, Boston, Charleston and Baltimore. According to Conrad and Irene B. Taeuber who are leading authorities on the growth of population in the United States:

The clustering of settlers in small compact groupings began early, but the leading places of the colonial period were small. Boston, the largest place in the American colonies, had about 4,500 inhabitants in 1680. Ten years later the number had climbed to 7,000, but it required nearly 50 years to double this number. A decline of some 1,500 persons in the 10 years after 1740 is attributed to smallpox and war. Before recovery to the 1740 figure had occurred, the Revolutionary War had begun, and with it came a further reduction. The estimates for 1780 place Boston's numbers at only 10,000. After that war, the city recovered rapidly, and by the time of the first census in 1790, its total population was reported as 18,000. But by then both Philadelphia and New York had overtaken Boston, with Philadelphia in the lead. In 1790, the leading cities were Philadelphia, New York, Boston, Charleston (South Carolina), and Baltimore.

As in the Old World, urban growth in the United States was stimulated by the rapid rate of population growth and the accelerating pace of technology. The abundance of fertile land could sustain an ever-growing urban population. Land was easy to own. People married early, had children early and had many of them.

The port cities were the first to grow, then as traffic on rivers and canals pushed industrialization beyond the coastal areas, new cities began to rise. After 1840, the railroads became the most important single factor in the formation of new cities and their growth.

Every decade since the first census in 1790, with the exception of that of 1870, urban population grew faster than rural. The decade of 1840 recorded the most rapid urban growth when the population in urban places almost doubled. But the urban increase was not numerically larger than the rural until the Civil War. Since 1860, with the single exception of the 1870's, every decade has shown greater urban than rural numerical growth. From 1880 until 1940, urban growth has accounted for from 60 to 90 percent of total growth. Between 1940 and 1950, United States population increased by 19 million, rural population declined 3 million while urban population grew by 22 million!

By 1900, the nation's population had grown to nearly 76 million. Almost 40 percent lived in urban areas—ten times as many people as in 1800. The number of urban areas with 2,500 population or more had increased to 1,737 by 1900. There were 38 places of 100,000 or more in the United States and, collectively, they claimed 19 percent of the country's population.

The first great city of over 100,000, New York, reached that mark in 1820. In 1790, New York City had only 33,131 people. By 1960, it had over 7.7 million, and that represents a 23,172 percent increase in 170 years.

The total population of the five largest cities has grown from 7.6 million in 1900 to 17.3 million in 1960. Now, one out of every ten United States citizens lives in these five cities.

While urban agglomeration and the growth of suburbs were well advanced by 1900, the nation had experienced nothing comparable to the rapid urban growth which was to take place during the next 60 years. By 1900, there were already 50 urban areas which would have qualified as "principal standard metropolitan areas" under the 1950 census definition, i.e., having a population of 100,-000 or over. These contained 24 million people, almost one third of the total U.S. population.

WORLD-WIDE URBANIZATION 1900-1960

World population is growing at an unprecedented rate today. The world still is far from a city world, even though it has been moving in that direction at an ever-accelerating rate since 1800. However, urbanization will continue to spread for some time to come as the under-developed areas strive for economic development.

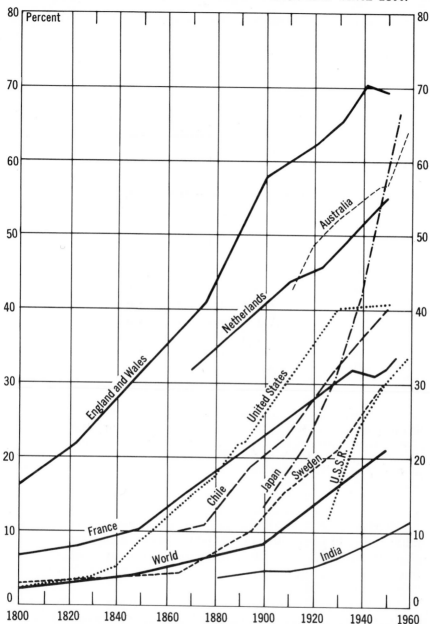

FIGURE 1-1. THE GROWTH OF URBAN POPULATIONS SINCE 1800.

Here is shown the percent of the total population of various countries living in localities of 20,000 or more. (The unit is 25 or more for the United States and Sweden.) For the world as a whole the proportion of dwellers in medium-size and large cities has quadrupled, from under 5 percent to over 20 percent. In the United States the proportion has increased tenfold as the nation has shifted from predominantly rural to one of the most highly urbanized countries. (Data from United Nations *Report on the World Social Situation* and other sources.)

FIGURE 1-2. THE INCREASE IN WORLD AND URBAN POPULATION.

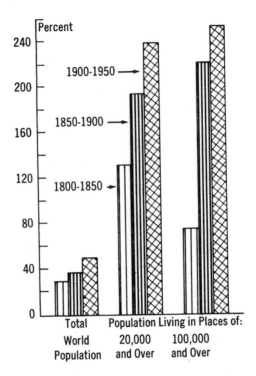

This graph shows the percentage increase in the total population of the world and of the population living in medium-size and large cities since the early part of the Industrial Revolution. During this time, world population increased at a rate unprecedented in previous history, but the movement into cities was far more rapid. In these explosive growing urban areas will be found some of the most serious political, social and economic problems in the next fifty years.

Today, over 20 percent of the world's people, or more than 500 million, live in urban areas of 20,000 or more, compared with only about 2 percent in 1800. Over three fifths of today's urbanites live in large cities of 100,000 or more, and they represent 13 percent of total world population.

In 1900, there were ten cities with one million or more population in the world: five in Europe, three in North America and only one in Asia and in Russia. In 1955, there were 61 cities of that size. Of the 28 in Asia, nine were in China and six in India. Europe had 16 cities of a million or more and the United States had five.

Urban growth rates reached their peak in Europe and America during the latter part of the 19th century and tapered off after that. They have been most rapid in Asia and Africa during the first half of the 20th century. The United Nations *Report on the World Social Situation*, published in 1957, carries a detailed discussion of world urbanization which includes chapters on "Social Problems of Urbanization in Economically Underdeveloped Areas," "Urbanization in Africa South of the Sahara" and "Urbanization in Latin America." The Report utilizes the research of many leading students of urbanization, and its tables and graphs summarize historical and present growth trends. This [account] draws heavily on that important document.

TABLE 1-2. POPULATION IN LARGE CITIES (100,000 AND OVER) BY MAJOR
CONTINENTAL REGIONS

Area	Population (in millions) in large cities				As percent of total population			
	1800	1850	1900	1950	1800	1850	1900	1950
World	15.6	27.5	88.6	313.7	1.7	2.3	5.5	13.1
Asia	9.8	12.2	19.4	105.6	1.6	1.7	2.1	7.5
Europe*	5.4	13.2	48.0	118.2	2.9	4.9	11.9	19.9
Africa	0.30	0.25	1.4	10.2	0.3	0.2	1.1	5.2
America	0.13	1.8	18.6	74.6	0.4	3.0	12.8	22.6
Oceania	—	—	1.3	5.1	—	—	21.7	39.2

* Including USSR
Source: United Nations, *Report on the World Social Situation*, New York, 1957, p. 114. (Based on data from Kingsley Davis and Hilda Hertz.)

The speed-up in population growth in the economically underdeveloped areas of the world is accompanied by the traditional acceleration in the growth of cities in those areas. Discussing present and future trends, the Report states:

A major factor in the present and the anticipated future acceleration is the sudden spurt of urban growth in economically under-developed countries. Between 1900 and 1950, the population living in cities of 100,000 or more in Asia mounted from an estimated 19.4 million to 105.6 million (a gain of 444 percent), and in Africa from 1.4 million to 10.2 million (a gain of 629 percent).
... the large-city population of Asia and Africa has increased much more rapidly during the twentieth century than it did during the nineteenth century while in Europe and America, urban growth reached its peak in the latter part of the nineteenth century and slowed down thereafter. These shifting rates of growth have meant that Asia, which contained nearly two-thirds of the world's population in large cities in 1800, had less than a fourth by 1900; but then the trend started to reverse, and by 1950 Asia had one-third of the world's large-city population.

The Report compares the difference between the present trend of urban growth and urbanization in Asia and Africa with the trends in Europe during the first half of this century:

In spite of rapid urban growth, the increase in degree of urbanization in Asia and Africa still did not equal the increase in Europe during 1900-1950. The reason for this paradox lies in the distinction . . . between urban growth and urbanization. While the population of Asia living in cities of 100,000 or more increased prodigiously from 19.4 million in 1900 to 105.6 million in 1950, the percentage of the total population living in such cities increased only from 2.1 per cent to 7.5 per cent; in other words, there was only a 5.4 per cent shift in the structure of the total population, while in Europe there was an 8 per cent shift in the same period. Because the urban population still represents only a small proportion of the total population in Asia (and other less developed regions), a small change in the degree of urbanization will produce a large amount of urban growth; or conversely stated, a large amount of urban growth is required to make a significant impact upon the population structure.

In the majority of the less developed countries, the rural population has continued to grow along with the urban population, although at a slower pace, but in many of the developed countries the absolute size of the rural population has remained constant or even declined in recent decades, so that the national population increase has been absorbed by the already heavy urban population.

Noting that there are important differences in the levels and trends of urbanization among the industrially more advanced countries and among the less developed countries, the Report states:

. . . Several of the economically less-developed countries, particularly in Latin America, have higher levels of urbanization—as measured by this particular criterion—than certain European countries.

. . . Some of the more urbanized and industrialized countries experienced a marked slowing-down of their urbanization rate during the period between 1930 and 1950 . . . France, the United States and (between 1940 and 1950) Japan; England and Wales actually experienced a slight drop between 1941 and 1951. Such a slowing-down or regression may be due to several possible factors: the reaching or approaching of a natural limit of urbanization, depending upon the economy of the country; the effects of the depression of the 1930's and of the Second World War; a shift from city growth to suburban growth—with the improvement of transportation and the overcrowding of cities, suburban localities are growing much more rapidly than cities proper in a number of countries (the United States is an outstanding example). The relative weight of these different factors is not known.

Other countries have shown a remarkable increase in degree of urbanization since 1930. This includes Puerto Rico and the USSR. In the latter country, between 1926 and 1955, while the total population increased only 34 per cent, the population in cities of 100,000 or more increased more than four times.

. . . Ceylon on the other hand, is remaining relatively stable at a low level of urbanization.

DIFFERENCES IN THE PATTERN OF URBANIZATION

In 1950, the world's major regions of industrial urban settlement were Australasia, Northwestern Europe, Northern America, Northeast Asia and Southern South America. These areas included about 25 percent of total world population, but 52 percent living in cities of 100,000 or more. By major world areas, Africa was the least urbanized, with only 9 percent of the population in cities of 20,000 or more. Australasia was the most heavily urbanized, with 47 percent in cities of that size.

During the past 25 years, the two largest countries of the communist world, USSR and China, have experienced very rapid urbanization. In the USSR in 1959, 48 percent of the total population was living in cities, compared with only 32 percent in 1939. In 20 years, the urban population grew by almost 40 million, an increase of two thirds. In 1959, 23 percent of the total population and almost 50 percent of the urban population lived in cities of 100,000 or more. Since 1939, many new cities have risen in the USSR. The seven largest are: Kaliningrad, 202,000; Angarsk, 134,000; Klaypeda, 89,000; Yuzhno-Sakhalinsk, 86,000; Volzhskiy, 67,000; Vorkuta, 65,000; Oktyabrskiy, 65,000.

It has been estimated that 20 million Chinese migrated from rural to urban areas between 1949 and 1956. This almost equals the total population of the three Benelux countries and "undoubtedly constitutes one of history's largest population shifts in so short a time ..." China's inland cities have experienced fantastic growth. Estimates indicate that in the western provinces alone, Lanchow grew from 200,000 in 1950 to 680,000 in 1956; Paotow from 90,000 in 1949 to 430,000 in 1957; Kalgan from 270,000 in 1949 to over 630,000 in 1958; Sian from less than one-half million in 1949 to 1,050,000 in 1957.

Furthermore, there is a heavy concentration of China's urban population in her large cities. In 1953, 103 cities of 100,000 or more accounted for 49 million people, or 63 percent of the total urban population. However, only 13 percent of the total population lived in cities. In contrast, about 46 percent of the United States urban population lived in cities of 100,000 or more in 1950, and 64 percent of our total population lived in urban localities.

The growth rate of the urban population of the USSR between 1950 and 1959 was 4 percent per annum. In China between 1949 and 1956 the urban growth rate appears to have been at the rate of 6.5 percent per annum.

Within countries, there are great variations in extent and rate of urbanization. For example, in 1950, the northeastern part of the United States had one quarter of the total population and one third of its urban population. Within this region, Vermont had the lowest degree of urbanization (36 percent), while New Jersey had the highest (87 percent).

In some regions of the world, a single large city—usually the capital city—contains a high proportion of a nation's total popula-

TABLE 1-3. ESTIMATED POPULATION OF WORLD'S 20 GREATEST METROPOL-
ITAN AGGLOMERATIONS

Metropolitan Area	Year	Population (in thousands)	Principal City	Year	Population (in thousands)
New York—	1960*	14,577	New York City	1960*	7,710
Northeastern New Jersey					
Tokyo—Yokohama	1955	11,349	Tokyo	1955	6,969
London	1956	10,491	London	1956	3,273
Moscow	1956	7,300	Moscow	1959	5,032
Paris	1954	6,737	Paris	1954	2,850
Osaka—Kobe	1955	6,405	Osaka	1955	2,547
Shanghai	1953	——	Shanghai	1953	6,204
Chicago—Northwestern	1960*	6,726	Chicago	1960*	3,493
Indiana					
Buenos Aires	1955	5,750	Buenos Aires	1955	3,575
Calcutta	1955	5,700	Calcutta	1955	2,750
Los Angeles—	1960*	6,690	Los Angeles	1960*	2,448
Long Beach					
Essen—Dortmund—	1955	5,353	Essen	1955	691
Duisburg (Inner Ruhr)					
Bombay	1955	4,400	Bombay	1955	3,600
East & West Berlin	1955	4,245	East Berlin	1955	1,140
			West Berlin	1955	2,195
Phila.—New Jersey	1960*	4,289	Philadelphia	1960*	1,960
Mexico City	1955	3,900	Mexico City	1955	2,800
Rio de Janeiro	1955	3,750	Rio de Janeiro	1955	2,900
Detroit	1960*	3,761	Detroit	1960*	1,672
Leningrad	1955	3,500	Leningrad	1959†	2,888
Sao Paulo	1955	3,300	Sao Paulo	1955	2,600

Source: International Urban Research, *The World's Metropolitan Areas,*
Berkeley, University of California Press, 1959, unless otherwise indicated.
* U.S. Bureau of the Census; 1960 data are preliminary.
† USSR All-Union Population Census of 1959.

tion and its urban population. In many countries, well over 50 percent of all the urban population is concentrated in the capital city.
This is especially true of several Latin American countries, and the
trend there was discussed in an earlier *Population Bulletin,* August
1958:

The unique feature in Latin America's urbanization is the high concentration of people in relatively few metropolitan areas, usually the
national capitals. Except in Brazil and Colombia, the largest city has
more inhabitants than all the other cities of 100,000 and more combined.
In 13 of the 20 countries, at least 10 percent of the people live in the largest city or metropolitan area, usually the capital city. In six of these

countries the largest city contains one-fifth or more of the national population: 33 percent in Uruguay, 29 percent in Argentina, 23 percent in Chile and Panama and 21 percent in Cuba and Costa Rica. One out of six Venezuelans lives in Caracas.

If 20 percent of the United States' population lived in the capital city, Washington, D. C. would have 34 million people!

In 1955, the world had 1,107 metropolitan areas of 100,000 or more. Asia contained almost one third of these or 341 and Europe over one fourth or 279. Northern America had 202, Latin America 78 and Oceania only 11. The nations with the largest number were the United States, 189; USSR, 148; and China, 103. Of the world's 108 metropolitan areas with one million or more, 34 were in Europe, excluding USSR, 32 were in Asia, and 26 were in North America.

The four largest metropolitan areas in the world have a total population of almost 44 million people. The Tokyo-Yokohama urban agglomeration with 11.3 million people in 1955 (almost 7 million of them in Tokyo) by now may be almost as large as the New York-New Jersey metropolitan area (over 14 million people in 1960). London's metropolitan area had 10.5 million people in 1956, 3.2 million of them in London proper. Suburbia has not reached the USSR, for in 1955, Moscow's metropolitan area, although the fourth largest in the world, was considerably smaller than the three other giants. It had 7.3 million people; and slightly over 5 million of them lived in Moscow itself.

New York City's five boroughs have a population of 7.7 million. The borough of Manhattan with 1.7 million in 1960 records a decline of 15 percent from the 1950 census. Its population density is 75,900 people per square mile!

Japan, with 92 million people and a land area about the size of Montana, is one of the most highly urbanized nations. She has 64 cities of 100,000 population or more, and their combined total is over 21.3 million. That is about a fourth of Japan's total population, and about 7 percent of all the people in the world who reside in cities of that size.

CONTRASTS IN CITY LIFE

Despite the ever-accelerating rate of urbanization since 1800, modern man continues to be tied to the land. Four out of every five people in the world still live in the country. However, the trek to cities will accelerate during the decades ahead as the economically underdeveloped countries strive to become industrial societies. But the speed-up in the rate of social change makes the urbanization process a very different one today in those countries than it was in the Western world. Since the Industrial Revolution began, the continuous migration in the West from country to city has been a flight from low-paid rural jobs to more lucrative jobs and greater opportunities in urban areas. But in underdeveloped countries today the movement to cities is more of a shift from unproductive rural situations to even less productive urban situations with no income gain and with grievous drain on limited savings due to higher living costs.

Because there is such a vast gulf between life in the traditional village and life in a large city, the rural-urban transition can be a painful experience. More often than not, the migrant ends up in a flimsy shantytown shelter, with no means of transportation and no job. Thus, in this pattern of urbanization, rural poverty is transferred to the cities where it becomes more concentrated and conspicuous. . . .

THE CITY OF TOMORROW

When the city of antiquity first began to emerge, transportation was by foot, communication by word of mouth, and space—that playground of 20th-century man—was thought to be an inverted bowl with holes punched in it. In the field of transportation and communication, invention and technology have moved farther in one century than in the preceding two thousand centuries.

Generations of scientific research and highly sophisticated planning have brought man to the stage where he can bounce messages off a balloon orbiting in space. By jet plane he can reach any spot on the planet in less than a day. But in the area of social invention man's approach to many urgent problems, among them population control and city planning, still smacks of the Dark Ages rather than the technological age of invention and creative improvization. A do-nothing, know-nothing approach or a Micawberish hope that "something will turn up" does not resolve crises.

It is very likely that in the city man first will have to face the fact that space is the finite factor in the multiplication of people. In all probability, projections which indicate that a century hence Calcutta's population could increase by 35 to 66 million, or that New York City could be half or two thirds that size will never materialize. However, they serve to warn of nightmares to come unless man begins to apply his foresight and his great inventive skills to check his unprecedented population growth and to solve the problems which that growth has created.

The Changing Functions of Latin American Cities

T. LYNN SMITH

University of Florida

The functions of the city are legion; and to a certain extent every city in Latin America performs nearly all of them. Trade and commerce, manufacturing and processing, communication and transportation, government and public administration, educational and cultural activities, religious and ceremonial observances, financial and personal services, servicing and repair, and recreation and welfare work, are a few of the better known categories. This list does not include, however, residence per se which is one of the principal *raisons d'être* of cities in general. Moreover, even these better known urban functions can be subdivided into many varieties and classes, without in any way being exhaustive. Familiar examples are wholesale and retail trade; motor, rail, water, and air transportation; light and heavy manufacturing; and national, provincial, and local government and administration. In addition some of them tend to overlap, as in the cases of educational and cultural activities, or government and protection. Finally, the absolute and relative importance of any one of the functions, or of any particular combination of them, varies greatly from one city to another and in the same city from one time to another.

One of the most significant classifications of cities is that based upon the number and complexity of the fundamental functions which they perform. Those which existed at the dawn of history were multi-functional in the strictest sense. They seem to have performed almost all of the social and economic functions necessary for life in that remote past; and the same was true of the fortress

First published in *The Americas*, Volume XXV, Number 1, pages 70–83, (July, 1968). Reprinted by permission of the author and the Academy of American Franciscan History.

cities of the early Roman state. In sharp contrast with these are the extremely limited functions of the cities which developed during the Middle Ages, as symbolized by the houses and shops of the tradesmen which were huddled at the base of the hill or cliff on which the castle was built. Protection was at first the fundamental function of the village or town, gradually supplemented by trade and commerce. In more recent times in Spanish America, Cartagena of the Indies, long the world's greatest fortress city, was during the entire colonial period one of the most highly specialized urban centers that man has built. As is stressed below, however, the functions of colonial Latin American cities were extremely limited, and the major concern of this paper is with the diversification that has taken place as a strong fever of urbanization has suddenly seized the twenty countries involved.

By some queer aspect of sociological and anthropological reasoning that it is difficult to explain, it seems that the study of the functions of cities has offered little or no challenge to the scientists working in those fields. Is it because so many of us are preoccupied with matters which belong largely to the study of psychology and even to the psychology of the individual? Is a societal entity or group par excellence, such as the city, actually outside the scope of our professed concern? In any case the failure for any of us to focus attention upon the functions of Latin American cities is almost total.

The absence of such effort certainly cannot be attributed to the lack of basic data nor to the difficulty of making significant first-hand observation. Any perceptive observer, equipped with a sound sociological frame of reference, may gather highly pertinent and useful materials by bare observation alone; and if he will take the trouble to examine the great quantities of statistical information gathered and published in recent decades, he will discover a rich mine of quantitative information bearing directly upon the subject. Most useful of all, for the various cities of Latin America, are the facts about the labor force. These, for example, enable one to ascertain the absolute and relative importance of the workers who are classified in the principal industrial and occupational categories such as trade and commerce, manufacturing, transportation, and so on, a sound basis for many significant and highly pertinent inferences. . . .

Before we concentrate our attention upon the current revolutionary changes in the functions of Latin American cities, two essential preliminaries must be handled. The first of these is to sketch briefly the functions of those cities during the colonial epoch, or from the time they were founded (largely in the sixteenth century) to about 1825 when most of the colonies had gained their independence; and the second is to outline the nature of the changes in their functions during the national period up to about 1935 or 1940.

THE FUNCTIONS OF LATIN AMERICAN CITIES DURING THE COLONIAL PERIOD

During the long colonial period the functions of Spanish American cities were extremely limited. Founded in accordance with carefully planned specifications they were closely similar in their ecological features and much alike in the roles they played in colonial society. In a word they were locations for the residences of the Spaniards from which these overlords exercised their dominion over the lands, peoples and mines in their particular part of the possessions of the Spanish Crown. Administrative centers and military posts or garrison towns best describes the *raison d'être* of the hundreds of new towns in which the Spaniards lived. Almost all of them were founded in the sixteenth century, and all except the very first ones were planned in accordance with the detailed plans and specifications set forth in the *Laws of the Indies*. Moreover, the learned jurists who formed the Council of the Indies sent out, over the Spanish sovereign's signature, decree after decree intended to maintain a rigid separation of the races in the colonies. The Spaniards were required to have houses (and later "inhabited" houses) in their towns and forbidden to have any buildings (and later even to spend the night) in any of the Indian villages.[1] Very early rings of huts of the mestizos and other outcasts sprang up on the outskirts of some of the Spanish towns, not too different from the "bands of misery" which have grown up like mushrooms or toadstools adjacent to most contemporary Latin American cities. However, the presence of these miserable segments of humanity did little to affect the basic functions of the cities involved.

Nor were most of them to change their social and economic functions very much throughout the whole colonial epoch. Practically none of them developed as centers in which manufacturing and processing furnished a significant number of jobs for the breadwinners of the family. The few feeble attempts actually made along these lines, such as the making of a crude brown sugar, the production of syrup and molasses, the spinning and weaving of cotton and woolen textiles, and so on, took place on the haciendas and other large landed estates. The few powerful owners of the large proper-

[1] Cf. T. Lynn Smith, "Some Neglected Spanish Social Thinkers," *The Americas*, XVII, No. 1 (July, 1960), 37–52.

ties involved lived in the cities, of course, but the rest of the urban residents functioned only as consumers of the few products involved.

Likewise trade and commerce were insignificant among the occupations of those who lived in the Spanish American cities during the centuries of Spanish domination. Given Spain's colonial policies it could not have been otherwise. These seem to have had two principal objectives: (1) to make the colonies into producers of gold, silver, and precious stones; and (2) to limit their consumption of manufactured goods strictly to those produced in Spain, shipped in convoys from Spanish ports, and destined for a few strongly fortified seaports, of which the principal ones were Vera Cruz, Cartagena, and Callao. Even certain types of agriculture, such as the planting of vineyards and the growing of tobacco, were strictly limited or prohibited altogether.

The effects of concentration upon the part of mining which involves precious metals and stones, including those relating specifically to the functions of cities, have been summarized by one highly perceptive Spanish American as follows:

> ... Spanish Americans saw themselves excluded from industry, foreign trade and agriculture to a high degree, by the innumerable monopolies and prohibitions of the colonial regime. Mining, reduced to that of gold and silver, was the cardinal element of riches. But mines of gold and silver enriched no one except their proprietors, few in number and exempt from genuine social activity by the extreme ease with which they made their fortunes. Gold travels to all parts in small and valuable bars; it does not stimulate the building of roads, agriculture, the arts, the growth of population, schools, etc.; it concentrates enormous fortunes in the hands of a few who live in the comfortable cities; it leaves the mass of the proletariat in misery, idleness, ignorance, and stagnation; it favors social inequalities; and it is a powerful stimulant to gambling, ostentatiousness, sterile luxury, dissipation, laziness, and all similar vices and consequences.[2]

The throttling of trade and commerce which effectually blocked the development in Spanish American cities of some of the most important functions was accomplished by several specific policies, including: (1) the prohibition of manufacturing in the new world; (2) the exclusion of the ships of all nations but Spain from the ports in the colonies; (3) the establishment of the *Casa de Contratación* in Seville with a monopoly on trade and shipping to the fortress ports in the western hemisphere; and (4) the restriction of shipping to the convoys sent out once a year.

[2] José M. Samper, *Ensayo sobre las Revoluciones Políticas y la Condición Social de las Repúblicas Colombianas (Hispano-Americanas)*, (Paris: Imprenta de E. Thunot y Cie, 1864), pp. 114–115.

Samper bitterly compared the effects of these deadly restrictions on commerce to the puerile and ineffectual work of the Holy Office of the Inquisition.

But the work of the fiscal inquisition was a different matter. In the view of the *Santo oficio fiscal* every piece of dinnerware from England, every bottle of wine from Bordeaux and every box of spaghetti from Genoa were scandalously heretical.[3]

For present purposes the basic importance of all this is the fact that trade and commerce were insignificant as bases for urban life in Spanish American cities all through the centuries of Spanish domination. The few important seaports, of which more is said later on, were entrepots for receiving the annual convoys from Seville, for outfitting the fleets of canoes and the trains of mules that carried the goods from the fortresses to the other parts of the Spanish dominions, for assembling the treasures to be sent to Spain, and for loading and outfitting the convoys for the voyage back across the Atlantic.

Of all the heavily fortified seaports Vera Cruz and Cartagena far outranked the others in importance. The former was the key in the supply of New Spain and the dispatch to Spain of the Aztec treasures; and the latter was long the greatest port in South America as well as the strongest fortress in the world. Cartagena's role as a center of commerce was enhanced by the prohibition of the transportation of goods across the Isthmus of Panama for reshipment to Pacific ports. (The routes to Valparaiso and Callao were via Cape Horn.) From it fleets of canoes left for the interior, and especially for Honda about 500 miles up the Magdalena River. This trip took about six months. There the cargoes were transferred to the backs of mules, and here the trains began the climb up the rough, steep, rocky, and slippery trail to Bogotá, capital of New Granada. Others set out on the much longer trip to the south, to Popayán first and then on to Quito. From Cartagena to Quito required from about 20 months to a full two years.[4] Obviously transportation being what it was, a thriving merchant class was not a prominent feature of Spanish American cities when the new places were established in the sixteenth century; and the same element was largely lacking when the various provinces began as independent countries during the first half of the nineteenth century.

Unusual interest should be attached, however, to the extent to which colonial Spanish American cities served, or failed to serve, as

[3] *Ibid.*, p. 119.
[4] *Ibid.*, p. 121.

hubs in the important systems of transportation and communication. As has just been indicated since the vast portions of America involved were possessions of the Spanish Crown, it was inevitable that a few places in the New World would function importantly as seaports. Havana, Santo Domingo, Vera Cruz, Cartagena must be mentioned in this connection, and perhaps Buenos Aires, Montevideo, Valparasio, Callao, Guayaquil, and Acapulco should be added. Definitely, though, this should not be taken as an endorsement of the widely held social and economic generalization which maintains that the location of cities is determined largely by breaks in transportation. Perhaps many of the data for the United States support such a proposition. But in Europe, where the origins of contemporary cities go back largely to the Middle Ages, such a thesis is untenable. These European cities (fortresses at first and later on fortresses with markets attached) sprang up along established trade routes at points where robber barons could most effectively interrupt travel and exact tribute from everyone who wished to pass. Still more interesting and important, however, in connection with this thesis are the locations of the Spanish American cities.

Suppose we examine this briefly by glancing over the list of the national capitals. Santo Domingo and Havana have already been mentioned, as have Buenos Aires and Montevideo. Panama City should be added. They are the five in a total of 18 that were favorably located from the standpoint of transportation facilities. But if we consider Mexico City, Guatemala City (or Antigua as well), San Salvador, Tegucigalpa, Managua, and San José we must conclude that a favorable location for the purposes of transportation was least in the thoughts of those selecting the sites for such major places. Mexico City was even established on an island in a lake! Much the same is true of the South American capitals: Bogotá, Caracas, Quito, Lima, La Paz (Sucre, too), and Santiago certainly owed little of their importance in colonial times to the transportation factor. Moreover, the vast majority of all the other cities and towns founded by the Spaniards during the colonial era were fully as limited in functions performed, if not more so, than the national capitals just enumerated. They were merely strong points, garrison towns and administrative and religious centers (these two functions had hardly been differentiated in the colonial period) from which the Spaniards exercised overlordship over the vassals they had conquered, the slaves they had imported, and the choicest expanses of the land they had seized and transformed into pastures.

The cities of colonial Brazil differed from those in the Spanish dominions in several significant ways which can be summarized briefly. In the first place they were built to no standard plan, such as that prescribed by the Laws of the Indies for the new Spanish settlements. Hence the former lack prominent features of the latter such as the central plaza, the *solares* or house lots all uniform in size and shape, and the grid work of streets all intersecting at right angles. Second, unlike the Spaniards who were granted immense holdings of land, but who chose to live in the cities, the owners of the large estates in Brazil resided in the country, each in the mansion which served as the center for the small barony over which he reigned. His vassals included slaves, often in large numbers, free retainers of many kinds, a small private army, and so on. Among his many retainers was the priest, frequently one of his less opulent kinsmen. Third, largely because the city served to a limited extent only as a residence for the affluent families of colonial Brazil, those that did exist were extremely limited in functions. Throughout the sixteenth, seventeenth, and eighteenth centuries the finest of harbors were closed to the ships of all nations except Portugal. Imports in any case were small; and the exports were limited largely to sugar, fine timber (much of this illicitly and from little-frequented anchorages), and precious metals and stones. Even such splendid natural facilities as those at Santos, Rio de Janeiro, Bahia, and Recife were not sufficient to make any of them into a great seaport. The cities that did exist, other than Rio de Janeiro which eventually became the seat of colonial government, and Bahia, once seat of both religious and administrative powers, and later on of ecclesiastical affairs only, were few in number and weak in importance. Trade and commerce, shipping, and the terminus of mule trains radiating into the interior were their chief features.

THE FUNCTIONS OF LATIN AMERICAN CITIES IN THE PERIOD 1825 TO 1945

Remarkably little change took place in the cities of Latin America during the first century of existence as independent nations of the various Spanish American countries and Brazil. With a few exceptions, of which Buenos Aires and Montevideo are the most prominent examples, the social and economic roles of these cities were about the same at the close of the first world war as they had been at the termination of the struggle for independence. Between 1918 and 1940 more fundamental changes got underway, but the effects of most of the new factors influencing the situation did not become fully apparent until after the second world war.

Throughout the nineteenth century and well along into the twentieth, government and administration and residence for the best families, their numerous servants, and for the craftsmen and artisans required to meet their needs, continued to be the bases of urban life. Consider, for example, the fact that the era of canal building, which determined largely the location and basic functions of many important cities in the United States, in the "opening of the West," never fired the imaginations of those responsible for the policies of Latin American countries. Similarly, the river steamboats, a transportation factor which determined many of the important features of dozens of other important cities of the United States (Cincinnati, Louisville, St. Louis, Memphis, and New Orleans to mention a few of the major ones), played virtually no role in the development of Latin American cities. In this case there was interest involved, and as Spanish domination crumbled emissaries from the United States were among the first on the scene in the various capitals seeking, among other things, concessions for the operation of steamboats on such rivers as the Magdalena and the Orinoco. Some lines were actually established on these, on the Paraná-Paraguay system, on the São Francisco (Brazil), and other lesser streams. In fact the services on a few still linger. Steam navigation on the greatest of all river systems (Amazon), however, was via ocean-going vessels, including those from Liverpool and other European ports and Brazilian coastal ships operating out of Rio de Janeiro and Santos. With a few possible exceptions, though, the role of the steamboat was practically nil in the transformation of Latin American cities into centers specializing in the transportation and commercial functions.

Due to the reciprocal relationship between transportation facilities, on the one hand, and trade and commerce, on the other, in the vast majority of Latin American cities and towns trade and commerce were slow in developing. However, in Argentina the heavy flow of immigrants of European origin, the settlement of new lands, and the development of farms and farming to go along with the traditional pastoral activities, brought forth huge amounts of wheat, flax, corn, and other products for sale and export. As a result, Buenos Aires and Rosário, to mention the two most important cities, grew with great rapidity, and greatly diversified their functions. Both emerged as great transportation centers in which the transfer from land to sea forms of transportation took place; both became bustling centers of trade and commerce; and both experienced a level of financial activities previously unknown in Latin America. Except for the lack of manufacturing and processing to furnish employment for large parts of their labor forces, by the close of the nineteenth century these Argentine cities had come to be multi-functional centers in the truest sense of the term.

Elsewhere in Latin America, the transformation got underway later and proceeded more slowly, so that most Latin American cities in the opening quarter of the twentieth century were strikingly like what they had been in the middle of the nineteenth. Argentina's cities, however, felt the full impact of the revolution in transportation on land brought about by the use of mobile steam engines to move trains of cars over railroads. Buenos Aires, particularly, became the hub of a great system of transportation.

On a much lesser scale during the years from 1850 on systems of railroads also were constructed in parts of some of the other countries. However, only São Paulo and Rio de Janeiro in Brazil, along with Santiago (and perhaps Valparaiso) in Chile, and Panama City actually were changed very much by the coming of the epoch of the railways. Mexico City, Bogotá, Caracas, Quito, Lima, La Paz, and Montevideo are among the capitals which felt only a minimum impact of the new revolutionary factor in transportation which elsewhere had a huge role in transforming the functions of cities.

Along other lines as well this particular aspect of social differentiation proceeded very slowly. The functions of most of the cities remained limited and comparatively little division of labor between various centers and specialization on the part of individual places took place. All of this set the stage that was to come in the middle of the twentieth century when the fever of modernization and development finally struck the Latin American countries in a vigorous form.

CURRENT METAMORPHOSIS OF LATIN AMERICAN CITIES

Following the close of the Second World War the functions of Latin American cities have changed and diversified almost as if accomplished by the wave of a magic wand. The populations of these urban centers have increased at a dizzy pace; at long last they quickly have become important commercial and transportation centers; many have developed substantial bases for their economies in the manufacturing and transforming industries; their financial roles have been modernized and greatly expanded; and their construction activities have doubled and redoubled time after time. Already the functions of most Latin American cities resemble much more closely those of important urban centers in Western Europe, the United States, and Canada, than they do the ones they themselves were performing in 1900 and in large numbers of cases as late as 1940. This metamorphosis deserves thorough-going consideration and study.

Before we focus our attention upon some of the details of the radical transformation that is underway, however, it is well to re-emphasize that the exact timing of the revolutionary developments differed considerably from country to country and city to city. As indicated above, the progress began earliest of all in Argentina, probably due largely to the immigration of large numbers of Europeans. These newcomers were thoroughly imbued with a venturesome commercial spirit, and they were not dominated largely by a feudalistic and pastoral outlook on life. In any case the promotion of agriculture by D. F. Sarmiento and others, the building of a web of railways with Buenos Aires as the hub, the construction of docks and storage facilities, the establishment of essential financial institutions, and so on, all were accomplished before the close of the nineteenth century.

In other countries Montevideo, São Paulo-Santos, and Rio de Janeiro, to a limited extent, were among the first places to experience some of the impact of the modern stream of urban development. Before the opening of the Panama Canal, however, all the West Coast cities were virtually shut off from effective means of promoting trade and commerce; and the extreme cost in time and money in bringing centers such as La Paz, Quito, Bogotá, Caracas, San José, Guatemala City, and Mexico City into the circulatory system of international trade meant that they would be among the last to feel the impulse of modern urban transformations. Moreover, in some cases, of which Mexico's cities are prime examples, bloody revolutions and protracted civil wars were to delay for decades any substantial start on overwhelming the basic functions performed by the cities.

Trade and Commerce

Perhaps the change, almost a societal mutation, in trade and commerce has best claim to primacy in the fundamental transformation of the basic functions of Latin American cities. Perhaps, too, the commercial outlook on life of a few Europeans who established residences in Latin American cities, sometimes as representatives of foreign companies and often as immigrants, was the factor which set the wheels in motion. Refugees from the Hitlerized Central Europe of the 1930's probably played a role inordinately out of proportion to their number. By ship and train the present writer travelled with hundreds of these people as they were seeking new locations in the Latin American countries; and only a few years afterward friends were indicating to him large sections of the shopping centers of city after city in which they were reputed to own and control every store in block after block of the commercial districts. Be this as it may, suddenly in the 1940's and 1950's great department stores, highly specialized retail outlets, and all the appurtenances of modern commerce sprang up as though by magic. Simultaneously, in city and country alike, the handicrafts began to become more standardized, it became obvious many things were being made for a specific market, barter became less prevalent, the practice of selling at established and marked prices became the rule in the stores, the metric system of weights and measures became of importance functionally, and in brief the commercial spirit waxed in importance in the cities themselves and even throughout their hinterlands. By 1968 it is likely that commercial enterprises lead all others in furnishing employment to those living in Latin American cities and towns, and probably the same is true in a majority of all the places if each were considered separately.

Transportation

From what has already been said it should be evident that in the great nineteenth century transformation of urban functions, in a figurative sense and also in a very literal one, most Latin American cities "missed the boat" and they also "missed the train." In the present century, though, as the motor vehicle worked its revolutionary effect upon urban places, Latin American centers did not entirely "miss the bus," even though they were somewhat late in catching it. Specifically, as Latin American cities took on important roles as transportation centers, neither river steamboats nor rail facilities played any very great parts in the transformation. The former continues to be vital in a few cases, such as that of Asunción; but interestingly enough in places such as Belém, Manaus, Iquitos, and Pulcalpa, to mention only four of those in the great Amazon Basin, transportation by means of motor launches and canoes propelled by outboard motors have been of major importance in the development of transportation. With respect to railroads, some extension of lines is still taking place, and there also are some efforts to modernize facilities for commuters within the metropolitan communities. On the relative basis, though, the lines and rolling stock get more and more inadequate every year, for the additions fail by huge margins to keep pace with tremendous annual increase in the urban and suburban populations.

The automobile, the motor truck, and improved roads are the great agents now swelling the importance of the Latin American cities as transportation centers. One must stress, however, the recency with which the impact of these factors has been felt and the fact that they by no means have lost their force in making for change. . . . As late as 1940 the role of the motor vehicle in moving goods and people in and out of Latin American cities was a very limited one. If all of the automobiles and trucks I encountered in an entire month of travel in Mexico, Brazil, and Colombia had converged on Mexico City, Rio de Janeiro or São Paulo, or Bogotá, respectively, their volume of traffic would not have equalled that which now moves into each of those cities daily, during half a day, and perhaps even hourly. More and more paved highways and superhighways choked with motor traffic, radiating out from the capitals are indicative of the high degree in which those large cities have greatly enhanced their function as centers of land transport. But the revolution involved goes far beyond the limits of the metropolitan centers. Its impact is great in cities of all sizes, towns in the most remote recesses of the various countries, and even in almost 100 per cent of the villages.

The principal Latin American cities also have great centers of air transportation. The very same places which missed the boat, missed the train, and almost missed the bus, were among the first in the world to take to the plane. Again, though, almost all of this development has taken place since 1940. That year one who had the temerity to travel by plane or even took the trouble to drive out to an airport encountered no huge, scrambling masses of humanity, and no extensive depot for the reception and the shipment of goods such as now must be contended against in hundreds of teeming terminals. In 1968, air transport competes with motor transportation for the place of primary importance in moving people, produce, and manufactured goods to and from the city. Much of this, of course, involves tremendous sleek jets which link the Latin American cities to others in all parts of the world. Shipments between the United States and many places, particularly the once remote cities such as Bogotá, Quito, and La Paz, cost less if the goods are moved by air freight than if they are sent via surface transportation. The international traveler, though, is likely to be most impressed by the hordes of people with whom he competes for breathing space in various greatly over-crowded passenger terminals. The people move between various parts of their nation in fleets of older, smaller and slower planes. Finally, one who himself undertakes to go to many still remote places in the various countries may find himself in a "mixed" carrier along with a motley array of fellow passengers, crates of livestock and poultry, boxes and bales of merchandise, and sacks of various kinds of produce. In short, the emergence, perfection, and proliferation of the means of moving people and things by air has been a powerful factor in bringing the transportation function to the fore in Latin American cities and, simultaneously, of altering substantially the basic forms of life and labor in the Latin American countries.

Manufacturing and Processing

The rapid development of light and heavy industry and urban locations for most of the greatly expanded numbers of processing plants constitutes the third of the major features of the recent and current diversification of the functions of Latin American cities. These trends, although getting well underway only in the recent past, are hemisphere-wide. Before World War II the Latin American countries were almost exclusively dependent upon imports for manufactured goods, and most of the processing of their own products (the making of sugar, the cleaning and drying of coffee, the milling of rice, the preparation of flour and meal, the slaughter of livestock and the chilling of meat, and so on) were carried out on the plantations and other estates. Moreover, except in connection with products for export, the processing of products was minimal: most of the foodstuffs for domestic consumption showed up in the large, open air, public market in about the same form as they were when dug, cut, pulled, or picked as the case might be. Now all this has changed to a radical degree. Almost to a man those who succeed one another at the helms of national policies seem to regard industrialization as the cure-all for each nation's host of chronic and acute social and economic problems. Immense amounts of public and private funds from at home and abroad are being expended for the purpose of promoting the industrial plants which are springing up by the thousands. The processing and marketing of food and other products for domestic consumption are being modernized at a rapid pace.

As a result, manufacturing and processing industries are now significant functions in hundreds of Latin American cities in which only 25 years ago they were conspicuous by their absence. All of the great cities, such as Buenos Aires, Rio de Janeiro, São Paulo, Mexico City, Lima, Bogotá, and Santiago, now include substantial industrial activity as important items in their highly diversified set of functions, and one of them (São Paulo) is rather highly specialized along this line. Moreover, on the basis of the high proportion of all those in the labor force who are engaged in manufacturing, it now is possible to characterize a few important Latin American cities as being rather highly specialized in the industrial function. The list of these could take on an impressive length if the smaller industrial centers such as Volta Redonda (Brazil), Oroya (Peru), and Paz del Rio (Colombia) were included. For our purposes, though, it probably is best to limit it to the few great cities which properly belong in a category of places specializing in manufacturing, all places that were in existence in the colonial period and once were primarily governmental and administrative centers. Even so at least São Paulo, Monterrey, Cali, and Medellín must be specified.

Other Diversification of Urban Functions

It is hoped that enough has been said to call attention to the rapid change and diversification in the functions of Latin American cities which is going on during the second half of the twentieth century. The vast majority of these cities entered the twentieth century performing functions that had changed very little since the sixteenth and seventeenth centuries when they were founded by the Spaniards and the Portuguese. For well over 300 years they continued to be largely governmental and administrative centers. Since 1900 in many cases, and since 1940 in almost all, they have rapidly diversified by taking on important roles as commercial, transportation, and, in many cases, industrial centers. This growth has been covered in our analysis.

It also would be possible to discuss in some detail the important changes in other functions such as communication, construction, repair and service work (which mounts by leaps and bounds in an age of automobiles and electric equipment), commercialized recreation, professional and cultural activites, and so on. There has even been the establishment of Brasília, another purely governmental and administrative center (where the haste with which banks in all parts of the Republic established their branches in the new city is an object lesson in the close interdependence of government and finance in the modern state). It is believed, though, that enough has been presented to demonstrate adequately the thesis of this paper that the functions of Latin American cities are rapidly undergoing a complete metamorphosis.

Chapter 2

URBANIZATION AS A PROCESS

Throughout the world cities are growing and, in most areas of the earth, they are growing rapidly. To be sure, the range in the degree of urbanization today is very wide. A few very small nations, newly achieving independence, still are almost entirely rural. At the other extreme is the United Kingdom, where approximately 80 percent of all residents are classified as urban.

Wide as are the variations, the process of urbanization creates certain common or similar adaptations and problems wherever cities expand. The very fact that growth itself has occurred within the metropolitan area (if not always in the city as such), and that such growth is expected to continue, gives a dynamic, future-oriented character to cities.

Precise study and interpretation of the process of expansion is often difficult within a given society, and more difficult among societies, because the "city" in an ecological sense is often not the unit of statistical reporting. In 1960, for example, Houston as a political entity was nearly a third more populous than the city of Boston, yet metropolitan Houston had fewer than half the residents of metropolitan Boston.

The selection to follow from the Bureau of the Census presents the basic concepts of the greater city, as these are used in current American data: the urbanized area and the standard metropolitan statistical area. The urbanized area which, in quite nontechnical phrasing, consists of the "built-up" area, is largely coexistent with the ecologist's idea of the city. This is the "metropolitan community" as it might be viewed from the air; in this sense it is the "true" greater city.

It is the "true" greater city, however, only at that particular moment in time. If growth continues, each new subdivision on the periphery is added to the urbanized area. The precise limits of the urbanized area are constantly changing.

For many purposes it is useful to delineate an area that can be compared from one census period to another, an area for which other data of various kinds are available. Births and deaths, school enrollments and tax assessments, crimes and accidents—these and many other kinds of data are collected and recorded, not by the ever-shifting bounds of the "built-up" area but by existing political units. Information of these types is collected for the political entity of the city and for the county or counties which surround it, and are closely linked with it.

Such an entity of city and surrounding county or counties (except in New England, where townships are used as the delimiting local units) is known as the standard statistical metropolitan area. It includes more territory than the urbanized area; it may even include some territory distinctly "rural" in its characteristics. Enclosed within it, however, is the large city with its environs. If the designation is a little less the "pure" ecological city than that of the urbanized area, it is far more useful for many purposes because of the wealth of contemporary and historical data that may be obtained for the metropolis so designated.

In some of the more thickly settled and highly industrialized areas of the world, supermetropolitanization is under way. Metropolitan areas are growing toward metropolitan areas, tending to fill in the interstices, creating long, chain-shaped conurbations far exceeding any past urban development in both size and complexity of regional interdependence. Such areas are emerging in the British Midlands, along the Ruhr and Rhine, in the Kyoto-Osaka-Kobe section of Honshu, in the Netherlands, and elsewhere. Most spectacular of all such areas, however, is that of the northeastern United States, reaching from below the Potomac to north of Boston, designated by Gottman as "megalopolis".[1]

It is appropriate that this largest of all megalopolitan developments be in the United States, the nation probably containing the largest aggregate (not relative) urban population on earth. Cer-

---

[1] Jean Gottman, *Megalopolis*, New York: The Twentieth Century Fund, 1961

tainly the United States has come to epitomize both the modern industrial system that creates massive metropolitan areas and the perplexing problems that such areas can produce. Although at present the most intense concern about the "urban crisis" seems to be in the United States, that "crisis" well may become worldwide in its scope. In his selection included here, Vandiver summarizes some of the major trends in urbanization in the United States.

If comparisons of the actual degree of urbanization and metropolitanization are often difficult within one country, they become all the more perplexing on an international basis. In research carried out some years ago, Gibbs and Davis met the challenge of making international comparisons by establishing criteria of metropolitanization which could be applied to data presented in the census materials of most of the nations that contained large cities. They demonstrate that in most instances it is possible to designate reasonably comparable metropolitan units. They further establish that the degree of metropolitanization thus designated is highly correlated with the published figures of urban population in these countries, despite the variable basis of such definition. They therefore conclude that published estimates and enumerations of urban population, while not precisely comparable from one country to another, are nonetheless meaningful for most descriptive needs. They also conclude that if an international criterion of minimum urban size is to be established for comparative purposes, this size should not be lower than 10,000 persons.

The most rapid urban growth of all today, on a proportional basis, is taking place in the nations of the "third world"—that is, those nations which belong neither to the industrialized family of nations (including Japan), nor to the Communist bloc. Except in Latin America, most of these nations have only recently moved from colonial status. They are nations often referred to by such terms as "underdeveloped," "developing," or "emerging." In the final selection of this chapter, Harroy summarizes the conclusions reached by participants in a study session devoted to the problems of urbanization in such countries, and sponsored by the International Institute of Differing Civilizations (INCIDI).

Harroy refers to the "primary" sector of the economy (that devoted to the production of raw materials), to the "secondary" sector (that devoted to the processing of such materials), and to the "tertiary" sector (that devoted to providing needed services in the economy, ranging from such things as servants, refuse collectors, and law enforcement through educational, cultural, medical, banking, and other essential requirements of modern urban existence). In the nations of the "third world," the growth of cities has often taken place despite relatively lagging development in the primary and secondary sectors of the economy, leading to an "over-tertiarisation" of the labor force. He presents many of the imbalances and problems that have accompanied the very rapid growth of cities in such lands in recent years, noting at the same time some of the advantages and opportunities that such urban growth has represented for these nations.

Urban Places, Urbanized Areas, and Standard Metropolitan Statistical Areas

URBAN PLACES

The count of urban places in 1960 includes all incorporated and unincorporated places of 2,500 inhabitants or more, and the towns, townships, and counties classified as urban. Under the previous urban definition, places of 2,500 or more and the areas urban under special rules were urban places.

URBANIZED AREAS

The major objective of the Bureau of the Census in delineating urbanized areas was to provide a better separation of urban and rural population in the vicinity of the larger cities, but individual urbanized area outside incorporated places was defined in terms of respond to what are called "conurbations" in some other countries. An urbanized area contains at least one city of 50,000 inhabitants or more in 1960,[1] as well as the surrounding closely settled incorporated places and unincorporated areas that meet the criteria listed below. An urbanized area may be thought of as divided into the central city, or cities, and the remainder of the area, or the urban fringe. All persons residing in an urbanized area are included in the urban population.

From United States Census of Population, 1960.

[1] There are a few urbanized areas where there are "twin central cities," neither of which has a population of 50,000 or more but that have a combined population of at least 50,000. See the following section on "standard metropolitan statistical areas" for further discussion of twin central cities.

It appeared desirable to delineate the urbanized areas in terms of the 1960 Census results rather than on the basis of information available prior to the census, as was done in 1950. For this purpose a peripheral zone around each 1950 urbanized area and around cities that were presumably approaching a population of 50,000 was recognized. Within the unincorporated parts of this zone small enumeration districts were established, usually including no more than one square mile of land area and no more than 75 housing units.[2]

Arrangements were made to include within the urbanized areas those enumeration districts meeting specified criteria of population density as well as adjacent incorporated places. Since the urbanized area outside incorporated places was defined in terms of enumeration districts, the boundaries of the urbanized area for the most part follow such features as roads, streets, railroads, streams, and other clearly defined lines which may be easily identified by census enumerators in the field and often do not conform to the boundaries of political units.

In addition to its central city or cities, an urbanized area also contains the following types of contiguous areas, which together constitute its urban fringe:

1. Incorporated places with 2,500 inhabitants or more.
2. Incorporated places with less than 2,500 inhabitants, provided each has a closely settled area of 100 housing units or more.
3. Towns in the New England States, townships in New Jersey and Pennsylvania, and counties elsewhere which are classified as urban.
4. Enumeration districts in unincorporated territory with a population density of 1,000 inhabitants or more per square mile. (The areas of large nonresidential tracts devoted to such urban land uses as railroad yards, factories, and cemeteries, were excluded in computing the population density of an enumeration district.)
5. Other enumeration districts in unincorporated territory with lower population density provided that they served one of the following purposes
   a. To eliminate enclaves.
   b. To close identations in the urbanized areas of one mile or less across the open end.
   c. To link outlying enumeration districts of qualifying density that were no more than $1\frac{1}{2}$ miles from the main body of the urbanized area.

[2] An enumeration district (ED) is a small area assigned to an enumerator which must be canvassed and reported separately. The average ED contained approximately 250 housing units.

STANDARD METROPOLITAN STATISTICAL AREAS

Definition

It has long been recognized that for many types of analysis it is necessary to consider as a unit the entire population in and around a city, the activities of which form an integrated economic and social system. Prior to the 1950 Census, areas of this type had been defined in somewhat different ways for different purposes and by various agencies. Leading examples were the metropolitan districts of the Census of Population, the industrial areas of the Census of Manufactures, and the labor market areas of the Bureau of Employment Security. To permit all Federal statistical agencies to utilize the same areas for the publication of general-purpose statistics, the Bureau of the Budget has established "standard metropolitan statistical areas" (SMSA's). Every city of 50,000 inhabitants or more according to the 1960 Census of Population is included in an SMSA.

The definitions and titles of standard metropolitan statistical areas are established by the Bureau of the Budget with the advice of the Federal Committee on Standard Metropolitan Statistical Areas. This committee is composed of representatives of the major statistical agencies of the Federal Government. The criteria used by the Bureau of the Budget in establishing the SMSA's are presented below. (See the Bureau of the Budget publication *Standard Metropolitan Statistical Areas*, U.S. Government Printing Office, Washington 25, D.C., 1961.)

The definition of an individual standard metropolitan statistical area involves two considerations: first, a city or cities of specified population to constitute the central city and to identify the county in which it is located as the central county; and, second, economic and social relationships with contiguous counties which are metropolitan in character, so that the periphery of the specific metropolitan area may be determined.[3] Standard metropolitan statistical areas may cross State lines.

Population Criteria

The criteria for population relate to a city or cities of specified size according to the 1960 Census of Population.

[3] Central cities are those appearing in the standard metropolitan statistical area title. A "contiguous" county either adjoins the county or counties containing the largest city in the area, or adjoins an intermediate county integrated with the central county. There is no limit to the number of tiers of outlying metropolitan counties so long as all other criteria are met.

1. Each standard metropolitan statistical area must include at least:
   a. One city with 50,000 inhabitants ore more, or
   b. Two cities having contiguous boundaries and constituting, for general economic and social purposes, a single community with a combined population of at least 50,000, the smaller of which must have a population of at least 15,000.
2. If two or more adjacent counties each have a city of 50,000 inhabitants or more (or twin cities under 1b) and the cities are within 20 miles of each other (city limits to city limits), they will be included in the same area unless there is definite evidence that the two cities are not economically and socially integrated.

Criteria of Metropolitan Character

The criteria of metropolitan character relate primarily to the attributes of the contiguous county as a place of work or as a home for a concentration of nonagricultural workers.
3. At least 75 percent of the labor force of the county must be in the nonagricultural labor force.[4]
4. In addition to criterion 3, the county must meet at least one of the following conditions:
   a. It must have 50 percent or more of its population living in contiguous minor civil divisions[5] with a density of at least 150 persons per square mile, in an unbroken chain of minor civil divisions with such density radiating from a central city in the area.
   b. The number of nonagricultural workers employed in the county must equal at least 10 percent of the number of non-agricultural workers employed in the county containing the largest city in the area, or the county must be the place of employment of 10,000 nonagricultural workers.
   c. The nonagricultural labor force living in the county must equal at least 10 percent of the number of the nonagricultural labor force living in the county containing the largest

[4] Nonagricultural labor force is defined as those employed in nonagricultural occupations, those experienced unemployed whose last occupation was a nonagricultural occupation, members of the Armed Forces, and new workers.
[5] A contiguous minor civil division either adjoins a central city in a standard metropolitan statistical area or adjoins an intermediate minor civil division of qualifying population density. There is no limit to the number of tiers of contiguous minor civil divisions so long as the minimum density requirement is met in each tier.

city in the area, or the county must be the place of residence
of a nonagricultural labor force of 10,000.
5. In New England, the city and town are administratively more
important than the county, and data are compiled locally for
such minor civil divisions. Here, towns and cities are the units
used in defining standard metropolitan statistical areas. In New
England, because smaller units are used and more restricted
areas result, a population density criterion of at least 100 persons per square mile is used as the measure of metropolitan
character.

Criteria of Integration

The criteria of integration relate primarily to the extent of economic and social communication between the outlying counties and
central county.
6. A county is regarded as integrated with the county or counties
containing the central cities of the area if either of the following criteria is met:
    a. 15 percent of the workers living in the county work in the
county or counties containing central cities of the area, or
    b. 25 percent of those working in the county live in the county
or counties containing central cities of the area.
Only where data for criteria 6a and 6b are not conclusive are
other related types of information used as necessary. This information includes such items as average telephone calls per subscriber
per month from the county to the county containing central cities
of the area; percent of the population in the county located in the
central city telephone exchange area; newspaper circulation reports prepared by the Audit Bureau of Circulation; analysis of charge accounts in retail stores of central cities to determine
the extent of their use by residents of the contiguous county; delivery service practices of retail stores in central cities; official traffic
counts; the extent of public transportation facilities in operation
between central cities and communities in the contiguous county;
and the extent to which local planning groups and other civic organizations operate jointly.

Criteria for Titles

The criteria for titles relate primarily to the size and number of
central cities.

7. The complete title of an SMSA identifies the central city or cities and the State or States in which the SMSA is located:

    a. The name of the standard metropolitan statistical area includes that of the largest city.

    b. The addition of up to two city names may be made in the area title, on the basis and in the order of the following criteria:

        (1) The additional city has at least 250,000 inhabitants.

        (2) The additional city has a population of one-third or more of that of the largest city and a minimum population of 25,000 except that both city names are used in those instances where cities qualify under criterion 1b. (A city which qualified as a secondary central city in 1950 but which does not qualify in 1960 has been temporarily retained as a central city.)

    c. In addition to city name, the area titles contain the name of the State or States in which the area is located. . . .

STANDARD CONSOLIDATED AREAS

In view of the special importance of the metropolitan complexes around New York and Chicago, the Nation's largest cities, several contiguous SMSA's and additional counties that do not appear to meet the formal integration criteria but do have strong interrelationships of other kinds, have been combined into the New York-Northeastern New Jersey and the Chicago-Northwestern Indiana Standard Consolidated Areas, respectively. The former is identical with the New York-Northeastern New Jersey SMA of 1950, and the latter corresponds roughly to the Chicago SMA of 1950 (two more counties having been added).

Urbanization and Urbanism
in the United States

JOSEPH S. VANDIVER

University of Florida

A legal and political struggle is underway in nearly every state of the American union concerning the reapportionment of state legislatures in order to give urban areas just representation on the basis of their populations. To persons elsewhere who have regarded the United States as the very epitome of industrial urbanization, it may be surprising to learn that hope for fuller urban representation is as recent as a United States Supreme Court decision in 1962, which invalidated the top-heavy rural apportionment of most state legislatures. Since state legislatures also delineate Congressional districts, membership in the national House of Representatives has similarly been shaped in a pro-rural mould. It is not exaggerating to say that the political structure of the nation, from state houses to Washington, is being remade. Clearly, in the future, metropolitan residents, in great cities and sprawling suburbs, will exert much more political power than formerly.

The industrial expansion which accompanied World War I provided the final spurt of growth needed to change the nation from one predominantly rural to one in which the majority of people lived in cities. By the census of 1920, for the first time, a slight majority of the American people were classified as urban as then defined (essentially, residents of incorporated places of 2,500 or more inhabitants; certain special rules applied to a few states, mostly in New England, in which townships function as units of local government for smaller communities, thus discouraging incorporation). In the United States, then, the emergence of a society in which city dwellers predominate has been recent.

From *International Journal of Comparative Sociology*, E. J. Brill, Leiden, Holland, Vol. 4, No. 2, pp. 259–273 (September, 1963). Reprinted by permission of publisher and author.

Even today, the United States is by no means the most complete example of urbanization. Among major powers, the United Kingdom has a markedly greater proportion of urban dwellers than the United States. Several other nations also exceed the United States in their urban proportions. (Such comparisons, to be very meaningful, involve coping with varying definitions of "urban," making allowance for different dates of enumeration, and so on).

It is difficult to know what the "saturation point" of urbanization in any society may be. Davis notes that the United States may eventually reach the stage of urbanization which England seems already to exemplify, the stage in which large urban centers begin to "eat up" the little ones, so that it is no longer rural communities, but smaller urban centers, which are being engulfed.[1] However this may be, there may well remain in America a core of rural residents sufficiently numerous to prevent it from becoming the extreme example of urbanization. The vast territory, with its extensive agricultural areas, presumably will always provide residence for a considerable number of at least technically rural persons.

As the reapportionment struggle indicates, in some respects the United States has yet to complete its transition into an urbanized society. American self-conceptions still draw heavily on the folklore of the agrarian society of the early days of national existence. It is true that the United States lacks the heritage of a sturdy peasantry with centuries-old ties to village and region, but this does not preclude a continuing emotional bias, based partly, no doubt, on nostalgia, depicting farmlands and villages as the "real" America. Even advertisers, when drawing on themes of national identity and the cultural heritage, tend to illustrate their appeals with scenes of "Main Street" suggesting either New England or the Middle West. Indeed, Wood emphasizes that the small-town model has invaded the metropolitan areas themselves. Suburban communities, to the damage, he maintains, of themselves, the cities, and the nation, seek to perpetuate their version of a "grass roots" tradition which developed under quite different circumstances.[2]

Moreover, despite the tremendous influence of New York, American administrative, intellectual, and "cultural" activities are less centered in one great metropolis than is true in many other nations. An obvious contributing factor is the separation of the seat of the government from the financial and "cultural" capital.

[1] Kingsley Davis, "Urbanization—Changing Patterns of Living," Chapter 3 in *The Changing American Population;* A Report of the Arden House Conference, Hoke S. Simpson (ed.), New York: Institute of Life Insurance, 1962, p. 62.
[2] Robert C. Wood, *Suburbia*, Boston: Houghton Mifflin Company, 1958.

The functional advantages offered by centralization have not been reinforced in America by a policy of deliberate centralization, as long exemplified (before 1955) in French history. As Robertson says:

> With a sixth of the national population, Paris today contains a quarter of the industrial labor force . . . With new industries there is often an even greater degree of concentration; seventy per cent of the workers in car manufacturing, eighty-two per cent in electronics and sixty-two per cent in pharmaceuticals, for example, are employed in Paris. It is thus not surprising that before restrictions were introduced, Paris accounted for thirty-one per cent of the area of new factory building in France. An even greater percentage of companies has their headquarters in the capital.[3]

Many predominantly rural nations, such as Cuba, Mexico, or Iran, are similarly capital-centered and are more dependent, in many respects, on a single city than Americans are on New York.

Despite all such reservations, the United States remains a, and in many ways, *the* great exemplification of industrial urbanism. By the current definition, approximately seven of every ten Americans, some 125,000,000 persons, are urban, probably the largest number so categorized in any nation. Urban residents outnumber the rural population in 39 of the 50 states. The population living in large cities is also very great, probably the largest such total in the world.[4] In 1960, 96,000,000 urban Americans lived in "urbanized areas," and almost 113,000,000, or 63 percent of the national population, resided in "standard metropolitan statistical areas." (See Table 4-1; clarification of the concepts, "urbanized areas" and "standard metropolitan statistical areas," is presented below.)

America symbolizes urbanization also because of the vast size and international influence of its greatest cities, particularly New York. Whether or not this was the world's "largest city" long depended on the willingness of the classifier to accept the London

---

[3] B. C. Robertson, *Regional Development in the European Economic Community*, London: Allen and Unwin, 1962, p. 44.
[4] Such statements can only be made tentatively, because of the difficulties of international comparisons even when full data are available. The populations of American cities were compared with those of the Soviet Union and China, as these are presented in: International Urban Research: *The World's Metropolitan Areas*, Berkeley: The University of California Press, 1959. By their estimates, central cities of such metropolitan areas in the United States exceeded by less than 2,000,000 persons the population in Chinese cities, and by about 7,000,000 persons the population in Soviet cities. Comparisons of the entire "urban zones" could not be made, because such areas could be delineated for few Russian and no Chinese cities. It seems safe to assume, however, that such comparisons, if possible, would have the effect of enlarging the American excess over the metropolitan population of China and the U.S.S.R.

Metropolitan Police District and the municipality of New York as comparable. As every schoolboy now is aware, this debate became obsolete with the recent emergence of Tokyo as a city, larger than either, but neither London nor Tokyo is the center of so intricate a megalopolitan network of city, satellites, and suburbs as is New York. In 1960, there were 14,115,000 residents of this urbanized area, and its separation from a string of contiguous areas in Connecticut was purely arbitrary.

TABLE 4-1. POPULATION, 1960 AND 1950, INCREASE DURING DECADE, AND PROPORTION OF NATIONAL TOTAL, FOR SMSA'S, URBAN, RURAL-NONFARM, AND RURAL-FARM CATEGORIES (All Totals in 000's)

| | Population | | Increase | Percentage | Percentage of National Population, |
| | | | | Increase, | |
	1960	1950	1950–1960	1950–1960	1960
UNITED STATES	179,323	151,325[1]	27,997	18.5	100.0
Living in SMSA's as defined in 1960	112,885	89,315	23,570	26.4	63.0
In Central Cities	58,004	52,390	5,614	10.7	32.3
Outside Central Cities	54,881	36,925	17,956	48.6	30.6
URBAN: TOTAL	125,269	96,848	28,421	29.3	69.9
In Cities of 100,000 and more	51,013	44,560	6,453	14.5	28.4
In Cities of 50,000–99,999	13,836	8,931	4,905	54.9	7.7
In Cities of 10,000–49,999	32,519	20,713	11,806	57.0	18.1
In Cities of 2,500–9,999	17,360	14,722	2,638	17.9	9.7
OTHER URBAN	10,541	7,922	2,619	33.1	5.9
RURAL-NONFARM	40,597[2]	31,424[3]	9,173[2]	29.2[2]	22.6
RURAL-FARM	13,445[2]	23,053[3]	−9,608[2]	−41.7[2]	7.5

Source: 1960 Census of Population

[1] 1950 totals revised to include Alaska and Hawaii.
[2] Change in definition of rural-farm population produced a net change in classification of an estimated 4,200,000 persons. If this number is added to the 1960 rural-farm population and subtracted from the rural-nonfarm population, the percentage change of the two becomes −23.5 and 15.8, respectively.
[3] 1950 totals include estimated rural-nonfarm and rural-farm populations of Alaska and Hawaii.

In recent years, observers have noted how some major American metropolitan areas are growing *toward* each other by expanding, in a vast complex of residential, commercial, and industrial development, along the transport lines linking them. Such "strip cities" or "supercities" appear to be emerging along the Great Lakes, the Pacific Coast, and very recently, the Florida east coast, but all these are dwarfed by the string of metropolitan areas starting north of Boston, extending through Massachusetts and Connecticut into New York, across New Jersey and through Philadelphia, Wilmington, and Baltimore to the southern suburbs of Washington. It is incorrect to imply that throughout this vast area, 500 miles in length, urban density prevails without gaps. This series of mammoth metropolitan areas, however, developing in response to a common functional impulse, is achieving an interpenetration of urban and rural which Gottman sees as a portent of future trends in metropolitan development in the industrial world.

Borrowing the term "megalopolis" to apply to this region, he observes that, within 10,000 square miles of densely settled territory, it contains one-fifth of the national population, one-tenth of the manufacturing capacity of the entire world, and perhaps one-fifth of the big business management of the globe. It has become "the most active crossroads on earth, for people, ideas, and goods, extending its influence far beyond the national borders. . . ."[5]

Not only urbanization, in the demographic sense, but urbanism as a design for living, has permeated the United States. In this sense virtually all Americans are urban. Agriculture itself has developed urban-like characteristics in its rationalization of production, its market orientation, its functional specialization. Large farms, usually remote from great cities, produce the basic staples—indeed, produce embarrassing surpluses of these staples. Specialized farming areas, providing perishable items for the cities, are highly concentrated in easy access to them or in particular climatic zones. The dairy industry has often been cited as the example *par excellence* of thoroughly urbanized agricultural operations. Gottman reports what must surely be the ultimate in urbanized agriculture—the establishment of a "cow-sitting" service for New Jersey dairy farmers who must be away from their herds.[6]

Thus, the density of the farm population itself increases in the vicinity of cities, despite competing demands for land. Within the ten percent of the national territory included in the standard metropolitan statistical areas live almost 15 per cent of America's

---

[5] Jean Gottman, *Megalopolis*, New York: The Twentieth Century Fund, 1961, pp. 9 and 385.
[6] *Ibid.*, p. 216.

farmers. This reflects to some degree the prevalence of part-time farming near the city, enabling a man to farm while also holding an urban job. As Anderson says, this may, for many, be a substitute for migration to the city.[7] A variant, or perhaps a reversal, of this pattern is that of the successful urbanite who moves to the nearby countryside as a "gentleman farmer." As Gottman comments, such men are farmers because they are "gentlemen" rather than being gentlemen because they own large farms, as was the historical relationship.[8]

In patterns of thought and levels of aspiration, the impact of urban values has made rural Americans part of an essentially urbanized society. A generation ago, Charles S. Johnson reported that Negro children in plantation cabins verbalized urban professional and white-collar occupational ambitions. Recently, in another supposed "backwater" of American rural life, Ford found that Southern highlanders express similar occupational and educational aspirations for their children.[9] That such goals, in the plantation or mountain setting, are often unrealistic and may be seriously pursued by few is beside the point; recognition of, and reaction to, status-yielding urban activities influence the thinking of these people who, by American standards, are the very prototype of rurality. The beginning, during the 1950's, of systematic placing of selected American Indians in cities suggests the inevitable yielding to the urban-industrial nexus of the society of the last stronghold of resistance—the Southwestern reservations.

Except perhaps in degree, this interpenetration of urban and rural is not uniquely American, but is a part of industrial society as such. As Anderson states, villages which have retained, largely uninfluenced by urban patterns, their traditionally rural perspectives have become rare in Belgium, Holland, West Germany, and the United Kingdom as well as the United States.[10]

The United States has been in the process of urbanizing throughout its national existence. In 1790, with but two cities of over 25,000 people, only five per cent of the population was urban. Throughout the 19th century, the unprecedented growth of the nation produced a dramatic expansion of both rural and urban populations, but, except during the decade, 1810–1820, the urban

[7] Nels Anderson, The Urban Community, New York: Henry Holt & Co., 1959, p. 99.
[8] Gottman, op. cit., p. 231.
[9] Charles S. Johnson, Shadow of the Plantation, Chicago: University of Chicago Press, 1934; Thomas A. Ford, The Southern Appalachian Region, Chapter 2, "The Passing of Provincialism," Lexington: The University of Kentucky Press, 1962.
[10] Anderson, op. cit., p. 79.

population grew faster. A century after the initial census, the urban population was more than one-third the total; in 1900, it was almost two-fifths. As noted previously, by 1920 it was half, and now is 70 percent, of the national population.

In 1790, Philadelphia was the nation's largest city, but by 1820, New York passed the 100,000 mark and assured its supremacy as the North American metropolis. By 1850, this city had over 500,000 residents and Brooklyn had passed 100,000. Thirty years later, New York had over a million people, and in 1900, after the union of the five boroughs, the enlarged city contained 3,500,000 persons. The growth of Chicago, after the census of 1840, and the growth, during the present century, of the Los Angeles area, have been equally impressive. It is possible to find Texans who maintain that Houston has entered a cycle of metropolitan expansion which will repeat the historical pattern of these great cities.

By 1960, there were 5,445 urban "places"—not all of them incorporated—of 2,500 or more persons. Of these, 130 were cities with more than 100,000 persons within their city limits; there were 154 urbanized areas of more than 100,000 people.

Many factors contributed to the rapid development and to the distinctive characteristics of urbanization in this new land. The abundant resources, the technological revolution in production and transportation, and the demographic processes in Europe and America, providing the population for such expansion, were obviously among the necessary factors. Other, somewhat less obvious, factors contributed. The role of New England in establishing industry and, indeed, in shaping so much of the ultimate American culture reminds one of the oft-assumed and sometimes-disputed functions of the Calvinist ethic in facilitating the development of industrial urbanism in America. Sjoberg observes that the United States was unique in lacking the "dead weight" of the past to retard adaptations. His point specifically is that the lack of an entrenched feudal elite made possible a strong development of industrial organization with a minimum resistance.[11] On a somewhat similar point, Anderson notes that European cities, with roots in unique developmental patterns arising in the medieval period, defy categorization more than the relatively standardized American cities; we can think of "typical" American cities of particular sizes to an extent inappropriate in older countries.[12]

Anderson also stresses the importance of the American frontier in encouraging industrial and urban development, at first in

---

[11] Gideon Sjoberg, *The Preindustrial City*, Glencoe: The Free Press, 1960, p. 336.

[12] Anderson, *op. cit.*, p. 71.

Britain, but indirectly in this country too, by creating a brand of individualism well suited for later application in industrial development.[13] Strauss denies that land was the exclusive attraction of the frontier, as popular traditions sometimes suggest. Towns emerged along with agricultural settlement, and when railroads cut through unsettled areas, towns established on the new railroads were the actual nuclei from which homesteaders dispersed. Nor was there anything modest in the aspirations of these "urban" pioneers—the towns did not just grow. They were promoted. Each was to become the Western metropolis, the city of the future.[14]

The stream of immigrants who entered the United States became, with the passing of time, increasingly urban-directed in their migration. The Irish, fleeing famine in the late 1840's, and needing immediate wages to aid destitute kinsmen at home, became the first immigrant group to rely much less heavily on the quest for land than on employment in industry, construction, and transportation. This pattern so early established persisted among the Irish immigrants, but by the 1890's, virtually all immigrant groups were primarily remaining in the expanding cities. By this date, the so-called "new immigration" from southern and eastern Europe was underway. Thus, American cities became markedly more heterogeneous in ethnic and religious composition than was most of rural America, a factor which long influenced rural-urban relations. Indeed, this is even yet not entirely a matter of the past; the election returns of 1960, when President Kennedy became the first Catholic to achieve the presidency, reflected a rural-urban contrast in voting patterns.

During the present century, the automobile has contributed not only to the continued urban and industrial expansion of the nation, but has been instrumental in altering urban ecology. The megalopolitan character of contemporary growth is intricately linked with automotive transport. Greater Los Angeles which, with more than 6,000,000 persons, has experienced nearly all of its growth since 1900, has come to symbolize the metropolis shaped by the car—witness its sprawl; its far-flung suburbs; its drive-in establishments ranging from laundries to churches; its giant multilaned expressways with their elaborate clover-leaf intersections; yes, even its smog, of which automobile exhaust is a major component.

In the South, the plantation system resulted in a lagging urbanization, with fewer and smaller cities. As Smith observes, the

[13] *Ibid.*, pp. 158–161.
[14] Anselm Strauss, *Images of the American City*, New York: The Free Press of Glencoe, 1961, pp. 93–96.

course of urbanization in the South resembled that of the nation as a whole except that it followed about fifty years behind the national pattern.[15] Southern cities, with few exceptions, developed as transportation and commercial, rather than industrial, centers. Economically, Southern urbanization, as Heberle remarks, followed essentially a "colonial" development, dependent on the North in somewhat the same manner that Polish and Balkan cities were long subsidiary to economic interests of Western Europe. Industrialization and urbanization under such circumstances produce a late development of secondary industries, very largely limited to the extraction and first processing of resource-based primary industries; a predominance of low-wage industries producing low-grade consumer goods; a sparsity of large cities, with smaller ones functioning as market centers; and out-migration to industrial centers elsewhere.[16] Although this is now changing, in many ways the urban, as well as the rural, South still lags by American standards. Whether explained by a "colonial" economy, the cumulative costs of racial discrimination, the reservoir of cheap rural labor, or a combination of these and other factors, Southern cities provide distinctly lower average incomes than other American cities. This is true despite the white-collar occupational structure and relatively high median educational attainment of residents of many Southern cities.[17]

As Table 4-2 indicates, Southern, and especially Western, cities have recently increased much more rapidly than the national average. The fastest proportionate increase was in the Mountain states, where a very rapid expansion of urban population transformed Arizona, Colorado, and New Mexico. The appeal of the desert is much extolled in America today, but the figures suggest that most persons prefer to combine their desert way of life with full urban amenities. The largest gross increment of urban population occurred in the Pacific states, which added more than 6,000,000 persons to the urban category during the 1950's.

[15] T. Lynn Smith, "The Emergence of Cities," in Rupert Vance and Nicholas Demerath, *The Urban South*, Chapel Hill: The University of North Carolina Press, 1954, p. 32.
[16] Rudolf Heberle, "The Mainsprings of Southern Urbanization," in Vance and Demerath, *op. cit.*, pp. 7–8.
[17] In 1959, the median family income for urban Americans was $6,163, an average rarely approached by Southern cities. The median family income of all Americans, urban and rural, was $5,660. Of 154 urbanized areas with 100,000 or more residents, 50 recorded median family incomes lower than this latter figure. In the South, 40 of 58 areas had family incomes lower than those of the national population. Outside the South, only 10 of 96 urbanized areas had incomes this low. Moreover, the cities in the census South with the highest incomes are peripheral to the region, being located in the southern reaches of "Megalopolis" and in Texas.

It was evident, by 1950, that reliance on incorporated centers as the basis of the urban definition was classifying as "rural-nonfarm" millions of persons who in fact lived in thickly settled areas. The definition of urban was therefore revised to include not only incorporated, but also unincorporated, centers of 2,500 or more, plus densely settled areas around cities of 50,000 or more. Procedures were also revised concerning townships in certain states; these are now divided into urban and rural segments. The 1950 and 1960 censuses presented data following both definitions. In 1960, the difference between the two (Table 4-2) exceeded 12,000,000, or about 10 percent of the urban population by the "new" definition.

In the immediate vicinity of great cities, the two definitions diverge widely. Nassau County, adjacent to New York City on Long Island, is an extreme example. In 1960, this small county of only 300 square miles contained 1,300,171 persons. The county-wide density of 4,000 per square mile was much greater than that of such municipalities as San Diego or Houston. Within this county, 34 incorporated places of 2,500 or more had 426,384 people, which would be the entire urban population under the standard procedures of the "old" definition. Virtually all of the remainder would be "rural-nonfarm." Of these, 715,862, more than half the population of the county, lived in 31 areas designated as "unincorporated places" by census procedures. An additional 31,021 lived in 27 municipalities which, covering very small territories, had less than 2,500 persons each. An additional 122,383 people lived in no designated "place," but in territory meeting urban standards of density. Only in its northeastern corner was the county too sparsely settled to be considered urban. Under the current definition, Nassau County was 99.7 percent urban, having but 4,521, rather than 873,787, rural residents.

American census sources also designate "urbanized areas" and "standard metropolitan statistical areas," ordinarily referred to as SMSA's (called in 1950 simply "standard metropolitan areas," or SMA's). Urbanized areas and SMSA's are established around one or more "central cities" of 50,000 or more persons. (Twin cities, such as Champaign-Urbana, Illinois, and Texarkana, Arkansas-Texas, are sometimes combined as a functional central city, although neither unit alone has as many as 50,000 persons). The designation of central cities for the two concepts differs slightly; currently delineated are 213 urbanized areas, 212 SMSA's. In the great majority of instances, of course, the designation of central cities is identical.

The "urbanized area," expressed simply, consists of the central

TABLE 4-2. 1960 TOTAL, "NEW" AND "OLD" URBAN, CENTRAL CITY, URBANIZED AREA, AND SMSA POPULATIONS, PERCENTAGE URBAN, AND PERCENTAGE INCREASE OF URBAN POPULATION, FOR CENSUS REGIONS AND DIVISIONS

(All Population Totals in 000's)

	Total Population	"New" Definition Urban Population, 1960	Percentage Urban, 1960	Percentage Increase of Urban, 1950–1960	Urban Population, 1960, "Old" Definition	Population in Central Cities of SMSA's	Population in Urbanized Areas	Population in SMSA's
U.S. TOTAL	179,323	125,269	69.9	29.3	113,056	58,004*	95,848	112,885
NORTHEAST	44,678	35,840	80.2	14.2	32,542	17,322	30,611	35,347
New England	10,509	8,032	76.4	13.1	7,888	3,246	6,368	7,393
Middle Atlantic	34,168	27,808	81.4	14.6	24,654	14,076	24,244	27,954
NORTH CENTRAL	51,619	35,481	68.7	24.5	32,994	16,511	26,550	30,960
East North Central	36,225	26,435	73.0	24.8	24,377	12,660	20,789	24,294
West North Central	15,394	9,046	58.8	23.8	8,617	3,851	5,761	6,666
SOUTH	54,973	32,160	58.5	40.1	28,966	15,062	21,501	26,447
South Atlantic	25,972	14,852	57.2	42.9	12,755	6,220	10,373	13,041
East South Central	12,050	5,831	48.4	30.0	5,253	2,411	3,451	4,344
West South Central	16,951	11,478	67.7	42.1	10,958	6,430	7,677	9,063
WEST	28,053	21,787	77.7	55.3	18,554	9,110	17,186	20,131
Mountain	6,855	4,601	67.1	65.1	4,145	2,047	2,837	3,348
Pacific	21,198	17,186	81.1	52.9	14,409	7,063	14,349	16,783

Source: 1960 Census of Population

* Population of central cities, as defined in urbanized areas, 57,975,000. Several specific divergences between the two classifications create distinct differences between the totals in a few states. On the national level, as the closeness of the totals indicates, these differences largely cancel each other out.

city (or cities), plus essentially contiguous territory of sufficient density per square mile (500 residences in 1950; 1,000 or more persons—a less dense measure—in 1960) to be considered urban. Thus, the urbanized area, the ecological city, expands as a city grows outward. For this reason, comparison from one census to another will always potentially overstate growth; some persons will not be new residents, but residents of districts with changed classification.

The SMSA consists of the county containing the central urban aggregate, plus any additional counties classified by established criteria as functionally integrated with it. In New England, townships are used in designating such areas, a point to remember when comparing this and other census divisions. New England SMSA's are usually much smaller in area, with much less peripheral territory, than those elsewhere. Enormous Western counties provide the opposite extreme. (San Bernardino in California, and Maricopa in Arizona, are larger in area than all of New Jersey.) Temporal comparisons, vital statistics, and economic and political information can be obtained easily for SMSA's through use of data presented by county units.[18] The built-up territory outside the central city in an urbanized area is referred to as the "urban fringe"; the area outside the central city within an SMSA frequently is called the "metropolitan ring."

Helpful as is the "new" definition of urban in bringing American demography into closer contact with reality, there remains an underenumeration of the essentially urban population, particularly in two respects. First is the failure to designate an "urban fringe" adjacent to cities under 50,000 persons. In the Northeast particularly, many cities as small as 15,000 and 20,000 have recorded declines during one or more of the last three decades. An increasing rural-nonfarm population in adjoining minor civil divisions suggests that a marked "urban fringe" often surrounds quite small cities. A second major source of underenumeration of the functionally urban population derives from the fact that the "interpenetration" of urban and rural extends far beyond areas of sufficient density to qualify as "urban fringe." The leap-frog nature of American suburban development has placed many persons in small subdivisions or isolated homes well beyond the urbanized area. Surrounding very large cities, an extensive area exists with a pop-

[18] For discussion of the utility of these two concepts, see Donald J. Bogue, "Urbanism in the United States, 1950," *American Journal of Sociology*, LX, No. 5, March, 1955. Bogue's presentation applies, of course, to the 1950 designation of such areas, but his comments apply to the current usage, except that the expense and labor of delineating urbanized areas as in 1950 has been eliminated.

ulation density below urban, but far above "normal" American rural, levels. Participants in a rather spectacular form of super-suburban living are described and dubbed "exurbanites" by Spectorsky.[19]

As shown by Tables 4–1 and 4–2, most of the expansion of the urban and of the national population during the 1950's occurred within the "metropolitan ring." The national growth, in round numbers, was 28,000,000; the increase within SMSA's was almost 18,000,000, or 64.1 percent of the national growth. Central cities increased by only 10.7 percent, as compared with a national growth of 18.5 percent and a "ring" growth of 48.6 percent. Much of the rapid growth of communities of less than 100,000 during this dec-ade, incidentally, arose from the hundreds of new places, some incorporated, some not, which appeared for the first time in the 1960 tabulations. In California alone, fifty such places had 10,000 or more people. Most of these new places are within existing SMSA's.

Even so, the material just presented understates the actual decentralization of metropolitan areas during the 1950's. Schnore demonstrated that nearly all of the growth of central cities resulted from annexations which occurred in 160 of the 212 SMSA's. The 1950 territory of the central cities increased only 1.5 percent in population (rather than 10.7), and the growth of the metropolitan rings is correspondingly adjusted from 48.6 percent to 61.6.[20]

Schnore further notes that, if annexation is ignored, the cities of the West South Central and Mountain divisions appear to be cen-tralizing rather than the reverse. In these states, extensive annexa-tion has been the rule, so that much of the suburban fringe is incor-porated as soon as, or even before, it develops. The extreme exam-ple is an annexation "war" currently underway between Oklahoma City and a number of smaller municipalities. The contrast between Western and Southwestern cities and those elsewhere is more apparent than real, more a legal than an ecological difference.

Schnore also cites the need to differentiate between actually diminishing centralization and the peripheral expansion which is "normal" when any city grows. Duncan, Sabagh, and Van Arsdol conclude that most of the so-called "flight to the suburbs" reflects normal outward growth of cities, made more dramatic by the pil-

[19] August C. Spectorsky, *The Exurbanites*, Philadelphia: J. B. Lippincott Co., 1955.
[20] Leo F. Schnore, "Municipal Annexations and the Growth of Metropolitan Suburbs, 1950–60," *American Journal of Sociology*, LXVII, No. 4, January, 1962, pp. 406–417.

ing-up of population before 1946 and by the rigidity of city limits of most very large cities.[21] Davis suggests that a useful and simple index of urban concentration or deconcentration is the ratio of the territory of the aggregate to its population. When territory is growing more rapidly than population (which is usual today), deconcentration is occurring. The process, underway since 1811 in London, began accelerating, there as elsewhere, about 1920, with the coming of the automobile.[22] For American cities, Strauss similarly observes that suburbanization as such is not at all a new phenomenon. He quotes an advertisement of 1823 proclaiming the rustic virtues of Brooklyn Heights and reproduces a handbill from suburban Chicago, dated 1874, which is strikingly contemporary in its appeal. Distance to the city is presented in minutes rather than miles; a low down payment is announced, with reasonable monthly payments "until paid for," and the final inducement is "This is cheaper than renting!"[23]

What *is* new, of course, is the magnitude of outward movement made possible by modern transportation and the sheer massiveness of modern cities. Whether "normal" peripheral expansion or "flight to the suburbs," this has altered the patterns of existence of almost half the metropolitan population of the nation.

So numerous a suburban population is sometimes interpreted, in itself, as proving the desirability of suburban living, but as Whyte insists, many middle-income families have little choice other than to move to suburbia. He maintains that if cities could provide middle-income groups with suitable housing and neighbourhoods, many would prefer the city, and finds some indications of a return to the city of certain segments of the population.[24]

The tendency of suburbs, composed often of adults of about the same age and income levels, to be overly homogeneous is a frequent indictment. Certainly, particular small suburban cities are, in terms of median family income, among America's wealthiest communities. Some of these are lovely, but one must avoid thinking of suburbs exclusively in the image of Scarsdale or Grosse Point. There are suburbs for all economic levels except the very poor, and many have been built hastily, with little planning and cheap construction. Already some post-World War II tract developments are

[21] Beverly Duncan, Georges Sabagh, and Maurice Van Arsdol, "Patterns of City Growth," *American Journal of Sociology*, LXVII, No. 4, January, 1962, pp. 418–429.
[22] Davis, *op. cit.*, p. 64.
[23] Strauss, *op. cit.*, pp. 231–235.
[24] William H. Whyte, Jr., "Are Cities Un-American?" in *The Exploding Metropolis* by the editors of *Fortune*, Garden City: Doubleday and Co., Inc., 1958, pp. 23–38.

deteriorating rapidly. In Los Angeles, the expressive term "slurb" refers to such areas.

Any problems escaped by the millions moving from the cities have been exchanged for perplexing new suburban difficulties. These are fascinating, important, and complex, but cannot be considered here. A whole new literature, much of it exhortatory, much of it popular, has developed around suburbia and its life styles.

Two points concerning suburbia should be made, perhaps, before the topic is reluctantly left behind. First, the increased fertility of urban families has not only produced the unexpectedly rapid accretion of the national population since 1940, but now accounts for more of the growth of American metropolitan areas than does migration. This trend toward somewhat larger families has no doubt been an impetus to suburbanization. The reverse may be true also; suburban living has perhaps encouraged a continuation of the higher fertility pattern.

Second, much popular literature has ascribed characteristics to suburbia which may indeed be found there, but which are essentially middle-class characteristics rather than distinctively suburban products.[25]

The effects of the suburban movement on the large cities themselves are also complex. The cities have lost heavily from their young, married, middle-income, white populations. Much of the residual population of the cities, because of poverty, racial discrimination, or both, is denied access to outward movement. The word "flight," applied to the influx of Negroes from the plantation South, whites from the upland South, and Puerto Ricans, involves little exaggeration. The central cities of urbanized areas now have 51.4 percent of America's Negro population, but the "urban fringe" contains only 8.2 percent of our Negroes. Much of this small proportion is located adjacent to Southern cities where long-established Negro neighbourhoods on the outskirts are within the present "urban fringe." Sizable "urban fringe" Negro populations also live in industrial satellites, as in New Jersey; very few Negroes have participated in the suburban stream. Within the cities, the over-representation of the impoverished, the elderly, the unmarried, and the minorities adds up to staggering costs of social services.

A high degree of territorial mobility has always characterized Americans—another respect in which the demands of a specialized, expanding economy and the heritage of the frontier reinforce each other. In 1960, more than one of every six urban Americans (17.6 percent), five years of age or older, lived in a county other than

[25] Wood, *op. cit.*, p. 8.

that of their 1955 residence. The range is very great, from less than 4 percent for the Pennsylvania anthracite cities of Scranton and Wilkes-Barre to almost 50 percent in Fort Lauderdale-Hollywood, Florida. In a number of smaller southern and western urbanized areas, the proportion of migrants was above one-third. State-of-birth data for the native-born population provide additional information on migration patterns. In all urbanized areas, something less than two-thirds—64.8 percent—lived in the state where born. The percentage is above 90 in several smaller Pennsylvania urbanized areas and exceeds 80 for both Boston and Pittsburgh. At the other extreme, it is below 33 percent in Washington and in a number of western and southern communities, falling to 20.8 percent in St. Petersburg, Florida. Neither of these indexes measures intervening migration, and each includes moves merely within an urbanized area, because intercounty and interstate migration is possible within the limits of many such areas.

All large cities are diverse in the services they offer, the functions they fulfill, but a marked division of labor differentiates cities concerning their predominant activities. From the occupational data of the census, Smith devised a useful, easily applied technique of classifying American cities into functional types.[26] This technique, when applied to the cities of 100,000 or more in 1950, yields seven differentiating types: 1. Manufacturing cities, in which only manufacturing engages 17.5 percent or more of the male labor force. Detroit is an example of the 16 such cities. 2. Manufacturing and trading centers in which manufacturing employs larger numbers than trading. The 47 such cities are typified, perhaps, by Cincinnati. 3. Trading and manufacturing cities where trading is more significant. Seattle exemplifies the 18 cities of this type. 4. Diversified centers in which trading, manufacturing, and transportation each employ at least 17.5 percent. Of seven such centers, Omaha, as a rail center, Duluth, as a port, seem typical. 5. Trading centers. Little Rock exemplifies these eleven cities. 6. Transportation and trading centers. New Orleans, Jacksonville, and El Paso are the three such cities. 7. Public administration and trading centers. Again there are three: Washington, Norfolk, Sacramento.

Cities extremely high or low in particular occupational categories illustrate urban functional specialization. In two cities, for

[26] T. Lynn Smith, "The Functions of American Cities," in *The Sociology of Urban Life*, eds., Smith and C. A. McMahan, New York: The Dryden Press, 1951, pp. 97–103. For a somewhat more elaborate classification of cities in functional terms, see Howard J. Nelson, "A Service Classification of American Cities," in Jack P. Gibbs, ed., *Urban Research Methods*, Princeton: D. Van Nostrand Co., 1961, pp. 353–374.

example, more than 60 percent of the male workers were in manufacturing. These cities, Gary and Flint, were of necessity very low in most other occupational categories. By contrast, in Washington, Miami, and Austin, fewer than 10 percent were in industry. The high rank in professional and related services of three relatively small cities containing great universities—Berkeley, Austin, and Cambridge—causes as little surprise as the ascendancy of Los Angeles, Miami, Pasadena, and New Orleans in entertainment and recreation. Hartford and New York led in the proportion employed in finance, insurance, and real estate. In trading, Phoenix, Miami, and Tampa, with seasonal opportunities to sell to more than their base population, exceeded such cities as Charlotte and Dallas.

Certain uniformities emerge from the occupational data. A Southwestern-and-Florida pattern, high in trade, entertainment, personal services, construction, and finance, low in manufacturing, is evident. "White-collar" cities (such as Dallas, Atlanta, Denver, Des Moines) show basic resemblances in occupational structure despite their differences in region and rate of growth. Heavy-industry cities of the Middle West (South Bend, Gary, or Flint) show rather typical divergences from light-industry cities of the Northeast (such as Paterson or Fall River). An "Old South" type (such as Nashville or Montgomery) is very high in personal services, high in professional services and trade, low in manufacturing.

The study of the urban community as an entity, particularly in its ecological aspects, is a distinctly American contribution to the discipline of sociology. The impetus to urban sociology given by the Chicago studies continues, but has broadened during the past two decades to include much more than the designation of spatial patterns and the observation of their correlation with a variety of social phenomena. At the same time, critics—none more challenging and influential than Lewis Mumford—have thoroughly emphasized the flaws of the metropolis, particularly in its American form, adding an antidote to the overly mechanical perspective of early urban sociology. That the demographic tradition in urban studies continues strong is accounted for, at least in part, by the unprecedented wealth of information concerning urban communities provided by recent censuses. The quest for interdisciplinary consensus between sociologists, geographers, economists, political scientists, and the "practical" men of city planning and administration, engineering, and architecture, is grounded on the hope that the dynamic American urban world, in which seven of ten Americans live and of which all are truly a part, can retain its demonstrable advantages while miminizing its perplexing shortcomings.

Conventional versus Metropolitan Data
in the International Study of Urbanization

JACK P. GIBBS
University of Texas at Austin
and
KINGSLEY DAVIS
International Population and Urban Research,
University of California, Berkeley

Most of urban sociology rests upon observations made in countries representing a small and biased sample of the world as a whole. Any attempt, however, to remove this narrow restraint—that is, any attempt to extend comparative urban analysis to include all parts of the earth—runs into the complex problem of comparability. In the present paper we have no solution to offer for this problem as it affects all aspects of urban sociology, but we do have some information bearing upon the validity of one type of international comparison—namely, the degree of urbanization as between one country and another. This is perhaps the type of urban statistic most frequently used in comparing countries. The proportion of people living in urban places or in cities of a given size is considered a fundamental trait of any society. The data required for computing such proportions are, for many countries at least, readily obtainable and hence widely used.

In view of the importance and wide use of data on the degree of urbanization in countries and regions, it is essential that such data be at least approximately comparable from one area to another. There must be assurance that persons included as city residents in one country are not excluded in other countries, and vice versa. The researcher who makes comparisons of the extent of urbanization must normally, however, rely on the statistics that governmental agencies provide on cities. He therefore has control neither over the type of data reported nor over the demarcation of

From *American Sociological Review*, Vol. XXIII, No. 5, pp. 504–514 (October, 1958). A publication of International Population and Urban Research, University of California, Berkeley. Reprinted with permission of authors and the American Sociological Association.

towns and cities as statistical units. Since, as is well known, different governments follow different procedures in delimiting their urban units, there is great danger that apparent differences among countries in the proportion of the population living in towns or cities may be in part the result of contrasting definitions and statistical practices. Even within the same country there may be little uniformity from one province or state to another or from one city to another in drawing the urban boundaries.

The lack of comparability stems, of course, from the fact that the so-called "city" is often a political or administrative unit. As such, its boundaries may or may not approximate the actual limits of the demographic or ecological "city." Some cities, as defined by the government concerned, are "underbounded" in the sense that their territory embraces only a part of the total area that makes up the ecological city and their population includes only a part of the total urban aggregate; others are "overbounded" in the sense that their limits extend far beyond the city as a continuous urban area, embracing land that is rural by virtually any standard.[1]

This situation obviously poses a dilemma for the student of urban phenomena. On the one hand, he must of necessity often work with data on administratively defined cities; yet on the other hand he knows that the data are not strictly comparable. One way to resolve this dilemma would be to provide the student of international urbanization with an idea of the actual degree of comparability or incomparability of official data on urban proportions in the world's nations. This could best be done, of course, if by some magic we had information on the populations of the actual demographic cities of the earth, for then we could compare the official data with the correct data. Since we do not generally have this information, the next best procedure is to compare the official statistics with the data on metropolitan areas delimited throughout the world according to a roughly comparable standard. Such a task is now possible because the International Urban Research office has just finished a world-wide delimitation of Metropolitan Areas of 100,000 or more inhabitants. The present paper therefore attempts to assess the validity of international comparisons of degree of urbanization based on official statistics by checking such compari-

[1] In most industrial countries, the "cities" are underbounded. In the United States in 1950, for example, the central cities held only 70 per cent of the residents and only 49 per cent of the land encompassed in the Urbanized Areas. In the case of the Philippines, on the other hand, some of the "Chartered Cities" are overbounded to an extreme degree, for they embrace great stretches of purely rural and sometimes uninhabited land. A fuller treatment of the question of urban delimitation will be found in International Urban Research, *The World's Metropolitan Areas,* to be published in 1959 by the University of California Press.

TABLE 5-1. PER CENT OF TOTAL POPULATION URBAN AND PER CENT IN METROPOLITAN AREAS AND LOCALITIES OF SIX SIZE RANGES BY COUNTRIES, *Circa* 1950

Countries by Type of Locality*	Per Cent of Total Population in Localities by Size Ranges**						Per Cent Urban**	Areas*** Per Cent in Metropolitan
	2,000 +	5,000 +	10,000 +	20,000 +	50,000 +	100,000 +		
Type A								
Argentina, 1947	62.5	56.9	52.7	48.3	42.1	37.2	62.5	43.8
Australia, 1947	74.2¹	66.4¹	61.6¹	57.3¹	52.4¹	51.4¹	68.9	55.4
Cuba, 1953	50.9¹	45.0¹	40.9¹	36.5¹	28.5¹	21.9¹	57.0¹	26.0
Denmark, 1950ᵃ	58.8	55.7	51.4	44.8	36.7	33.5	67.3	45.5
France, 1954	50.2¹	42.4¹	36.8¹	29.8¹	21.2¹	15.0¹	55.9	34.4
India, 1951	37.7	21.1	15.3	12.0	8.7	6.6	17.3	7.8
Ireland, 1951	40.5	35.5	32.2	28.3	23.7	17.6	41.5	23.4
Israel, 1949ᵇ	73.6¹	66.2¹	61.9¹	51.3¹	45.6¹	45.6¹	71.3¹	55.9ᵉ
Italy, 1951	56.5¹	45.4¹	37.5¹	30.3¹	21.9¹	17.0¹	40.9¹	27.3
Netherlands, 1947	72.6	63.6	56.1	49.8	41.3	32.7	54.6	45.6
Norway, 1950	44.1	40.3	38.4	32.7	26.0	19.8	32.2	21.8
Pakistan, 1951	10.2¹	10.0¹	9.1¹	8.0¹	5.9¹	5.1¹	11.4	5.1
Portugal, 1950	31.2	24.6	19.4	16.4	12.7	12.7	31.2	19.6
Sweden, 1950	51.9	45.4	40.3	33.0	25.5	19.4	47.5	31.8
United States, 1950ᵈ	65.1¹	60.3¹	56.2ᵉ	52.0ᵉ	46.8¹	43.9¹	64.0	55.9
Type B								
Australia, 1947	71.5¹	62.9¹	55.4¹	43.9¹	17.2¹	3.0¹	68.9	55.4
Brazil, 1950	30.8	26.8	23.4	20.2	16.3	13.2	36.2	17.6
Canada, 1951	50.7	45.3	40.2	35.1	27.5	23.3	61.6	45.5
Ceylon, 1946	15.2	14.8	14.0	11.4	8.7	5.4	15.4	9.5
Colombia, 1951	34.7¹	29.1¹	25.5¹	22.4¹	18.2¹	14.7¹	36.3	18.6
Costa Rica, 1950	28.6	23.7	18.8	10.9	10.9	0.0	33.5	19.9
Dominican Republic, 1950	21.5	18.5	16.0	11.1	11.1	8.5	23.8	11.2
Ecuador, 1950	27.7	24.0	21.3	17.8	14.6	14.6	28.5	14.9
El Salvador, 1950	27.6	21.7	17.3	12.9	11.5	8.7	36.5	11.9
Finland, 1950	35.1	31.6	28.2	22.2	14.2	14.2	32.3	17.0
Greece, 1951	49.7¹	38.3¹	33.9¹	26.8¹	16.0¹	12.7¹	36.8	22.0
Guatemala, 1950	23.9	16.8	12.5	11.2	10.2	10.2	25.0	10.6
Haiti, 1950	10.0	8.2	6.3	5.1	4.3	4.3	12.2	6.0
Honduras, 1950	17.2	11.8	9.8	6.8	5.3	0.0	31.0	7.3

Locality								
India, 1951	17.3[i]	16.7[i]	14.4[i]	11.9[i]	9.0	7.2[i]	17.3	7.8
Japan, 1950	59.6[i]	58.0[i]	50.7[i]	42.1[i]	33.2[i]	25.6[i]	37.5	36.3
Malaya, 1947	24.3	21.2	19.0	17.1	10.2	7.4	26.5	12.7
Mexico, 1950	45.5[i]	34.6[i]	28.9[i]	24.0[i]	18.7[i]	15.1[i]	42.6[i]	20.3
New Zealand, 1951	65.7	60.2	57.0	54.2	41.6	32.8	61.3	43.6
Nicaragua, 1950	28.0	21.7	19.0	15.2	10.3	10.3	34.9	13.3
Panama, 1950	42.5	33.8	27.8	22.4	22.4	15.9	36.0	23.9
Paraguay, 1950	28.1	20.2	18.4	15.2	15.2	15.2	34.6	15.6
Peru, 1940	25.5[i]	20.4[i]	17.5[i]	13.9[i]	10.5[i]	8.4[i]	36.1[i]	10.4
Philippines, 1948	21.0[i]	13.8[i]	8.9[i]	6.3[i]	4.1[i]	3.4[i]	24.1[i]	10.3
Thailand, 1947	9.9[i]	9.8[i]	8.9[i]	6.7[i]	4.5[i]	4.5[i]	9.9	6.8
Turkey, 1950	28.7	22.4	18.7	14.5	10.1	8.2	21.9	14.0
Union of South Africa, 1951	39.8	36.2	33.2	30.7	28.2	24.0	42.6	31.5
United Kingdom, 1951	79.7[i]	77.6[i]	74.0[i]	66.9[i]	50.8[i]	36.1[i]	80.3[i]	77.0
United States, 1950	59.8[i]	54.4[i]	49.0[e]	43.0[e]	35.3[i]	29.4[i]	64.0[i]	55.9
Venezuela, 1950	49.7[i]	42.4[i]	36.8[i]	32.2[i]	24.7[i]	20.6[i]	53.8	26.2
Type C								
Austria, 1951	65.7	49.3	43.1	39.8	35.2	32.9	49.2	38.9
Belgium, 1947	82.3	62.7	46.6	32.0	17.9	10.5	62.7	41.4
Egypt, 1947	90.9	64.1	40.3	29.1	22.7	19.3	30.1	19.6
France, 1954	62.6	49.8	41.5	33.3	23.1	16.8	55.9	34.4
Germany, East, 1950[f]	70.1[e]	57.2[e]	47.7[i]	39.2[i]	25.6[i]	20.8[i]	67.6[i]	37.9
Germany, West, 1950[g]	72.5	59.5	50.9	44.1	35.7	30.3	72.4[i]	51.2
Greece, 1951	55.4	42.0	36.3	28.1	16.2	12.7	36.8	22.0
Iraq, 1947	99.9	99.5	94.7	76.9	34.9	16.6	33.8	17.5
Italy, 1951	93.1	73.9	55.4	41.2	28.0	20.4	40.9[i]	27.3
Japan, 1950	98.0	75.1	53.9	42.4	33.2	25.6	37.5	36.3
Philippines, 1948	99.4	97.2	85.7	55.5	17.5	9.3	24.1	10.3
Spain, 1950[h]	83.2	66.3	51.8	39.8	30.3	24.1	37.0	24.2
Switzerland, 1950	68.1	48.1	36.4	29.1	24.7	20.6	36.5	41.2
Thailand, 1947	100.0	99.9	99.4	95.2	57.4	13.3	9.9	6.8

---

* See text for a description of the three types of localities.
** Unless designated otherwise the percentages shown in these columns are based on figures reported in the *Demographic Yearbook, 1955,* Tables 7 and 8.
*** Based on provisional figures prepared by International Urban Research.
a Excluding the Faeroe Islands; b Per cent urban for the year 1952; c 1951; d Urbanized Areas and incorporated or unincorporated places outside of Urbanized Areas treated as localities; e Estimate made by International Urban Research; f Including East Berlin; g Including West Berlin; h Including Canary Islands; i Census reports or official yearbooks used as source.

sons against those made with our data on Metropolitan Areas. The question is not only whether or not *any* comparison of national urbanization based on official statistics is valid, but also which kinds of official statistics on urbanization are *most* valid.

TREATMENT OF DATA AND SOURCES

Since the procedures employed in our world-wide delimitation of Metropolitan Areas are set forth at length in another publication,[2] we shall describe them only briefly. We began with a list of all administratively defined cities or continuous urban areas of 50,000 or more, designating them as principal cities. Then the administrative or territorial units around these cities were examined to determine the percentage of their labor force engaged in agriculture and their distance from the principal city. To be included in a Metropolitan Area, an administrative unit had to (1) touch upon the principal city or an administrative area already included in the M.A.; (2) have at least 65 per cent of its labor force engaged in non-agricultural occupations; (3) be located close enough to the principal city to make commuting feasible. In some cases the lack of data made it necessary to substitute a density criterion for the non-agricultural criterion, in which case any unit included in the M.A. had to have a density either equal to half or more of the density of the principal city (or the next inner ring) or twice that of the next outer ring. If the boundary of the area established by these criteria failed to include at least 100,000 people, we dropped it from the list.

This procedure for delimiting metropolitan areas, crude as it may be, is sufficiently standardized to guarantee a high degree of comparability. Furthermore, it can be applied to most of the world's countries and particularly to those containing numerous cities. It therefore furnishes a yardstick for assessing the validity of comparisons made on the basis of officially reported urban statistics.

The present analysis is made with reference to the 50 independent countries shown in Table 5-1, representing approximately half of the world's population and 42 per cent of its inhabited land area. For each country, as explained above, we utilize two kinds of data: our M.A. delimitations derived from the last census prior to 1954;[3] and the officially reported data on localities. Localities for which populations are officially reported fall into different classes

[2] International Urban Research, *op. cit.*
[3] This dating was violated in two cases: France, where the census was taken *in* rather than *prior* to 1954, and Ceylon, where the census of 1946 was used instead of that of 1953 (which was unavailable).

according to how the areas are delimited by the government concerned; and this fact in part accounts for the scepticism of many people concerning the comparability of urban data from one country to another. The United Nations, in its latest report on the population of localities by countries,[4] distinguishes three classes, as follows: Type A—agglomerations or clusters of population without regard to official boundaries or administrative functions; Type B—localities having fixed boundaries and an administratively recognized "town" status, usually characterized by some form of local government operating under a charter or terms of incorporation, and normally called by some such term as "city," "borough," "urban district," or "municipality"; Type C—minor civil divisions (often the smallest of the administrative divisions) which have fixed boundaries and which together comprise the entire territory of the country.[5] Our analysis in this paper undertakes to deal with each of these classes separately. For officially reported populations of localities in each class we have drawn upon the valuable data provided by the United Nations Statistical Office in the *Demographic Yearbook* (cited above), where the localities are grouped by ten size-classes. It has proved necessary, however, to go beyond the Statistical Office's data, either by including additional countries or data on one of the types of locality not provided for a particular country.[6]

For each of the 50 countries the reader will find in Table 5-1 the percentage of the nation's total population residing in localities of six open-ended size-classes. The countries are grouped in this table according to the type of locality used as a reporting unit—Types A, B, and C. Some countries appear twice in the table because for them two types of localities are reported. To be sure, questions concerning the proper classification of countries by type of locality used as a reporting unit present a problem. In several cases it is difficult to ascertain the exact status of the localities, and in other cases it appears that the localities constitute a mixture of Types A and B. The seriousness of this problem is lessened, however, by our results, as will be seen presently.

Having, on the one hand, the percentage of the population living in M.A.s of 100,000 or over based on our own delimitations[7] and, on the other hand, the officially reported data for percentage

[4] United Nations, *Demographic Yearbook, 1955*, New York: 1955, Table 8, pp. 198–215.
[5] *Ibid.*, p. 17.
[6] In the case of France, for example, the localities reported by the United Nations are minor civil divisions (Type C). We have made use of these figures in our analysis, but have also obtained data from French census reports on agglomerations (Type A).
[7] The M.A. percentages given in Table 5-1 must be considered provisional.

"urban" and percentage in six size-classes of locality (grouped into three definition-classes), we proceeded to run correlations as a test of the validity of the officially reported information.

ANALYSIS OF FINDINGS

The results, shown in Table 5-2, strikingly belie the hypothesis that officially reported statistics on either urban agglomerations (Type A) or administratively defined cities and towns (Type B) are grossly non-comparable as between countries. The product-moment coefficients of correlation (r) between the percentage in any size-class of urban agglomerations or clusters (Type A) and the percentage in M.A.s is .91 or above. As could be expected, the correlations are generally lower between the percentages in cities and towns defined administratively (Type B) and the proportion in M.A.s; but the difference between this and the Type A case is amazingly small.

   Special interest attaches to the last column of Table 5–2. The proportion of the population said to be "urban" presumably varies from one country to the next in part because the dividing line between "rural" and "urban" is arbitrary and unstandardized. The United Nations *Demographic Yearbook* for 1955 (p. 16) lists several reasons for noncomparability in this respect, and Table 7 [not shown here] in this issue, showing the proportion urban by countries, is careful to include in each case the definition of "urban."[8] As the last column of our Table 5–2 shows, however, the defects in the official distinction between "rural" and "urban," although real and admittedly undesirable, do not render meaningless the reported figures on the percentage urban. In fact, so long as the countries are using definitions that relate to Type A or Type B localities, regardless of the exact rural-urban dividing line they prescribe, the proportion urban constitutes an index of national urbanization that can be used with some degree of confidence.

   Because the boundaries of Type A and Type B localities are drawn on a different basis, one might infer that an index of urbanization based on the one is not comparable with an index based on the other. Although this is true in the sense that there is an obvious danger in mixing the two, especially if individual countries are being compared, the fact remains that both classes are highly cor-

[8] The *Demographic Yearbook* for 1952 followed the same procedure in giving data by countries for the proportion urban. It also included a discussion of the validity of the data, concluding (on pp. 9–10) that international comparisons of the percentage urban should be avoided "except in the most general way." However, it was found (p. 11) that the percentage urban correlates with the percentage in cities of 100,000 or more to the extent of 0.84.

TABLE 5-2. COEFFICIENTS OF CORRELATION (r) BETWEEN PER CENT IN METROPOLITAN AREAS AND SEVEN INDICES OF URBANIZATION BY COUNTRIES, *Circa* 1950

Countries by Type of Locality	Per Cent in Localities by Size Range						Per Cent Urban*
	2,000+	5,000+	10,000+	20,000+	50,000+	100,000+	
15 Countries with Type A Localities (urban aggregates or clusters)	+.91	+.96	+.96	+.96	+.96	+.95	+.94
30 Countries with Type B Localities (administratively demarcated "towns" and "cities")	+.92ᵃ	+.94ᵃ	+.95ᵃ	+.95ᵃ	+.95ᵃ	+.90ᵃ	+.92
14 Countries with Type C Localities (minor civil divisions)	−.56	−.68	−.68	−.59	−.19	+.59	+.86
Countries with Types A or B Localities	+.92ᵇ	+.95ᵇ	+.96ᵇ	+.95ᵇ	+.95ᵇ	+.91ᵇ	+.92ᶜ

* Per cent urban as administratively defined. These figures have no necessary connection with the types of localities as defined in the stub, but simply characterize the countries in question.
ᵃ Excluding Australia, N=29. If Australia is included as a Type B country (N=30), the correlations for each size-class, from left to right, are as follows: .93, .95, .95, .95, .89, and .74.
ᵇ Excluding Australia as a Type B country, N=44. With Australia included as a Type B country (N=45) the corresponding correlations, from left to right, are: .93, .95, .96, .95, .91, and .82.
ᶜ Excluding all Type B countries which are also included as a Type A, N=42.

related with the proportion in M.A.s. Furthermore, when the two groups are combined, as in the last line of Table 5–2, the correspondence with the proportion in 100,000-plus M.A.s remains very high. We can thus conclude that in comparing groups of countries with reference to urbanization, those that define localities in Type A terms can be compared to those that define localities in Type B terms with relative safety.

Our results, however, are by no means uniformly positive. We shall have occasion below to sound a warning about the use of official data on urban places *in general*. For the moment, let us cite the results referring specifically to countries that publish data on localities defined in Type C terms. It will be recalled that these are minor civil divisions (usually the smallest in the country) which, taken together, comprise the entire national area. In other words, they are territorial divisions like "counties" in the United States, "taluks" or "thanas" in India, or "municipios" in Latin America. As shown by line 3 in Table 5–2, the proportion of the population in such localities by size-class varies inversely with the proportion of the population in Metropolitan Areas. The only exception involves the minor civil divisions having a population of 100,000 or more; for when they become this large they apparently are in many cases urban and there is a correlation, albeit not a strong one, with the percentage in M.A.s. It seems clear that the proportion of the population in Type C localities, regardless of size-class, cannot be used with any security for purposes of international comparison.

A GENERAL WARNING

In addition to noting the unacceptability of Type C data for urban comparisons, it must be stressed that no international statistics on towns and cities should be used without critical examination. The point can be illustrated by reference to two cases, Australia and Thailand. Australia follows the extremely unusual practice of cutting up its urban agglomerations into very small politically-defined "cities." Therefore, if the figures for these "cities" (which are Type B units) are utilized uncritically as they stand, one winds up by reporting what is actually one of the world's most urbanized countries as having only 3 per cent of its population living in "cities" of 100,000 or more! When Australia is included in Table 5–2 as one of the countries in the Type B category, the correlations drop markedly, as shown in the table's footnotes. Fortunately, Australian census reports cover actual aggregates as well as politically defined places, and, as shown in Table 5–1, we need not depend on the Type B data for an index of urbanization in that country. But it is clear that uncritical use of Australian statistics for political localities might easily produce erroneous conclusions.

The case of Thailand shows the error of the uncritical use of the percentage urban as administratively defined. In this country the communes of more than 2,500 inhabitants are evidently designated in official reports as urban.[9] Since the commune is a minor civil division, this practice is tantamount to according urban status to all counties in the United States having a population of, say, 10,000 or more.

When the percentage urban in Thailand as reported in the Thai Yearbook (90.85) is used rather than the figure provided by the U.N.'s Statistical Office, the correlation between the percentage urban and the percentage in M.A.s is $+.69$ among Type B countries, $+.22$ for Type C countries, and $+.76$ when Types A and B countries are combined. The discrepancy between these correlations and the corresponding ones in Table 5–2 indicates that the percentage urban as administratively defined may in certain isolated cases bear no relationship whatever to the true extent of urbanization in a country. This is particularly the case when, as in Thailand, the urban-rural distinction is based on the population size of minor civil divisions (Type C localities).

THE CUTTING POINT FOR THE RURAL-URBAN DISTINCTION

One reason, of course, why the correlations in Table 5–2 show so little variation is that the size-classes are open at the top and therefore cumulative. In other words, the size-class 5,000 and over behaves statistically much like the class 10,000 and over because it is made up principally by the latter class. In the United States, for example, the 10,000-plus class of places includes 90.1 per cent of the population of all places of 5,000-plus.

To what extent, then, will the size-classes correlate with the metropolitan percentage when they are defined as mutually exclusive classes? The expectation, of course, is that on the whole the correlations will be reduced—and this is what happens, as Table 5–3 shows. But the variations are interesting. In Column 1, for exam-

[9] *Statistical Yearbook of Thailand, 1952,* Bangkok: Central Statistical Office, 1953, Table 15, p. 42. Interestingly, the United Nations, in its *Demographic Yearbook, 1955,* p. 193, does not utilize the figure given in the Thai yearbook, but instead gives a much more realistic figure for the percentage urban—9.9. This is the figure we have used in Table 5-1. How this percentage was obtained is not known, but in another table, p. 207, the *Demographic Yearbook* places the Thai localities into Type C and gives figures showing 99.9 per cent of the population as living in localities of more than 5,000 inhabitants.

TABLE 5-3. COEFFICIENTS OF CORRELATION (r) BETWEEN PER CENT IN
METROPOLITAN AREAS AND FOUR COMPONENT INDICES OF URBANIZATION
BY COUNTRIES, *Circa* 1950

Countries by Type of Locality	Per Cent in Localities by Size Range of Locality			
	2,000–4,999	*5,000–9,999*	*10,000–19,999*	*20,000–49,999*
Countries with Type A Localities N=15	−.08	+.26	+.55	+.40
Countries with Type B Localities* N=29	+.01	+.43	+.54	+.75
Countries with Types A or B Localities* N=44	+.07	+.43	+.58	+.67

* Australia excluded as a Type B country.

ple, it appears that the percentage of the population in places of
2,000 to 5,000 bears no relation to the percentage in metropolitan
areas of 100,000 or more. The explanation is doubtless the following: The proportion of people who live in places of this size is not a
function primarily of economic development or per capita wealth,
but a function of the pattern and the density of rural settlement. In
a country such as India, for instance, the proportion in places of
this size would be comparatively high, not because India is highly
urbanized but because the Indian countryside is very densely settled and its rural people follow the custom of congregating in villages rather than living in isolated farmsteads. In the United
States a lesser proportion can be expected to be in such places,
because the farmers tend to live on farmsteads and the business
people tend to live in places larger than 5,000. Inspection of the
actual proportions shows the expectations to hold true, as follows:

POPULATION IN PLACES OF 2,000–4,999

	Number	*As % of Total Population*	*As % of Population in All Places 2,000+*
India, 1951, Type A	59,108,973	16.6	44.0
U.S.A., 1950, Type A	7,290,205	4.8	7.4

We know that the United States is far more urban than India. The fact that it has a lesser proportion in towns of 2,000 to 5,000 inhabitants has nothing to do with the degree of urbanization in the two countries but a great deal to do with the average density and the residential agglutination in rural areas.

The data of Table 5–3 suggest that the cutting point between rural and urban should not be assumed, as most governments so do, to be somewhere between 2,000 and 5,000. This may be the appropriate range for a cutting point in some countries but not in others. An arbitrary boundary applied to all countries within this range would thus lead to distortion rather than to comparability. Actually, the best cutting point probably does not lie even in the 5,000 to 10,000 range. If a lower limit to the size of places to be called urban is to be adopted for international comparison, we believe that it would best be set at nothing less than 10,000 population. This may seem unorthodox, but the fact is that at best we are always using an *index* of urbanization; there is no absolute measure. An index based on the proportion of the population in places of 10,000 and over will correlate highly with the proportion in Metropolitan Areas of 100,000 or over. Putting the floor at this level not only has the advantage that data are easier to secure, but the virtue that the distortion introduced by the "standard" definition as between one type of country and another is minimized.

THE DEVIANT CASES AND URBAN ANALYSIS

In all studies of statistical association, special interest attaches to the deviant instances. In the present case, we may view the marked divergence of any country from the regression line as an invitation to investigate either the validity of the Metropolitan Areas delimited for it or the validity of its reporting for Type A or Type B localities.

In Figure 5–1, which shows a scatter diagram involving countries that supply data on Type B localities, the United States appears to be quite deviant, having a higher proportion in metropolitan areas than the percentage in cities and towns of 20,000 or more would seem to justify. Since the Standard Metropolitan Areas delimited by the Census Bureau were used for the United States, does this deviation from the trend line mean that the S.M.A.s are larger than they should be, as many critics have alleged; or does it mean that localities of over 20,000 are not fully representative of the degree of urbanization because, by the Type B definition, many places that are parts of big urban agglomerations are necessarily omitted? On the basis of Figure 5–1 alone, we would have no way of settling this issue, but the solution is suggested by Figure 5–2. There it is seen that when Type A units are used—that is, actual urban aggregations, in this case Urbanized Areas delimited by the Census Bureau—the proportion in M.A.s in the United States is much nearer the line of best fit. In other words, it looks as if the deviation of the United States in Figure 5–1 is the fault of the "cities of 20,000 and over" rather than the fault of the "Standard Metropolitan Areas."

A situation similar to that in the United States is found in the case of Australia. Whereas it deviates from the trend line in Figure

FIGURE 5-1. THE RELATIONSHIP BY COUNTRIES BETWEEN THE PERCENTAGE OF THE POPULATION IN TYPE B LOCALITIES OF OVER 20,000 AND THE PERCENTAGE IN THE METROPOLITAN AREAS, *Circa* 1950.

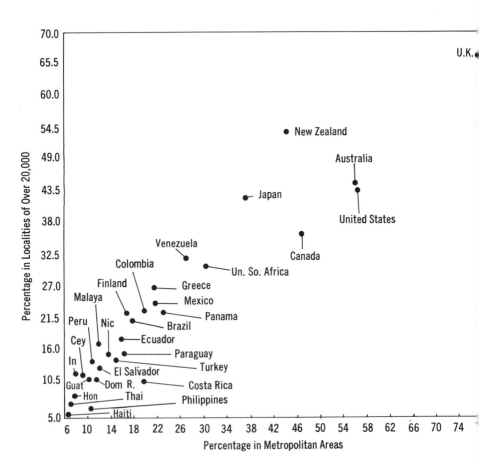

5-1, it is very close to the line in Figure 5-2. Thus, as suggested earlier, the Type A localities provide the most valid gauge of urbanization in Australia.

We cannot pursue this line of analysis in the present paper, but Figure 5-1 suggests that Canada, the United States, Australia, and the United Kingdom all fail more than most countries to include the whole urban population in their administrative "cities"

FIGURE 5-2. THE RELATIONSHIP BY COUNTRIES BETWEEN THE PERCENTAGE OF THE POPULATION IN TYPE A LOCALITIES OF OVER 20,000 AND THE PERCENTAGE IN METROPOLITAN AREAS, *Circa* 1950.

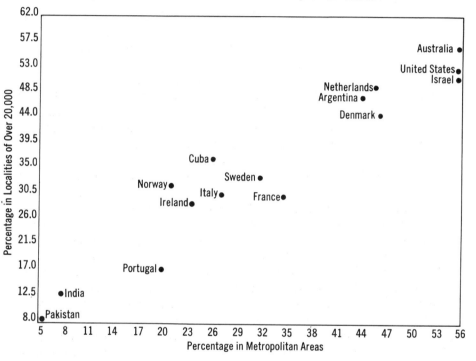

and "towns." In such countries there is particular reason to develop data of both the type called "metropolitan areas" and the type called "urbanized areas." Further analysis of this situation would greatly contribute to a clarification of the weaknesses and strengths of existing types of urban statistics.

CONCLUSION

Since official statistics on urbanization have been and will continue to be used for international comparisons, their validity should be assessed as carefully as possible. Although no absolute yardstick exists by which the accuracy of the official data can be judged, we have utilized as a means of assessment an index of urbanization that is more standardized than any other available—namely, the proportion in Metropolitan Areas of 100,000 or more inhabitants, areas we delimited according to common criteria. The correlations between this index and indices of urbanization based on official statistics run so high as to justify the conclusion that the latter, when carefully selected and critically used, possess a high degree of validity for comparative research purposes. Since the individual researcher lacks the resources necessary to construct measures of urbanization that go beyond official statistics, this conclusion should encourage scholars to make full though careful use of officially published urban statistics for comparative research.

Of course, the results of our analysis do not prove that the boundaries of all cities are comparable. The findings indicate only that selected current official statistics on urban aggregates or administratively defined cities and towns (Type A and B localities) contain no bias so serious as to yield an unrealistic index of urbanization. The question of the comparability of the official boundaries of individual cities is a matter not dealt with here.

A further consequence of our investigation is the conclusion that the size-classes of places from 2,000 to 10,000 are of little use in constructing an index of the degree of urbanization. The frequency of towns of this range in a population is so much a matter of the particular circumstances of the country concerned that a standard definition of "urban" in terms of a cutting point within this range (for example, 2,500 inhabitants) would introduce distortion rather than standardization into comparative analysis. If a cutting point is desired, it seems better to take 10,000 as the floor of the "urban" class than anything smaller.

Finally, it is worth noting that the relationship between proportions urban according to reported urban statistics and the proportions urban according to M.A. data offers means of finding countries with weak types of statistics on either side. By developing estimating equations from the regression lines, the expected proportion of the population in "urban" or in "metropolitan" areas can be derived for any particular country. If the expected differs sharply from that actually found, this is a signal to investigate carefully the data making up the actual fractions on both sides of the equation.

The Political, Economic, and Social Role of Urban Agglomerations in Countries of the Third World

JEAN-PAUL HARROY
*International Institute
of Differing Civilizations,
Brussels, Belgium*

PRELIMINARY REMARK

The attempt to treat the problem at the level of the Third World as a whole is a risky undertaking and these general comments will probably not be entirely valid for any particular country. They apply in the first place to those developing nations, whose number is on the increase, where a very big town—perhaps several—has been undergoing for the last ten or twenty years an extremely rapid population increase. And it is only in a somewhat more accessory way that they will also touch on the question of towns of secondary importance, which will allow them, in particular, to sidestep the question of the lower population limit below which an agglomeration loses the right to the designation of town.

THE BIG TOWN IN AN INTEGRATED NATION

Essentially it was the industrial revolution which, especially by promoting the concentration of powerful sources of energy in relatively limited areas, primarily in Western Europe, allowed the more or less peaceful birth of very big towns in an "economically developed" region where, provided there is a minimum of social justice and fair distribution of the means of production and of incomes, the peasant producers of agricultural produce can enjoy a happy lot as well as the citizens of small relaytowns and those of the very big cities.

From Jean-Paul Harroy, *Civilizations*, Vol. XVII, No. 3, pp. 166–184 (1967), International Institute of Differing Civilizations, Brussels. Reprinted by permission of author-publisher.

A balance of this kind has so far been more or less completely achieved in about thirty countries with a capitalist or socialist economy. It should be noted:

1. That its achievement has often taken more than a century;

2. That their industrial development was generally due to internal factors and usually preceded the process of urbanization;

3. That this balance was finally reached only at the cost of much suffering and social strife in which the country-dwellers often came off worse (let us remember that it was more than fifty years ago that the Belgian poet Emile Verhaeren wrote his celebrated works: Octopus Towns and the Hallucinated Countryside); and

4. That the maintenance or improvement of this balance now require, mainly if not exclusively on the part of the public authorities, great vigilance and serious efforts within the framework of more and more complex and burdensome planning, both national and regional.

THE ORIGIN OF TOWNS IN THE THIRD WORLD

In the pre-industrial era a few cities of more than one hundred thousand inhabitants grew up in Asia, Africa or Latin America, thanks to the convergent action of indigenous factors, either geographical (ports, etc.), political (a strong central power), or economic (trade routes). The colonial system had the effect of expanding such cities and of creating others. In spite of almost general decolonisation, the process of artificial urbanisation which started in colonial times and was characterised by industrialisation based on capital, equipment and technicians from abroad, and an export trade arising partly from this industrialisation (including mining) and partly from the introduction and generalisation of cash crops, is by no means at an end in these countries.

The real origin of large-scale urbanisation in Third World countries must therefore usually be sought not in the action of internal factors as in Western Europe in the XIX century but in that of external factors which have not always had either as aim or result the economic development of those countries. The cycle thus set in motion, moreover, did not have all the cumulative local effects which could have been observed in Europe in connection with the same phenomena; on the contrary, in some of these countries there developed a wealthy upper crust, grown rich from the export of raw materials, which on the one hand strove to hamper the progress of indigenous industrialisation and, on the other, preferred to export their capital rather than invest it in their native country.

As much for these historical reasons as on account of the rural discontent which we shall look at in a moment urbanisation in Third World countries has therefore only rarely been the result of economic development; on the contrary, it has often preceded the latter.

THE BIG TOWN IN A THIRD WORLD COUNTRY WHICH HAS ACHIEVED NATIONAL INTEGRATION

In such a nation, just as in developed countries, the population should be divided into three groups: peasants, inhabitants of relay-towns and inhabitants of very big towns, each member of these three groups enjoying a sufficiently desirable lot not to be tempted to give it up for one of the other groups.

In brief, the peasants of this nation in course of development ought to be sufficiently free—that is to say sufficiently emancipated from the present too often oppressive political, social or economic structures—to be able through an increase in their agricultural productivity to leave the subsistence level substantially behind and to produce abundant surpluses which they could sell for their own profit (and not for the indirect profit of a landowner, an overlord, an usurer or an extended family) at favourable commercial prices for disposal either to the town dwellers, national industry or international trade.

Such peasants would constitute a valuable market for services, or investment or consumption goods produced by national industry, and would contribute to enabling the town to provide sufficient and adequately paid work for its inhabitants logically confined to the secondary and tertiary sectors. Again, real national integration is only conceivable with a minimum of social justice and equity in the distribution of incomes and the ownership of the means of production.

In this case, in those Third World countries where societies with traditional structures were until recently predominant, the harmoniously conceived big town would see the triumph of the "modernity" which makes much slower progress in the countryside. But the peasant of a balanced nation of that kind would only leave his land because his temperament led him to prefer this modernity of the town and not because poverty and misfortune had driven him from his birthplace.

DESERTED COUNTRYSIDE IN THIRD WORLD

With all due reservations about the danger of drawing general conclusions valid for the whole Third World, the impression was nevertheless left by the Study Session [of the International Institute of
Differing Civilizations] that in the great majority of countries considered there is much rural discontent, causing the peasants to
leave the countryside and take refuge in the towns instead of raising agricultural productivity.

It seems that Third World countries are very rare where the
conditions set out in the preceding paragraph are adequately met.
Often the "oppressive structures" prevail: bad system of land
tenure, rack-renting, the toils of money lenders, feudal structures,
tribal solidarity directed in a one-way traffic for despoiling any
member of the clan showing a spirit of enterprise. To these oppressive socio-political structures are added economic factors: inefficient local marketing and, at the world level, the ever increasing
deterioration of the terms of trade for raw materials. Other factors
may have a local effect in causing peasants to leave the countryside: war (the problem of refugees), the disorganisation of traditional social structures in the village, unsuitable school arrangements emphasising the decline of the calling of farmer, the growing dearth of arable land.

The net result is a very low standard of living for the peasant,
sometimes lower than the vital minimum, and a lack of motivation
for any effort to produce better and more. His low productivity
together with the need to provide for a dramatically increasing
number of mouths to feed (in both countryside and town) leads to
an ever increasing destruction of the renewable natural resources
of agriculture. Erosion, deforestation, disappearance of water
resources and wild life are the most serious effects, all further
accentuating rural misery.

The final outcome is in very many cases—in forms and intensities varying from place to place in Asia, Africa and America—a
veritable exodus from the inhospitable countryside towards the
town where, through a psychosociological process sometimes encouraged by the enchantment of occasional visits to town and the stories
of relatives who have migrated there, everyone decides to seek
"freedom": freedom of the individual in respect of his traditional
group, freedom through the wage which puts an end to the night-
mare of bad harvest, freedom for women, freedom for the teenager,
freedom even from the dark forces of nature against which there is
a feeling of better protection in town, freedom finally acquired

through emancipation from that field work which is despised both by the town dweller and the nomad, and the popularity of which is unfortunately constantly decreasing. And so we see enormous migrations which a Norwegian author has rightly called a "substitute for revolution."

THE CONGESTION OF BIG TOWNS

Here again it is hard to draw any general conclusion. The following comments apply particularly, as has already been pointed out in the introduction to this paper, to the countries where a very big town—usually the capital—has undergone an extremely rapid rate of growth in the last few decades. This very big town often forms a pole of attraction rather than a pole of growth or even less of development. In some very large countries the same phenomenon may occur in several big towns at the same time (India, Brazil). As a general rule however we mostly see the existence of only one very big town favoured by the public authorities and thereby exerting a much bigger attraction than the country's other towns.

If the process of urban development had been able to proceed harmoniously, the inhabitants of the very big town—which in harmonious conditions would not be the only one in a country—would all have a properly paid job or a source of income ensuring them and their families a comfortable existence. And the public treasury would be in a position to equip this very big town with the infrastructure and services to provide the framework for this comfortable existence for all the inhabitants, without needing to neglect the creation of comparable infrastructures and services (i.e. on a reasonably smaller scale) in the other towns, in the small agglomerations and in the countryside.

The achievement of this harmonious development seems to require various conditions which have so far been fulfilled only partially or not at all:

—an annual rate of growth of the town population which is not too high (from 4 to 6% seems to be the figure representing the maximum potential of assimilation) ;

—substantial industrialisation, sufficiently independent of foreign influence ;

—an economic, and above all a politico-social system ensuring a fair distribution of incomes ;

—an agricultural hinterland supplying the town dwellers with produce at reasonable prices through marketing arrangements leaving a large part of these prices to the peasant producer ;

—public authorities with the will and the power to impose, at cost of inevitable unpopularity, effective planning of this urban expansion.

Observation of the facts shows that these conditions are practically never fulfilled entirely in the very big towns of the Third World, and as regards more particularly the first condition, we are witnessing in these towns, alongside of a natural demographic growth of about 2.5 to 3% a year, a constant and enormous influx of immigrants leading to real overcrowding, even if the overall rate of urbanisation of these countries remains on the whole relatively low, often definitely lower than that of the industrialised countries of Western Europe.

MAIN HARMFUL EFFECTS OF OVERCROWDING IN THE BIG TOWNS

Failure to meet the various conditions set out in the preceding paragraph entails, in particular, the following harmful effects:

A. — The possibilities of economic activity for town dwellers are almost exclusively in the secondary and the tertiary sectors. As a general rule, however, these sectors prove quite incapable of providing work for the whole of the considerable mass of workers seeking it. Unemployment and underemployment often reach high levels. The situation may be further worsened by the poor qualifications of the available manpower, as well as by the tendency of industrialists to use the most modern technological equipment requiring, of course, only a small but highly qualified labour force.

B. — The villagers crowding into the very big town for one thing rarely find conditions allowing them to become real town dwellers quickly; for another, they have a marked tendency to keep at least partially their former rural characteristics and, in particular, their links with the countryside. Some of them even are only seasonal town dwellers returning periodically to resume their village life. Others form groups with a rural mentality in the town, a phenomenon of cultural contact well worth profound study. It has been said that what happens is the "ruralisation" of the town rather than urbanisation; the new arrivals, although obviously recruited among the most dynamic and gifted elements, are unable or sometimes even unwilling to join the working class, forming rather what has been termed a "subproletariat" living mainly at the expense of a "tertiary-refuge" or "pseudo-tertiary" sector. Hence the well documented phenomena of marginality, of over-tertiarisation, of pauperisation, of shanty towns with their corollaries of crime, especially juvenile, and prostitution.

C. — Often too in these very big towns of the developing countries there is a politico-social system in force which leads, through the cumulative process described in particular by Gunnar Myrdal, to extreme inequality in the distribution of incomes. Alongside the sub-proletariat, the manual and nonmanual workers and an often all too thin layer of real middle class, these towns have a kernel of the politically strong, of beneficiaries of the oppressive structures of the countryside or of the owners of the tools of production, whose desire is to be able to keep up a way of life imitating if not surpassing that of the very rich of the western world. This is perhaps the place to repeat that this group of beneficiaries of a formerly predominant primary sector (export of raw materials) have seen it to be in their interest, have endeavoured and have succeeded in hampering the industrialisation which could have provided better conditions for the development of urbanisation. These big owners, through their political influence, sometimes successfully persuade the public authorities to protect some of their privileges by legislation, to apply with lenience progressive legislation attacking those privileges or else to finance from public funds investments in infrastructure calculated to serve their interest at the expense of those of the population both rural and urban.

D. — This desire to please the economically and politically strong which too few governments manage to shake off does not prevent another political problem taking shape and developing: the huge mass—a formidable force if roused to anger—of inhabitants of the very big town, especially the subproletariat, disquiets the political leaders who, in order to remain in power, must not only depend on the army but also above all satisfy some of the demands expressed by political spokesmen with the necessary talent for flattering and handling the masses. Comparison with the "bread and circuses" of imperial Rome is sometimes tempting. But at the present juncture the problem is to be seen primarily in the disproportionate use of the country's financial resources in giving priority to the very big town in the provision of infrastructure, equipment and services. This preferential treatment works to the serious detriment of the other towns and the countryside. Yet it is often far from sufficient to provide all the necessary equipment, infrastructure and services in due time, especially as these investments are often in the nature of prestige achievements and in consequence their unit costs are needlessly high.

E. — To this diversion, essentially political in origin, of an exces-sive part of the nation's public investment to the very big town, are added other forms of concentration of wealth and resources: the frequent fixation in or in the immediate neighbourhood of the very big town of foreign capital and of many national industries, not to mention a highly developed bureaucracy, the white collar army whose serried ranks are also to some extent the result of political pressure or the desire to satisfy electoral clients. In the same con-nection mention also has to be made of the excessive concentration of the nation's elite in the big town to the detriment above all of the countryside where medical services, for example, are often quite inadequate in proportion to the cities which are swarming with doctors. Sometimes almost a majority of the nation's political, administrative and technical personnel are thus to be found clus-tered in the capital, an imbalance whose impact is further aggra-vated by the very high level of salaries and benefits which they, especially the political elite, often manage to attain at the expense of the national treasury.

F.—All these imbalances have to be seen in relation to the dualism of the economies of Third World countries as much as to the socio-cultural dualism of the modern and the traditional. It should be remembered and forcibly underlined to what extent these dual-isms and imbalances have been accentuated for many of these societies, until recently unmechanised, by their entry into the cycle of a monetary economy. The self-regulating forces of the subsist-ence economy have disappeared. The taxation machinery which many of these recently independent countries have wished to alter in recent years in order to spread the taxation burden more fairly between town and country has also been profoundly influenced by them, if only by the action, unfortunately much too frequent, of inflation which sometimes strikes hard at those engaged in the sec-ondary and especially the tertiary sectors, that is to say the town-dwellers, sparing—shall we say by poetic justice?—the countryfolk, but creating tragic situations such as that, for example, which the Indonesian civil service is now experiencing.

G.—The considerations set out [in an earlier paragraph] regarding the widespread destruction of renewable natural resources in the Third World—soil, forests, flora, fauna, water—apply with par-ticular force to the outskirts of the big towns where marginal ele-ments indulge in a ceaseless over-exploitation of all these resources. Thus one can sometimes see from an aeroplane in the middle of the equatorial forest a circular clearing 30 to 40 km in diameter, totally denuded of vegetation: it is a tropical town's belt of complete disaf-forestation whose radius is fixed by the maximum distance a fire-

E. — To this diversion, essentially political in origin, of an excessive part of the nation's public investment to the very big town, are added other forms of concentration of wealth and resources: the frequent fixation in or in the immediate neighbourhood of the very big town of foreign capital and of many national industries, not to mention a highly developed bureaucracy, the white collar army whose serried ranks are also to some extent the result of political pressure or the desire to satisfy electoral clients. In the same connection mention also has to be made of the excessive concentration of the nation's elite in the big town to the detriment above all of the countryside where medical services, for example, are often quite inadequate in proportion to the cities which are swarming with doctors. Sometimes almost a majority of the nation's political, administrative and technical personnel are thus to be found clustered in the capital, an imbalance whose impact is further aggravated by the very high level of salaries and benefits which they, especially the political elite, often manage to attain at the expense of the national treasury.

F.—All these imbalances have to be seen in relation to the dualism of the economies of Third World countries as much as to the socio-cultural dualism of the modern and the traditional. It should be remembered and forcibly underlined to what extent these dualisms and imbalances have been accentuated for many of these societies, until recently unmechanised, by their entry into the cycle of a monetary economy. The self-regulating forces of the subsistence economy have disappeared. The taxation machinery which many of these recently independent countries have wished to alter in recent years in order to spread the taxation burden more fairly between town and country has also been profoundly influenced by them, if only by the action, unfortunately much too frequent, of inflation which sometimes strikes hard at those engaged in the secondary and especially the tertiary sectors, that is to say the town-dwellers, sparing—shall we say by poetic justice?—the countryfolk, but creating tragic situations such as that, for example, which the Indonesian civil service is now experiencing.

G.—The considerations set out [in an earlier paragraph] regarding the widespread destruction of renewable natural resources in the Third World—soil, forests, flora, fauna, water—apply with particular force to the outskirts of the big towns where marginal elements indulge in a ceaseless over-exploitation of all these resources. Thus one can sometimes see from an aeroplane in the middle of the equatorial forest a circular clearing 30 to 40 km in diameter, totally denuded of vegetation: it is a tropical town's belt of complete disaf forestation whose radius is fixed by the maximum distance a fir

through emancipation from that field work which is despised both by the town dweller and the nomad, and the popularity of which is unfortunately constantly decreasing. And so we see enormous migrations which a Norwegian author has rightly called a "substitute for revolution."

THE CONGESTION OF BIG TOWNS

Here again it is hard to draw any general conclusion. The following comments apply particularly, as has already been pointed out in the introduction to this paper, to the countries where a very big town—usually the capital—has undergone an extremely rapid rate of growth in the last few decades. This very big town often forms a pole of attraction rather than a pole of growth or even less of development. In some very large countries the same phenomenon may occur in several big towns at the same time (India, Brazil). As a general rule however we mostly see the existence of only one very big town favoured by the public authorities and thereby exerting a much bigger attraction than the country's other towns.

If the process of urban development had been able to proceed harmoniously, the inhabitants of the very big town—which in harmonious conditions would not be the only one in a country—would all have a properly paid job or a source of income ensuring them and their families a comfortable existence. And the public treasury would be in a position to equip this very big town with the infrastructure and services to provide the framework for this comfortable existence for all the inhabitants, without needing to neglect the creation of comparable infrastructures and services (i.e. on a reasonably smaller scale) in the other towns, in the small agglomerations and in the countryside.

The achievement of this harmonious development seems to require various conditions which have so far been fulfilled only partially or not at all:

—an annual rate of growth of the town population which is not too high (from 4 to 6% seems to be the figure representing the maximum potential of assimilation);

—substantial industrialisation, sufficiently independent of foreign influence;

—an economic, and above all a politico-social system ensuring a fair distribution of incomes;

—an agricultural hinterland supplying the town dwellers with produce at reasonable prices through marketing arrangements leaving a large part of these prices to the peasant producer;

—public authorities with the will and the power to impose, at cost of inevitable unpopularity, effective planning of this urban expansion.

Observation of the facts shows that these conditions are practically never fulfilled entirely in the very big towns of the Third World, and as regards more particularly the first condition, we are witnessing in these towns, alongside of a natural demographic growth of about 2.5 to 3% a year, a constant and enormous influx of immigrants leading to real overcrowding, even if the overall rate of urbanisation of these countries remains on the whole relatively low, often definitely lower than that of the industrialised countries of Western Europe.

MAIN HARMFUL EFFECTS OF OVERCROWDING IN THE BIG TOWNS

Failure to meet the various conditions set out in the preceding paragraph entails, in particular, the following harmful effects:

A. — The possibilities of economic activity for town dwellers are almost exclusively in the secondary and the tertiary sectors. As a general rule, however, these sectors prove quite incapable of providing work for the whole of the considerable mass of workers seeking it. Unemployment and underemployment often reach high levels. The situation may be further worsened by the poor qualifications of the available manpower, as well as by the tendency of industrialists to use the most modern technological equipment requiring, of course, only a small but highly qualified labour force.

B. — The villagers crowding into the very big town for one thing rarely find conditions allowing them to become real town dwellers quickly; for another, they have a marked tendency to keep at least partially their former rural characteristics and, in particular, their links with the countryside. Some of them even are only seasonal town dwellers returning periodically to resume their village life. Others form groups with a rural mentality in the town, a phenomenon of cultural contact well worth profound study. It has been said that what happens is the "ruralisation" of the town rather than urbanisation; the new arrivals, although obviously recruited among the most dynamic and gifted elements, are unable or sometimes even unwilling to join the working class, forming rather what has been termed a "subproletariat" living mainly at the expense of a "tertiary-refuge" or "pseudo-tertiary" sector. Hence the well documented phenomena of marginality, of over-tertiarisation, of pau-

perisation, of shanty towns with their corollaries of crime, especially juvenile, and prostitution.

C. — Often too in these very big towns of the developing countries there is a politico-social system in force which leads, through the cumulative process described in particular by Gunnar Myrdal, to extreme inequality in the distribution of incomes. Alongside the sub-proletariat, the manual and nonmanual workers and an often all too thin layer of real middle class, these towns have a kernel of the politically strong, of beneficiaries of the oppressive structure of the countryside or of the owners of the tools of production whose desire is to be able to keep up a way of life imitating if not surpassing that of the very rich of the western world. This is perhaps the place to repeat that this group of beneficiaries of a formerly predominant primary sector (export of raw materials) have seen it to be in their interest, have endeavoured and have succeeded in hampering the industrialisation which could have provided better conditions for the development of urbanisation. These big owners, through their political influence, sometimes successfully persuade the public authorities to protect some of their privileges by legislation, to apply with lenience progressive legislation attacking those privileges or else to finance from public funds investments in infrastructure calculated to serve their interest at the expense of those of the population both rural and urban.

D. — This desire to please the economically and politically strong which too few governments manage to shake off does not prevent another political problem taking shape and developing: the huge mass—a formidable force if roused to anger—of inhabitants of the very big town, especially the subproletariat, disquiets the political leaders who, in order to remain in power, must not only depend on the army but also above all satisfy some of the demands expressed by political spokesmen with the necessary talent for flattering and handling the masses. Comparison with the "bread and circuses" of imperial Rome is sometimes tempting. But at the present juncture the problem is to be seen primarily in the disproportionate use of the country's financial resources in giving priority to the very big town in the provision of infrastructure, equipment and services. This preferential treatment works to the serious detriment of the other towns and the countryside. Yet it is often far from sufficient to provide all the necessary equipment, infrastructure and services in due time, especially as these investments are often in the nature of prestige achievements and in consequence their unit costs are needlessly high.

wood collector can cover on foot in a day. A strange contrast at a time where every modern town is thinking of creating its green belt, the city's lungs, and recreational zone for town-dwellers dogged more and more by air pollution, that ransom of industrialisation. A strange contrast too when one thinks that, at the very time the poor world offers the spectacle of the flight from the countryside to the towns, the rich world sees its privileged classes fleeing the town for the countryside at every holiday season, every weekend, for that matter, every evening if they can.

H. — Another important disadvantage of the overcrowding of the very big towns is the difficulty entailed in elaborating and especially in applying good planning. We have already seen how this is thwarted by the pressures exerted on the leaders by the economically strong and the popular masses of the capital. It is often complicated too by a bureaucratic invasion, another political consequence of over-tertiarisation. It is still further disturbed, and unfortunately the Third World is not sufficiently sheltered from this danger, by political instability and especially by public insecurity, riots, civil strife, guerrillas and war.

ADVANTAGES OF URBANISATION

It will be much quicker to state the advantages of the process of urbanisation, which are classical. Whatever the present function and historical background of the town, the beneficent effects of the "advantage of number" will be the clearer, the rarer and more attenuated are the imbalances described above.

In the town's "modern" context, the assimilated inhabitant and, to an appreciable degree, the newcomer awaiting or starting his assimilation have the benefit of the services provided, mainly perhaps in the matter of education and public health, including under the latter heading the distribution of drinking water. Sometimes the State offers facilities in the matter of housing and electric supply. They find certain possibilities of spiritual and cultural enrichment, or of entertainment, in particular sporting events, processions, plays, etc. which are so numerous only in the towns. And their economic efforts which on average bring them higher earnings than those of the peasants are helped by all the resources of the urban equipment in transport, banking and credit arrangements, facilities for supply and marketing and many others.

The advantages which, from the psycho-sociological point of view, particularly as regards "freedom", the peasants see in their arrival in town have been abundantly described above.

Finally, it is proper to emphasise strongly the decisive role which the town, as a pillar of modernity, can and almost everywhere is starting to play in spreading that modernity into the countryside.

Without any real antagonism opposing it yet to the rural masses, the town must through its beneficent action absolutely prevent any such antagonism arising. The frequent comings and goings of many town dwellers, especially the newcomers, to and from their native villages facilitate the propagation of its ideas of modernity. The development of the mass media contributes to accentuating this awakening of the countryside, where some governments have already succeeded, particularly by encouraging town dwellers to invest in their native villages, in bringing about a coexistence of the traditional and the modern.

The town, rich in potentialities, has a mission to fulfil as a centre of development, a mission which it is still carrying out only imperfectly, but which it must become capable of carrying out better. ... Since it too upholds the coexistence of the traditional and the modern, it facilitates the discharge of this task, on the one hand, by offering newcomers wide possibilities of welcome among members of their extended family who have remained conscious of traditional duties and, on the other hand, by allowing the despatch by the town dweller of gifts in money or kind to members of his family who have stayed in the village.

Finally, in a sufficiently favourable political climate, the very big town also constitutes a meeting point for different tribes and can thus contribute effectively to the strengthening of national unity.

CONCLUSIONS

An irreversible phenomenon, the process of accelerated urbanisation which the Third World as a whole is now undergoing involves indisputable and serious disadvantages arising chiefly from its excessive speed and a gigantism which some see as a sign of underdevelopment.

On the other hand it is getting into stride all too slowly with its indispensable role of auxiliary development motor which the nations concerned have the right to expect of it.

Only bold and far-seeing planning, based on infinitely more copious and scientifically better controlled information and knowledge than that available today and able, moreover, to win a race against time could succeed in putting the hands of the clock back before it is too late.

■ ■ ■

A list of the current processes which have to be stopped without delay brings the immediate conviction that the remedies must be applied throughout the whole national territory and even beyond if geography requires it. The effort will have to aim simultaneously at an acceptable attack on the basic problem of population growth, at the redevelopment of the countryside through land reform conceived in the fullest possible sense of the term, at the establishment of a state of equilibrium in the big town with really revolutionary town-planning innovations and at the construction of a balanced urban network equipped with good communications ensuring the optimum economic development of the whole territory.

Seen from this pragmatic viewpoint, the solution can be found only in a series of regional plans, integrated within the framework of the national plan and steered to final completion by leaders possessing the courage to take painful political options in full view of a public opinion already schooled to understand the meaning of the welfare of the nation and to be ready to pay the price for it.

Chapter 3

URBANISM AS A WAY OF LIFE

The title of this chapter is borrowed from Louis Wirth, for his famous article, published in 1938. Ever since that time, Wirth's presentation has been a point of departure for many of the discussions of the sociology of urban life.[1]

In his article, Wirth acknowledged the numerous studies dealing with the dramatic urbanization of the United States and of other countries, but he called for an adequate framework within which to interpret such urbanization. He sought to demonstrate the need for a theoretical orientation and to present the fundamentals of such an urban theory. He offered his classic definition of the city as a "relatively large, dense, and permanent settlement of heterogeneous individuals,"[2] and he identified a number of characteristics of cities which were, in his view, related to these factors of size, density, and heterogeneity. In a very thorough critique of Wirth's urban theory, Morris has rephrased these characteristics in the form of twelve propositions, which he then examines and evaluates, one by one.[3]

Essentially, Wirth's views of the characteristics of the city were consistent with that tradition of polar typology in which

[1] Louis Wirth, "Urbanism as a Way of Life," *American Journal of Sociology*, Vol. 41 (July, 1938), pp. 1–23.
[2] *Ibid.*, p. 8.
[3] R. N. Morris, *Urban Sociology*, Studies in Sociology: No. 2, New York: Frederick A. Praeger, 1968.

trends in modern society are contrasted with presumed previous conditions. Such constructed typologies vary in emphasis, but in the ideal types of *gemeinschaft* and *gesellschaft* as described by Tönnies, in the mechanical-organic society contrast of Durkheim, in the presentation by Maine of status society and contract society, in the sacred-to-secular conceptualization of Becker, and in the folk-urban contrast of Redfield, there existed the underlying assumption of social and cultural transformation. In such typologies, man is seen as moving from a relatively simple, undifferentiated network of relationships, largely based upon primary relationships, strong in tradition and in emotional bonds, toward the opposite conditions. To be sure, Wirth carefully avoided the assumption that "urbanism" was limited to cities or was typical of all persons in them. To him, urbanism as a way of life was differentiated from urbanization as a process, and the essence of urbanism was a pattern of living which can and does diffuse beyond the limits of urban areas. Even so, there was strongly implied in his essay a rural-urban polarity in ways of living, thereby linking his conceptualization with those of Tönnies, Maine, Durkheim, and Redfield.

In his selection included here, Anderson fully acknowledges his obligation to Wirth. Like Wirth, Anderson sees the outreaching or "centrifugal" influence of urban life as penetrating all areas of contemporary societies; urban symbols are ubiquitous. He notes some of the uniformities, particularly structurally, which cities show on a global scale, and he identifies a number of the distinctive elements of the "urban way of life." While some of these were also emphasized by Wirth, Anderson stresses additional urban traits in his presentation, including the subordination of urban man to mechanical time, the development of expectations that change will occur and a high degree of adaptability to such change, and a remarkable dependency upon records.

Bascom tests some aspects of Wirth's theory in a setting very different from the Chicago which Wirth knew so well. In sub-Saharan Africa, indigenous urbanization along characteristic African patterns developed long before the coming of the European colonial epoch. Particularly impressive was the urbanization among the Yoruba of western Nigeria, where the combination of highly intensive agriculture, a system of trading, and marked specialization of crafts and services enabled a number of cities to develop. As Bascom notes, these cities meet criteria of size, of population, and of density. It is less clear whether or not they meet Wirth's third criterion of urbanism, that of heterogeneity.

By raising the question, Bascom emphasizes that the concept of heterogeneity was not developed in very specific terms by Wirth:

heterogeneous in respect to what? In any event, Bascom establishes that in the Yoruba cities, the assumed diminution of importance of lineage and kinship ties seemed not to occur. Traditional principles of social organization were strongly maintained, and ethnic homogeneity was typical. Such cities could meet the criterion of social heterogeneity, Bascom suggests, only in terms of some degree of craft specialization, of stratification, and of social and political segmentation. Bascom suggests that one might replace the loosely defined criterion of "heterogeneity," at least in cross-cultural comparisons, with another criterion. He suggests that the existence of a formalized government, which exercises authority over primary groups within the city and which incorporates them into the community, be used for this purpose.

Oscar Lewis is most widely known today for his writing on the culture of poverty, first in Mexico City, then in Puerto Rico, and the United States. In the selection included here, Lewis used field data collected in Mexico City to take issue with Wirth's theory in some fundamental respects. He questions the basic assumption of a necessary polarity as implied in the concept of a rural-urban continuum. He disagrees with various emphases which Wirth assumed characterized the urban way of life, including the assumption that the nuclear family becomes more typical, and the extended family declines, in the city. On the contrary, Lewis holds that many rural migrants into Mexico City maintain their extended family ties and their ties through the Mexican institution of *compadrazgo* (a linking of individuals in a mutual relationship of intimacy and dependence). Indeed, primary groups in general can be as important to the urbanite as to the countryman. The urban dweller, because of the complexity of his setting, does indeed have a much wider range of alternatives concerning his forms of participation than does the rural man, but the choices concerning participation which he makes do not necessarily, or even typically, contrast with rural practices. The emphasis which Lewis places upon the maintenance of family, kinship, and neighborhood ties in Mexico City is consistent with the results of much research during the past two decades in North American cities, as we shall see in Chapter 5.

The Urban Way of Life

NELS ANDERSON
University of New Brunswick

While industrialism and urbanism are separate concepts, neither can be understood without considering the other.[1] In this article, however, attention is focused on urbanism, and particularly on the urban way of life. Urbanism and, secondarily, industrialism, are seen in the perspective mainly of the West. As a way of life, urbanism is seen as the dynamic opposite in many respects of the rural way of life.

MODERN INDUSTRIALISM

Industrialism, as Lewis Mumford observed its evolution in his "Technics and Civilization," has been developing over several centuries, and much of this development has been associated with the life of towns and cities. It has been a cumulative development which accelerated with each succeeding century, most of it taking place since about 1750, and most of that since about 1850. Industry's evolution has been paralleled by other developments; in the arts of local government, in public education, in standards of living, for example.

From *International Journal of Comparative Sociology*, E. J. Brill, Leiden, Holland, Vol. 3, pp. 175–188 (September, 1962). Reprinted by permission of the publisher and author.
[1] Some of the thought here follows that in an article by the late Louis Wirth, "Urbanism as a Way of Life," *American Journal of Sociology*, Vol. 41, No. 1, July 1938, pp. 1–23. Wirth also recognized the industrialism-urbanism linkage. Herein I have extended the thought to include management and technical aspects of the urban way of life, also areas of cumulative urban experience. These elements Wirth considered in his writings on urban planning.

The evolution of industrialism moved from relatively local areas of operation to ever wider areas, which for many industries have become global. Certain industries, in fact, have become world networks.

Industrial evolution, for obvious reasons which need not detain us, has moved faster in some world regions than in others. Thus we speak of advanced countries, developing countries, and underdeveloped countries. These terms are relative, since even in the advanced countries can be found underdeveloped areas, and developed industrial areas can be found in underdeveloped countries.

It is true that modern industries may be located far from cities, and in some important cities few industrial establishments are found. Such remote industries are not outside the urban-centered economy, or detached from urban-centered control. They are as much linked with their particular global networks (oil, metals, rubber, etc.) as if actually located in cities. However, most industries, for reasons of transportation, access to markets, and the essential labor supply, must locate in or near cities. They are the sustaining instrumentalities of urban man by which he produces goods and services for exchange with rural man for food, fiber and other raw materials.

As we speak of industry, industrial work or industrialism, these terms are descriptive of work and enterprise which is non-agricultural. It includes work in commerce and transportation as well as in manufacture. It would include public and private services as well as the leisure industries.

MODERN URBANISM

One measure of urbanism is statistical; the number of inhabitants in towns and cities of different magnitude, cities by size in a country or region, changes in the composition of the population over time, etc. This demographic approach is pertinent to any effort to understand urbanism. Demographic data are usually presented in studies of urbanization, in fact many urbanization studies go little beyond demographic data.

Through the demographic approach, cities can be seen in relation to their locations and their growth. It permits comparison as between countries or between regions and makes possible the drawing of curves and graphs comparing population change against time. Thus we know that cities in most world regions are growing. In some regions the population growth is faster than the capacity of industry to provide employment.

Urbanization in these terms concerns the movement of population from agricultural to industrial work, and from rural to urban places of residence. People are attracted to cities by visions of a better life, or they feel compelled to leave rural places because they are disadvantaged there. For most urbanization, migration, the attractions and compulsions are intermingled. For most such migrants, urbanization means a transition from one way of life to another. They become urbanized by going to where the urban way of life is.

Urbanization through migration to urban centers is a global phenomenon. It is not only found everywhere, it is also centuries old and has always been more or less necessary to keep cities alive, since city populations are seldom able to reproduce themselves. They draw new inhabitants full-grown from their hinterlands. The modern city needs more than the migrant who is fullgrown and ready for work. Before he can be put to work he needs the kind of experience and training that can be used.

The understanding of urbanization only begins with counting people and making statistical comparisons. The demographic approach is useful as one measure of the urbanization process, as it is a very definite measure, but mainly of cityward and toward-industry migration. There is also the nonmigration aspect of urbanization; one can be urbanized by going to the city, but urbanization can also come to him in a non-urban place. In this sense, urbanism is outward reaching. People may be urbanized without migrating to cities and without changing from agricultural to non-agricultural work.

Urbanization as it radiates to non-urban people carries in dynamic everchanging forms the urban way of life. As a result, the rural population in such countries as Denmark, Germany or Holland are as urban as city people in their thinking and behavior. They differ from urbanites in their occupations, which are agricultural and not industrial.

ELEMENTS OF THE URBAN WAY OF LIFE

Work and life in towns have always had a character of their own. The beginning of towns marked a division of labor between agricultural and nonfarming people, and the beginning of interdependence between the two. Initially the towns were exploitative, the centers of authority (ecclesiastical, civil) and administration, and some towns had military functions. But whatever other functions they performed, all towns and cities have ever been places of special work. They harbored the artisans who made things of leather, wood, metal or other raw materials. They made glass, pottery or cloth, and they converted cloth into clothing. Here also gathered the medicine makers, men of magic, music makers, dancers and the wise men who propound the law, or who governed.

The rural-urban division of work continues, but the relationship is now less one of exploitation of the country and more one of exchange, although in the bargaining the urbanite still has the advantage, or he takes it. There are still regions where most rural villages are owned by urban families, or where rural people remain in continuous debt to urban money lenders.

In the entire evolution of cities, urbanism has remained a distinctive way of life, but never more clearly distinctive than in our time. An attempt will be made here to list some of the generally-recognized elements which distinguish the urban way of life from the rural. In doing this, attention is mainly on those places which may be called most urban, as against non-urban places which are quite rural. The order of these items does not reflect their relative importance, and each tends to overlap the others.

1. Mass division of labor accompanied by high specialization in work, and mass production of goods and services for the widest distribution,

2. Almost total commitment to the use of mechanisms and mechanical power, whether in places of work or non-work,

3. Increasing detachment of the individual from traditional controls and loyalties, greater transiency in his contacts, and his increasing dependence on secondary groupings,

4. High mobility in the individual's daily circulation, changes of residence, job changes and changes of occupation, leading often to changes in social status,

5. Continuous change in the man-made elements of the urban environment, especially in structural renewal and technological advance,

6. Almost complete subordination of the individual and groups to mechanical time, and increasing control by the clock over appointments and the coordination of movements,

7. High transiency in acquaintance and contact relations of the individual, accompanied by considerable anonymity in his relations with the crowd,

8. Attitudes of expectancy toward all forms of change, and an increasing capacity for adaptation, with attitudes of devotion to change,

9. Increasing commitment to records and conformity to their use for the verification of actions, contacts, pledges, and presences.

Most of these essential elements of urban living are found in the urbanism of all industrial countries. It would be surprising if they did not exist to some degree in the least industrial countries. They are some of the minimal elements for order and convenience in mass living. Other elements might be added to the list; for example: a) the natural mechanisms of social control which evolve through secondary organizations in urban agglomerates; and b) mass arrangements for the economic security of the individual as new types of collective security arrangements assume the functions that earlier forms of familial security arrangements can no longer serve.

Let us now consider these elements in the order presented.

Specialization in Modern Work

Division of labor between urban workers is not new, but that of modern industrial urban centers differs radically from earlier divisions of labor in which the work of the artisan was associated with one or another traditional craft. Crafts exist in modern industry, but mainly for special branches (construction, printing), but even here they have been greatly modified. Or they are found in occupations above the level of handwork (secretary, engineer, accountant, physician), and are identified as technical or professional. The mass of industrial workers have neither tools nor special skills.

But the mass of workers do have general skills, which may be called "skill sophistication." As individuals, they are not skilled workers, but as a group they are a skilled labor force out of which can be selected workers to operate any kind of factory, with very little previous "job training." Specialization is found in groups of workers associated in a particular production process. In this collective sense, specialization is found in plants, shops, or offices. Thus all workers in a metropolitan area are integrated impersonally into a community-wide division of labor with which hundreds of occupations and "semi-occupations" are associated. The network of work exchange and interdependence may become so integrated that the strike of a small group of workers in a small specialized plant may inconvenience or even stop work in many other plants.

Since most forms of industrial production call for vast investments of capital, and since each industry is faced with continuous competition and must continually adapt its methods, the organization of its work must be ever flexible. A flexible labor force is a skilled one because it can be used in many combinations. This could not have been done in the time of the preindustrial guilds, nor can it be done in the less developed countries where the mass of workers do not have "skill sophistication." From managers, engineers and technicians to supervisors and machine operatives, there must be this capacity to meet change. It is characteristic of the urban way of life. Even the housewife and the schoolchild must have this sophistication, and upon this basic training more precise specializations may be built.

Mechanisms and Mechanical Power

One measure of industrialism in a country is the per capita consumption of electric power or other mechanical energy. Except as they function in leisure preoccupations, animals (pets, race horses) are more and more excluded from the urban way of life. They require too much space, and their work is performed better with mechanical power. The amount of such power per worker used in a month or year gives some clue to the level of industry in a community, just as the amount of such power used per household is a clue to the level of family living. The amount of mechanical power used by public departments is evidence of the level of public service in a city. The more advanced a community becomes in its way of life, the more uses it has for mechanical power in its work places, its homes and in its public services.

The urban way of life is one that makes increasing and more varied use of constructed facilities and mechanisms. We use the term "mechanism" in its wide applications to include street patterns, water systems, electric power networks, transport systems, etc. It is possible to judge the efficiency and urbanity of a city by the amount and condition of such collective mechanisms and properties, or the effectiveness of their use by the inhabitants. The service potential of such facilities depends for the most part on the "skill sophistication" of the inhabitants in a community.

If a great urban agglomerate would be clean and healthy, and it has taken centuries to learn this, then the water system must be a service to all, and all must be served by the sewer system. These two systems must be coordinated as they meet in the home, at the work place, in hotels, and at other points of contact with the people. In these same places we find the service outlets for gas and electric lines, for telephone lines and the pipes that bring heat into living space. These are complex mechanisms that all the people must learn to use; the result would be chaos if they did not know. Then there are the secondary mechanisms, the power operated machines found at the work place, in the home and elsewhere. Acquaintance with their use is no small part of the learning associated with the urban way of life.

The urban man's automobile is a mechanism that demands great skill in getting safely from place to place, and in its use the safety of others is also involved. This applies to most mechanisms; one exposes himself to hazard but he also exposes others. To be well adapted to this form of mass use of mechanisms one must acquire certain attitudes and habits of collective safety. He must also maintain a constant awareness of mechanisms until alertness becomes a constant element in his behavior.

Detachment of the Individual

Particularly in the modern urban community, the individual lives in a variety of roles. He is a worker, a family member, and a citizen. He may have membership in a political party, a work organization, a cooperative society, a church, and so on. Each relationship tends to be a role somewhat separate from his other roles. His roles may differ in many respects from those of other members in his family. Each role relates to some special interest, but his total personality is not involved in any one role; family, for example. The fully urbanized person is said to be "individuated," which does not mean that he is personally disorganized; the contrary is usually true.

In the urban way of life the individual is detached from the traditional loyalties and groupings, so characteristic of non-urban societies. In his situation he must at times be responsible to himself and for himself. His most important decisions tend to be his rather than a family responsibility. He must assume responsibilities that would not be permitted to him in earlier societies. In his roles as student, worker, citizen, member of a formal group, etc., he has his own identity and his status is rarely other than individual.

While the extended family manages to survive after a fashion in some urban situations, it has difficulty exercising there its ancient functions. In its stead the nuclear family gains in stature, but even the nuclear family tends to become (except as families have wealth or power) a one-generation institution. In Western regions the three-generation urban household is rare, and three-generation familial contacts tend also to be transient. But the bonds between members of the nuclear family show a special resiliency, especially during child-rearing years (this in spite of increasing divorce). The familial relationship, however, tends to cultivate individual responsibility in each family member, assuming that he must often stand alone. Thus, while the modern nuclear urban family has high cohesion through the child rearing phases of its cycle, it is an assembly of individuals. After it has served its basic functions it may fall apart in the old age of the parents. This is to be expected, since it is held together by internal bonds, not outside pressure.

Participation of the individual in urban life hinges on two special kinds of contact. In the personal and more intimate sphere is the personal contact network; relatives, near friends and acquaintances. His other contact is less personal and includes his relationships with organized groups.

Contact networks are made up of the persons in the individual's acquaintance circle. These include long-time close friends, long-time acquaintances not so close and chance acquaintances. Some contacts are known only in the area of work. Others may be known in the area of politics only, of church only, or in leisure activity only. Some may be known in two or more spheres of contact. If all persons in one's network, or most of them, are known to one another, the network is said to be "closed." If there is little acquaintance between persons in the individual's network, it is "open." Living in the changing scene, the individual is ever making new contacts, while the firmness of other contacts may diminish, or they may be discontinued.

Participation by the individual in secondary organizations may lead to close personal relationships with members of the organization, but not with the membership as a whole. His attachment to the organization concerns some interest that can be served. The labor organization protects his work interests, something he cannot do standing alone. His political party affords an arena for expression as a citizen. His membership in one formal group may be quite unrelated to his membership in another. In the organization he pays membership dues, which is much like paying service fees. The kinds and number of organizations to which the individual belongs depend on his occupation, income, social position, and other marks of his status. As this status changes with the years, his affiliations with formal groups may also change. As in his personal contact network, he may join organizations to which he did not belong previously, while he may withdraw from others. These are individual actions in keeping with his participation in community life.

Implications of Mobility

A fourth to a third of the inhabitants in American metropolitan centers were not born in the cities where they live. An equal number born in these cities are the children of parents born elsewhere. Perhaps less than a fourth of the residents of Chicago or New York are of families that have been for generations in these cities. This kind of mobility, or some degree of it, is found in most great cities, and in all of them it is continuous. They receive and assimilate, but rarely export population, except to other cities.

Looking closer at the life of cities, we find that mobility assumes other aspects. There is in the younger cities, especially, a great amount of residential mobility as people move from house to house or from one area to another. As cities grow there is a mobility of business enterprises. A single unit of ground in the course of a century may experience a series of different uses. Buildings are replaced by more modern ones. Workers move from one job to another and in doing so may move from one occupation or profession to another. This is professional mobility and it may lead to persons leaving one social class level to enter another. This is social mobility and is normally found in cities that are growing and being rapidly industrialized. These different manifestations of mobility are not characteristic of the rural way of life.

Creativity and Renewal

Cities as areas of mobility have never ceased to attract the restless and footloose. They have also attracted dreamers, venturers, and men of genius for whom there would be meager opportunity in the rural community. While the creative man may be attracted to the city, he is not the only stimulus to its creativity. It is also stimulated by the competitive and unusually free way of life in the urban center.

Perhaps more so today than ever, cities must be resourceful and creative if they would survive. Besides food supply they must have raw materials in which to invest their labor in goods and services for exchange. Because of this exchange, in the newer countries especially, farmers have been stimulated to produce more, and to be more efficient in their production. Almost all improved farm machinery is the result, not of rural inventiveness, but of urban genius. Good roads in some countries came initially because of urban demand, and practically all modern improvements in transportation have been urban creations stemming from urban efforts to survive. This is one phase of urbanizing the hinterland, stimulating rural advance. For example, the farmer knew about manure fertilizer, but the city man had to persuade him to use manufactured fertilizer.

Inventiveness and creativity are continually evident in urban life, in the mechanisms used and in other elements of the man-made urban environment. Particularly in the more industrial countries, cities are rebuilding and renewing themselves as if in ceaseless struggle against obsolescence. To meet increasing demands for access, street systems must be reconstructed. To meet demands for better service, such facilities as hotels, restaurants, office buildings, large stores and often public departments must undergo reconstruction and renewal; an apartment building, designed for a life of 80 years, is outmoded before the end of 40 years.

This urge for renewal in structures, equipment and work ways, so much a part of the urban way of life, is not understood in rural places, and may even be resisted there. In the city it reflects the continuous contest between inventiveness and obsolescence. Obsolescence becomes such a relative concept that in extreme cases we see the old machine, while still in prime condition, replaced by a new one. It would have the aspect of waste were it not that the new machine performs better and faster. Measured against conservative standards, renewal does involve waste. Progress in this sense, while being somewhat wasteful, is also callous to sentimental values; for example, feeling for historic buildings, replaced by modern structures.

Renewal is not stimulated alone by efforts for gain; sometimes the changes are demanded by the organized groups who will not have their city seem less progressive than some other. This sentiment of community pride often results in visible evidence of local progressiveness to impress visitors.

Urbanism and the Clock

When cities acquired importance as centers of administration and commerce, they confronted difficulties in measuring time. The arrival or sailing of a ship, the meeting of an appointment, rates of speed, durations of work could not be marked by the old measures of natural time. It was in the town, therefore, that the clock was invented. It was the result of a series of inventions which enabled the use of bells to mark time at regular intervals. Later clocks with hands and faces appeared. Nearly four centuries passed before the arrival of the pocket watch. The clock was the forerunner of most other mechanisms and, without it today, few mechanisms could be effectively operated. Without it today, urban life could hardly function, although rural life could.

Urban man, with the aid of the clock, established a new relation with time. He was freed from the natural limitations imposed by night and day sequences and the cycle of the seasons. With this regulating instrument, industry was able to evolve with precision: revolutions of a wheel per second, prints per minute, unit output per hour; all values could be measured against it, the work of machines as that of man.

Industrial workers are sellers of time, as workers for hire have always been, but selling time for the urban industrial worker has come to be an exact transaction involving clock-measured units. Rural man never needed to draw a clear line between his work time and non-work time, but this is the great mandate of urban work. It is strictly separated from all activity and interests of a non-work nature. One does not play, laugh or talk trivialities at the work place. Conversely, modern workers give little thought to their jobs when away from the work place. This separation of work from non-work had little importance in the days of the 72-hour or the 84-hour week. It becomes a matter of great importance now that the 40-hour week arrives among us, and the worker in a few decades has gained a gift of leisure of at least 40 hours. He is earning more money than before, which makes him the most important consumer.

What is pertinent to our subject is that this transition is mainly urban-centered. It is here where industry, as work time becomes more costly, must use this time more efficiently. The use of work time becomes more concentrated, and more "tempo" is injected into work processes. Liaison between departments and plants in an industry must be more exactly timed. Great promptness is needed in deliveries. Speed is demanded in the movement of persons, in the transfer of goods and the dispatching of information.

This modern "tempo" starts in the work place and all work places are in step with it, but it cannot be confined to places of work. All related life in the community is affected. There is not (and could hardly be) one tempo in the community for work and another for non-work. Whatever the tempo is, all the mechanisms in the man-made environment pulsate with it, and so the individual, whether at work or leisure, must keep his eye on the clock. This tempo element of urban life tends also to become accepted by rural man. It is one of the most impelling of urbanizing influences, that the farmer too must carry a watch.

Anonymity and Transient Contact

Rural people are sometimes overwhelmed by the seeming chaos, the unremitting tempo, and the impersonal demeanor of urban life. The newcomer learns eventually that, in fact, this flow of life has an order of its own. Once he adapts himself to the impersonality of urban life, he finds the anonymity of the crowd a convenient kind of privacy. We must also see it as an essential to urban order.

Transiency of contact and acquaintance turn out also to be essential in adjustment to urban living. Considerations of time set a limit to the number of friends the individual can maintain contact with and there must be a limit to casual acquaintances. If he changes his place of residence or his work, or if his income increases or decreases, some faces will disappear from his personal contact network, but others will be added. For one in a changing situation, transiency in contacts is inevitable.

In his secondary contacts with interest groups the individual can be a "colleague" of hundreds or thousands and yet know but a small fraction of the total. His main contact with them is through the impersonal organization. The agglomerate *en masse* is a collection of many such secondary groups. The individual may have membership in four or five of these, although there are many others. Through such memberships he participates in the life of the agglomerate. This relationship that permits him to feel at home in the crowd is essentially anonymous. No one seems to mark his going and coming and he appears to disregard the going and coming of others.

These qualities of the urban way of life, anonymity and social transiency, are regarded with concern by some. In this anonymity one can hide himself, or he can do evil and not be discovered. In the remote village one can also do evil and hide it. Actually, the well adjusted urbanite spends his day moving from contact to contact. He is often under a greater variety of controls than the rural man. Even when moving through the anonymous crowd he is subjected to multiple controls peculiar to the urban way of life.

Expectations and Change

Urban living is more than a special way of behaving; it is also a special way of thinking. The sophisticated urbanite may be naïve in some respects and provincial in others, but he is rarely surprised by the new and the strange. Interest would be more descriptive of his reaction than surprise. He has a general interest in many things, but he is able to focus attention on those interests that pertain to him. Of the rest he tends to be tolerant. For example, he is not disturbed by the presence in his city of people belonging to other races, religions, or national groups than his own. His tolerance tends to be more evident in his secondary than in his primary relations, but even in his primary contacts he is more tolerant than the ruralite. He is more than tolerant of change, as if change were something to be expected.

As the urbanite expects next year's model to be an improvement over previous models, so he expects advancement in all technological change. Unlike his great-grandfather on the farm who was overwhelmed on seeing a railroad train or his grandfather who was skeptical about the practicability of the automobile, he is seldom overwhelmed or skeptical; technological change he takes for granted.

This does not mean that the urban man accepts change without concern. He may not be surprised about the invention of a labor-saving machine, but he may resist having the machine in his work place. If the machine is installed there, he may urge his trade union to demand a higher wage for its operation. He sees nothing new in the idea of automation, since every factory is automatic to some degree, and some will become more so. When he thinks how automation will affect him, he may come forward with demands for his future economic security. He may demand that the public school system be made more efficient, so that his children will be better trained than he was. Thus the individual, when faced with technological change, may stimulate other change.

Attitudes of expectation regarding change in urban work and living are often dynamic in that they are often also attitudes of approval. Believing that he can stimulate change for his own advantage, the urban man tends to regard creativity as a virtue. Attitudes of expectation and approval regarding creativity, although native to the city, are not confined there. They are among the urbanizing influences that radiate outward.

Records and Their Utility

The bigger an industry becomes and the wider the reach of its contacts, the larger must be its front office. Paper work increases with the growth of commerce and industry, and without paper work neither could function, nor could government in the urban community function without records. For the urban individual, paper work and records begin with his birth certificate (and somewhat before) and they begin to end with his death certificate. Between the two certificates may be volumes of records that witness events in his education, his work life, and in his different roles as citizen, church member, member of formal groups, even his record as a consumer. Most of these records will concern his earnings and his spending. Some records are public, but mostly they are private. Each tells something about the individual relative to time and place of actions. This control device is a precising element in urban life.

Records and record keeping in this sense are a necessary concomitant of industrial urbanism, since here memory is an unreliable witness, and the person giving the pledge here today may be absent tomorrow. Many transactions involve persons in distant places. They have a surety function in the life of the individual whose record is commendable, but they may be a problem for one who has something to hide. Record consciousness for the child begins when he must bring from school each month his report card. Again, here is a necessary element in the urban way of life which tends to become universal and here is another reason why illiteracy is a handicap for urban living.

SYMBOLS OF URBANISM

It would be difficult in many countries to find places where the rural way of life exists in its peasant-like purity. Where extremely rural communities are found they are likely to be extremely isolated. In European countries the peasant has passed into history, although he still exists as a stereotype in the thinking of most urbanites. The term continues in the French language, and when the urban Frenchman speaks the word "paysan" much of the imagery is still attached to it. Urbanites in other countries have similar ideas.

Urban and rural are relative terms. In countries being rapidly industrialized and where rural to urban migrants are numerous, some observers are quick to point out that the city is being "ruralized." But since ruralism is passive, or active mainly in its resistance to change, it does not survive long against the dynamic force of urbanism. In this sense, some cities are more urban than others, and that may be said of small places also.

There are certain specific symbols of the urban life that can be seen and enumerated. One of these would be the streets in a village, whether they are paved, drained and lighted, and the condition of roads in the vicinity. The place may or may not have a water supply system. Adherence to or departure from traditional housing and house furnishings, and the amenities in these houses indicate urban or rural orientation. The kind of stores and the goods offered reflect urban influence or its absence.

In the work places of rural localities town influence can be seen in the extent to which machines are used to supplement or replace handwork. Most tests are focused on the homes, the percentage of homes with refrigerators, washing machines, bath rooms, telephones, etc., or the extent to which newspapers, periodicals, radios, or television sets are found there. Looking at the people on the street, their dress and deportment; these tend to reveal rural or urban orientation.

To look for and tabulate such symbols of the urban way of life is to tacitly recognize the outreaching character of urbanism, sometimes called the centrifugal influence of urban life. Insofar as these influences disturb the stabilities of rural life, there may be local resistance to them. Some of these influences may be regarded as intrusions, threatening local traditions and undermining local moral and social values. The urbanite is less concerned about traditions, and he is quite ready to accept change in those artifacts or behavior forms which stand as symbols of urbanism. He tends to be devoted to the mode in which change itself becomes institutionalized. The mode, incidentally, in its influence on rural life, is the most dynamic symbol of urbanism.

URBANISM AND ITS UNIFORMITIES

While truly pertinent to our definition of the urban way of life, space does not permit an examination of such related subjects, for example, as the ecology of urban places or the principles of urban growth. In different respects urban ways of life are influenced by the ecology and geography of cities. So also their ways of life may be influenced by their history. Other influences would be the climate and the natural resources in the hinterlands of cities. Admittedly, differences in ecology, geography, history, climate and natural resources, in different combinations, make for differences between urban places regarding their work, structure, organization and way of life.

These differences are not always evident in measurable terms. They may be largely qualitative, and we lack research material about them. Often they come to attention when we compare urban places for uniformities. These may relate to demographic and economic information, but the most visible of uniformities concern the elements in the man-made part of the environment. These would include buildings, streets and transit facilities. The traveler may look at the hotel facilities and restaurant menus, or the contents of newspapers.

But the most evident are those uniformities pertaining to the engineering aspects of urbanism. A pressing problem in most cities is downtown congestion and space crowding. The approach of the engineer differs little. He devises traffic constructions and control to facilitate access to central areas. He multiplies the use of space by erecting higher buildings and he devises a more efficient use of space in these buildings. Principles of construction are much the same, and the same basic materials are used: stone, brick, concrete, glass, steel, etc. Hotels, private office buildings, public office buildings, factories, multiple-dwelling apartments, hospitals, etc., may differ in architecture but for each type there is considerable region-to-region uniformity. This is necessary to meet the mandates of uniformity in their uses.

Water system, sewers, electric power systems, streetcar, and bus services tend to be globally standardized. So also are telephone systems and other communication facilities. Such uniformities are in part due to the imperatives of economy; industries tend to make fairly similar products, designed for fairly standard uses. Similar equipment from country to country has other advantages; for example, uniformity enables comparison of performance. A safety element may also be involved. The railroads of 17 European countries have established a single purchasing corporation, which helps promote the standardization of equipment.

Most machines and work tools used in factories, garages, and other work places are designed to insure uniformity in the quality of work. This is also true of office equipment, and it tends to be true of apparatus used in the homes; automatic mixers, vacuum cleaners, electric or gas stoves and many others.

These fairly standard artifacts from the autobus to the fountain pen, from the electric fan to the airplane, are among thousands of concrete items in the urbanite's environment wherever he may live. Like the winding of his watch, he must learn to manipulate them according to the technical requirements of each. His day is spent in manipulating them, looking at them, hearing them and thinking about them. They become increasingly part of his way of life.

In this uniforming process, the most effective "educators" are the leisure industries, although all industries are involved. But the industries that cater to man's social and leisure needs are especially effective in training whole populations in how to dress and ornament themselves, how to beautify their homes and how to use free time. The popular song may be translated in different languages and in a few weeks millions of records are sold, and within weeks, too, the latest dance may become a global fad. The transmission from region to region is from city to city. While the great cities are preoccupied with urbanizing their own hinterlands, they also stimulate and influence one another.

Notwithstanding these influences that make for inter-regional uniformity in the urban way of life, the city is far from being a global stereotype. The stereotype is there but it pertains to phases and not to the whole of the community's life. To multiply the technological uniformities may serve to make them globally much alike, but this does not encroach upon the qualities of difference, some of which are social, others psychological. Each continues to retain its own individuality.

Nor does this individuality of urban places diminish with the increase of the city's cosmopolitanism. In its cosmopolitanism the city takes its stance with reference to the outside. Its unique qualities relate more to internal relationships and with respect to which the city is itself "in its own house." In the same sense a university may be proud of its cosmopolitanism, but at the same time it may be proud of its uniqueness.

Urbanization Among the Yoruba

WILLIAM BASCOM
University of California, Berkeley

Wirth has defined a city as "a relatively large, dense, and permanent settlement of socially heterogeneous individuals."[1] His final criterion is not clearly defined; and, in the absence of specific standards which can be applied cross-culturally, it is difficult to distinguish between heterogeneity and homogeneity. Miner has recently commented on "the lack of any concise benchmark from which to appraise the degree of homogeneity"[2] in his study of Timbuctoo, although he concludes that "Timbuctoo is a city. It has a stable population of over six thousand persons, living in a community roughly a square mile in area and patterning their lives after three distinct cultural heritages. The size, density, and heterogeneity of the city are all evident."[3] Miner admittedly rests his case for heterogeneity on the ethnic diversity of the Songhai, Tuareg, and Arabs who inhabit it, but neither he nor Wirth suggests that ethnic diversity is essential to the definition of the city. Many Western cities include groups of different racial, linguistic, and cultural backgrounds, but this can be regarded as a secondary feature of the process of urbanization and a basis for distinguishing cosmopolitan from noncosmopolitan cities.

The shortcomings of Wirth's criterion of social heterogeneity are suggested by the equivocal conclusions of those who have

Reprinted by permission of publisher and author from *American Journal of Sociology*, Vol. LX, No. 5, pp. 446–453 (March, 1955). Copyright 1955 by the University of Chicago.

[1] L. Wirth, "Urbanism as a Way of Life," *American Journal of Sociology*, XLIV (1938), 8.

[2] H. Miner, *The Primitive City of Timbuctoo* (Princeton: Princeton University Press, for the American Philosophical Society, 1953), p. 268.

[3] *Ibid.*, p. 267.

attempted to apply it to traditional African communities. Miner describes Timbuctoo as a "primitive city" and its inhabitants as a "city-folk." Schwab, in a study of a Yoruba city, concludes that "if Oshogbo was viewed on the level of form, it was an urban community; if viewed in terms of social organization and process, it was folk."[4] If the concepts of "folk" and "urban" are useful, it should at least be possible to distinguish between them.

Contrasted to Timbuctoo's 6,000 inhabitants, the Yoruba have six cities of more than 100,000 including Ibadan, the largest Negro city in Africa (Table 8-1). Only Lagos, which is both the principal port and the capital of Nigeria, is ethnically heterogeneous and follows the familiar African pattern of the growth of cities at mining and trading centers, ports, and colonial administrative headquarters.

Nine out of the ten largest cities in Nigeria in 1931 were Yoruba, excepting only Kano, with 97,031 inhabitants. In these nine cities of over 45,000 lived 901,262, or 28.4 percent, of the 3,166,164 Yoruba recorded in the *Census of Nigeria, 1931*, while 1,077,691, or 34 percent, lived in sixteen cities of over 20,000 (including, in addition to those listed in Table 8-1, Ijebu-Ode, 27,909; Ikirun, 23,874; Ikire, 20,920; and Ondo, 20,859). In addition, there were 27 other Yoruba centers with populations between 10,000 and 19,999; 55 with populations between 5,000 and 9,999; and 180 with populations between 2,000 and 4,999.[5]

Taking the average populations of the last three groups as 15,-000, 7,500, and 3,500 and counting only the 77 percent of the population of Lagos who were Yoruba, we arrive at the distribution of urban Yoruba in 1931 given in Table 8-2. For comparison, the figures for European and North American countries cited by Davis and Casis are included, and, following these authors, the index of urbanization has been completed as the average of the previous four columns.[6] The estimated index of urbanization of Yoruba cities falls between that of the United States and Canada, and the distribution of population in urban centers is remarkably similar to that in France.

Official figures on population density are lacking except for Lagos Island (25,000 in 1901, 50,000 in 1921, 58,000 in 1931, and 87,000 in 1950; in 1950 the three wards of Lagos Island had densities of 67,000, 111,000, and 141,000 per square mile). It has been possible to calculate approximate densities for three other cities,

[4] W. Schwab, "Urbanization and Acculturation" (MS).
[5] There were also 7,338 communities with populations under 2,000.
[6] K. Davis and A. Casis, "Urbanization in Latin America," *Milbank Memorial Fund Quarterly*, XXIV (1946), 186–207.

TABLE 8-1. YORUBA CITIES WITH POPULATIONS OVER 40,000*

	1952 (Census)	1931 (Census)	1931 (Non-natives)	1921 (Census)	1911 (Census)	Estimates by Millson (1890)	Estimates by Bowen (1856)	Estimates by Tucker (1853)
Ibadan	459,196	387,133	226	238,094	175,000	200,000	70,000	60,000
Lagos	267,407	126,108	1,443	99,690	73,766	......	20,000	......
Ogbomosho	139,535	86,744	0	84,860	80,000	60,000	25,000	45,000
Oshogbo	122,698	49,599	31	51,418	59,821	35,000—40,000	......	......
Ife	110,790	24,170	5	22,184	36,231	......	......	......
Iwo	100,006	57,191	4	53,588	60,000	60,000	20,000	......
Abeokuta	84,451	45,763	66	28,941	51,255	......	60,000	80,000
Oyo	72,133	48,733	19	40,356	45,438	40,000	25,000	......
Ilesha	72,029	21,892	7	......	......	......	......	......
Iseyin	49,680	36,805	0	28,601	33,362	40,000—60,000	20,000	70,000
Ede	44,808	52,392	0	48,360	26,577	30,000—40,000	20,000	......
Ilorin	41,000	47,412	27	38,668	36,342	......	70,000	......

* Other estimates, not included above, are as follows: Ogbomosho: 50,000 (1860, Campbell); Abeokuta: 45,000 (1842, Freeman), 50,000 (1843, Townsend), 100,000 (1852, Irving), twice the usual figures of 60,000—100,000 (1855, Consul Campbell), 80,000 (1858, Bowen), 100,000 (1874, Chause and Holley); Iseyin: 20,000 (1860, Campbell); Ilorin: 100,000 (1858, Bowen). The 1952 figures were kindly made available by the Nigerian government in advance of publication.

TABLE 8-2. PERCENTAGE OF YORUBA IN CITIES BY SIZE CLASS

	Over 2,000	Over 5,000	Over 10,000	Over 25,000	Over 100,000	Index of Urbani- zation
Yoruba (1931)	78.8	58.9	45.9	29.6	15.3	37.4
Great Britain (1931)	......	81.7	73.6	63.1	45.2	65.9
Germany (1939)	......	57.4	51.7	43.5	31.8	46.1
United States (1940)	......	52.7	47.6	40.1	28.8	42.3
Canada (1941)	......	43.0	38.5	32.7	23.0	34.3
France (1936)	......	41.7	37.5	29.8	16.0	31.2
Sweden (1935)	......	37.1	33.4	27.0	17.5	28.7
Greece (1937)	......	33.1	29.8	23.1	14.8	25.2
Poland (1931)	......	22.8	20.5	15.8	10.7	17.4

using 1931 census figures and official maps[7] for that period. Abeokuta's area is calculated roughly as 8 square miles, giving a density
of 5,720; Oyo's area is about 3½ square miles, giving a density of
13,914; Ogbomosho's area is calculated, probably more accurately
than the others, at 2 square miles, giving a density of 43,372 per
square mile. Because of the higher ratio of inhabitants per room
and per square foot and the greater compactness of the traditional
Yoruba housing, the size of the older Yoruba cities is easily underestimated by outsiders. Abeokuta, for example, appears much
larger than Ogbomosho, which is actually something like half again
as large and eight times as dense.

The permanency of Yoruba cities is partially documented in
Table 8–1. Bowen's estimates of a century ago are conservative but
incomplete; he visited Ogbomosho but does not estimate its size,
and he states: "The eastern parts of Yoruba, and the countries of
Ifeh (Ife), Ijesha (Ilesha), Igbona (Igbomina), and Effong
(Effon-Alaive) have not been visited by the missionaries. We are
assured that there are many large towns in that region."[8] The interior of Yoruba country was first reached in 1825 by Clapperton and
Lander, who visited Katunga (Old Oyo) and other large cities,
some of which were obliterated before Bowen's arrival in 1849. The
wars of the last century destroyed or reduced many Yoruba cities
and resulted in a very considerable depopulation of the entire area.

Earlier historical materials can be found in the accounts of
Benin, to the east, and Dahomey, to the west, which indicate that

[7] Abeokuta: Scale 1:12,500; drawn and reproduced by Land and Survey Department, Lagos, 1947; surveyed in 1930. Oyo: 300/723/3-50; scale 1:12,500;
drawn and reproduced by Land and Survey Department, Lagos. Ogbomosho
Town: 300/684/1.50; scale 400 feet to 1 inch; surveyed in 1938 and reproduced
by Land and Survey Department, Lagos, 1939; reprinted in 1950.
[8] The principal historical sources are listed in the bibliography.

both were subject to some measure of political control by Yoruba cities as early as 200-500 years ago. When the Portuguese explorer d'Aveiro first visited the city of Benin in 1485, it was learned that the sanction of the Ogane, a powerful king in the interior, was required when the king of Benin was crowned; the Ogane has been identified by Talbot as the King of Ife. In 1505-8 Pereira mentions "a very large city called Geebuu," which is unquestionably Ijebu-Ode. In 1668 Dapper mentions the kingdom of Oedobo, and D'Anville's map of 1729 locates Oudobo in the region of the province and city of Ondo. Dapper also mentions the kingdom of Ulkami, which Talbot identifies as Old Oyo; Old Oyo may also be referred to in Bosman's account of the invasion of Arder in Dahomey in 1698. Old Oyo was certainly an important and powerful center by 1724, if not earlier, and was able to collect annual tribute from Dahomey for almost a century (1747-1837). Between 1830 and 1841 Old Oyo was evacuated and the present city of Oyo was founded.

Urbanization can therefore be considered a traditional Yoruba pattern and not the outgrowth of European acculturation. It cannot be explained in terms of the development of colonial administrative centers, ports, mines, or industry. The real basis of the Yoruba economy is, and was, farming. Yet the farmers are city dwellers, and the city is not really a "nonfarm area" as we view it. A belt of peripheral farms which are visited regularly surrounds the city, extending as much as fifteen miles or more outside it. Families whose farms are more distant may have farm huts, where they spend several days at a time during the height of the farming activity, but they maintain a residence in the city and regard it as their real home. Some Yoruba, of course, live on farms or in very small villages.

Nearly all Yoruba engage in farming, but the production of many other goods is specialized. Weaving, dyeing, ironworking, brass-casting, wood-carving, ivory-carving, calabash-carving, bead-working, and leather-working, as well as drumming, divining, the compounding of charms and medicines, and certain other activities, are crafts, whose techniques are known only to a small group of specialists. These specialists, who are organized into guilds, supply all other members of the community with their particular goods and services. Formerly these occupations tended to be more hereditary within the clan or lineage, but the apprenticeship system provided a method by which individuals from outside the kinship unit could be taught a craft. Specialization, however, was only on a craft basis and never reached the extent to which it is found in industrialized societies with the adaptation of labor to the machine.

Trading in local produce within the community is a necessary outgrowth of craft specialization, and both intercommunity and intertribal trade are apparently traditional. The Landers met one hundred wives of the king of Old Oyo trading for him at "Jadoo," north of Ilaro and "Egga." Clapperton and Lander met Hausa and Nupe caravans at "Coosoo" and "Jaguta" between Shaki and Old Oyo and at Kiama, north of Yoruba country, who traded with Yoruba and Dahomeans, with Gonja, Ashantee, and Accra in the Gold Coast, and with Bornu in northeastern Nigeria. In at least Ife, Abeokuta, and Ijebu-Ode, guilds of male traders held monopolies on imported goods from other Yoruba towns and from Europe, buying them in wholesale lots and letting them out to women traders for retail in the markets. Tolls levied on all trade, which provided an important source of income for Yoruba chiefs and kings, are mentioned by Lander on his first visit to Old Oyo. These, and the monopolies on imported goods held by the guilds of male traders, were actively opposed and eventually broken by the British in their efforts to extend trade in Nigeria. The desire to control trade routes to the sea and insure a supply of European imports, including arms, and an outlet for slaves led Ibadan, Abeokuta, and other inland cities to attack coastal enemy towns and defend those of their allies.

Trading is the third basis of the Yoruba economy, and the size and importance of Yoruba markets impress the visitor today as they did the early explorers. Retail trade in the markets is primarily in the hands of women, who also tend to specialize in yams, corn, chickens, cloth, and other commodities, as they become successful, and who are organized into guilds. Trade does not involve a simple exchange of goods between the producer and the consumer but is carried on by middlemen whose role and motivation are similar to those in our own society. In the simplest case a trader buys from the producer and sells at a higher price for a monetary profit; but in some cases goods are sold and resold through a chain of middlemen which has so many links that it becomes difficult to distinguish between wholesaler and retailer. True money in the form of the cowrie shell was used by the Yoruba probably even before European contact, and early European officials received their pay in cowries. Barbot (1732) mentions that "cauries" or "boejies" were being imported from the Maldive Islands in the East Indies as ballast, "no other people in the universe putting such a value on them as the Guineans," but their use as money at Benin is mentioned as early as 1589. Some Yoruba traditions speak of the institution of barter, but others suggest that cowrie shells were used as money before even the Portuguese arrived and that the pecuniary economy of the Yoruba is of long standing. To say the least, it is difficult to imagine how the European traders would have hit upon cowrie shells as an importable commodity which the Africans would accept in exchange for goods if the shells had not been already known and valued. One may conclude that the traditional Yoruba pattern of trade involved large markets, true middlemen, and true money.

The earliest available evidence indicates an important and well-developed trade between Yoruba cities and with other tribes but does not suggest that these cities developed as trading centers of the type represented by Timbuctoo, Kano, and other Sudanese cities. Under British rule, trade in European goods has increased tremendously, and as has trade in local produce, owing to the development of new occupations such as those of clerk, carpenter, and mechanic and to the increasing amounts of farm land devoted to cocoa. The typical pre-British markets, however, excluding those which specialized in the buying and selling of slaves, dealt mainly with local produce rather than with goods from abroad, from other tribes, or from other Yoruba cities. In other words, trade was based upon specialization within the city rather than the city itself being based upon trade growing out of extensive regional or tribal specialization.

It is important to distinguish between industrial and nonindustrial cities. Industrialization, where it has occurred, has produced a kind and degree of specialization that are unknown in nonindustrialized societies. Industrialization has given rise to urbanization in Western societies, but this is not to say that it is its prerequisite or its only cause. On this point, Wirth has stated specifically: "It is particularly important to call attention to the danger of confusing urbanism with industrialism and modern capitalism. The rise of cities in the modern world is undoubtedly not independent of modern power-driven machine technology, mass production, and capitalistic enterprise. But different as the cities of earlier epochs may have been by virtue of their development in a preindustrial and precapitalistic order from the great cities of today, they were, nevertheless, cities."[9]

The Yoruba cities were nonindustrial and lacked the degree of specialization based upon the machine. Nevertheless, the craft form of specialization made each individual economically dependent upon the society as a whole. The weaver depended upon the blacksmith for tools and upon the farmer, the hunter, and the trader for his food; the blacksmith depended upon others for his food and upon

[9] Wirth, op. cit., pp. 7–8.

the weaver for his clothes; the farmer depended upon the hunter and the trader for his meat, the smith for his cutlass and hoe, and the weaver for his clothing. Each of these, moreover, had to rely upon the diviner, the herbalist, the priest, the drummer, the potter, the wood-carver, and other specialists for goods and services which they could not provide for themselves.

Aside from craft specialization, the Yoruba cities were heterogeneous only in terms of their social stratification and their social and political segmentation. Nine social strata can be distinguished in the Yoruba city of Ife. Oversimplifying for the sake of brevity, the five lowest strata, comprising perhaps 95 per cent of the population, may be described as positions which are ascribed on the basis of clan or lineage, while the four highest strata are primarily achieved, although often only within specified clans or lineages.[10] The patrilineal lineage or clan is basic to Yoruba society, rural or urban. The large cities are composed of many such segments based on kinship, organized politically into permanent, clearly defined wards or "quarters" and precincts or subquarters, while the small villages may contain only a few or even only a single lineage. In Ife heads of each lineage constitute the precinct council, one of their number serving as its chief. Precinct chiefs constitute the ward council, headed by a ward chief. The five ward chiefs and three other city chiefs represent the interests of the townspeople and, with eight chiefs chosen from the palace retinue, serve as the king's council and in former times served as a chief tribunal. The king, whose position is hereditary within the related lineages of the royal clan, is responsible for the affairs of the capital and of the outlying towns and villages within the kingdom.

Within the lineage, individual relationships are dependent upon such circumstances as seniority, sex, wealth, personal qualities, and status as slave, pawn, or free; but between lineages individual relationships are dependent upon the relative rank of the lineage.[11] The individual counts for little except as a member of the lineage. Further, in Wirth's words, "interests are made effective through representation."[12] Representation or delegation is clearly illustrated in the system of lineage, heads, precinct councils and precinct chiefs, ward councils and ward chiefs, city council with its city chiefs, representatives of the palace officials, and the king himself.

The city is a secondary group, while the lineage is primary.

[10] W. Bascom, "Social Status, Wealth and Individual Differences Among the Yoruba," *American Anthropologist*, LIII (1951), 490–505.
[11] *Ibid.*; W. Bascom, "The Principle of Seniority in the Social Structure of the Yoruba," *American Anthropologist*, XLIV (1942), 37–46.
[12] Wirth, *op. cit.*, p. 14.

Wirth says "The contacts of the city may indeed be face to face, but they are nevertheless impersonal, superficial, transitory and segmental." All these characteristics are exemplified in Yoruba market transactions. As in our own urban communities, one may have regular customers with whom relations are not impersonal, but one also must deal with casual customers of whom one must always beware in either buying or selling. Miner notes the cheating of a gullible buyer or seller in Timbuctoo. Among the Yoruba the principle of *caveat emptor* is also well established, as is illustrated by an edict of the king of Ife prohibiting the "hawking" or peddling of palm wine through the streets so as to restrict the possibility of its being watered down. Furthermore, the counterfeiting of government currency was so perfected by one Yoruba subgroup that counterfeit coins became known throughout Nigeria as "Ijebu money." Another new kind of cheating was made possible by the "money doubling" machines of the early thirties. Into these Westernized gadgets the up-country dupe would put shillings and pounds in increasing amounts and have double value returned, until he became greedy for the big kill and put in all the cash he could; at this point the operator explained that the machine had stuck and would take overnight to digest such a large amount, and skipped out of town under the cover of darkness.

Wirth emphasizes that urbanization refers to a distinctive mode of life. This is evident among the Yoruba in clothing, food habits, manners, and attitudes toward each other of even the non-Europeanized city dweller and the people from the small village, the rural farm area, and the hinterland. The city dwellers ridicule the unsophisticated "bush" people; their attitudes, as expressed in conversation and proverbs,[13] closely parallel our concepts of "rube" or "hick." The attitudes of the rural Yoruba toward the city dweller also seem to resemble those in our society. On the other hand, the anomie stressed by Durkheim and later sociologists does not seem to be apparent, unless it is to be found among the rural Yoruba who find themselves in the city. Since the lineage is the residential unit and involves reciprocal social and economic obligations, the city dweller need not feel lonely or insecure. Competitiveness is strong, and economic failure can lead to frustration or suicide but not to starvation.

There is no evidence that the old pattern of city life tended to weaken the lineage, or produce the increased mobility, instability, and insecurity which Wirth suggests are the results of heteroge-

[13] E.g., "They don't call a man a man; they don't call a human a human; therefore the farm people (*ara oko*) wear a breechclout to town," meaning that they do not have enough respect for others to dress properly in public.

neity. To the extent that the lineage has been weakened, the causes have been other conditions, such as the increased ease of travel with the ending of warfare and the development of Western forms of transportation, the introduction of a valuable permanent crop in cocoa, the super-imposition of British control and European ethics over the traditional Yoruba authorities and mores, and the emphasis on the individual in the teaching of Christian missions, which have affected the Yoruba over the last fifty to a hundred years.[14] All these things are today producing changes in Yoruba cities similar to those in the newer African cities, and to the Western cities of which Wirth speaks; kinship bonds, traditionally a basic element in the structure of the city, are weakening.

Wirth states that "the bonds of kinship, of neighborliness, and the sentiments arising out of living together for generations under a common folk tradition are likely to be absent or, at best, relatively weak in an aggregate the members of which have such diverse origins and backgrounds. Under such circumstances competition and formal control mechanisms furnish the substitutes for the bonds of solidarity that are relied upon to hold a folk society together." This statement is undoubtedly true of the cosmopolitan cities in the United States and perhaps elsewhere, but in the Yoruba cities the bonds of kinship and living together which unite the lineage were strong, and the elements of competition and formal control mechanisms were not developed as *substitutes* for kinship control mechanisms but, rather, as mechanisms of control on a suprakinship, secondary level, transcending the primary groups, such as lineages, which were very much alive and functional.

Although Wirth dismisses forms of political organization as an arbitrary and therefore unsatisfactory criterion for urbanism, the presence or absence of a formalized city government which exercises authority over neighboring primary groups and incorporates them into a community seems, on the contrary, no less arbitrary and certainly far less subjective than social heterogeneity. When coupled with size, density, and permanency, formalized community government would seem to be a useful criterion of urbanism for cross-cultural comparisons. It is the factor which differentiates the urban Yoruba from the Ibo of eastern Nigeria, whose total population is comparable and whose over-all population densities are about double[15] but the growth of whose cities has been recent. We

[14] The effects of these factors cannot be analyzed here. They are touched on partially in W. Bascom, "African Culture and the Missionary," *Civilisations* (Brussels), III (1953), 491–504.
[15] Population densities in 1931 for the Yoruba provinces in Southern Nigeria run as follows: Ondo, 56; Abeokuta, 74; Oyo, 94; Ijebu, 125; and the Colony, 153; for the Ibo provinces: Ogoja, 94; Owerri, 268; and Onitsha, 306. In 1931 the Ibo numbered 3,184,585, as against 3,166,164 Yoruba in Nigeria.

do not know why the Yoruba developed cities and city government while the Ibo did not, but city life is definitely a part of the Yoruba tradition.

Some Yoruba cities, such as Oyo, Ife, Ilesha, Ijebu-Ode, Ondo, and Ketu, were metropolitan in that, as capitals, they served as centers of the entire kingdom and can be considered metropolitan. The capital city maintained regular communication with the outlying towns over which they ruled, and representatives of the king were stationed in them. Taxes of several kinds were collected throughout the kingdom and brought to the capital for the king. Death sentences had to be referred to the capital, where executions were performed and where each case could be reviewed by the king's court. Other large cities, such as Iseyin, Ogbomosho, and Ibadan, were not metropolitan except as they served as centers of trade or warfare, but these also had formalized city government. Each was ruled by a "town" chief (*bale*) under the authority of the king (*oba*), who lived elsewhere and to whom allegiance was owed. Ibadan became so powerful as a military center that it achieved a measure of independence from Oyo and could command the allegiance of many surrounding towns, but its ruler is still a *bale*, not an *oba*.

Ethnically the Yoruba cities were homogeneous. With the end of the wars of the last century, individuals from the Hausa, Ibo, Jekri, and other cultural and linguistic groups have settled in them, but in relatively small numbers except for Lagos. One may assume that in earlier times the non-Yoruba consisted mainly of slaves and transient traders. The wars of the last century flooded some cities with refugees, including those from other Yoruba kingdoms and subcultures; but one may also assume that even on the level of subcultural and dialectical variation Yoruba cities were previously noncosmopolitan.

Despite the absence of industrialization and ethnic heterogeneity and despite the continued importance of kinship units, the Yoruba had cities even before European penetration. They had cities because they had large, dense, permanent communities whose inhabitants were economically independent, socially stratified, and politically unified. These cities were based on farming, craft specialization, and trading. Only Lagos represents the common type of recent growth of African cities as ports, mining and trading centers, and colonial administrative headquarters. Some Yoruba cities were metropolitan, serving as capitals and centers of the Yoruba kingdoms; others were nonmetropolitan. Some were founded as defensive or predatory centers during the wars of the last century; others undoubtedly existed when the Portuguese arrived and before the beginning of the slave wars. Although the cause of their growth is still not fully known, they were definitely a part of the traditional Yoruba pattern, providing permanent residences for farmers and markets for trade within, as well as beyond, the city's boundaries.

It is difficult to decide whether or not the Yoruba cities were heterogeneous in Wirth's sense, because social heterogeneity is not clearly defined. At best, it is a relative criterion which is difficult to apply cross-culturally. Perhaps the answer may be to define it in terms of specialization to the extent that each individual is economically dependent on the production and the special skills of the other members of his community. It is necessary at least to distinguish between industrial and nonindustrial cities and between cosmopolitan and noncosmopolitan cities. It is also suggested that the existence of a formalized government which exercises authority over the primary groups and incorporates them into a political community may be more useful than heterogeneity when applied cross-culturally, since it is less subjective. It is hoped that these points may broaden the concept of urbanization so that it is less dependent upon the historical conditions of Western urbanization and so that it can be applied more profitably to the study of the urban centers of India and Southeast Asia.

Further Observations on the Folk-Urban
Continuum and Urbanization
with Special Reference to Mexico City

OSCAR LEWIS

University of Illinois

. . . I would like to present in brief some of my own research findings in Mexico which can serve as a starting point for the discussion. The relevant findings of my first Mexico City study of 1951
can be summarized as follows: (1) Peasants in Mexico City
adapted to city life with far greater ease than one would have
expected judging from comparable studies in the United States and
from folk-urban theory. (2) Family life remained quite stable and
extended family ties increased rather than decreased. (3)
Religious life became more Catholic and disciplined, indicating
the reverse of the anticipated secularization process. (4) The
system of *compadrazgo* continued to be strong, albeit with some
modifications. (5) The use of village remedies and beliefs persisted.

In the light of these findings I wrote at the time, ". . . this
study provides evidence that urbanization is not a single, unitary,
universally similar process but assumes different forms and meanings, depending upon the prevailing historic, economic, social, and
cultural conditions."[1]

Excerpts from Chapter 13 in Philip M. Hauser and Leo F. Schnore (eds.).
The Study of Urbanization, New York, John Wiley and Sons, Inc., pp. 494–502
(1965). Reprinted by permission of Professor Lewis.
[1] Oscar Lewis, "Urbanization Without Breakdown: A Case Study," in *The
Scientific Monthly*, 75, No. 1 (July 1952). In this article I have suggested a
number of specific Mexican conditions which might explain the special findings. More recently, Joseph A. Kahl has restated and elaborated upon some of
these points in his article "Some Social Concomitants of Industrialization and
Urbanization: A Research Review," *Human Organization*, 18 (Summer 1959),
pp. 53–74.

Because of the unusual nature of my findings, I decided to test them in 1956-1957 against a much wider sample of non-Tepoztecan city families. I selected two lower-class housing settlements or *vecindades*, both located in the same neighborhood within a few blocks of the Tepito market and only a short walk from the central square of Mexico City. In contrast with the Tepoztecan city families who represented a wide range of socioeconomic levels and were scattered in twenty-two *colonias* throughout the city, my new sample was limited to two settlements whose residents came from twenty-four of the thirty-two states and territories of the Mexican nation.[2]

On the whole, my research findings tended to support those of the earlier study. The findings suggested that the lower-class residents of Mexico City showed much less of the personal anonymity and isolation of the individual which had been postulated by Wirth as characteristic of urbanism as a way of life. The *vecindad* and the neighborhood tended to break up the city into small communities that acted as cohesive and personalizing factors. I found that many people spent most of their lives within a single *colonia* or district, and even when there were freqent changes of residence, they were usually within a restricted geographical area determined by low rentals. Lifetime friendships and daily face-to-face relations with the same people were common, and resembled a village situation. Most marriages also occurred within the *colonia* or adjoining *colonias*. Again, I found that extended family ties were quite strong, as measured by visiting, especially in times of emergency, and that a relatively high proportion of the residents of the *vecindades* were related by kinship and *compadrazgo* ties.

In spite of the cult of *machismo* and the overall cultural emphasis upon male superiority and dominance, I found a strong tendency toward matricentered families, in which the mother played a crucial role in parent-child relations even after the children were married. In genealogical studies I found that most people recalled a much larger number of relatives on the mother's side than on the father's side.

I also found that the *vecindad* acted as a shock absorber for the rural migrants to the city because of the similarity between its culture and that of rural communities. Both shared many of the traits which I have elsewhere designated as "the culture of poverty." Indeed, I found no sharp differences in family structure, diet, dress, and belief systems of the *vecindad* tenants according to

[2] Oscar Lewis, "The Culture of the Vecindad in Mexico City: Two Case Studies," *Actas del III Congreso Internacional de Americanistas*, Tomo I, San Jose, Costa Rica (1959), pp. 387–402.

their rural-urban origins. The use of herbs for curing, the raising of animals, the belief in sorcery, and spiritualism, the celebration of the Day of the Dead, illiteracy and low level of education, political apathy and cynicism about government, and the very limited membership and participation in both formal and informal associations, were just as common among persons who had been in the city for over thirty years as among recent arrivals. Indeed, I found that *vecindad* residents of peasant background who came from small landholding families showed more middle-class aspirations in their desire for a higher standard of living, home ownership, and education for their children than did city born residents of the lower-income group.

These findings suggest the need for a reexamination of some aspects of urban theory and for modifications which would help explain the findings from Mexico City and other cities in underdeveloped countries, as well as those from Chicago.

Wirth defines a city as "a relatively large, dense, and permanent settlement of socially heterogeneous individuals." By "socially heterogeneous" he had in mind primarily distinctive ethnic groups rather than class differences. Wirth defines urbanism as the mode of life of people who live in cities or who are subject to their influence. Because Wirth thinks of the city as a whole, as a community (and here, I believe, is one of his errors), he assumes that all people who live in cities are affected by this experience in profound and similar ways, namely, the weakening of kinship bonds, family life, and neighborliness, and the development of impersonality, superficiality, anonymity, and transitoriness in personal relations. For Wirth the process of urbanization is essentially a process of disorganization.[3]

This approach leads to some difficulties. For one thing, as Sjoberg has pointed out, ". . . their interpretations [i.e. those of Park, Wirth and Redfield] involving ecology have not articulated well with their efforts to explain social activities."[4] Wirth himself showed some of the contradictory aspects of city life without relating them to his theory of urbanism. He writes of the city as the historic center of progress, of learning, of higher standards of living, and all that is hopeful for the future of mankind, but he also points to the city as the locus of slums, poverty, crime, and disorganization. According to Wirth's theory both the carriers of knowledge and progress (the elite and the intellectuals) and the ignorant slum

[3] Louis Wirth, "Urbanism As a Way of Life," *American Journal of Sociology*, 44 (July 1938), pp. 1–24.
[4] Gideon Sjoberg, "Comparative Urban Sociology," *Sociology Today* (New York: Basic Books, 1959), p. 340.

dwellers have a similar urban personality, since presumably they share in the postulated urban anonymity and so on.

It is in the evaluation of the personality of the urban dweller that urban theory has gone furthest afield. It leaps from the analysis of the social system to conjecture about individual personality; it is based not on solid psychological theory but on personal values, analogies, and outmoded physiopsychological concepts. Some of the description of the modern urbanite reads like another version of the fall of man. The delineation of the urbanite as blasé, indifferent, calculating, utilitarian, and rational (presumably as a defensive reaction to preserve his nervous system from the excessive shocks and stimuli of city life), suffering from anonymity and anomie, being more conscious and intellectual than his country brother yet feeling less deeply, remain mere statements of faith.[5]

Besides the lack of an adequate personality theory, it seems to me that some of the difficulty stems from the attempt to make individual psychological deductions from conditions prevailing in the city as a whole. The city is not the proper unit of comparison or discussion for the study of social life because the variables of number, density, and heterogeneity as used by Wirth are not the crucial determinants of social life or of personality.[6] There are many intervening variables. Social life is not a mass phenomenon. It occurs for the most part in small groups, within the family, within households, within neighborhoods, within the church, formal and informal groups, and so on.

Any generalizations about the nature of social life in the city must be based on careful studies of these smaller universes rather than on a priori statements about the city as a whole. Similarly, generalizations about urban personality must be based on careful personality studies. The delineation of social areas within cities and a careful analysis of their characteristics would take us a long way beyond the overgeneralized formulations of "urbanism as a way of life."

Basic to this Simmel-Wirth-Redfield approach are the supposed consequences of the predominance of primary relations in small rural communities versus the predominance of secondary relations in large cities. It seems to me that the psychological and social consequences of primary versus secondary relations have been mis-

---

[5] Wirth, "Urbanism As a Way of Life," in *Community Life and Social Policy* (Chicago: University of Chicago Press, 1956), pp. 119–120.

[6] Sjoberg has correctly criticized the logic of comparison inherent in the writings of Redfield and Wirth on folk-urban theory on the ground that they were comparing a whole society with a part society. Here my criticism is that Wirth treated the city as a whole society for purposes of social relations and personality.

understood and exaggerated for both the country and the city. I know of no experimental or other good evidence to indicate that exposure to large numbers of people per se makes for anxiety and nervous strain or that the existence of secondary relations diminishes the strength and importance of primary ones. Primary group relations are just as important psychologically for city people as they are for country people, and sometimes they are more satisfying and of a more profound nature. And although the sheer number of secondary relations in the city is much greater than in the country, these relations can also be said to be secondary in the sense that their psychological consequences are minor.

The number of profound warm and understanding human relationships or attachments is probably limited in any society, rural or urban, modern or backward. Such attachments are not necessarily or exclusively a function of frequency of contact and fewness of numbers. They are influenced by cultural traditions which may demand reserve, a mind-your-own-business attitude, a distrust of neighbors, fear of sorcery and gossip, and the absence of a psychology of introspection.

George Foster's recent comparative analysis of the quality of inter-personal relations in small peasant societies, based on anthropological monographs, shows that they are characterized by distrust, suspicion, envy, violence, reserve, and withdrawal.[7] His paper confirms my earlier findings on Tepoztlan.

In some villages, peasants can live out their lives without any deep knowledge or understanding of the people whom they "know" in face-to-face relationships. By contrast, in modern Western cities, there may be more give and take about one's private, intimate life at a single "sophisticated" cocktail party than would occur in years in a peasant village. I suspect there are deeper, more mature human relationships among sympathetic, highly educated, cosmopolitan individuals who have chosen each other in friendship, than are possible among sorcery-ridden, superstitious, ignorant peasants, who are daily thrown together because of kinship or residential proximity.

It is a common assumption in social science literature that the process of urbanization for both tribal and peasant peoples is accompanied by a change in the structure of the family, from an extended to a nuclear family. It is assumed that the rural family is extended and the urban, nuclear. It must be pointed out that not even all primitive or preliterate people are characterized by a pre-

[7] George Foster, "The Personality of the Peasant," paper read at the 58th Annual Meeting of the American Anthropological Association, Mexico City, 1959.

ponderance of the extended family as the residential unit. The
Eskimo is a good example. Among peasantry, also, one finds a wide
range of conditions in this regard. In most highland Mexican villages the nuclear family predominates as the residence unit. Very
often and without any evidence, this fact is interpreted as a symp-
tom of change from an earlier condition. In India, one finds a
remarkable difference in family composition by castes within a
single village. For example, in Rampur village in the state of Delhi,
the Jats and Brahmans, both of whom own and work the land, have
large, extended families, whereas the lower-caste Sweepers and
Leatherworkers have small nuclear families.

I suggest that we must distinguish much more carefully
between the existence of the extended family as a residence unit
and as a social group. In Mexico the extended family is important
as a social group in both rural and urban areas where the nuclear
family predominates as the residence unit. In Mexico the persistence of extended family bonds seems compatible with urban life
and increased industrialization. Moreover, the *compadre* system,
with its extension of adoptive kinship ties, is operative, though in
somewhat distinctive ways, on all class levels. I suspect that
increased communication facilities in Mexico, especially the telephone and the car, may strengthen rather than weaken extended
family ties.

One of the most distinctive characteristics of cities, whether in
the industrial or preindustrial age, is that they provide, at least
potentially, a wider range of alternatives for individuals in most
aspects of living than is provided by the nonurban areas of the
given nation or total society at a given time. Urbanism and urbanization involve the availability of a wide range of services and alternatives in terms of types of work, housing, food, clothing, educational facilities, medical facilities, modes of travel, voluntary
organizations, types of people, and so on.

If we were to accept these criteria as definitive traits we could
then develop indices of the degree of urbanization of different sectors of the population within cities. For example, if the population
of any subsector of a city had fewer alternatives in types of clothing, foods, and so on, either because of traditional ethnic sanctions
or lack of economic resources, we could designate this population
sector as showing a lower degree of urbanization than some other
sector. This does not apply to the city alone; the scale of urbanization can also be applied to villages, towns, and to their respective
populations.

As I see it, therefore, there are two sides to the urbanization
coin: one, the amount and variety of services and the like to be
found in any city, and two, the extent to which different sectors of

the city residents can partake of these services. From this distinction it follows that two cities may show the same urbanization index in terms of the number and variety of services per capita but may be very different in terms of the degree of urbanization (cosmopolitanism) of the various sectors of its inhabitants.

It also follows that there are many ways of life which coexist within a single city. This is particularly evident in the underdeveloped countries where class or caste differences are sharp. In Mexico City, for example, there are approximately a million and a half people who live in one-room *vecindades* or in primitive *jacales*, with little opportunity to partake of the great variety of housing facilities available for the tourists and the native bourgeoisie. Most of this large mass still have a low level of education and literacy, do not belong to labor unions, do not participate in the benefits of the social security system, make very little use of the city's museums, art galleries, banks, hospitals, department stores, concerts, airports, and so on. These people live in cities, indeed, a considerable portion were born in the city, but they are not highly urbanized. From this point of view, then, the poor in all cities of the world are less urbanized, that is, less cosmopolitan, than the wealthy.

The "culture of poverty" is a provincial, locally oriented culture, both in the city and in the country. In Mexico it is characterized by a relatively higher death rate, a higher proportion of the population in the younger age groups (less than 15 years), a higher proportion of gainfully employed in the total population, including child labor and working women. Some of these indices for poor *colonias* (districts) of Mexico City are much higher than for rural Mexico as a whole.

On another level the "culture of poverty" in Mexico, cutting across the rural and the urban, is characterized by the absence of food reserves in the home, the pattern of frequent buying of small quantities of food many times a day as the need occurs, borrowing money from money lenders at usurious interest rates, the pawning of goods, spontaneous informal credit devices among neighbors, the use of secondhand clothing and furniture, particularly in the city which has the largest secondhand market in Mexico, a higher incidence of free unions or consensual marriages, a strong present-time orientation, and a high proportion of pre-Hispanic folk beliefs and practices.

In the preoccupation with the study of rural-urban differences, there has been a tendency to overlook or neglect basic similarities of people everywhere. In a recent paper Bruner[8] has illustrated

[8] Edward M. Bruner, "Urbanization and Culture Change: Indonesia," paper read at the 58th Annual Meeting of the American Anthropological Association in Mexico City, December 28, 1959.

this point for Indonesia where he found that the urban and rural Toba Batak are essentially part of a single social and economic ceremonial system.

Mexico-India contrasts also illustrate his point. In Mexico, Catholicism gives a similar stamp to many aspects of life in both rural and urban areas. The nucleated settlement pattern of most Mexican villages with the central church and plaza and the barrio-subdivisions, each in turn with its respective chapel, makes for a distinctive design which is in marked contrast to the north Indian villages where Hinduism and the caste system have made for a much more segmented and heterogeneously organized type of settlement pattern. It is my impression that a similar contrast is to be seen in some of the cities of these two countries and I believe this merits further study. Taking another example from India, we find that the way of life of the urban and rural lower castes, such as Washermen and Sweepers, have much more in common with each other than with the higher caste Brahmans in their respective urban and rural contexts.

Although I agree that number, density, permanence of settlement and heterogeneity of population is a workable definition of a city, I believe we need an additional, more elementary set of variables, with a narrower focus, to explain what goes on within cities. The sheer physical conditions of living have a considerable influence on social life, and I would include, among the variables, such factors as stability of residence, the settlement pattern, types of housing, the number of rooms to a family, and property concepts.

A type of housing settlement like the *vecindad*, which brings people into daily face-to-face contact, in which people do most of their work in a common patio, share a common toilet and a common washstand, encourages intensive interaction, not all of which is necessarily friendly. It makes little difference whether this housing and settlement pattern is in the city or in the country, indeed whether it occurs among the tribal peoples of Borneo or the Iroquois Indians. In all cases it produces intense interaction, problems of privacy, quarrels among children, and among their parents.

Stability of residence too has many similar social consequences wherever it occurs. As I have already shown, in Mexico City the *vecindades* make for a kind of community life which has greater resemblance to our stereotyped notions of village life than to Wirth's description of urbanism. Stability of residence may result from a wide variety of factors, both in rural and urban areas. Nor can we assume that it is a necessary concomitant of nonurban societies; witness the nomadism of the Plains Indians or of agricultural workers in parts of the Caribbean.

Certain aspects of the division of labor stand up well as an elementary narrow-focus variable. When the family is the unit of production and the home and the work place are one, certain similar consequences follow for family life, both in the country and the city. I have in mind similarities in family life of small artisans in Mexico City and rural villages. In both, husband and wife spend most of the day together, children are early recruited into useful work, and there is much interaction among family members. Thus, in terms of the amount of time husbands spend away from home, there is much more similarity between a peasant and a factory worker than between either of these and an artisan.

What we need in comparative urban studies as well as in rural-urban comparisons, within a single culture and crossculturally, are carefully controlled, narrow-focus comparisons of subunits. . . .

Chapter 4

SUBURBANIZATION AND SUBURBANISM AS A WAY OF LIFE

Already documented in previous selections is the statistical fact of the growth of the fringe surrounding the great American cities. Similar trends have been underway in many other nations. The dependence of the North American pattern of suburbanization upon the automobile, however, limits this particular type of suburbanization to those portions of the world and/or those classes in which the car is a usual family possession.

In the United States, all indications point to continued rapid growth of the suburban fringe around large cities. It is difficult to obtain intercensal estimates which can be considered sound for the population of cities, but from time to time the Census Bureau has released estimates of the population of standard metropolitan statistical areas, including the populations of component counties. If one takes five large cities (Baltimore, Denver, New Orleans, San Francisco, and Washington) for which the political city is also a county or federal district, one may compare central city and suburban growth. Between 1960 and 1967, for example, the population of these five metropolitan areas increased 18 per cent. The population of the central cities (excluding Oakland) had increased hardly at all—less than one per cent. The growth of the remaining area within the five standard statistical metropolitan areas was 31 per cent during the seven-year period. These cities were selected merely because data for them could conveniently be obtained in the needed form; there is no reason to assume that their pattern of growth differed from that elsewhere in the United States.

Suburbanization as a process, then, is indisputable. Not so suburbanism as a way of life. A voluminous literature, both by those whom Dobriner calls "commentators," as well as the "scientists," is devoted to the alleged life styles of suburbia. The stereotype is familiar; suburbia is the home of families, stratified by age and income into homogeneous neighborhoods. The father leaves the community daily as he commutes to the city, with the mother thereby inheriting the responsibilities of the family and the community. These are status-oriented families, conformity-minded, engaged in a great deal of neighborly contact. Politically they are Republicans, made conservative by the gradually accruing equity in home ownership and the sometimes more rapidly increasing tax assessments necessary to provide educational and other services for the child-centered populace. The picture has been embellished endlessly. Each reader will recognize it and can furnish his own additions to the familiar image of the American suburb.

In discussing urbanism and suburbanism, Gans made a useful differentiation when he distinguished the inner city from the outer city and suburbs. The inner city consists of the central business district, of course, but also includes residentially a heterogeneous population consisting of "cosmopolites," the unmarried or childless, the "ethnic villagers," the "deprived," and the "trapped" and downwardly mobile. Beyond the inner city are the stable residential areas of the outer city, including residences both of the working and the middle classes. Still more distant, newer, less thickly settled, and often politically distinct lie the suburbs, but sociologically these represent to Gans largely an extension of the outer city.[1] From this perspective, the most meaningful distinctions, then, are those between the ways of life in the inner city and those of the outer and suburban areas.

Many observers have challenged the overly simplified stereotype of suburbia which developed following World War II. Among sociologists, Bennett Berger has been instrumental in dispelling some elements of "the myth of suburbia." In an article carrying that title[2] and in a book describing a suburban area of industrial workers in California,[3] he questioned the idea that transplantation

[1] Herbert Gans, "Urbanism and Suburbanism as Ways of Life: A Re-evaluation of Definitions," in Arnold Rose, ed., *Human Behavior and Social Processes*, Boston: Houghton-Mifflin Company (1962), pp. 625–648.
[2] Bennett M. Berger, "The Myth of Suburbia," *The Journal of Social Issues*, Vol. XVII, No. 1, pp. 38–46.
[3] Bennett M. Berger, *Working-Class Suburb (A Study of Auto Workers in Suburbia)*, Berkeley, University of California Press, 1960.

into the suburban setting should so remake the life styles of the persons involved. He found, indeed, that working-class suburbanites showed little indication of conforming to the model of suburban life which had become so popular.

In short, there are different kinds of suburbs. Berger suggested that the characteristics of suburban life which have so often been ascribed to that setting are instead the characteristics of the American middle classes. In an incisive discussion of the function of the "myth," he maintained that to various segments of the population, the beliefs in their image of suburbia and of suburbanites were useful. Some approved the characteristics imputed to suburbia—realtors and market-oriented mass communications industries, for example. Some disapproved—and intellectuals were conspicuous among these. Those approving and those objecting alike found the "myth" convenient.

In a later essay, Berger has added another possible explanation to the "myth" of suburbia, which, as he notes, persists despite the growing number of studies confirming the inaccuracy of basic elements of the popular picture. He has hypothesized that the "myth" may ease the unresolved dilemma in American values of the melting-pot versus the pluralist models of society. The suburb of the popular image is a homogeneous projection of America, a replacement for the picture of Main Street which was so popular during an earlier and less metropolitanized era. Our ambivalence concerning our own racial, ethnic, religious, and class diversity, he suggests, causes us to find comfort in an image of a homogeneous world of young American families, marked by no apparent differences.[4]

The selections upon suburbanization and suburbanism presented in this volume include a discussion by Schnore of the distinction between "satellites" and "suburbs," and a consideration of characteristic features of each of these kinds of communities of the urban fringe. The rapid movement of industry and of white-collar companies to the suburban ring has continued since the article was written and is creating a situation in which some residents of the central city commute into the fringe for employment, and many suburban residents commute "horizontally," often to a newly-developed "satellite" district on or near the belt highways circling the metropolis.

---

[4] These comments are based upon Bennett M. Berger, "Suburbs, Subcultures, and the Urban Future," in Sam Bass Warner (ed.), *Planning for a Nation of Cities*, Cambridge, Massachusetts, The M.I.T. Press, Massachusetts Institute of Technology, 1966, pp. 143–162. The same article was printed under the title, "Suburbia and the American Dream" in *Public Interest*, 2 (Winter, 1966).

The excerpts from *The Organization Man,* the classic account by William H. Whyte, Jr. of the rising members of young executives or executives-to-be in the corporation world, give the reader some feeling for the life style Whyte so graphically depicted in this book. Much which Whyte describes became, by extension, a part of the popular stereotype applied to all suburbs. Refutation of the overgeneralization of the description does not invalidate the relevance of the description to the particular setting which was observed. Whyte's book is the starting point for much of the subsequent literature upon suburban life.

In the selection from Dobriner, he adds his emphasis to the point that suburbia is heterogeneous. A given suburb may have a relatively high degree of homogeneity in an economic sense, and perhaps in other respects, but suburbs are not necessarily homogeneous internally, and they differ markedly, one from the other. In the work from which the selections are quoted, Dobriner goes on to identify the variations in social class in suburban America. He also notes that, whatever the class-linked behavior patterns may be, they are expressed to some degree in the suburban setting in ways which differ from the city. The suburban dweller, for example, is more "visible" in his pattern of living, more open to scrutiny, than is his counterpart in many sections of the city.

In the concluding section of the chapter, Riesman presents his own interpretation of some features of suburban life. It seems reasonable to assume that the picture he had in mind as he described the "suburban dislocation" was that of the upper-middle class style of suburban living. The dependence of suburban life upon the automobile is emphasized, as are a number of other suburban characteristics.

At the time he wrote, Riesman found few indications that young people, whether or not they were themselves the products of the suburban setting, had any particular disillusionment with that setting. He found little hint among them of resistance to the prospect of immersing themselves in suburban life upon completion of their university training. It is interesting to note that a decade later, among students protesting the structure and the practices of American society, many seem to come from the background of the comfortable upper-middle class suburban community. Among the things that some of these young people, judged by their own rhetoric, protest against is what Riesman himself calls "the aimless quality of suburban life."

Satellites and Suburbs

LEO F. SCHNORE
University of Wisconsin

INTRODUCTION

The purposes of this paper are threefold: (1) to set forth an explicit distinction between two types of metropolitan sub-center—suburbs and satellites; (2) to summarize presently available information on these two basic types; and (3) to suggest some important and immediate implications for research that seem to follow from these considerations.

SUBURBS VERSUS SATELLITES

The distinction made here cannot be claimed as original. In a book published over forty years ago, Taylor discussed the unique functional position of "satellite cities." Such places were recognized by Taylor as basically subordinate to larger centers, yet retaining a high degree of independence stemming from their importance as production and employment centers.[1] It was Douglass, however, who first made this distinction in clear-cut terms when he discussed two broad types labelled "suburbs of production" and "suburbs of consumption."[2]

From *Social Forces*, Vol. XXXVI, pp. 121–127 (December, 1957). Reprinted by permission of the University of North Carolina Press and the author.
[1] Graham R. Taylor, *Satellite Cities* (New York and London: D. Appleton and Co., 1915).
[2] Harlan Paul Douglass, *The Suburban Trend* (New York and London: The Century Co., 1925), pp. 74–92. See also his article, "Suburbs," in *The Encyclopaedia of the Social Sciences* (New York: The Macmillan Co., 1934), XIV, pp. 433–35. This distinction can also be found in Louis Wirth, "Urbanism As a Way of Life," *American Journal of Sociology*, 44 (July 1938), pp. 1–26, and in C. D. Harris and E. L. Ullman, "The Nature of Cities," *The Annals*, 242 (November 1945), pp. 7–17.

By "suburbs of production," Douglass referred to the type of sub-center discussed by Taylor—the satellite offering employment for at least its own residents, and frequently for other commuting workers as well. By "suburbs of consumption," Douglass referred to the suburb as it is described in its popular connotation, i.e., as a "dormitory town" or "bedroom city." The key functions of such sub-centers are not production or employment, but rather the provision of residential amenities. They serve, in a sense, as reservoirs of the manpower required to staff the productive enterprises in the central city, in satellite employing places, and elsewhere.

In one form or another, this distinction has gained some currency. In a 1943 article on "Suburbs," Chauncy Harris claimed that "the commonest types of suburbs are housing or dormitory suburbs and manufacturing or industrial suburbs."[3] More recently, Reiss has noted that "suburbs often are polarized as 'residential' and 'industrial suburbs,' the residential suburb being considered the modal type."[4] Despite this seeming agreement, a careful and systematic definition has yet to become established among sociologists. As Shryock has indicated, "in the literature, *suburb* is used almost as loosely by the social scientist as by the layman. . . . We badly need some basic concepts here to guide our operational definitions."[5]

The most logically conceived set of definitions appears to be the one recently outlined by Walter T. Martin. To quote Martin at length,

In general, the term "suburb" refers to the relatively small but formally structured community adjacent to and dependent upon a large central city . . . Certain features of suburban communities may be designated as definitive characteristics. These are the characteristics essential to suburban status. In combination they differentiate invariably between suburban and non-suburban communities. The two definitive characteristics treated first are a unique ecological position in relation to a larger city and a high rate of commuting to that city. . . .

Ecological position. By definition suburban areas, however subcategorized, are *primarily residential areas* having a peculiar location; that is, they are farther away from the center of the major city than urban neighborhoods but closer than rural neighborhoods. They lie outside the limits of the central city but remain dependent upon the city as a source of necessary goods and services. The ecological position thus differs from both urban and rural positions. . . .

Commuting. Commuting to work, the second definitive characteristic

[3] C. D. Harris, "Suburbs," *American Journal of Sociology*, 49 (May 1943), p. 6.
[4] Albert J. Reiss, Jr., "Research Problems in Metropolitan Population Redistribution," *American Sociological Review*, 21 (October 1956), p. 575.
[5] Henry S. Shryock, Jr., "Population Redistribution within Metropolitan Areas: Evaluation of Research," *Social Forces*, 35 (December 1956), pp. 155–56.

of suburbs, is a direct outgrowth of the ecological position. Thus communities located adjacent to larger urban centers but *providing jobs for their own residents as well as others* are classified as *satellite cities* rather than suburbs. . . .[6]

Taking Martin's core definitions as a basis, it seems desirable to make explicit some of the outstanding structural and functional differences between the two types.

Structure

In *spatial* terms, both suburbs and satellites are often physically indistinguishable from adjacent areas, hemmed in on all sides by other municipalities. Many of these sub-centers, of course, were originally independent and self-contained cities in their own right; now engulfed by the expanding metropolis, they have somehow resisted annexation and have retained at least political autonomy. Other suburbs and satellites apparently had their origin in the exhaustion of space in the nearby central city, developing as the metropolis spilled over its former boundaries. Yet they are treated as separate legal entities.[7] Whatever their past history, however, *all* suburbs and satellites have one structural feature in common. Although they are treated as separate units for a limited range of purposes, including the reporting of data, *they are themselves merely constituent parts of a larger urban complex*—the metropolitan structure as a whole.

The structure of suburbs and satellites can also be treated in *temporal* terms.[8] Like other parts of the entire metropolitan area, they represent *sources* and *destinations* of the internal circulation of commodities and people that makes up the daily rhythm of community activity. It is at this point, however, that the two types can

---

[6] Walter T. Martin, "The Structuring of Social Relationships Engendered by Suburban Residence," *American Sociological Review*, 21 (August 1956), pp. 447–48; italics added. A highly similar—though less detailed—distinction was previously outlined by Harris and Ullman, as follows: "Satellites differ from suburbs in that they are separated from the central city by many miles and in general have little daily commuting to or from the central city, although economic activities of the satellite are closely geared to those of the central city." Chauncy D. Harris and Edward L. Ullman, "The Nature of Cities," *The Annals*, 242 (November 1945), pp. 7–17.

[7] These diverse historical origins comprise a key dimension in an interesting typology of suburbs developed by Stuart A. Queen and David B. Carpenter. See *The American City* (New York: McGraw-Hill Book Co., 1953), pp. 116–31.

[8] For a complete discussion of the temporal aspect of community structure, see Amos H. Hawley, *Human Ecology* (New York: The Ronald Press, 1950), pp. 288–316.

be distinguished most clearly. We can say that *goods and services* tend to flow out of the *employing satellites* to other areas (both local and non-local), while *persons* are attracted into these areas for employment. On the other hand, *residential suburbs* send out *workers* and tend to receive an influx of *goods and services* for consumption by their inhabitants. These are the major components of the daily ebb and flow of movement that gives the whole metropolitan community its temporal organization.

Functions

The general functions of the two types of sub-center can thus be conceived as polar in nature. Stated in most succinct terms, (1) *residential suburbs are suppliers of labor and consumers of commodities. Conversely, (2) employing satellites are consumers of labor and suppliers of commodities.* This conception is in accord with Douglass' original idea that manufacturing sub-centers represent the decentralization of production, while residential suburbs manifest the decentralization of consumption.

CHARACTERISTICS OF SUBURBS AND SATELLITES

Assuming the validity of this simple dichotomy, the first question that occurs is the sheer number of sub-centers of each type that may be found within metropolitan areas. Here we are able to draw upon two studies using essentially similar methodology. Kneedler presented an "economic base" classification of all of the incorporated places of 10,000 or more inhabitants lying within the Metropolitan Districts defined in the 1940 census.[9] In this study, 160 "dormitory" suburbs were identified, together with 173 satellite sub-centers, with the latter classified accordingly to their major economic functions (manufacturing, retail trade, wholesale trade, mining, education, and government). The same general economic types were recognized in a follow-up study by Jones, who classified 183 suburbs and 180 satellites lying within the Standard Metropolitan Areas identified in the 1950 census.[10]

[9] Grace M. Kneedler, "Functional Types of Cities," *Public Management,* 27 (July 1945), pp. 197–203; reprinted in Paul K. Hatt and Albert J. Reiss, Jr. (eds.), *Reader in Urban Sociology* (Glencoe: The Free Press, 1951), pp. 49–57.
[10] Victor Jones, "Economic Classification of Cities and Metropolitan Areas," in *The Municipal Year Book 1953* (Chicago: The International City Managers' Association, 1953), pp. 49–57.

Despite minor differences in the operational definitions used by Kneedler and Jones, the two studies yield the same general picture. First of all, the relative balance between the two types appears to have been similar at both dates, with satellites slightly outnumbering suburbs at the earlier date. However, it must be remembered that these data refer only to incorporated places of 10,000 and over; other data (to be presented below) suggest that satellites tend to be larger in size than suburbs. Thus if data were available for the full size range of sub-centers, it is probable that residential suburbs would predominate numerically.

Secondly, with respect to the *economic bases* of satellites, both studies reveal that the overwhelming majority (81 percent in 1940 and 77 percent in 1950) are manufacturing sub-centers. The next most frequent major activity is retail trade (12 percent in 1940 and 18 percent in 1950). Mining is the major function of only a few metropolitan satellites, while areas in which wholesale trade, education, and government predominate are even more infrequent.[11]

In general, then, employing satellites are typically industrial sub-centers, so that their characterization as producing places seems most appropriate. Unfortunately, these studies give us no detailed information on the economic activities predominating in residential suburbs. However, it can be generally stated that the bulk of employment that does occur in this type of sub-center lies in the general categories of retail trade and services—particularly in the lines that are relatively inexpensive and frequently needed by a residential population.

The economic characteristics of these sub-centers serve to document the basic distinction under discussion. But what of the other characteristics of the two major types? Are there any other general features that serve to distinguish between them? Fortunately, the use of Jones' classification of 1950 metropolitan sub-centers allowed the present writer to make a summary comparison of the two basic types. At the risk of oversimplification, the results of that study can be summarized very briefly.[12]

In general, *employing satellites* tend to be concentrated in the heavily industrialized areas of the Northeastern and North Central regions. They appear relatively more frequently in the metropolitan areas with smaller central cities, but they tend themselves to be larger than residential suburbs. Satellites also tend to be older than

[11] It is rather interesting to note the specialties in which *no* satellites are represented—transportation, and resort, retirement, and recreational services. These functions are more likely to be found in independent cities, far from metropolitan centers.

[12] Leo F. Schnore, "The Functions of Metropolitan Suburbs," *American Journal of Sociology*, 61 (March 1956), pp. 453–58.

suburbs. Although satellites appear throughout the metropolitan area, they are more frequently found beyond the limits of the densely settled urban core. As distance from the central city increases, in fact, satellites are found with relatively greater frequency. Finally, these employing satellites are typically characterized by low rent levels.

In contrast, *residential suburbs* are distinctly different, although they are found in the metropolitan areas of all the major regions. They tend to appear with increasing relative frequency near larger central cities, but they are themselves smaller than satellites. Residential suburbs predominate among the more recently incorporated sub-centers. Very few of them lie either outside the densely occupied urbanized area or farther than 30 miles from the central city. Finally, rents are higher than average in these residential suburbs.

These data throw further light on the nature of satellites and suburbs, and they also serve to underscore the utility of the distinction. Still further insights can be gained, however, by a closer look at more detailed data on *the characteristics of the populations* occupying these two types of place. At this point we can draw upon a case study of the Chicago Metropolitan District (1940) by Dornbusch.[13] Dornbusch used the basic dichotomy discussed here, further subdividing residential suburbs according to rent level. However, rather than discuss the detailed comparisons between the three resulting types, we will continue to confine our attention to the major differences between satellites and suburbs in general.

Dornbusch's research shows that residents of Chicago satellites tend to have lower average education, and they contain higher proportions of foreign-born whites. In the matter of housing, these employing satellites exhibit lower average rent levels, they have higher proportions of tenant-occupied dwellings, and they have higher proportions of crowded dwellings. The satellites appear to have slightly higher fertility than residential suburbs. In fact, the satellites contain somewhat younger populations. In terms of occupational make-up, roughly two out of three of the employed residents of satellites are found in the "blue-collar" categories, as contrasted with one out of three in the suburban population. At the

[13] Sanford M. Dornbusch, "A Typology of Suburban Communities: Chicago Metropolitan District, 1940," Urban Analysis Report No. 10 (University of Chicago: Chicago Community Inventory, May 1952). Wirth long ago presented the hypothesis that "A one-industry will present *different sets of social characteristics* from a multi-industry city, as will . . . *a suburb from a satellite, a residential suburb from an industrial suburb.* . . ." See Louis Wirth, "Urbanism as a Way of Life," *American Journal of Sociology,* 44 (July 1938), pp. 1–24; italics added.

same time, a somewhat smaller percentage of persons is found to be employed in satellites.

In general, the images that emerge from Dornbusch's results are those of two rather clearly contrasting types: (1) *employing satellites containing younger populations of lower than average socio-economic status*—as measured by educational, ethnic, residential, and occupational variables; and (2) *residential suburbs containing slightly older populations of higher than average socio-economic status*. Suggestive as these data may be, it must be remembered that they refer to the suburbs and satellites of only one Metropolitan District in 1940. However, the conceptual significance of the results—together with the relative simplicity of the methodology employed—would seem to recommend replication for other areas and more recent periods.

SATELLITE AND SUBURBAN GROWTH

Having reviewed the relative numbers of satellites and suburbs, as well as some of their more distinctive characteristics, we may now turn to the matter of their relative rates of growth in recent years.

A study by Harris provides information for the 1930-1940 decade. On the basis of an examination of growth rates in all places of 10,000 and over in 11 Metropolitan Districts, Harris reported that the growth rates of residential suburbs (average 11.7 percent) were well in excess of the rates found in industrial satellites (average 1.7 percent).[14]

A more recent study by the present writer revealed that the same general tendency persisted in the 1940-1950 decade. Suburban growth (average 31.9 percent) was well in excess of that of satellites (average 17.0 percent). This study covered all of the suburbs and satellites of 10,000 and over in all of the Standard Metropolitan Areas of the United States, and the relatively large number of cases (416) permitted the successive control of a number of relevant variables.

On the average, suburbs grew faster than satellites in all regions, in all central city size classes, in all satellite and suburban size classes, in all concentric distance zones, and in metropolitan areas of every major type of economic activity. One minor exception appeared when rent level was controlled, for the prevailing differential was reversed in the high-rent category. The only major reversal

[14] C. D. Harris, *op. cit.*

was found when suburbs were classified according to their dates of incorporation; the differential in favor of residential suburbs was found to characterize only the older places, i.e., those incorporated before 1900. Thus the control of six out of seven relevant factors did not alter the over-all pattern of growth differentials in any significant respect. Suburban growth appears to have continued well in excess of that of satellites in the most recent intercensal decade.

These findings may be viewed as reflections of a fundamental alteration of metropolitan organization in the direction of greater functional and territorial complexity. In many respects, it can be argued that these growth differentials simply mirror the changing distribution of housing opportunities emerging as a result of new patterns of building activity in these areas.

Residential suburbs appear to be growing more rapidly because they are becoming even more residential in character, by means of large increments in housing construction. At the same time, employing satellites appear to be growing less rapidly because they—like the central cities themselves—are becoming more *exclusively* devoted to industry and other employment-producing activities. In these employing satellites, the process of land-use conversion—from residential to industrial, commercial, and transportation uses—is apparently (a) driving out pre-existent residential uses of land and (b) discouraging new construction of housing.[15]

RESEARCH IMPLICATIONS

The first research question that presents itself concerns the *source* of these growth differentials. However, "source" can be taken to mean either of two things. First of all, we can pose the question in broad demographic terms, by asking "what are the relative contributions of (a) natural increase and (b) net migration to these observed differentials?" In addition, we can ask about the areal or geographic sources of the migrants contributing to the growth of suburbs and satellites. The question then becomes "what are the relative sizes of migrant streams from (a) the central city, (b) other suburbs, satellites, and nearby fringe areas, and (c) areas outside the metropolitan community in question?" Both of these detailed questions are in need of answers. Moreover, the basic dis-

[15] See Leo F. Schnore, "The Growth of Metropolitan Suburbs," *American Sociological Review*, 22 (April 1957), pp. 165–73. It might also be noted here that this general process of land-use conversion has yet to run its course. See Dorothy K. Newman, "Metropolitan Area Structure and Growth as Shown by Building-Permit Statistics," *Business Topics*, 4 (November 1956), pp. 1–7.

tinction between suburbs and satellites should be kept in the fore-front of the analysis, for these two types appear to differ with respect to the relative importance of natural increase and net migration, and they may also differ with respect to the geographic sources of persons migrating to them.

Demographic Sources of Growth

The data from Dornbusch's study of Chicago suburbs and satellites might suggest that natural increase contributes more importantly to the growth of satellites than to suburbs. After all, his data indicate that satellites have higher fertility ratios. In addition, satellites tend to have lower proportions of persons over 65 years of age, so that they might be expected to have lower death rates.

However, the apparent trends in population growth and residential construction in metropolitan areas suggest that this hypothesis be given more elaboration. On the basis of a preliminary analysis of the growth of satellites and suburbs between 1940 and 1950, it appears that natural increase may indeed be especially important to the typical satellite because it offsets net losses of migrants. In other words, satellites may be able to exhibit growth only because of recent high rates of natural increase. Suburbs, on the other hand, appear to be growing more rapidly from *both* demographic sources—natural increase and net in-migration. Thus it appears that employing satellites—which are *functionally* similar to the central city, in that they draw workers from other areas—are also highly similar to the metropolis in their sources of growth.[16]

[16] This analysis was confined to the suburbs and satellites of 10,000 and over in the five largest Standard Metropolitan Areas (New York, Chicago, Los Angeles, Philadelphia, and Detroit), and utilized the general method described in detail in Donald J. Bogue and Emerson Seim, "Components of Population Change in Suburban and Central City Populations of Standard Metropolitan Areas: 1940 to 1950," *Rural Sociology*, 21 (September-December 1956), pp. 267–75. In this study, Bogue and Seim present compelling evidence to the effect that recent central city growth was largely a function of natural increase, high enough to offset migration losses. This reverses the long-term situation, in which net in-migration offset extremely low rates of natural increase or even natural decrease. Ideally, of course, suburbs and satellites should be compared with *parts* of the central city, rather than with the central city as a whole. (See Reiss, *op. cit.*) It should also be noted that *individual* suburbs and satellites exhibit considerable variation within each of these types. Much of this variation may be due to variations in size, age, location, and other characteristics that were not controlled here. One major difficulty that has yet to be surmounted in studies of suburban growth stems from a lack of appropriate data; there are no reliable statistics on the amount of vacant land available for residential development in sub-centers throughout the nation.

Geographic Sources of Growth

Unfortunately, available census data do not permit investigation of the detailed geographic sources of recent migrants to satellites and suburbs. The 1950 census data on migrants are coded in categories (based on county units) that are inappropriate to the type of study needed here. For the moment, we will have to be content with inferences drawn from scattered case studies and older census data.

Case studies of outlying areas indicate that the popular notion of "decentralization" as simply a "flight from the city" is a gross oversimplification.[17] In addition, studies by Thompson and Hawley, based upon 1935-1940 migration data, show that a substantial component of metropolitan ring growth comes from other areas.[18] Much of this growth—which may be labelled "accretion at the periphery" in contrast to outward relocation from the city—must have taken place in satellites and suburbs, as well as in the "fringe" and open country.

It seems feasible to use the same survey technique in studies focussed *specifically* upon the geographic sources of migrants to suburbs and satellites. In view of the lack of appropriate census data on this question, such case studies will probably remain the major source of our information for some time.

The Question of Classification

We need more data on daily commuting (recurrent movements) as well as migration (nonrecurrent movements). In fact, a major research question concerns the very basis of the distinction between these two functional types of area. Up to this time, we have had to depend upon manipulation of census data in order to classify subcenters in these terms. The work of Harris, Kneedler, and Jones has been particularly ingenious, but deficiencies in the basic data reduce the potential value of their contributions.

In *theory*, the types developed by these writers depend essen-

---

[17] See Myles W. Rodehaver, "Fringe Settlement as a Two-Directional Movement," *Rural Sociology*, 12 (March 1947), pp. 49–57; Walter T. Martin, *The Rural-Urban Fringe* (Eugene: University of Oregon Press, 1953), pp. 60–63; Wendell Bell, "Familism and Suburbanization," *Rural Sociology*, 21 (September-December 1956), pp. 276–83.
[18] Warren S. Thompson, *Migration Within Ohio, 1935-40* (Oxford, Ohio: Scripps Foundation for Research in Population Problems, 1951); Amos H. Hawley, *Intrastate Migration in Michigan, 1935–40* (Ann Arbor: Institute of Public Administration, University of Michigan, 1953).

tially upon a comparison of (a) the number of employed people *living* in a given area with (b) the number of people *working* in that area. This is basically a question of "day-time" versus "night-time" population, for suburbs and satellites are dispensing and attracting areas in the daily ebb and flow of movement. Subordinate centers that attract more workers every day than the number of employed people who sleep there every night are labelled satellites, while those having substantially more residents than jobs are classified as suburbs.

In *practice,* however, many difficulties are encountered in the use of census data in classifying particular areas in these terms. For one thing, the requisite data on employment (the number of jobs in a given area) are not generally available for smaller places—those under 10,000 inhabitants. Moreover, the data for larger places are inadequate in many respects. The employment data have been derived from the Censuses of Business and Manufacturing, while the numbers of employed residents have been drawn from the Population Census. The discrepancy in the very dates of these censuses (e.g., 1947, 1948, and 1950), means that inaccuracies enter the final results. Annexations comprise a major source of difficulties. In addition, any substantial change in employment opportunities or in available housing between these dates can seriously distort the basic "employment-residence ratio." The statistics for the numerator and the denominator of this ratio refer to different time periods, and changes in either element can artificially raise or lower the true value of the ratio. Still another weakness is the fact that all job categories have not been included in the computation of the ratio.

Many of these difficulties may be surmounted in the forthcoming population census. It seems almost a certainty that the 1960 census will contain a question on the individual's place of work. It remains to be seen, however, whether the Census Bureau will be able to present tabulations in sufficient detail to permit the accurate classification of individual suburbs and satellites in these terms. Considerations of cost will undoubtedly prohibit full detail for smaller places, and other priorities will inevitably compete for the funds available. In view of these considerations—and mindful of the additional fact that published census data are at least five years away—we might do better to consider alternative sources of data.

Because the fundamental distinction between satellites and suburbs is essentially a question of commuting flows, our attention is immediately drawn to traffic data as a possible source of information. "Origin-and-destination" data available from sample studies permit the identification of satellites and suburbs in a number of metropolitan areas. Punchcards for individual workers contain information on place of employment and place of residence, together with other characteristics. All work-trips to a given satellite or suburb can simply be tabulated by the place of residence of the workers. The simple balance between residents and job opportunities yields an identification of the two main types of sub-center discussed here. In addition, detailed information can be gained on main streams of commuters, and the direction of these streams throughout the entire area—centripetal, centrifugal, and lateral. Furthermore, the characteristics of the workers in these various commuting streams can be compared.

In summary, these detailed commuting data can be used to identify individual suburbs and satellites according to their basic type in many metropolitan areas. Comparison of such results with those derived from analysis of census data should be particularly interesting. In addition, these commuting data will yield information that is not presently available from census sources.

CONCLUSION

As Woodbury has observed, "dormitory towns are only one species of suburb."[19] This paper calls attention to the available evidence supporting a fundamental distinction between satellites (employing sub-centers) and suburbs (residential sub-centers). However, it may well be that these two types are too broadly defined for many research purposes. Dornbusch's study indicates that rent level is another variable of real significance, while Martin suggests population size and density as additional criteria. The demographic source of growth may even be an important distinguishing characteristic. On the face of it, it seems that a place growing or maintaining its size by natural increase might be significantly different from one expanding mainly via net migration.

Whetten has argued that "there is need for further identification and classification of suburban populations into meaningful groupings or community types."[20] The present writer can only agree—and hope that this paper will help to fill this gap in our knowledge of metropolitan areas. But there are other gaps to be closed. A single example will suffice. One closely related concept that has been ignored in this presentation is that of the "fringe."

[19] Coleman Woodbury, "Suburbanization and Suburbia," *American Journal of Public Health*, 45 (January 1955), p. 2.
[20] Nathan L. Whetten, "Suburbanization as a Field for Sociological Research," *Rural Sociology*, 16 (December 1951), p. 325.

Although it is used with increasing frequency, there is still little agreement on the fundamental meaning that should be assigned to the term. However, if we are careful to build upon the theoretical and research foundations already established, it should not be too long before we have a much more complete understanding of the structure and functions of the metropolitan area and *all* of its constituent parts.

The New Suburbia

WILLIAM H. WHYTE, JR.

To find where the mobility of organization life is leading, the new package suburbs may be the best place of all to look. For they are not merely great conglomerations of mass housing. They are a new social institution, and while the variations in them are many, wherever one goes—the courts of Park Forest, the patios of Park Merced in San Francisco, Philadelphia's Drexelbrook, the new Levittown, Pennsylvania—there is an unmistakable similarity in the way of life.

It is a communal way of life, and the residents are well aware of it. They are of many minds how to describe it. Sometimes they lean to analogies like the frontier, or the early colonial settlements. Other times they are a little more wry: "sorority house with kids," a projection of dormitory life into adulthood, or, slightly better, a lay version of Army post life. But no matter how sharp the coinages—"a womb with a view," "a Russia, only with money"—it is a way of life they find suited to their wants, their needs, and their times. They are not unwitting pawns; educated to be more aware of social trends than their forebears, they discuss their situations with considerable sophistication; at times, the way they casually toss out words like "permissive" and "kid-centered," it almost seems as if everyone was his own resident sociologist.

In part, these communities are a product of the great expansion of the middle class, for the new suburbs have become a mecca for thousands of young people moving up and out of city wards. It

From William H. Whyte, Jr., *The Organization Man*, New York: Simon and Schuster, Inc., Copyright © 1956, by William H. Whyte, Jr.; pp. 280–281; 298–300; and 302–306. Reprinted by permission of Simon and Schuster, Inc., and Jonathan Cape, Ltd., London.

is not these people, however, who are dominant. In his wanderings, the organization man has found in the new suburbs an ideal way station. He is the one who is most quick to move out, but as soon as he does another replaces him, and then another. It is he who sets the tone, and if he is as uncertain as any in keeping up with the Joneses, it is because he *is* the Joneses.

Park Forest, the community I studied most intensively, has its unique features, but its most salient characteristic is that it is virtually a controlled sample of organization people. As elsewhere, there are other kinds of people too, and for many a newcomer from the city such communities are an education in middle-class values. What might be called the modal man, however, is a twenty-five-to-thirty-five-year-old white-collar organization man with a wife, a salary between $6,000 and $7,000, one child, and another on the way.

If one wishes to study the next generation of organization men, a pretty good form chart is the record of how the younger ones handle their problems when they are away from their elders. Because they are jammed into such propinquity with one another in their new suburbia, everything they do carries a certain degree of exaggeration: the schools are a little more modern than elsewhere, the politics a little more intense, and most certainly the social life is a lot more social. Abnormal? Or the portent of a new normality? The values of Park Forest, one gets the feeling, are harbingers of the way it's going to be.[1]

■ ■ ■

As far as social values are concerned, suburbia is the ultimate expression of the interchangeability so sought by organization. It is classless, or, at least, its people want it to be. As in The Organization, so in its dormitories there has been a great broadening of the middle, and a sort of "declassification" of people from the older criteria of family background. But there is also another parallel. As in The Organization, the more that distinctions are broken down, the more exquisite they become. The suburbanites' impulse to the Social Ethic is understandable; to live without social class you must be socially skillful—consciously and continuously.

Like the office with no division between carpet and linoleum, suburbia demands perception. How in the world, you wonder when you see Park Forest, can anyone tell rank—or, for that matter, pull it? To the stranger's eye the usual criteria of status are almost

[1] These chapters are based on research I did for a *Fortune* study in 1953, and on subsequent research in 1955 and 1956. . . .

entirely absent. There are a few exceptions; in the rental area there are some duplex units situated on roads rather than grouped court fashion, and these, renting for $117 (versus $92 to $104 for most court units) make something of a local Gold Coast. Similarly, though most homes are in the $13,000 bracket, there are a few areas with houses around $10,000, several in the $17,000 to $20,000 class, and a small area with "custom" houses ranging anywhere from $17,000 to developer Klutznick's $50,000 home. These differences, as I will touch on later, are not without significance. For the great bulk of residents, however, the houses are uniform enough in cost as to make them comparatively unimportant as a prestige factor, and physically they are so uniform that if it weren't for paint and trim, newcomers would have trouble finding their unit in the labyrinth.

Cars aren't much help, either. Of the thousands that lie in the parking bays, few are more expensive than the Buick Special, and rakish touches are not too frequent. Only in near-by industrial towns do people show exuberance in the captainship of the American car; foxtails and triumphant pennants, like Cyrano's plume, fly defiantly on cars there, and occasionally from the radiator a devil thumbs his nose at the passing mob. Not at Park Forest; whatever else it has, it has no panache.

Suburban residents like to maintain that their suburbia not only looks classless but is classless. That is, they are apt to add on second thought, there are no extremes, and if the place isn't exactly without class, it is at least a one-class society—identified as the middle or upper middle, according to the inclination of the residents. "We are all," they say, "in the same boat."

They are not. People may come out of the new suburbs middle class; a great many who enter, however, are not. Middle-class, college-educated organization people give the communities their dominant tone, but there are other residents for whom arrival in the Park Forests and Levittowns is, psychologically at least, a crossing of the tracks. This expansion of the lower limits of the middle class is happening in towns and cities as well, but it is so pronounced in the new suburbs that it almost seems as if they were made for that function.

They have become the second great melting pot. The organization man furnishes the model, and even in suburbs where he is a minority he is influential out of all proportion to his numbers. As the newcomers to the middle class enter surburbia, they must discard old values, and their sensitivity to those of the organization man is almost statistically demonstrable. Figures rather clearly show that people from big, urban Democratic wards tend to become

Republican and, if anything, more conservative than those whose outlook they are unconsciously adopting. Pondering the 1952 Park Forest vote, the *Chicago Tribune,* with vengeful pleasure, attributed the large Republican majority to the beneficial influence of fresh country air on erstwhile Democrats. Whatever the cause, it is true that something does seem to happen to Democrats when they get to suburbia. Despite the constant influx of Democrats, the size of the Republican vote remains fairly constant from suburb to suburb. (The vote for Eisenhower in 1952: 66 percent in Levittown, Long Island, 69.4 percent in Park Forest.)

■ ■ ■

For newcomers, the teaching of sociability is perhaps the greatest achievement of suburban education. The newcomers need it. They are more lonely than the others, for they are strangers to this world, yet they markedly lack the social skills by which to overcome their loneliness. This is particularly apparent in a new block that does not have the leavening influence of one or two organization couples. Often it is months before the people even strike up a conversation with the neighbors about them. They don't know how, and they want so desperately to know that they will respond to any activity, no matter what the ostensible purpose, that furnishes a catalyst. This is one of the reasons for the popularity of the "home commercial parties" in such neighborhoods. In one small subdivision outside Hartford, Connecticut, it was not until ten months after everyone had moved in that they got to know one another, and a Stanley Home Party was the cause; the first party broke the ice, and in a surge of gratitude all of the wives pleaded to be hostesses in turn. It was the best way they knew of to get friendship started.

To understand how suburbia fills this kind of void, an understanding of the nature of turnover within them is necessary. It is not a subject suburbanites like to talk about. When I first went to Park Forest, I found the residents rather touchy about the fact that the turnover in the rental apartments was running at roughly 35 percent annually, and in the homes area at about 20 percent. Only temporary, many assured me. One man even went to far as to work up an ingenious mathematical formula to demonstrate the imminent decline of turnover. Of every 100 persons moving in, he argued, a given number will stay permanently; the more these people move in, accordingly, the fewer apartments and houses there will be on the market for the transient type—*ergo,* in time there should be practically no turnover at all.

Meanwhile, the turnover continues. In the rental courts a third of the tenants still move out every year. In 1954, out of 3,000 rental apartments there were 1,059 move-outs; in 1955, 1,100. As Park Foresters are quick to point out, some of these move-outs didn't leave the community but moved to the homes area, and this movement has lent a measure of stability to the community. Nonetheless, over-all turnover remains high. A comparison of the 1954 phone directory with the 1955 directory indicates that in one year's time 18 percent of Park Foresters had moved on to other communities (948 families out of a total listing of 5,363). A closer check on one court shows that since 1953 all of the original thirty-nine couples had left save eight; of the couples who left, a third had moved to other parts of Park Forest, while the rest moved away.

It is a perfectly normal phenomenon. Some of the people who leave Park Forest do so because they want something "better," but most leave because they *have* to. In 1953, 44 percent of the move-outs were corporation couples being transferred away from the Chicago area; 12½ percent were Army and Navy couples assigned to new stations. Since then there has been little shift in this pattern and little shift in the kind of people who are moving in to fill up the vacancies. Periodic checks on the occupational breakdown of the rental people show that from year to year the proportion of engineers, junior executives, and such remains roughly the same.[2]

This constant replenishing assures that, as the community ages, there will always be a cadre of young, middle-class organization people on the way up. People who stay are not necessarily less successful; Park Forest has a strong adhesive power for those who have become involved in its activities, and many people who ordinarily would have moved away to the North Shore or its equivalent have stayed on. But the transients are still the key. Whether they actually move or not, it is the people successful enough to have the option who set the dominant style of life in suburbia.

While it cannot be called a "class" division, there is an important difference in attitude between these transients and the others, and to explore it is to recognize the great amount of insecurity many of the latter have over their middle-class status. A resident's attitude toward the community is an index. The usual organization man tends to affect an attitude of fond detachment—swell place, lots of kicks, but, after all, the sort of place you graduate from. For

[2] As of April 1954, a check made by Thomas McDade of ACB of 700 rental families showed the following breakdown: business administration, 28.2 per cent; professional, 25.2 per cent; sales, 22.1 per cent. Of the remaining 24.5 per cent: supervisors, production workers, and independents, 6.3 per cent; publicity, 4.2 per cent; retail workers, 5.7 per cent; transportation workers, 6.1 per cent; miscellaneous, 2.2 per cent.

others, however, such an attitude is impossible. It is most impossible of all for the man who has expected to go ahead in the organization world but finds that he will not. He dislikes thinking about turnover, not so much that he sees it as a slur on the community, but as a slur on himself. For him, the ever-present moving van is a standing rebuke—a reminder of an organization world to which he does not truly belong.

Then there are the people for whom suburbia is a social achievement. They are not envious, like the unsuccessful organization man, of those who leave; much as enlisted men feel toward a comrade who has won a bid to officer's training, they can speak quite equably, sometimes proudly, of ex-neighbors who have gone on to better things. But it is the permanence of the community, not its impermanence, that they wish to see. They cannot joke about it with detachment, and they can be extraordinarily sensitive about references that no one else would think invidious. When I first started interviewing, one of the women's magazines had just come out with a picture story on life in the homes area. It was a pleasant story, full of praise, but the housewives were very annoyed. "Those pictures they published are absolutely disgraceful," one exclaimed to me. "Why did they have to take so many of back yards? The way they angled them makes it look like a development!"

Let us pause briefly to retrace their steps back through suburbia. It is important to remember that the move is not a sudden one from the lower to the middle class but rather the most critical of several moves. To a degree the people affected have been moving simultaneously with others—which is to say, the mobility hasn't been a case of the individual outracing the people he was brought up with, but a concurrent movement. Yet it is not so uniform a movement that some have not gone past others, and the awareness of this competition has produced some very powerful tensions.

This was brought home to me when I made a study of several new Philadelphia row-house neighborhoods of the kind that are the stepping stones to suburbia. There were many similarities to suburbia—the median income was only slightly beneath the Park Forest and the Levittowns; the population was predominantly a young one, and they give it the look of the new market wherever you see it: the great forest of television aerials, the hard-top convertibles, the housewives in blue jeans and plaid slacks *Kaffee-klatsching* on the lawns, the hundreds of husbands stopping off at the giant supermarket to pick up the extra groceries on the way back home from work.

But there were differences, and if I had to single out the one that impressed me most, it would be, simply, the amount of plain, ordinary disagreeableness. Compared to the suburban communities, the tensions seemed much closer to the surface, the jealousies more intense. Nobody seemed to have settled down to take a long breath; the notion of survival of the fittest was omni-present, and few blocks seemed to have the graces, the rules of the game that suburbia has acquired to muffle the conflict. These neighborhoods happen to be in Philadelphia, and there are factors peculiar to them. Yet I was persuaded by the talks I had there that this somewhat intangible atmosphere was a reality which all sensed and which had its roots in causes fairly universal.

As a check of former addresses indicated, these people are members of the great outward movement from the inner city wards—as they have been moving geographically toward the suburbs, they have been moving socially as well. But it is a *transition*, and there is the rub, for though they have left one world—the close-knit society of the *padrone*, for example—they have not quite joined another, and the influx of Negroes into the houses they left behind is a specter they do not for a moment forget. Except for the older people, for whom such neighborhoods can be ideal, suburbia is the dream, and the neighbor who puts the "For Sale" sign up as he prepares to move to suburbia does so with a feeling that he has made it.

It is not stretching the sense of the word too much to say that he has not *made it* so much, but that he is *passing*. Still fundamentally urban and lower middle class in his reflexes, he has a long acculturation ahead of him, and if he is not entirely sure how it is going to end up, neither can we be. His social enfranchisement is a great tribute to the vigor of our democracy, but we would do well to recognize the pitfalls of this dynamic.

Images of Suburbia

WILLIAM M. DOBRINER
Hofstra University

COMMENTATORS AND SCIENTISTS

It was perhaps inevitable that social scientists, politicians, journalists, and writers casting about for something refreshing to talk about would discover and set about interpreting the spectacular growth of suburbs in the years after World War II. An ever-swelling flood of suburban literature pours forth from two fountainheads of inspiration: those students of suburbs whom we may think of as *commentators* and those who are the *scientists.*

The commentators are an exuberant band of social impressionists who greatly outnumber the scientists. In the best tradition of scientism, they strive to paint the scope, the significance, the big picture of suburbia. In the broil, veracity and intellectual vigor sometimes suffer. Given as they are to the direct statement generated out of "holistic" thought, it is not surprising that the commentators incline to the view that the scientists may be confounded by illusory tempests in their empirical teapots. Since the late 1940's, an inspired series of suburban "studies" have given form and substance to a set of recurrent themes, images, stereotypes, and superstitions about "suburbia." Certainly Whyte's *The Organization Man* did much to establish the psychological and literary matrix from which these prevailing images were cast, but the currently active savants, numerous beyond counting, have ranged unbridled far beyond the relatively controlled and legitimate perspective of

Excerpts from Chapter 1, "Images of Suburbia," pp. 5–15, in William M. Dobriner, *Class in Suburbia* © 1963. Reprinted by permission of Prentice-Hall, Inc., Englewood Cliffs, New Jersey.

this pioneering work. The commentators simply do not like suburbs. Whyte indicts the "social ethic" which is brilliantly etched in the contemporary suburbs as "redundant . . . premature . . . delusory . . . static, and self-destructive." This is hardly in the staid, value-free tradition of the *American Sociological Review*.

The images of suburbia penned by the commentators can be reduced to these themes: suburbs are

1. warrens of young executives on the way up;
2. uniformly middle class;
3. "homogeneous";
4. hotbeds of participation;
5. child-centered and female-dominated;
6. transient;
7. wellsprings of the outgoing life;
8. arenas of adjustment;
9. Beulah Lands of returns to religion;
10. political Jordans from which Democrats emerge Republicans.

To the commentators, suburbia is not only classless (i.e., all middle class), it has been homogenized: social and personal differences are submerged beneath a great, wet blanket of conformity. The chief delineating feature of suburbia is compulsive, frenetic, outgoing social life—togetherness, belongingness, *Kaffeeklatsches*, PTA, back fence gossip confabulations, cocktail parties, car pools, and the "open door." Suburbia is the melancholia of those whose individuality has succumbed to the inexorable pressures of The Organization, bureaucracy, mass culture, uniformity, conformity, monotony—the symptoms of a false egalitarianism, mistaken as social democracy. They suggest, on the psychological level, a suburban population of "other-directed" men, passive and acquiescent, firmly convinced of the natural benevolence of society and nature, and whose chief anxiety is the fear of being different. They are the nomads of the modern world, who, like a swarm of corporate gypsies, passively follow the *ex cathedra* directives of a paternalistic Organization, moving whenever and to wherever it decides, from one section of the country to another—but always to another suburb. And all suburbs are pretty much the same, in the commentators' view. Suburbia is young, a couple with one child here and another on the way. Older people are unknown; Grandma is only a voice on the telephone. The essence of suburbia is monumentalized in its architecture "My God!—all the houses are identical!" Ideologically quiescent, escapist, frenetic on the social level, suburbs lack both the liberalism and vitality of the city and the unsophisticated simplicity and strength of the rural village. These are the qualities and characteristics imputed by the commentators to the suburbs. How much is myth, how much reality? The *scientists'* images of the suburban community are formed by inductive interpretations of reliable empirical materials. The Census is their bible; through statistical comparisons of census data they erect socioeconomic profiles of metropolitan areas and suburban and fringe zones. The *scientists* are relatively guarded in their approach to the suburbs. They strive to stay within the confines of their data and the rigorous discipline of scientific method. Bound ineluctably to objectivity, the images they build of suburbia are less colorful, perhaps, than those drawn by the commentators, but certainly more intellectually circumspect. However, in building their images of the contemporary suburbs, the scientists do go beyond conventional demography and ecology. They, too, like the commentators, are concerned with the factors behind metropolitan and suburban growth, in terms of social psychology as well as economic factors, and in the generic characteristics of the suburbs as a community type, and way of life.

■ ■ ■

In summary, both the scientists and the commentators agree in certain broad ways, on the basic features of the suburbs. Both proceed primarily from an ecological position which defines the suburb as physically removed from, but economically dependent on, the central city. The commuter, the definitive feature of the suburban work force, dramatically illustrates the characteristic of economic dependence. In addition, both schools of suburbia seem to agree on the middle-class nature of the suburbs and an unusually high degree of suburban homogeneity. To these suburban features, real or spurious, I should like to add another: *visibility.*

■ ■ ■

HOMOGENEITY

Communities or groups characterized by similar basic status positions, social roles, groups, norms, values, beliefs, ideologies, and the like are said to be "socially homogeneous." The best example of the principle of homogeneity are the simple folk villages of nonliterate cultures.

The concept of homogeneity is meaningless unless it is compared with something. Communities are more or less homogeneous, compared to other communities. The units of comparison employed to designate suburban communities as homogeneous have never been made clear. We must presume that the points of comparison are a "typical" residential suburb and a "typical" central city, then the city would emerge as significantly more heterogeneous. Cities, in terms of demographic, ecological, class, and institutional structures, are more complex and heterogeneous than suburbs. The classic portrait of the suburbs as significantly "homogenized" areas, however, grossly oversimplifies the character of the suburbs and obscures the vital and *significant differences between them*. Perhaps it would be best now to stop generalizing and look at suburbs with more attention to detail.

We have known that there are established differences between suburban units. Industrial or employing areas (satellite cities) and residential suburbs vary enormously. For example, there are the new, mass-produced suburbs of ten or fifteen thousand units on a single tract. Increasingly, suburban developments appeal to the skilled and semiskilled blue collar workers. Indeed, there are suburbs for the $8000 house buyer as well as suburbs for the $65,000 house buyer.

A hundred families move into a newly completed section of some new suburbs—like modern boom-towns—on a single day. Old, established rural villages, just on the border of the rural-urban fringe, are overrun by hordes of suburbanites. Such villages are in a process of transition from rural to suburban form. The differences between a suburb created out of the cornfields by a big business builder using modern technology and the "reluctant suburb," shaped by the forces of urban assault, are legion. The mass-produced suburb has no institutional vitals at all; these must be created by the transplanted population. The assaulted village, with its rural institutions and way of life, goes through the agony of transition from rural to urban within the span of comparatively few years. There is such a diversity of suburb forms it is misleading to label all suburbs "homogeneous." Suburbs differ greatly in the circumstances of their creation, in the price and use of their real estate, their degree of transiency, their size and institutional complexity, and the income, life style, occupation, and educational level of their residents. Perhaps the issue of suburban homogeneity has been compounded by a semantic blunder: are we talking about *suburbs* as the residential habitat of one out of every four Americans or are we talking about a single hypothetical suburb? If it is the suburbs that fall generically within the label "homogeneous" then we must take issue—the term simply forces us to make thin and rather useless statements about suburbs in general. In our legitimate quest to find patterns and regularities we bury under the general label "Homogeneity" any awareness of those real differences between suburbs that increase our knowledge of them. If, on the other hand, we isolate a given suburb, which is an empirical reality, and find that it has a median income of $15,000 a year, that it is 76 percent Protestant, that three quarters of the adult population is college educated and 72 per cent vote Republican, then we might feel safe in using the concept of homogeneity as a useful descriptive term. We might conclude, therefore, that the notion of homogeneity has usefulness as a description of some suburbs (indeed, of rural towns and some cities too) but not of suburbs in general. Unfortunately, many of the quasi-empirical studies of suburbs which gave rise to the homogeneity myth focused on upper-middle class areas around large central cities. In fact, many suburbs are not essentially middle-class and accordingly do not exhibit those middle-class patterns too often mistaken as suburban patterns. Indeed, Berger's study of a working-class suburb in California failed to sustain the findings of the Park Forest and Drexelbrook studies of William Whyte, the Crestwood Heights researches of Seeley and his associates, and those of the Gordons in *The Split-Level Trap.* Berger found that his working-class suburbanites still voted Democratic, they did not become Republicans as the Myth has it.[1] They did not rediscover religion—more than half of the respondents said they went to church rarely or not at all. They had no great mobility aspirations; the great majority did not regard their suburban homes as a transient watering place, but rather as "paradise permanently gained." Furthermore, recent studies by Lazerwitz[2] point out that the suburbs are losing whatever middle-class monopoly they might once have enjoyed, that streams of semi-skilled and skilled workers are steadily moving to the suburbs.

As Berger points out, the reports that have flowed from those interested in the growth and character of the suburbs are more often than not selective in terms of the socioeconomic level of the community, biased in favor of the middle- and upper-middle

[1] It is interesting to note that the myth of political conversion from Democratic affiliation to Republican, which Berger found little evidence of in his California study, has been reduced even further by another empirical study. A research conducted by David Wallace of the Bureau of Applied Social Research at Columbia (reported in the February 12, 1962, issue of *The New York Times*, p. 25) in the metropolitan New York suburb of Westport found little support for the theory of suburban political conversion. "If anything," the study maintained, "Democrats have retained more of their parental voting habits than have Republicans—and they retained it both in the place of their prior residence and in Republican Westport itself."
[2] Bernard Lazerwitz, "Metropolitan Residential Belts," *American Sociological Review*, XXV (April, 1960), pp. 245–252.

classes. Neither Levittown, Lakewood, Drexelbrook, Park Forest, Crestwood Heights, nor any of the others can be taken as models of the incredibly diverse suburban forms that currently exist. Homogeneity may also be a temporary condition of a suburb that time will eventually erase. The majority of the suburbs in which homogeneity was a characteristic were also new suburbs—not more than a few years old. In its early years, Levittown, Long Island, might have been comparatively homogeneous in some respects. It was born in the post-World War II housing shortage. The builder, William Levitt, financed much of the construction through government funds and for many years restricted purchases to veterans. Houses were bought on the "G.I. mortgage." The early Levittowners represented the many religious and ethnic groups of the New York area, but they had in common (as homogenizing features) their comparative youth, military background and veteran status, young families, modest incomes. By 1962, however, Levittown's population was significantly less "G.I."; the young families of 1948 were 14 years older, and the community was losing its upward mobile population to costlier, higher status suburbs elsewhere on Long Island. Over the years, the homogeneous aspects of Levittown have been blunted by tides of shifting, dissimilar populations.

Indicative of the current heterogeneity of Levittown's population, I counted the following on a single street: a Catholic second-generation Italian housepainter; a Protestant "old American" college professor; a Jewish second-generation automobile mechanic; a Catholic second-generation Italian plumber; a Protestant "old American" salesman; a Catholic third-generation German blue-collar worker; a Protestant "old American" skilled worker; a Jewish third-generation factory foreman; a Jewish second-generation clerk; a Catholic "old American" research physicist; a Catholic third-generation Irish semiskilled factory worker; a Protestant "old American" Wall Street "customer's man," and a retired elderly couple who had just moved in. The life styles, ideologies, folkways, values, aspirations, and child-rearing practices of these families defy generalization to "homogeneity." If any kind of meaningful pattern lies beneath the idiosyncratic surface of that neighborhood, analysis in terms of class rather than "suburban" variables seems to be the most profitable.

The point critical to our discussion is that the homogeneous image of the suburbs has been formulated on empirical materials, but based not only on selected upper-middle class suburbs, but also on suburbs that were selectively studied in time. The Drexelbrooks, Levittowns, and Park Forests were all brand new when they were first depicted as the home of the New Common Man. The image of the young organization family upward bound in the class structure and deeply involved in the institutionalized informality of the court and neighborhood has unfortunately persisted as the model for all suburbs. Where are the "young" couples of Drexelbrook today? Have they been replaced by younger cadres of new suburbanites who duplicate the social forms of ten years ago? Or have the intrinsic patterns of social relationships within the community also changed over time? The data and conclusions of ten years ago do not answer these questions.

Of all the factors which determine where a suburbanite lives, the economic probably plays the most decisive role. The first thing he must decide is his price range. Can he support a $17-, $25-, $35-, or $50-thousand house? His price decided, he looks for a "development," a neighborhood, or a village that falls within his price class. At this point he may look into the religious or ethnic character of the community. If homogeneity exists, income again probably plays the decisive role. In effect, occupational and income homogeneity becomes a function of another variable—the status and class structure. The crucial role of income in determining the class character of a suburb is, of course, not peculiar to suburbs. Cities have their "Park Avenues," "Little Italys," "Skid Rows," all reflecting homogeneity in the form of economic, ethnic, and honorific segments within the total city framework. The forces which make for economic homogeneity in city neighborhoods operate with equal facility in the suburbs.

The Suburban Dislocation

DAVID RIESMAN
Harvard University

The suburbs have become so characteristic of life "among democratic nations" that some of our most acute social observers in the
post-World War II years have seen in them the shape of the egali-
tarian future. William H. Whyte, Jr., in his *Fortune* series on "The
Transients" has emphasized the poignancy of the relaxed yet inescapable bonds in the new suburbs, notably Park Forest.[1] Others,
too, have been struck by a kind of massification of men in Levittown and other housing developments such as was once postulated
for the endless residential blocks of the cities created by the industrial revolution.[2] Even in a Canadian suburb, where one might
expect slightly more hierarchical traces, a team of social scientists
has found "the track of generations" barely visible.[3] In the light of
these commentaries, the emphasis on status in *Middletown, Yankee
City, Elmtown,* or the New York suburb which marks for Charlie
Gray in Marquand's novel the point of no return—this emphasis on

Excerpts from "The Suburban Dislocation," *Annals of the American Academy
of Political and Social Science*, Volume 314, pp. 123–125 and 129–143 (November, 1957). Reprinted by permission of the American Academy of Political
and Social Science and the author.
[1] *Fortune* (May, June, July, August 1953); also *The Organization Man* (New
York: Simon & Schuster, 1956), Part VII. See, also, an unpublished master's
thesis on Park Forest by Herbert Gans done in the Department of Sociology,
University of Chicago.
[2] Compare Frederick Lewis Allen, "The Big Change in Suburbia," *Harper's
Magazine* (June 1954), pp. 21–28, and (July 1954), pp. 47–53; and H. Hender-
son, "The Mass-Produced Suburbs," *Ibid.* (November 1953), pp. 25–32, and
(December 1953), pp. 80–86.
[3] See John R. Seeley, R. Alexander Sim, and E. W. Loosley, *Crestwood Heights:
The Culture of Suburban Life* (New York: Basic Books, 1956); and the perceptive discussion by William Newman, "America in Subtopia," *Dissent*, Vol. 4
(1957), pp. 255–66.

graded ranks seems almost archaic. In contrast, the new suburban-ite appears to suffer, less from exclusion, than from a surfeit of inclusions.[4]

Yet this is impression, based on a few soundings in a few per-haps strategic and surely highly visible locations. We know very little about the relatively settled suburbs, especially those leap-frogged by the waves of post World War II growth; and so far as I can see we know almost nothing about the suburbs (old or new) surrounding the smaller cities. The new developments which have altered the physical and moral landscape so strikingly may betoken a trend or a blind alley. They may fascinate us out of our contem-porary fears for the loss of liberty and individuality; and intellec-tuals, seldom unambivalent about the suburbs—whether or not they make them their own domiciles—may generalize from them too readily to middle-class life and leisure as a whole.

SOCIOLOGICAL STUDIES

Such considerations led me to a review of what sociologists have recently written, at their most empirical, about cities, suburbs, and the urban-rural fringe. Much of this work is based on census data or on such repeated explorations as the University of Michigan's Detroit Area Survey or the Metropolitan St. Louis Survey. Such studies tend to put a brake on extrapolative generalization. They indicate, for example, the presence of urban elements in rural areas, and vice versa.[5] The city is not necessarily the seat of urban-ism, and the suburban way differs from the city way only at the polarities of each and is based on variables not entirely dependent on ecology or visible from a helicopter.[6] Hence these investigations do support the common-sense observation that can find suburban styles in many cities and urban ones in many suburbs; that an

[4] As in the witty but unrevealing novel of exurbia, Max Shulman's *Rally Round the Flag, Boys!* (New York: Doubleday & Company, 1957); see, also, the slight topographical variations in exurbanite status dissected by A. C. Spectorsky, *The Exurbanites* (New York and Philadelphia: J. B. Lippincott Co., 1955).

[5] See Albert Reiss, Jr., "An Analysis of Urban Phenomena," in Robert M. Fisher, ed., *The Metropolis in Modern Life* (New York: Doubleday & Com-pany, 1955), pp. 41–49; Morris Janowitz, *The Community Press in an Urban Setting* (Glencoe, Ill.: The Free Press, 1952).

[6] See, for observant commentary, Gregory P. Stone, "City Shoppers and Urban Identification: Observations on the Social Psychology of City Life," *American Journal of Sociology*, Vol. 60 (1954), pp. 36–45; also Wendell Bell and Marion D. Boat, "Urban Neighborhood and Informal Social Relations," *Ibid.* Vol. 62 (1957), pp. 391–98, and references there cited; Sylvia Fleis Fava, "Suburban-ism As a Way of Life," *American Sociological Review*, Vol. 21 (1956), pp. 34–37.

urban fringe is growing which is neither country nor city nor quite bedroom suburb in the older mode.

If this is so, then it means that the differences which divide Americans today depend less and less on where one lives, what one does, or who one is in terms of lineage, but more and more it depends on style and social character. Of course, some self-selection will occur towards places to live and towards occupations—especially between the two sectors of our "dual economy" I shall describe later. However the sorting at any given time reflects chance and idiosyncracy and scarcely predicts the life cycle of individuals.[7] Occasional studies of suburban voting and a few intimations concerning suburban worship shed tangential light on such major questions of attitude. On the whole, however, it seems fair to say that empirical investigations—including those recently done on problems of zoning, planning, and recreational needs; on the location of industry and the journey to work; and on problems of suburban and regional administration—scarcely connect with the kinds of writing cited at the outset. Thus, we cannot link nation-wide data on changes in metropolitan areas with Whyte's descriptions of how Park Forest feels toward its pro tem inhabitants. This is the characteristic situation in sociology today—that research in the macrocosmic and in the microcosmic scarcely connect, scarcely inform each other.[8] At any rate, this is my excuse, or my opportunity, for dealing in this paper with quite general themes only illustratively and sporadically pinned down in empirical research: I speak for a point of view—at best for a seasoned subjectivity.

■ ■ ■

. . . For millions of suburbanites, their post World War II experience has been prosperous and open far beyond their depression-born expectations. For them, the suburbs have been one vast supermarket, abundantly and conveniently stocked with approved yet often variegated choices. The children are less of a worry there than on city streets; the neighbors often more friendly than those city folk who "keep themselves to themselves"; life in general is more relaxed. The confidence such people often have that things will continue to go well for them is revealed in the story told one journalist

[7] See the forthcoming book of G. E. Swanson and D. N. Miller in which they distinguish within the city of Detroit and within the middle-income strata between "bureaucratic" (inner-directed) and "mass-society" (other-directed) families.

[8] I may, of course, be unaware of important work in this area—work, for instance, of the scope of G. A. Lundberg, and others, *Leisure: A Suburban Study* (New York: Columbia University Press, 1934).

in a Southern California suburb where employment depends on nearby defense plants. When he asked people what would happen to them in case of a depression or cancellation of defense contracts they answered: "Why then the government will stockpile cars." Life on credit has worked out well for many such home owners, allowing them to have their children young and in circumstances far better than those in which they themselves grew up. Whatever the outsider might say about the risks blithely taken, with no allowance made for personal or social setbacks, or about the anemic quality of the relaxed life or its complacency, he would have to admit that such first-generation suburbanites have found the taste of abundance pleasant and, for the younger ones with wages rising faster than prices, not notably problematic.

REVOLT AGAINST INDUSTRIALISM

This subjective attitude does not, however, alter the fact that, among such suburban dwellers and in general in our society, we are witnessing a tremendous but tacit revolt against industrialism. It is a very different sort of revolt from either that of the machine smashers of the early nineteenth century or that of the various anti-industrial sects—socialist, anarchist, agrarian, etc.—of an earlier day. Large manufacturing industry is increasingly moving to the luxury side of the "dual economy," and back-breaking toil and harsh physical conditions are vanishing (except in industrialized farming and the service trades) with the coming of electricity, full employment, unions, and personnel men. But the luxury, which is often used to make the work more gregarious and less of an effort, is seldom used to make it less monotonous.[9] Naturally, men treat their work as delinquents treat school though schools are less likely than plants to pioneer the partial truancy of the four-day week, escaping and sabotaging when they can. Managers and foremen try in vain to restore the "old school spirit" to their employees and, failing, seek through automation and quality control to make up for the deliquescence of the "instinct of workmanship" once so painfully built into the labor force. Observers of factory life have repeatedly pointed out that status within the plant is no longer

[9] Cf. Peter Drucker's discussion of job enlargement and related measures in *Concept of the Corporation* (New York: Harper & Brothers, 1946). Union leaders who once were in the forefront of the drive to make work less exhausting—often an extrapolative matter of lowering hours, slowing the assembly line, lessening dirt and noise—have seldom moved into the more difficult area of making it less uncreative. (According to Nelson Foote, they have eliminated the former grim silence that suited a Puritanical management.)

gained by hard work and craftsmanship, but rather by one's consumer skills outside. Men dream, not of rising in the factory, but of starting a small business such as a motel, gas station, or TV repair shop in the shabby and open-shop underside of our dual economy.[10] For youngsters from subsistence farms, for hillbillies, and Southern Negroes, a Detroit or Gary factory is still glamorous or at least a liberation from drastic poverty and insecurity; but for second- and third-generation factory workers, it no longer holds much meaning other than as a (hopefully temporary) source of funds and fringe benefits.

To be sure, there is a new industrialism of electronics, plastics, aviation, and so on, which retains a certain appeal that the older industries have so largely lost. However, the new firms, increasingly located in suburbs or where people want to live: California, and the Southwest and Florida, speed the movement out of heavy industry and merge factory and suburban life in a blend Patrick Geddes would probably disown. But we see in these industries precisely the form that the revolt against industrialism has taken today, namely to partially incorporate the "enemy" so that industrialism is not compartmentalized but rather, in muted form, spreads into all parts of the culture. This is, of course, what happens in so many social struggles: One defeats the enemy by becoming more like him.

LIFE AND WORK VALUES

Let me pursue this further by looking at what is happening to the older form of industrial and commercial metropolis. When, a few years ago, I studied interviews done with several hundred college seniors at twenty representative universities, asking them what they would like or expect to be doing in fifteen years, I was struck by the fact that the great majority planned to live in the suburbs. They expected to be married, and in describing their prospective spouses they hoped for what we might call station-wagon types: educated, companionable, civic-minded, and profoundly domestic. There were few who recognized some incompatibility between focus on suburban life and focus on big-city ambitions (for instance, a senior who wanted to go into advertising, yet not live in or near New York). They were—with some exceptions especially among

[10] Cf., e.g., Ely Chinoy, *Automobile Workers and the American Dream* (Garden City, N.Y.: Doubleday & Company, 1955) and, on older patterns of work morality, Eugene A. Friedmann and Robert J. Havighurst, *The Meaning of Work and Retirement* (Chicago: University of Chicago Press, 1954).

the Southerners—willing to sacrifice the heights of achievement, though not the plateaus of the luxury economy, in favor of their goals of suburban domesticity and peace. Those who hailed originally from the suburbs suffered from no disenchantment and wanted to return to them—often to the same one—while both city-bred and small-town boys also preferred the suburbs. I assume that some of the latter in an earlier day would have wanted to leave Main Street behind and make their mark in the big city, whatever lingering agrarian fears and suspicions of it they still harbored.[11] The city today, for many, spells crime, dirt, and race tensions, more than it does culture and opportunity. While some people still escape from the small town to the city, even more people are escaping from the city to the suburbs.

The successful book and movie, *The Man in the Grey Flannel Suit*, dramatizes these values quite explicitly. The hero chooses unromantic suburban cosiness, with (in the movie version) a not altogether inspiring wife and progeny, in preference to a high-pressure but potentially exciting business opportunity.[12] The head of the business is portrayed as having destroyed his family life and as virtually alienated from all human contact. Very likely, some of his junior executives would describe the company as a "mink-lined rattrap," thus explaining and justifying their withdrawal of affect from the work itself, while recognizing that they are still competitive. A recent fragmentary survey presents evidence that managers are less satisfied with their work even than unskilled workers, and it is conceivable that the middle-class occupations in general will soon be regarded as sources of funds and of periodic contacts and activity, much as the working-class occupations are now largely regarded.[13] If work loses its centrality, then the place where it is done also comes to matter less, and the access to variety in work that the central city provides may also come to matter less. Indeed, so much is this the case already that advertising for engineers in *Scientific American* and in trade journals looks more and more like the vacation advertising in *Holiday*. Minneapolis-Honeywell offers

---

[11] Cf. "The Found Generation," *The American Scholar*, Vol. 25 (1956), pp. 421–36; see also Eric Larrabee and David Riesman, "Company Town Pastoral: The Role of Business in 'Executive Suite,'" reprinted in Bernard Rosenberg and David Manning White, *Mass Culture* (Glencoe, Ill.: The Free Press, 1956), pp. 325–37.

[12] There is an equivalent rejection of a wartime love affair with an Italian girl. The business in question is broadcasting—typical for the luxury economy and far removed from traditional industrialism.

[13] See Nancy C. Morse and Robert S. Weiss, "The Function and Meaning of Work and the Job," *American Sociological Review*, Vol. 20 (1955), pp. 191–98. It should be noted that many men in the professions (the study included only men) and many in sales express great satisfaction with their work.

seasons and skiing as a counter-lure to the aircraft and electronic suburbs of the Far West.[14] In this regimen, white-collar and blue-collar move towards one another, as each group now emphasizes the consumption aspects of life.

■ ■ ■

SUBURBAN WAY OF LIFE

This life, as just indicated, is increasingly focused on the suburbs which, since World War II, have grown so in quantity as to change their quality. For, although upper-class and upper-middle-class people have lived in the suburbs of our great cities since the 1880's or earlier, the cities before World War II still retained their hegemony: They engrossed commercial, industrial, and cultural power. The city represented the division and specialization not only of labor but of attitude and opinion: By discovering like-minded people in the city, one developed a new style, a new little magazine, a new architecture. The city, that is, provided a "critical mass" which made possible new combinations—criminal and fantastic ones as well as stimulating and productive ones. Today, however, with the continual loss to the suburbs of the elite and the enterprising, the cities remain big enough for juveniles to form delinquent subcultures, but barely differentiated enough to support cultural and educational activities at a level appropriate to our abundant economy. The elite, moreover, tend to associate with like-income neighbors rather than with like-minded civic leaders, thus dispersing their potential for leadership beyond township boundaries. Ironically, these people sometimes choose to live in communities which might be almost too manageable if millions of others did not simultaneously make the same choice.[15]

Indeed, the suburbs are no longer simply bedroom communities but increasingly absorb the energies of the men as well as the women and children. The men, that is, are not simply being good providers while still attached to the values of the industrial system: They are seekers after the good life in the suburbs on their own account. Early marriage and the rise in the birth rate are so

---

[14] An occasional ad is more work-minded and will feature opportunities for responsibility and creativity along with the suburban fringe benefits.

[15] This is somewhat analogous to fad behavior, for individuals no longer live in suburbs as, so to speak, statistical isolates, but live there with recognition of the suburban style as theirs and their country's. *Cf.* Rolf Meyersohn and Elihu Katz, "Notes on a Natural History of a Fad," *American Journal of Sociology*, Vol. 62, No. 6 (1957), pp. 594–601.

many rivulets of individual, only barely self-conscious protest against the values inherited from industrialism and the low-birth-rate middle-class metropolis—so many decisions to prefer companionship in the present to some distant goal, and so many mortgages of the future in the benevolent shadow of the luxury economy and its escalator of slow inflation, promotion, and protection. Whereas men once identified themselves with commerce and industry—with its power, its abstractions, its achievements—and forced women to remain identified with domesticity—save for those women who broke through the barrier and became man-imitating career girls—now, as many observers have pointed out, a growing homogenization of roles is occurring. Women take jobs to support the suburban ménage periodically while men take part in its work (do-it-yourself), its civic activities (Parent-Teacher Association, and so on), and its spirit. Rather than delegating religion to their womenfolk, men go to church in increasing numbers, occasionally as in an earlier day to be respectable or to climb socially, and occasionally out of a genuine religious call, but more typically because the church, like the high school and the country club, has become a center for the family as a social and civic unit.

DECENTRALIZATION OF LEISURE

All this brings with it an increasing decentralization of leisure. Just as the suburban churches tend, within the boundaries of the "three faiths," to an amiable syncretism, ignoring doctrinal or liturgical differences, so too the other leisure activities of the suburbs tend to reduce the specialized differentiations possible in a metropolis. What I mean here can be illustrated with reference to music. A metropolis has enough music lovers to organize highly differentiated groups: Mozart lovers may split off from Bach lovers and would never encounter lovers of Wagner, while in the suburbs the music lovers—if they are to support communal activities at all—must in some measure homogenize their tastes and hence create a local market for "classical music." Indeed, they will be exposed to a good deal of community pressure to support the musical activities of their friends in return for having their own enterprises supported. The same holds, *parri passu*, for the other arts—just as it does for the differentiation of specialty stores, churches, and museums found in a large city. By the same token, the suburban activist can feel that his own contribution matters, as he would likely feel in the big city only when he is very rich, very active, or very influential. People brought up in the suburbs may not realize what they are missing, and they may relate their emotional ties entirely to their locality, not going downtown to shop or to visit friends or to go to the theatre.[16]

Suburbs differ, of course, in what they make available, and so, as we noted at the outset, do central cities; thus, Morris Janowitz showed that many people who, to the visitor's eye, live in Chicago actually live in a small neighborhood that might as well be a suburb.[17] Moreover, central cities are increasingly influenced by suburban styles of life: People trained to a suburban attachment to their cars drive downtown even when good and commodious public transportation is available, and they wear the casual dress of the suburbs when they do.

The suburban dweller believes, in fact, that he has the best of both worlds. In the interviews with college seniors I referred to earlier, in which such stress was placed on suburban domesticity, many students also emphasized their wish not to lose the cultural amenities they had enjoyed in college.[18] Some of these amenities will certainly be distributed in the suburb though frequently in diluted doses: Piped in through television and radio and high-fidelity sets; the suburb may even support a theatre group and, in a few cases, amateur chamber music; the local high school will provide entertainment of a sort, as well as facilities for adult education.

However, as the radii lengthen on which people move away from the city—as they must with the crowding of the suburbs leading to the jump to the exurbs—people either learn as in California to drive great distances for dinner or confine themselves to their immediate environs: The central city as a meeting place disappears—a process which has gone further in Los Angeles and Chicago than in Boston or New York. The neighbors make up little circles based—as William H. Whyte, Jr., showed for Park Forest—largely on propinquity.

LOSS OF HUMAN DIFFERENTIATION

The decentralization of leisure in the suburbs goes further than this, however, as the home itself, rather than the neighborhood,

---

[16] I am indebted to unpublished work on the performing arts in the suburbs done by Philip Ennis at the Bureau of Applied Social Research of Columbia University.

[17] *The Community Press in an Urban Setting, op. cit.*

[18] Colleges themselves make the same claim that the suburbs do. I recently had occasion to go through a large number of college catalogues as well as the descriptions colleges give in brief compass in the *College Board Handbook;* all but the huge urban universities did their best to present themselves as near the advantages of a large city, but far enough away for suburban safety and charm. (Correspondingly, some teen agers, raised in safe suburbs, find glamor in going downtown, at least for a time.)

becomes the chief gathering place for the family—either in the "family room" with its games, its TV, its informality, or outdoors around the barbecue. And while there are values in this of family closeness and "togetherness," there is also a loss of differentiation as the parents play pals to their children and the latter, while gaining a superficial precocity, lose the possibility of wider contacts. At worst, there is a tendency for family talk and activity to seek the lowest common denominator in terms of age and interest.

Some of these matters are illustrated by an interview with a housewife who had recently bought a house in one of the wealthier suburbs north of Chicago. Her husband had been transferred to Chicago from a southern city and had been encouraged by his company to buy a large house for entertaining customers. Customers, however, seldom came since the husband was on the road much of the time. The wife and three children hardly ever went downtown—they had no Chicago contacts anyway—and after making sporadic efforts to make the rounds of theater and musical activities in the suburbs and to make friends there, they found themselves more and more often staying home, eating outdoors in good weather and looking at TV in bed. Observing that "there is not much formal entertaining back and forth," the wife feared she was almost losing her conversational skills; yet she felt that her family had been pulled closer together by the shared activities, in which the husband joined on weekends, around the home. After listening to her list and discuss the friends made at church and golf, it became evident that her immediate environment just missed providing her with people close enough to her in taste and interest for intimate ties to develop.

One interview, of course, proves little, and many factors are obviously involved in choice of friends; suburban location in an older, nonhomogeneous suburb is only one of them. I recall obtaining such interviews in Kansas City, too, among people who had lived there all their lives and had potential access to wide strata in the metropolitan area. Nevertheless, there seems to me to be a tendency, though not a pronounced one, in the suburbs to lose the human differentiations which have made great cities in the past the centers of rapid intellectual and cultural advance. The suburb is like a fraternity house at a small college—or the "close propinquity" to which Tocqueville referred—in which like-mindedness reverberates upon itself as the potentially various selves within each of us do not get evoked or recognized. For people who move to the suburb to live when adult, of course, matters are different than among those who never knew another milieu. And, to be sure, creative human contact need not be face to face but can often be vicarious, through print or other mediated channels. Certainly, highly differentiated human beings have grown up in locales which gave them minimal support. Moreover, though the nonneighborly seldom seek the suburbs,[19] a few doubtless manage to survive there. Ease of movement, in any case, permits periodic access to others, although as these others themselves scatter to the suburbs, this process becomes more difficult.

ROLE OF THE AUTOMOBILE IN SUBURBIA

Indeed, at least until each of us has his own helicopter or rocket, this pattern of life requires us to spend a great deal of time in automobiles, overcoming decentralization—but driving is itself a terribly "decentralized" activity, allowing at best for car-pool sociability, and at worst mitigated by the quiz-bits, frequent commercials, and flatulent music of AM radio. As compared with the older suburbanites who commuted by train and read the paper, did homework, or even read a book, the present and increasing tendency to travel to work by car seems aggressively vacuous and solipsistic.[20] Whereas in preindustrial cultures and in the lower classes in industrial society, people sometimes just hang on a corner or sit vacantly, it is striking that in a society which offers many alternatives, people will consent to drive vacantly but not refreshingly—woe betide the careless or unspry pedestrian or bicyclist who gets in the way of industrial workers pouring out of the factory parking lots or white-collar workers coming home on a throughway. The human waste here is most important, but the waste of resources and land, the roadside *dreck*,[21] the highways which eat space as railroad yards even in St. Louis or Chicago never did, are not negligible even in a huge rich country.

Where the husband goes off with the car to work—and often, in the vicious circle created by the car, there is no other way for him to travel—the wife is frequently either privatized at home or to

[19] *Cf.* Sylvia Fleis Fava, "Contrasts in Neighboring: New York City and a Suburban County," in William Dobriner, ed., *Reader on the Suburbs* (New York: G. P. Putnam's Sons).
[20] To be sure, driving may offer some commuters a change of pace and a chance to be alone. *Cf.*, for a general discussion of the elements of irrationality hiding under slogans of convenience in driving to work in the metropolis, see David Riesman and Eric Larrabee, "Autos in America: History Catches Up with Ford," Encounter, Vol. 8 (1957), pp. 26–36.
[21] A few superhighways have been designed to refresh the traveler and increase his sense of visual possibility as well as to speed him on his way; the Taconic State Parkway in New York is a fine example.

escape isolation must take a job which will help support her own car. Whereas the rental courts of developments like Park Forest provide companionship for the stranded wives—companionship which, given the age and sex homogeneity, is sometimes oppressive —other suburbs are so built and so psychologically "unsociometric" as to limit neighboring and leave many women to the company of Mary Margaret McBride and Arthur Godfrey. Indeed, in a few instances of interviewing in the morning in new suburbs south of Chicago, I have been struck by the eagerness of the housewives to talk to somebody (and not only to a man!) who is not a salesman— once they can be weaned away from the TV which amuses them as a kind of vicarious baby sitter. It is not only the visiting intellectual who finds the lives of these women empty, their associations fragmentary. My colleagues, Donald Horton and R. Richard Wohl, speak of the "parasocial intimacy" they attain with the celebrities of the TV variety shows.[22] The women themselves, if at all sensitive or well educated, complain of having their contacts limited to their young children and to a few other housewives in the same boat. And, as a result of efforts to understand the extraordinary philoprogenitiveness of the suburban middle classes (a theme recurred to below), I have come to entertain the suspicion that, once started in having children, these women continue in some part out of a fear of the emptiness of life without children and of the problems they would face of relating themselves to their menfolk without the static, the noise, the pleasure, the "problems" that the presence of children provides.

The children themselves, in fact, before they get access to a car, are captives of their suburb, save for those families where the housewives surrender continuity in their own lives to chauffeur their children to lessons, doctors, and other services which could be reached via public transport in the city. In the suburban public schools, the young are captives, too, dependent on whatever art and science and general liveliness their particular school happens to have—again contrast the metropolis, with its choice of high schools, as most notably in New York.[23]

[22] See Horton and Wohl, "Mass Communication and Para-Social Interaction: Observations on Intimacy at a Distance," *Psychiatry*, Vol. 19 (1956), pp. 215–29.
[23] I doubt if even the most superior schools of Scarsdale or Winnetka are as good in the arts as the High School of Music and Art, or in science as the Bronx High School of Science—or at least this was so when New York City was not yet a slum for the Southern and Caribbean migrants. The suburban schools, of course, can hardly cope with the crowding their very advantages have brought about—just as the suburbs, to which people go to escape the city's dirt, suffer from a water shortage and may shortly not be able to wash away their own dirt.

UNEVEN DISTRIBUTION OF LEISURE

Let me stress again that the themes I am discussing are peculiar neither to the United States nor to the twentieth century. Just as cities are older than industry so are suburbs, their splendors, and miseries. It is the democratization and extension of the phenomena I am describing, and the resultant constriction of alternatives, which give them a new and cumulative quality. The modern suburb is the product of the car, the five-day week, and the "bankers' hours" of the masses. As hours drop further, we can anticipate that still fewer families with children will willingly live in the city. Exceptions would be cities like Minneapolis where the inhabitants can focus their leisure around their cottages on nearby lakes. But the same developments which have reduced hours for those white-collar and factory workers who do not go in for "moonlighting" or extra jobs have in turn put additional pressure on the still limited leisure of certain professional groups. These latter, in one way or another, cater to those whose enhanced income and leisure time allows them greatly to increase their consumption of services. People, that is, can now afford both the time and money for better medical care, more professional advice (therapeutic and otherwise), additional schooling, and so on. And the professions and service trades that supply these wants do not benefit from automation. Thus, the very developments that have increased the leisure of the masses have greatly reduced that of certain of the classes: Doctors, civil servants, teachers, school and college administrators, and some groups of managers and intellectuals work almost as long hours as steel workers did in the nineteenth century. While some of these cadres, notably the doctors, have enough of a monopoly position to earn high incomes in partial revenge for being overworked, others, notably the civil servants and teachers, are poorly paid both in money and time. It is these groups who are becoming the principal victims of the anti-industrial or leisure revolution.[24]

Yet these victims, too, live in the suburbs where they are exposed to the styles of life of neighbors with at least equal incomes and a far easier schedule—neighbors, moreover, who need never bring work home at night. This developing pattern of uneven distribution of leisure has not been channeled into political slogans. We do not hear cries for the doctors of the world to unite and throw off their patients (a good many of whom have no better or

---

[24] *Cf.* the thoughtful comments on an "administrative depression" among white-collar workers in Harvey Wheeler, "Danger Signal in the Political System," *Dissent*, Vol. 4 (1957), pp. 298–310.

more socially mobile ways to spend their time than by absorbing doctors' time!) Few today would begrudge the masses their claims both on the landscape and on services; but few have asked what this portends for the leisure of the servicers. Even now, school superintendents sometimes poignantly say they should never have gotten married and had children, for they must continuously serve other families and other children. Nor can such a group partially make it up to their families through the status and ease that money can buy as, for example, do busy surgeons or top executives. Ministers and rabbis, too, are victims of the suburban style in "belongingness"; and they are likewise unprotected by celibacy from having their own families wish they were in some other line of work.

THE DILEMMA OF PROFESSIONALS

How do people feel who live in the suburbs without the comforts and indulgences the ads tell them they ought to have—and not only the ads, but the "propaganda of the deed" of their neighbors and their neighbors' children? Vistors to the metropolis have often been struck by the contrast of Gold Coast and slum, of majesty and misery. Suburban contrasts in housing and decor are less stark; majesty rides less high and misery less low. Yet, just because the suburb doesn't present poverty and deprivation as a given, the less self-evident lack of privileges must sometimes rankle and smolder. This is true even though some middle-class suburbanites, weary of the time on their hands, no doubt envy the doctor his busy rounds and his unquestioned usefulness.

Thus it would seem that a polarization is occurring between those who are dispensable to their jobs, and who therefore have a lot of time off, and those who, precisely as a result of this development, have no time off. A hundred years ago, doctors took it easy. In those days few could afford their services or were educated enough to recognize and discover sysmptoms; today illness is felt to be arbitrary, not one of the givens of life. A hundred years ago, civil servants took it easy: Their jobs were sometimes sinecures for impecunious writers. Today city and suburban officials, planners, highway engineers, and National Park personnel struggle in vain to cope with the problems created by mobile masses of Americans. The struggle is similar to that of a permissive mother with a brood of willful, well-fed and not wholly socialized children. In the novels of Trollope and other nineteenth-century novelists we glimpse this vanished world in which professional people led a leisurely existence. Today this is available only to those who can turn a deaf ear to importunate clients and customers, to colleaguial pressures, and to their own ambitions.

Of course, I have minimized in this account the fact that doctors and other professionals are often among the happy few who enjoy their work. They like the constellation of activities they perform; they find their colleagues and sometimes their clients stimulating; in the best case, they regard their work as play, with the freedom and creativity of the best play. We cannot speak of "overwork" where the task and the pace are freely chosen—even if there are included some inevitable marginal increments of boredom and compulsion.[25] Yet we must also recognize both that many intellectuals and professional people have entered their careers under some compulsion—even though their horizons are wider than those of most farmers and factory workers—and that the developments here discussed have sometimes trapped them beyond the point of no return. Their image of the career may have been formed on an older, less harrassed model. Furthermore, they may have chosen their careers, in part at least, out of such factors as a distaste for business and industry and ethical, ideological, or snobbish scruples against big business rather than out of a positive pleasure in, for example, scientific work. They may find themselves, then, in a quasi-big business of their own, but with none of the protections big business can give. They may retain the illusion of setting their own pace whereas in actuality the traffic sets it for them. In rejecting industry and commerce, only to be plunged right back into it as is the case with many professors and physicians, they resemble the suburbanite who flees the city and has it catch up with him.

SUBURBIA'S POSITIVE AND NEGATIVE ASPECTS

Our Center for the Study of Leisure has been conducting studies of limited scope in several Chicago suburbs in an effort, *inter alia*, to see what happens to people who leave the city for the suburbs in terms of new commitments and new demands. We have also done a very inconclusive study of how people in the city spend their week ends. We have the impression that the suburbanite, tied to his house as the doctor is to his practice, may actually be less likely to take off for a week end in the country than the urban dweller

[25] We must recall that, although play is by definition more freely chosen than work, it has also marginal compulsions: To finish the rubber, the sociable evening, the set of tennis—even, for many of us, the novel.

whose janitor can look after his apartment and even the cat. Indeed, it is the city people, freed by industrialism from long hours of grinding work, who (along, of course, with an ample supply of untied suburbanites) make up a large proportion of the outboard population of our lakes and rivers and of the thirty-five million fishermen—more than twice the number of those urban sportsmen, the bowlers. Although air-conditioning makes even the most humid and dirty city potentially habitable, people can't wait to leave town on week ends and during the summer, even though in many parts of the country it means spewing the city into the countryside and fighting with like-minded crowds for space on roads, lakes, and at motels.[26]

As I have indicated, I believe that snobbery and imitation of the rich play a declining part in this exodus to the suburbs and that the quiet revolt against the city and industrialism plays an increasing part. I would argue that there is often less"front" in the new suburbs than in equivalent sections of a metropolis, and less pressure for a lace-curtain life concealing backstage scrimping and meanness than there once was. People do not usually learn the idea of a garden suburb either from British models or Mumford or Clarence Stern: The idea, in its uncomplicated forms, is an omnipresent dream, carrying overtones of the Bible, peasant life and folk imagery. The urban wish for contact with nature has been crystallized for many Americans around the habits of the British gentry and their middle-class imitators. But, more modest than the aspidistra-lovers of the London suburbs, we prefer not to give fancy names to our own "villas" but to let this dumb show be done for us by the realtors. In the Chicago area, for instance, a great many suburbs have either "Park" or "Forest" in their names, and two of them have both! Furthermore, social mobility means that many, perhaps most urban dwellers will have suburban relatives or friends. The mass production of suburbs, especially in the postwar years, has made them accessible to almost everyone. Only in the rural and impoverished parts of the South and Great Plains farming regions are we likely to find many people who do not know anybody who lives in a suburb and have never had occasion to visit one. Beyond that, the vicarious socialization of Americans into the

[26] It is, however striking how much of this movement, though largely "private" and unorganized and unideological, is determined by fashion—in this respect, resembling residential location itself. On warm winter days Central Park and its rowboats are often nearly deserted, as is Jackson Park in Chicago; likewise, the Atlantic beaches such as Coney Island, in their off-season magnificence, are as unpopulated as the Labrador coast. People feel it is arbitrary to be cooped up in the city on a summer week end because they so largely accept the definitions of "living it up" provided by the media and conversation.

experiences of consumption they are about to have is the continuous task of the mass media. Many of these, and at a variety of
income levels, are devoted to expounding the suburban way of life
directly in ads and features; other media are indirect vehicles for
suburban styles in the homes pictured in stories, the sport shirts
worn, and the idols of consumption portrayed.[27] The whole American ethos, which once revolved about the dialectic of pure country
versus wicked but exciting city, seems to me now aerated by the
suburban outlook. This produces an homogenization of both city
and country, but without full integration.

While on the whole the lower-middle- and middle-income suburbs sponsor the relaxed life, there is one area where they impose
an imperative which many city dwellers have not met, namely that
of having some sort of garden—less as a cultural amenity than as a
minimum contribution to civic decency: A kind of compulsory outdoor housekeeping. Indeed, in the study of gardening in two Chicago suburbs conducted by our Center for the Study of Leisure[28]
we gained the impression that garden clubs were not extremely
active in either one (though we have found very active and pres-
tigeful clubs on the North Shore); garden clubs are much more
characteristic of older communities, where they represent a familiar activity of some of the established families, rather than of the
new suburbs, where gardening must compete with many other hob-
bies and activities, both outdoor and indoor. We found in Fairlawn,
a new developer's suburb, for example, that to many housewives
the garden was simply one more chore. It represented neither a
contrast with the asphalt jungle of the city, nor a pleasure in growing things, nor a rage for order. It was rather a tax imposed by
neighborhood consciousness—the neighbors often being interpreted
as more concerned and censorious than they, for the most part,
were. Thus, we find that many people who have moved newly to the
suburbs to escape the city come without awareness of the constraints they will find—or mistakenly interpret—in the suburb.
Like the appointment of Samara, they meet pressures they had
thought to leave behind, though altered in form and impact.

[27] Cf. Leo Lowenthal, "Biographies in Popular Magazines," in P. F. Lazarsfeld and Frank Stanton, Eds., Radio Research, 1942–43 (New York: Duell,
Sloane & Pearce).
[28] For a full report on this study, see Robin Jackson and Rolf Meyersohn,
"The Social Patterning of Leisure," address to the Annual Institute of the
Society for Social Research, Chicago, May 30, 1957. I also draw in this paper
on a study, now in the field under the direction of Prof. Donald Horton (with
the assistance of Robin Jackson), which is concerned with the conflict in styles
of leisure in one of the North Shore suburbs, and with the ways in which
the institutions of the suburb, particularly the high school, become the foci
of that conflict.

One of these pressures, already adverted to, is the metropolis itself; its traffic, its ethnic minorities, and its tax rates tend to catch up with them. The waves of succession within the city proper do not halt at its boundaries, and many old and established suburbs are finding themselves cut in two by freeways and by the new kinds of people they bring. In this situation, some of the old kinds of people are among those tempted to become exurbanites, putting the ever-approaching city another few miles away and hoping to solve the dilemma of distance versus intimacy by a superhighway.

However, in this quandary the emphasis on superhighways—and on supercars which require them—takes on much of the lunatic quality of an arms race. As highways get bigger and better, they invite more cars, destroy what undeveloped and unschematized country (or central city) remains, and require still more highways in an unending spiral.[29]

SUBURBAN STYLES OF LIFE AND THOUGHT

People have been drilled by industrialism in the values of efficiency—narrowly defined in terms of speed, performance, and a kind of streamlined look (what Jacques Barzun has referred to as "America's Romance with Practicality"). Thus even when they flee from the cities and the style of life industrialism has brought about, they cannot change the style of thought which sees the solution to ribbon developments in stretching them still further until our East and West coasts threaten to become continuous roadside slums.

What is true of the planning, or lack of it, of our road-centered culture as a whole is also true of domestic architecture. Efficiency here is less stark—and consequently often less attractive—since it must compete with traditional definitions of a suburban free-standing home. But, as many architects have pointed out, the interiors are highly modern in the sense of mechanization. Indeed, one reason why husbands have been willing to become domesticated is that they have been promoted from dishwashers to operators of dishwashers. Similarly, they use power mowers to give crew cuts to

[29] Highway engineers resemble guided-missile engineers in an understandable irritation with the tiresome "human factor" which is bound to produce accidents—and every effort has typically been made to reduce the functions of individual drivers or soldiers, thus making them more bored and more accident-prone.

Lewis Mumford has been pointing these things out for so long that he resembles the hero in Wells' story, "The Country of the Blind," who comes close to wishing he could share the visual defects of his fellow-men, for it would be more comfortable that way for everybody.

handkerchief-sized lawns and pierce their wives' and neighbors' ears with the screams of high-fidelity music. The open plan of the very newest ranch-style homes puts the TV set on a swivel in the center. Here it can be seen from all parts of the house so that urban news, fashions, gossip, and jokes can circulate in the home throughout the daily cycle of the members of the family. But all these improvements are bought at the expense of space for the individual whose bedroom in the suburban development is often smaller than in city tenements. This is especially true, as Albert Roland of *Household* magazine has pointed out to me, of the newest suburban homes. These have both a family room and a living room. The latter, like the old parlor, is used only for state occasions; the family room is big enough for games, the TV, an inside barbecue, and general clutter.

Nor does the lawn or backyard provide a bounteous free space in most of the new developments. In comparison with the size and cost of the house, plots are small (much as they have traditionally been in midwestern cities where people wanted to avoid the row house but not to be too far from their next-door neighbors). Moreover, the fact that there is both a front and a backyard—the latter being, in many developments, the "family room" and the former the "parlor"—means that what space there is becomes divided. And just as the homes have no interstitial spaces, no nooks and crannies, so the lots have no texture taken individually or together.[30] I keep asking myself what the lots will look like when the explosion of our population doubles the numbers in the suburban hegira without, in all probability, increasing proportionately the services that our new expectations crave. Will houses and lots get smaller when people can no longer spread further afield? People have been moving to the suburbs in many cases in pursuit of an inchoate dream of spaciousness. They have looked for a release from urban tensions, from crowded and ugly schools, from indoors. And ordinarily this release has more than compensated for losses in urban qualities which are difficult to sense or describe—qualities of possibility, often, rather than of actual use.[31] What will occur when the urban qualities have been dissipated, while the suburban ones elude all but the rich?

[30] It would seem as if Americans, gaining some of the feelings towards the city and its works and ways that Thoreau had, have succeeded in blending his values with those of Carnegie. However, as indicated earlier, they are far from having Andrew Carnegie's concern for hard work, wealth, and thrift—let alone his self-taught passion for literacy—but they do have his interest in serving an image of efficiency, modified by Dale Carnegie's concern for gregarious friendliness.
[31] My colleague, Anselm Strauss, has been engaged in a study of the informal tone or aura of cities, their images of themselves; I have profited from conversations with him about city life.

Such questions assume, as I have here been doing, that Americans have ceased being socially inventive outside the corporate or military spheres. They assume that we will not discover the governmental or voluntary channels either to give many people alternative satisfactions to large families or to create forms of life and livelihood appropriate to another age of population expansion—this time with no frontiers left. Certainly, there is now a kind of private inventiveness in the suburbs among people who, having lost "the track of generations" and traditional standards of judgment and taste, are somehow managing, with ambivalent aid from the media, to create new forms and styles. The leaders of Park Forest and several other new communities, surrounded by others as green as they, often managed to develop some communal decencies and controls; in that sense, the townmeeting spirit is far from moribund. It is easy to see the negative and ironical features of the suburbs— harder to see emergent crystallizations.[32]

But one trouble is that the suburbs, like the families within them, can scarcely control their own immediate environs, let alone the larger metropolitan and national orbits that impinge on them and decide their eventual atmosphere. And here is where the suburbanites' immense liking for Ike is portentous. It expresses the wish of so many of the college seniors mentioned above that civics and the Community Chest replace politics; it expresses the hope, built into the very structure of credit and the additive-extrapolative style of thought, that nothing serious will occur, that everything will go on as before. And it expresses this hope, of course, at the very moment when private decisions—irresponsibly influenced—to buy or not to buy, to propagate or not to propagate store up our destinies (quite apart from the similar activities of the rest of our small planet). In interviews done in Chicago suburbs by Louis Harris before the 1956 elections, he asked potential voters how they felt about a part-time, golf-playing president. Many were indignant, saying they would play golf too if they had such problems— though when asked to name serious problems facing the country, they could often get no further than high taxes. Plainly Ike's complacencies mirrored and supported their own (Eisenhower, of course, like most anyone in Washington, is far less complacent than these constituencies), and their defenses against untoward apprehension were too great to allow thought for the morrow.

---

[32] *Cf.* my discussion in "Some Observations on Changes in Leisure Attitudes," *Antioch Review*, Vol. 12 (1952), pp. 417–36; reprinted in *Individualism Reconsidered*. See also the thoughtful hopefulness concerning changed forms of inventiveness in Conrad M. Arensberg, "Work and the Changing American Scene," in Arensberg, and others, eds., *Research in Industrial Human Relations* (New York: Harper & Brothers, 1957).

THE AIMLESS QUALITY OF SUBURBAN LIFE

In the days of Lincoln Steffens and later, people emphasized the "shame of the cities," and in the 1920's major novelists emphasized the constraints of small-town and occasionally of small-suburban life. Today, the comparable worry, in the books dealing with the suburbs, is conformity—*Point of No Return*, with its concern for place and competition, strikes a somewhat older note; writers point to the uniformity of the ranch style, the ever-present television antennae, the lamp, if not the crack, in the picture window—which usually provides a view of the nearly treeless street, the cars, and someone else's picture window. Actually, uniformity and conformity are quite different matters as Georg Simmel has observed in his essay on "Fashion."[33] The former may dictate to men only in inessentials, whereas the latter involves some psychological mechanism. And the conformity of the new suburbs is, in some important ways, far less stringent than that of the old; if it is not quite the case that "anything goes," lots of things do go which once would, if known, have brought ostracism. If one does not seek to force the new suburbanite back across the ethnic tracks he has just crossed, he is quite tolerant, even bland. If he is political at all—rather than parochially civic-minded, tending to a "garden" which includes the local schools and waterworks—he is apt to be an Eisenhower Republican, seldom informed, rarely angry, and only spasmodically partisan.

No, what is missing in suburbia, even where the quality of life has not overtly deteriorated, is not the result of claustrophobic conformity to others' sanctions. Rather, there would seem to be an aimlessness, a pervasive low-keyed unpleasure. This cannot be described in terms of traditional sorrow but is one on which many observers of the American scene and the American visage have commented, notably Erich Fromm in *The Sane Society* and the Goodmans in *Communitas*. For millions of people, work no longer provides a central focus for life; and the breadwinner is no longer the chief protagonist in the family saga—just as Saturday night no longer provides a central focus for festivity. In fact, the decentralization of leisure in the suburbs is not only spatial but temporal, as evenings from Thursday through Sunday are oriented to play rather than work and are not individually accented or collectively celebrated.[34]

[33] The essay, which originally appeared in *International Quarterly*, Vol. 10 (1904), pp. 130–55, is reprinted in *American Journal of Sociology*, Vol. 62, No. 6 (1957), pp. 541–58.
[34] I sometimes consider the drive-in movie the archetypical symbol of decentralization where people go to the theater not in stalls which permit circulation of elites but in cars which keep the family or the dating couple together with no sense of the audience or any shared experience outside the sedan.

At the same time, leisure has not picked up the slack—as, in earlier writings, I was too sanguine that it might. Whatever balances of work and play might have been possible for preindustrial man, postindustrial man is keyed, as I remarked earlier, to greater expectations. He has learned more "needs" and cannot in any case reconstitute the institutions industrialism destroyed. It is almost inconceivable, for example, to imagine a reconstitution of the folk arts which everywhere—in Nigeria as in New Orleans, in Damascus as in Tennessee—prove fragile in the face of mass-produced music and imagery. In *Communitas*, the Goodmans devoted much ingenuity to suggesting how, in their New Commune, work could be made more varied and interesting: By job rotation on a grand scale, by alternating supervision and apprenticeship, by scrutiny of all work in terms of means as well as ends. But automation as presently interpreted moves us yet further away from such a re-examination of work routines, even though, were our values different, it could provide an opportunity for eliminating monotonous work and bringing far more variety and spark into it. . . .

Chapter 5

SOCIAL ORGANIZATION IN THE URBAN SETTING

Differences in social organization between rural and urban areas inevitably would result from the sheer contrast between the two settings in complexity, even if other bases of divergence were altogether lacking. A major theme in urban sociology has been to identify and to describe the characteristic aspects of social organization in the urban setting. Underlying much of the thought and much of the research upon social organization are questions of the type brought forth by Wirth in his classic statement of a theory of urbanism.

Of all of the aspects of social organization which could be considered, three themes were chosen for presentation in this chapter. Two selections each relate to the topics of the power structure, of voluntary associations, and of the family in the urban community.

The impetus to the study of the organization of power in the modern community came from the pacemaking study carried out in a southern metropolitan area by Floyd Hunter.[1] The very phrase "power structure" has entered our language, often to symbolize the established opponents of whatever changes the advocates of innovation are urging upon the community. In the city he studied, Hunter did find a definite concentration of the power to make decisions influencing the course of events in the city. Interlocking

[1] Floyd Hunter, *Community Power Structure* (Chapel Hill: The University of North Carolina Press, 1953).

cliques of leaders, drawn largely from business and finance, exercised power in Regional City.

The degree to which a relatively small number of decision makers is able to determine the policies of American society as a whole, as seen from one perspective, or the degree to which the countervailing influence of the various components of a highly pluralistic society prevents such concentration of power, as viewed from the opposing perspective, are topics outside the scope of this book. Even on the level of the specific city or metropolitan area, it well may be that Hunter's account of Regional City is by no means characteristic of all cities. The difficulty of maintaining near-monolithic control presumably increases with the size of the metropolitan area and its internal fragmentation into units.

Pellegrin and Coates studied a southern city considerably smaller than Hunter's Regional City, and yet discovered a less unitary power structure than that which Hunter had found. In "Bigtown," very rapid growth, made possible by industrial expansion, had weakened community integration and provided a convenient scapegoat for all acknowledged problems. In fact, the industrial expansion had brought into the community a number of local managers of national corporations, and these men immediately moved into positions of importance in the elite and decision-making organizations. Such participation was perceived by them as an appropriate extension of their role of corporate leadership. Because their participation in other community activities was more restricted than that of older leaders in the community, and because local political leadership, largely based upon an electoral appeal to the workers, had little influence upon the basic decision-making process, the entire pattern was one of less centralization and less ability to affect community policies than that described by Hunter.

Using Hunter's data for the Southern city in some of his interpretation, and drawing from his own research in a city of the Pacific Northwest and an English city, Miller compared the three communities in respect to the dominance of business leaders in community decision making. He found that when the key leaders of the community were identified sociometrically from the group of top influential leaders, definite differences emerged between the English city and the two in America. Key leaders in the English city were drawn more evenly from various bases of leadership, and therefore drew less preponderantly from business, than was true in the American centers.

Enthusiastic participation has been considered a preeminently American characteristic—and source of democratic strength—from the time of de Tocqueville to the present. Wirth held that such participation was especially characteristic of urban man. Zimmer and

Hawley wondered if residents of the urban fringe, of the suburbs, were characterized by a different degree of participation in such organizations than those of the central city itself. Some plausible grounds existed for assuming that this might be the case, but reasons, equally plausible on the surface, also suggested that participation in such associations might be quite strong in the fringe area. In their research, they discovered that participation in voluntary associations was indeed lower among residents in the urban fringe.

Although most writing about voluntary associations in American life has presented such activity as particularly characteristic of the middle class, Myrdal and other observers have indicated that Negro Americans of all class levels often have a high degree of organizational participation. Babchuk and Thompson investigated the membership in voluntary associations of the black residents of a Middlewestern city which contained a rather small Negro population. A high degree of affiliation with such associations was characteristic of the Negro community. This was true on all class levels, but the contrast with patterns of participation usually found among white people was greatest on the lower-class levels. The authors suggest that in some respects, such organizational activity may provide the lower-class black person some of the interpersonal satisfactions denied in the family. However that may be, while some of the organizational activity was race-oriented, most of it could not be accounted for in terms of preoccupation with a cause.

Wirth suggested that the extended family declined, creating marked dominance for the nuclear family, in the urban setting. As Litwak notes, Talcott Parsons has also indicated that only the isolated nuclear family is functional for our mobile, industrial society. Yet, a number of studies have shown that visiting with kin, giving aid to relatives, and otherwise acknowledging an important familial bond extending beyond the nuclear unit is characteristic even of the residents of very large metropolitan areas. Litwak disputes the assumption that we must consider the typological nuclear family and the classical extended family as being the only alternatives. He suggests that a modified extended family, able to sustain emotional identification even when migration creates spatial scattering, has become widespread. Such an extended family not only is meaningful to the individuals involved, but also has important implications for geographic mobility which are precisely opposite the usual assumption, in which the classical form of the extended family has been viewed as an impediment to territorial or social mobility.

In their recent article, Winch and Greer seek to clarify our understanding of the relationships among ethnicity, urbanism, and the extended family through identifying four differing measures of the extended family. Some interpretations of family relation-ships have looked at one, some at another, of these measures of the extended family, and as a result, a lack of interpretative clarity has resulted. No matter which index of extended familism was utilized, most of the respondents in a Wisconsin-wide probability sample reported involvement with kin. They found that ruralism correlated significantly with two of their indexes of the extended family—interaction with a number of kin and the functionality of such interaction. Their other measures of extended familism—called by them "extensity" and "intensity"—showed little difference between rural and urban respondents.

Absentee-Owned Corporations and Community Power Structure

ROLAND J. PELLEGRIN
Institute for Community Studies,
University of Oregon
and
CHARLES H. COATES
University of Maryland

The stratification system of a given community attains stability and remains basically unaltered over relatively long periods of time because, as shown in recent studies, the control of community affairs and policies resides in dominant interest groups which feel little incentive to disrupt the existing pattern of superordination and subordination. These groups exercise power[1] which is infinitely out of proportion to their number.

The mechanics of control by minority are clearly revealed in Floyd Hunter's work *Community Power Structure*.[2] Hunter examined the roles in community affairs and policy-making played by various cliques or "crowds" of leaders from the realms of business, finance, and industry. The power of these individuals and groups, he states, is effectively channeled through organizations, committees, and agencies which are concerned with community affairs —plans, projects, and policies.[3] Following his argument, this paper deals with the role played by executives of absentee-owned corporations in organized groups, such as associations, clubs, councils, and committees. Data were gathered between June, 1954, and May, 1955, through intensive interviews with fifty leading executives of

Reprinted by permission of publisher and authors from *The American Journal of Sociology*, Vol. LXI, No. 5, pp. 413–419 (March, 1956). Copyright © 1956 by the University of Chicago.
[1] "Power" is defined herein as the ability to direct and control the activities of others in the pursuit of goals which are established in accordance with a given set of social values.
[2] Floyd Hunter, *Community Power Structure: A Study of Decision-Makers* (Chapel Hill: University of North Carolina Press, 1953).
[3] Floyd Hunter, *Host Community and Air Force Base*, Air Force Base Project Technical Rept. No. 8, p. 5 (Maxwell A.F.B., Ala.: Research Institute, Human Resources, 1952).

the community and other persons who have worked with and observed corporation executives.

THE COMMUNITY SETTING

Bigtown, the nucleus of a southern metropolitan area of approximately 200,000 inhabitants, is a fictitious name for a rapidly growing city whose rise to economic prominence in the region and nation has been meteoric. Above all, its growth is a consequence of new industrial plants. The residents of Bigtown derive their livelihoods from a variety of sources, but the most vital elements in the economic structure of the city are a number of absentee-owned corporations which manufacture and process industrial products mainly for nonlocal consumption. The plants not only employ a large proportion of Bigtown's citizens and set the local wage pattern but make possible the existence of a multitude of smaller industrial and business concerns. The development of community facilities and services is in part dependent upon their financial contributions[4] and their cooperation in programs designed to improve the city. In short, they play a pre-eminent role in the dynamics of Bigtown life.

THE POWER STRUCTURE, CIVIC AFFAIRS, AND THE CORPORATION

American cities apparently vary considerably in the extent to which dominant interest groups are united effectively for coordinated control of community affairs. As Hunter describes the situation in Regional City, groups are drawn together through mutual interests and common values and are held together by strong leadership, which integrates their efforts.[5] The cliques or crowds "go along" with one another's projects in anticipation of future reciprocity.

The leaders of Bigtown, many of whom are of cosmopolitan backgrounds, tend to view this pattern of control as ideal. They dwell at great length upon the power structure of other cities in which they have resided, where an informal "Committee of 50," "Citizens' Council," or like group controls civic affairs with a firm hand. These glowing accounts are typically accompanied by a pes-

[4] Corporations not only pay taxes (directly and indirectly) but make outright gifts to community projects and collect contributions from their employees during various fund-raising "drives."
[5] *Community Power Structure*, Chap. iv.

simistic description of the situation in Bigtown. This community, as analyzed by some of its outstanding men, has a number of powerful interest groups but lacks effective liaison among them and leadership to unite them. Under these circumstances, a given "crowd" is unlikely to participate in a proposed project unless it foresees tangible gain.

This situation lends itself neither to effective community planning nor to adequate facilities and services for the citizenry. Many plans and projects are initiated by individuals and groups, but few indeed are carried through to fruition, either because of a lack of cooperation among powerful groups or negative reactions by one or more "crowds." The shortcomings of the city are popularly ascribed, however, not to power conflicts or apathy but to the rapid growth of the city and to the failings of its governmental officials.[6]

In the relative power vacuum which exists in Bigtown, community projects are usually doomed if they lack the approval of the industrial, absentee-owned corporations. There is no single crowd or clique of representatives of them, but their top executives communicate with one another informally and arrive at agreement on matters of policy. The executives of each corporation are then informed of the decision, making it possible for given community projects to be supported or vetoed through united action. Corporation support probably assures the success of a proposed project, while disapproval spells doom for it. Thus absentee-owned corporations are a decisive force in the power structure of Bigtown, since they constitute a balance of power among the competing interest groups of the community. On the other hand, as initiators of projects or policies, the corporations can ordinarily get support from a sufficient number of other enterprises to put across their goals.

Corporate participation in Bigtown's civic affairs has followed an intriguing pattern. While the interests of a corporation extend far beyond the local community and it is primarily concerned with furthering its own goals rather than those of cities in which its branches are located, there has been a tendency for absentee-owned

---

[6] The typical interviewee in this study described local government officials as relatively powerless figures who do not have the backing of influential groups but secured their positions through the support of working-class voters. Indeed, these officials were more often than not targets of ridicule for those who evaluated their positions in the power structure. Note the differences in roles between these officials and those of Regional City, where governmental figures are subservient to the dominant interest groups (see *ibid.*, p. 102). The relative lack of integration of Bigtown's interest groups makes it possible for governmental officials to sponsor civic projects which are sometimes successful, in spite of opposition from one or another of the "crowds." Interest groups find it difficult to express publicly opposition to projects which attract widespread public support. To do so would be "bad public relations," perhaps unprofitable in the long run.

corporations in the South to adopt local customs and practices, including a paternalistic attitude toward both their employees and the community.[7] The corporations of Bigtown have exhibited considerable interest in civic affairs, justifying their participation publicly in terms of "making this a better place for all of us to live." In past decades, of course, additional motivation for becoming community-conscious has been found in the corporation's concern for favorable taxation rates and good labor relations and for securing needed local facilities and services for its expanding enterprises. Thus a need for a favorable public conception of the corporation has been felt for a considerable period.

Recent changes in the region and nation, however, have also promoted the corporate concern with public sentiment. The threat posed by the gains of organized labor in the South has greatly stimulated the desire to develop and maintain a favorable public image as a weapon for use in labor-management controversy. There exists in Bigtown, as elsewhere in the nation, an almost incredible preoccupation with "public relations"—i.e., a constant and vociferous campaign designed to apprise the populace of the magnanimity and generosity of the corporations. Local media of communication constantly provide tangible evidence of corporate altruism in the form of statements concerning substantial financial contributions to civic projects and the heavy burdens of civic duties carried by top executives.

David Riesman has called attention to the emerging pattern of "conspicuous production" or "conspicuous corporate consumption," by means of which a corporation seeks prestige and plaudits for providing new employee benefits and services, luxurious buildings, machinery designed with aesthetic values in mind, and the like— much of which can hardly be justified economically.[8] In the same way, the corporations are contributing money and time to community projects as a favored means of creating and reinforcing a favorable public image of the corporation.

It must be strongly emphasized, however, that this active participation in civic affairs is motivated primarily by a desire to present the corporation to the citizenry in as favorable a light as possible and to maintain zealous guard over the corporation's interest and prerogatives. Not only does the corporation dictate the terms, but it decides what *social values* are to be implemented by its choice of projects and the policies followed by its agents. This is indeed

[7] Cf. Harriet L. Herring, "The Outside Employer in the Southern Industrial Pattern," *Social Forces*, 18:115–126 (October, 1939).

[8] "New Standards for Old: From Conspicuous Consumption to Conspicuous Production," in his *Individualism Reconsidered and Other Essays*, pp. 228–229 (Glencoe, Ill.: Free Press, 1954).

participation with a purpose, the purpose being a double one: to further corporate interests and to exercise control over civic affairs in order to preserve the values of a conservative, business-oriented ideology. This is clearly revealed by an analysis of the role of the corporation executive in civic affairs.

THE EXECUTIVE'S CIVIC PARTICIPATION

Extent and Types of Participation

The executives of Bigtown's absentee-owned corporations are discriminating in their choice of civic associations. The modal number of affiliations with local organizations per person is but two, as contrasted with a modal number of four organizational memberships for executives in all other types of industrial, business, and financial enterprises.[9] Citing the number of memberships, however, is likely to give a misleading impression of the influence of corporation executives in civic affairs. When the types of organizations to which they belong are analyzed, it is discovered that in 60 per cent of the cases they belong to *both* of the two most powerful organizations in the community.[10] These two are policy- and decision-making bodies that play a vital role in charting the course of Bigtown's plans and projects.

Conversely, the executives of the absentee-owned corporations are heavily under-represented in the less powerful organizations of the community. The restriction of their memberships primarily to

[9] In contrast, executives in absentee-owned corporations had twice as many memberships in state and national organizations as did the other executives (modal numbers, 2 and 1, respectively). These comparisons of local and non-local affiliations of the two groups may indicate the relative lack of dependence of the former upon the community for a livelihood, prestige, etc. The personal futures of the former group are much less tied in with the fortunes of Bigtown than are those of the latter.

[10] In 90 per cent of the cases, membership was held in at least one of these two top organizations. Executives from other types of enterprises were also well represented in the two organizations—42 per cent belonged to both, and 77 per cent to one or the other. Being from many enterprises, these persons outnumber the executives from absentee-owned corporations in these two organizations. It should be noted, however, that, because of the size and influence of the large absentee-owned corporations, each is allotted more memberships in these organizations than are given to smaller enterprises. Since there is agreement within the absentee-owned corporation as to policies and procedures to be followed by its executives, and since the interests of these corporations are generally not conflicting, their executives constitute an effective minority in dealing with the executives from other enterprises, which frequently represent conflicting interests.

the "elite" organizations not only shows a personal lack of interest in the lesser ones but means that the numerous youth, welfare, "uplift," fraternal, and other agencies are dependent upon others for support, direction, and sponsorship. A few of the top corporation executives participate in the work of these groups, primarily as members of boards of directors. They are especially likely to be found in organizations charged with the responsibility of disbursing large sums of money, since they are interested in the uses to which the money will be put. In general, however, the least influential organizations of Bigtown are forced to content themselves with membership from middle management and junior executive levels.[11]

The Assignment of Civic and Committee Memberships

Typically, the absentee-owned corporation in Bigtown has a list of executives eligible for membership in power-wielding civic organizations and for service on various "citizens' " committees and commissions created to plan for and supervise important special community projects. Community leaders generally expect the corporation to provide civic leadership commensurate with its size and influence; similarly, the corporation anticipates adequate representation in groups which chart the course of community affairs.

Almost without exception, the men chosen to represent the corporation are high-level executives with lengthy service. They have demonstrated time and again that they are familiar with corporation policies and that they can be relied upon to do a good job of representing the company and its interests. They will express opinions on any subject which indicate that they cherish the "proper" social values.

Executives are expected to belong to civic organizations and serve on committees as part of their jobs. The process by which an individual receives a committee assignment was described by an interviewee as follows:

Let's suppose that Mr. X, a community leader or government official, is lining up men to serve on an important new committee or commission.

[11] To his superiors, "excellent service" in these civic groups identifies the junior executive as responsible and clear-thinking. The young executive, in turn, may regard his civic duties as a means of demonstrating an ability to serve his employers in a higher capacity.

The assignment of junior executives to civic projects is discussed in Aileen D. Ross, "The Social Control of Philanthropy," *American Journal of Sociology*, 58:451–460 (March, 1953). This article provides keen insight into corporate participation in civic "drives" or "canvasses."

He will contact the top executive in a corporation, Mr. Y, and explain the situation to him. Mr. X will then ask Mr. Y to provide him with a certain number of men. Sometimes the two disagree concerning the number to be assigned. Mr. Y will demand more representation if he evaluates the matter as important to the corporation's interest or if it involves basic community policy. If he feels the matter relatively unimportant, he will try to cut down the number of men he has to assign. If Mr. X especially wants a specific executive, say Mr. Z, to serve on his committee, he might ask Mr. Y for him. Mr. Y may agree to this choice, or he may not. In any case, his decisions are the final ones. He can always justify denying the request by stating that Mr. Z is too busy.

Sometimes, if Mr. Z is widely known to have clearance for such activities from his superiors, Mr. X will contact him directly. In such a case, Mr. Z would O.K. the matter "upstairs" before committing himself.

If an executive is not on the "approved list," he is unlikely either to be given permission to serve or to absent himself from his job during working hours, even if he should volunteer. Interviewees emphasized that only if there were a great deal of "public pressure," would a man not on the list obtain clearance to serve.[12] Another interviewee, who is in a position to be well acquainted with the practices of his own corporation, put the matter this way:

Only a man who is naïve would accept invitations to participate in important community affairs without the blessings of Mr. A, the top executive in our company. For a man to ignore the usual procedures for getting clearance, he'd either have to be unconcerned about his career or else be a complete ass. In fact, in my company, *executives at any level have to clear all their organizational memberships with top management.*

Policy and Tactics

As an agent of his corporation, the executive is cautious in his public pronouncements. His superiors expect him to keep in mind company policies and interests, and he knows that he should emphasize at opportune moments a firm conviction that what is good for the corporation is good for the community. These expectations are not difficult to adhere to when he participates in organized groups, such as associations and clubs. The individual is informed ahead of time what the position of his company will be, and no decisions on his part are required. He merely has to proceed in accordance with predetermined policies and tactics.

---

[12] This "public pressure," the authors concluded, consists of demands for an individual's services after he had demonstrated at a lower level that he is either an unusually competent "idea man" or a workhorse.

It is through an examination of the executive's role in commit-tees and councils created for specific projects that we gain insight into the extent to which his behavior is conditioned by the expectations of his superiors. Prior to the first meeting of a given committee or other similar group, the executive usually receives a briefing from his superiors on the company's position in the matter involved. In committee meetings he listens carefully for sentiments expressed by others and then reports the proceedings to his com-pany. Thus his superiors are kept informed of what transpires, and he receives instructions as the project proceeds. If a committee unexpectedly seeks a vote on an issue which is not on the prepared agenda, the executive may plead for a recess in order to telephone for instructions. If the word must come from the national head office, he may seek a longer delay by suggesting "Let's sleep on it!"

In civic matters, as reworked, the corporation seeks not only to protect and foster its own interests but to promote a conservative, business-oriented ideology. The general procedure is for Bigtown's executives to state their opinions in such a manner as to imply that anyone holding different ones is stupid, uninformed, or possibly subversive. The implication is that all "right-thinkers" must believe as the executives do. Thus a dissenter would be forced into a defense not only of his social values but of his intelligence and his patriotism.

Executives are constantly on guard lest fellow committee members divert funds to new projects suggestive of the "welfare state." Advocates of such measures are speedily labeled "controver-sial" and, if they persist, are referred to as "cranks" or "subver-sives"—a term once used only for political traitors. Deviants of this nature are, in the long run, however, weeded out; they are not able to obtain appointments to other committees. An old-timer, involved in such measures scores of times during the previous thirty years observed:

We freeze out these New Dealers and other Reds. When we appoint people to important committee posts, we look at their record. If an indi-vidual has gone all out on some crazy idea, his goose is cooked. If I am chairman of a group that is making appointments, I go stone deaf when-ever someone suggests the name of one of these radicals. My hearing improves when a good, reliable person is mentioned as a possibility.

Said another informant:

It frequently happens in the course of a meeting that someone will call attention to the heavy burden of civic responsibilities that is being carried by a small proportion of the population. Someone will say, "My God, it's a shame that just a few of us have to do all the work. Why, this community is just full of talented people who could help a lot, if only they wouldn't shirk their civic duties."

At this point heads will nod vigorous assent, and comments along the same lines will be made by several persons. Then someone else will say, "Yes, all of this is true, but we have to select people we can depend on." Everybody agrees emphatically with this too, so the idea of enlarging the circle of policy-makers is dropped.

Thus a bow is made in the direction of what might be termed more democratic participation of the citizenry in policy-making. As Hunter has pointed out in the case of Regional City, however, community projects can be carried out successfully only if the small group of policy-makers can marshal the co-operation of large numbers of lower-level workers who will perform the labor required to transform the policies and decisions into reality.[13] When Bigtown's leaders speak of the desirability of increasing participation in community affairs, they are referring to their wish for more followers, not leaders.

The Individual's Motivation for Civic Participation

C. Wright Mills and Melville J. Ulmer have pointed out that the executive depends for his career advancement upon his superiors rather than upon local individuals or institutions, and hence he is much more concerned with the affairs of the corporation than he is with those of the community.[14] This correctly implies that his civic participation tends to be a by-product of his job and his desire for career advancement. In the modern corporation the executive role requires a considerable capacity for organizing and manipulating ideas, men, and materials. A demonstration of ability in civic matters may well lead a man's superiors to exploit his talents in the administration of the corporation's internal affairs. Moreover, in his work with influential people in civic organizations and committees, the individual acquires experience and contacts which contribute to his personal development. Hence the executive may, through his outside activities, gain promotion for himself within his own organization.

Top executives of Bigtown are afforded many opportunities for gaining publicity for themselves and their corporations. Not only are these men granted clearance for civic participation by

[13] *Community Power Structure,* p. 65.
[14] *Small Business and Civic Welfare: Report of the Smaller War Plants Corporation to the Special Committee To Study Problems of American Small Business,* Senate Doc. No. 135, 79th Cong., 2d Sess., p. 26 (Washington: Government Printing Office, 1946).

their superiors, but they are invited to join many civic organizations. It is even possible for an executive to migrate to Bigtown from outside the South and in a short time become known as an outstanding civic leader.

The junior executive, through his participation in the lower levels of civic organizations of less prestige and power, can likewise build a reputation in a hurry. This attention-getting activity is especially important for young men employed in corporations in which the individual tends to be just one of a large and "anonymous" mass of junior executives.

Thus the desire for advancement in his career motivates a man to play a part in civic affairs. It would be a mistake, however, to assume that executives are active in community affairs solely to promote their own careers or the interests of the corporation. Not only are there many reasons why men become concerned with the affairs of the community, but a given individual may have several reasons for his activities. Some executives, for example, seem quite concerned with the "sorry state" of community services in Bigtown and cherish an altruistic hope of contributing toward improvement.

It should be added that another motive for civic participation is emerging from the peculiar role which the corporation executive plays in modern society. As contrasted with the earlier elite of the capitalistic world, the business owner, the modern executive is not an entrepreneur. He manages his corporation, but he does not own it. He is usually not wealthy and cannot indulge in flagrant conspicuous consumption. Subject to control by his own superiors, he is not free and independent. This situation led several interviewees, both corporation and non-corporation men, to speculate on civic participation as a means of compensating for the executive's lack of real power. One of Bigtown's entrepreneurs, quite conscious of his own powerful position, made the following remarks:

> I've been observing these corporation executives in action for about thirty years. Two things about them have really impressed me. One is their frustrated desire to be free and independent—that is, to be able to make independent decisions and exercise personal power. The other thing is the lengths to which they will go to conceal from their subordinates and the public at large their subservience to their masters up above, either locally or in the corporation's national headquarters.
>
> The fact is that these fellows nurse a tremendous desire to be bigshot capitalists. But they are not, and they know it. Some of them try to hide this fact by holding a tight rein on their subordinates, using this means to demonstrate their power. Others try to further the impression that they are big shots by being hyperactive in community affairs.

Thus, lacking many of the satisfactions and powers of the entrepreneur, the corporation executive seeks means of displaying authority and independence which he knows to be functions of his position rather than his personal prerogatives. He may conceal his frustrations by playing to the hilt the role of entrepreneur, so long as his own superiors do not see fit to curtail his activities and restrict his powers.

This research report has focused upon the influence of absentee-owned corporations and their executives in the civic affairs of a single community; hence the extent to which the phenomena described and analyzed are typical of American cities must be determined by further comparative research. Future investigations may identify circumstances making for variation in the patterns of informal control in various types of urban environment.

It should be observed that this analysis of Bigtown's power structure has centered attention solely upon one interest group—the absentee-owned corporations. A broader investigation would examine the structures and functions of the multitude of other competing-cooperating factions which actively seek to influence policy-making in civic affairs.

Attention has also been concentrated in this study upon the role of executives in civic matters deemed important to those in control of the corporation and which are potentially controversial—i.e., matters involving decisions to be made in terms of goals and values. Happily, perhaps, not all community affairs are decided in an arena in which the combatants are hostile and competing interest groups. Some matters are resolved through quick consensus, since all agree on the desirability of certain goals.

Industry and Community Power Structure: A Comparative Study of an American and an English City

DELBERT C. MILLER

Indiana University

The role of business leaders[1] within a local community poses some challenging questions about the on-going processes of community decision making. Why do business leaders[2] take an active interest in community affairs? What is the extent of their influence in the community? How do they exercise this influence?

These questions have been asked by sociologists who have sought answers by conducting research on both the community[3]

From *American Sociological Review*, Vol. 23, No. 1, pp. 9–15 (February, 1958). This study is part of the comparative analysis of four world cities in Delbert C. Miller, *International Community Power Structures* (Indiana University Press, 1969). The four cities are Seattle, Washington; Bristol, England; Cordoba, Argentina; and Lima, Peru. Reprinted by permission of the author and the American Sociological Association.

[1] I am indebted for research assistance to Stuart D. Johnson, William Wilkinson, Esther Hirabayashi, and Anthony Baker, all of the University of Washington. Financial support by the Graduate School of the University of Washington is gratefully acknowledged. This report is one of a series describing tests of twelve hypotheses of community power structure in Pacific City (studied 1952–54; 1956–57) and English City (studied 1954–55). Other published work includes Delbert C. Miller, "The Seattle Business Leader," *Pacific North West Business*, 15:5–12 (February, 1956); and "The Prediction of Issue Outcome in Community Decision Making," Proceedings of the Pacific Sociological Society, *Research Studies of the State College of Washington*, 25:137–147 (June, 1957).

[2] Cf. Howard R. Bowen, *Social Responsibilities of the Businessman*, esp. Chapters 8 and 9 (New York: Harper and Bros., 1953); William H. Whyte, Jr., *Is Anybody Listening?*, Chapter 1 (New York: Simon and Schuster, 1952).

[3] Robert S. Lynd and Helen M. Lynd, *Middletown in Transition* (New York: Harcourt Brace, 1937); Floyd Hunter, *Community Power Structure* (Chapel Hill: University of North Carolina, 1954); James B. McKee, "Status and Power in the Industrial Community: A Comment on Drucker's Thesis," *American Journal of Sociology*, 58:364–370 (January, 1953); Roland J. Pellegrin and Charles H. Coates, "Absentee-owned Corporations and Community Power Structure," *American Journal of Sociology*, 61:413–417 (March, 1956); Don-

and the national level.[4] However, community power structure as a field of knowledge still has wide areas in which research data are lacking.[5]

The purpose of this paper is to describe and analyze the characteristics of decision makers in an American and an English city. It has been repeatedly asserted that business men (manufacturers, bankers, merchants, investment brokers, and large real estate holders) exert predominant influence in community decision making. This is the central hypothesis under test. Hunter has recently demonstrated this hypothesis in his study of a large regional city of southern United States.[6] This paper applies Hunter's basic methods to two cities of similar size and economic structure. The research design has been altered only to refine the conceptual framework and provide for more extensive data to test the hypothesis.

RESEARCH DESIGN

Two cities with similar economic, demographic, and educational characteristics were selected. "Pacific City" is located in the Pacific Northwest, U.S.A., "English City" in Southwestern England. Both are comparable in many features with Hunter's Southern City. All of the cities qualify under the Harris classification as "diversified types."[7] The following summary shows the close similarity of the three cities.

Southern Regional City in 1950 had a population of 331,000. It serves as the commercial, financial, and distributive center for the Southeastern section of the United States. It manufactures aircraft, textiles, and cotton waste products; is a transportation center of rail, air, bus, and truck lines; and is a center of education possessing a large university and many small colleges.

---

ald W. Olmsted, "Organizational Leadership and Social Structure in a Small City," *American Sociological Review*, 19:273–281 (June, 1954); Peter R. Rossi, J. L. Freeman, and James M. Shiften, *Politics and Education in Bay City* (forthcoming); Floyd Hunter, Ruth C. Schaffer, and Cecil G. Sheps, *Community Organization* (Chapel Hill: University of North Carolina Press, 1956).
[4] Robert S. Brady, *Business as a System of Power* (New York: Columbia University Press, 1939); C. Wright Mills, *White Collar, The American Middle Classes* (New York: Oxford University Press, 1951); C. W. Mills, *The Power Elite* (New York: Oxford University Press, 1956); Karl Mannheim, *Freedom, Power, and Democratic Planning* (New York: Oxford University Press, 1950).
[5] Ralph B. Spence, "Some Needed Research on Industry Within the Community," *The Journal of Educational Sociology*, 27:147 (December, 1953).
[6] Hunter, *op. cit.*, p. 113.
[7] Employment in manufacturing, wholesaling, and retailing is less than 60 percent, 20 percent, and 50 percent, respectively, of total employment in these activities. See Chauncey D. Harris, "A Functional Classification of Cities of the United States," *Geographical Review*, 22:86–89 (January, 1943).

Pacific City had a population of 468,000 in 1950. It is the commercial, financial, and distribution center for the Pacific Northwest. Major transportation lines are centered in the city and it has a fine port. The city is the largest educational center of the region, with a state university and many small colleges.

English City, also a regional city, serves as the commercial, financial, and distributive center of the West of England. Its population in 1950 was 444,000. The major manufacturers are airplanes, ships, beer, cigarettes, chocolate, machinery, and paper. It possesses an ocean port. The city houses a provincial (state) university and many private grammar schools.

The Community Power Structure[8] is composed of key influentials, top influentials, the community power complex, and those parts of the institutionalized power structure of the community that have come into play when activated by a community issue. When not active, the community power structure remains in a latent state. In this paper attention is centered upon the role of the top influentials and the key influentials as representative of a significant part of the community power structure.

The Top Influentials (T.I.) are persons from whom particular members are drawn into various systems of power relations according to the issue at stake.

The Key Influentials (K.I.) are the sociometric leaders among the top influentials.

Lists of leaders were secured from organizations and informants in nine institutional sectors: business and finance, education, religion, society and wealth, political and governmental organization, labor, independent professions, cultural (aesthetic) institutions, and social service. The initial lists included a total of 312 names in Pacific City and 278 in English City.

Ten expert panel raters were selected on the basis of the following qualifications: (1) knowledge of the leaders in one institutional sector with special thoroughness, (2) broad knowledge of the community, (3) many contacts with T.I. but not themselves K.I. Raters meeting these qualifications are commonly found among public relations officials, newspaper reporters, and some government officials. Raters were asked to designate each person as *most*

[8] Cf. Albert J. Reiss, Jr., "Some Logical and Methodological Problems in Community Research," *Social Forces*, 33:51–57 (October, 1954); Gordon W. Blackwell, "A Theoretical Framework for Sociological Research in Community Organization," *Social Forces*, 33:57–64 (October, 1954); Conrad W. Arensberg, "The Community Study Method," *American Journal of Sociology*, 60:109–124 (September, 1954). The theory and concepts used in this paper were developed jointly with William H. Form of Michigan State University.

influential, influential, or *less influential* on the specific criterion: "Person participates actively either in supporting or initiating policy decisions which have the most effect on the community." Those nominated most frequently as most influential were selected for interviewing.[9]

Personal interviews were held with a 50 per cent stratified random sample of 44 T.I. in Pacific City and 32 T.I. in English City. The sample had been stratified according to the nine institutional sectors enumerated above, and corresponding proportions of leaders from each sector were interviewed. During the interview each top influential was asked the following question: "If you were responsible for a major project which was before the community that required decision by a group of leaders—leaders that nearly everyone would accept—which ten on this list would you choose, regardless of whether they are known personally to you or not? Add other names if you wish."

Each respondent was asked to check a social acquaintance scale for each T.I. by don't know, heard of, know slightly, know well, know socially (exchange home visits). He was also asked to check each T.I. with whom he had worked on committees during the past two years.

The interview included questions on current issues, role played by respondent, persons and organizations that worked for and against issues. Ratings were also secured of influential organizations and associations in the community. The interview concluded with the question: "There are several crowds in (Pacific City) that work together and pretty much make the big decisions. Is this true or false?" The responses were probed.

A questionnaire was left with each respondent at the time of interview. The questionnaire called for background data, career history, business participation (other than own business), social, civic, and professional participation. These questionnaires were later collected through the mail or by a personal visit.

Newspaper accounts during the period of the study were used to record activities of T.I., committee appointments of T.I., activities of their wives, community issues, and interactions between institutions of the community.

Informants were interviewed to validate findings on clique behavior, and to describe activities of top influentials and the community power complex in the resolution of current issues.

[9] A valuable test of this technique has been conducted by Foskett and Hohle. See John M. Foskett and Raymond Hohle, "The Measurement of Influence in Community Affairs," *Research Studies of the State College of Washington,* 25:148–154 (June, 1957).

TEST OF THE HYPOTHESIS

Evidence for a test of the hypothesis that business men exert
a predominant influence in community decision making was
secured from three major sources: from *interviews*: (1) Degree
of sector representation based on panel selection of T.I., (2)
Sociometric rank of each T.I., (3) Committee participation
score of T.I.; from *questionnaires*: (1) Participation scores in
business, social, civic, and professional organizations of T.I.; from
newspapers: (1) Participation mentions (acts and opinions) of
T.I., (2) Current committee appointments of T.I. for community
activities.

In each of the three cities a panel of representative judges
from various institutional sectors designated the most influential
leader in the community. Table 15-1 shows the institutional affiliation of the T.I. selected by the panels in the three cities. Business
has the largest representation among the T.I., but there is a considerable spread over the other institutional sectors. A chi square
test applied to the frequency distribution in the three cities failed
to reveal any significant variation in the panel selections. However,

TABLE 15-1. TOP INFLUENTIALS BY INSTITUTIONAL AFFILIATION AS
SELECTED BY EXPERT CITIZEN PANELS

Institutional Affiliation	Pacific City (N=44)	English City (N=32)	Southern City (N=40)
	Per cent	Per cent	Per cent
Business	33	34	58
Labor	14	19	5
Education	10	9	5
Government	17	9	5
Independent professions*	12	13	15
Religion	7	9	0
Society and wealth	0	7	12
Social welfare and cultural leaders (combined)	7	0	0
Total	100	100	100

* Hunter says both of the lawyers in Southern City are corporation lawyers.
I have been inclined to clarify them as part of the business representation,
but I have not because they are lawyers of independent law firms. Lawyers
are classified under independent professions unless they were reported as
salaried employees in a business firm.

a different pattern emerged when the K.I. were selected by the T.I.
themselves.

The K.I. are a significant feature of any community power

structure for they are the sociometric leaders. The initiation and sanction of policy tends to be centered about them so that they may greatly influence the values which dominate in decision making. The K.I. are those persons who were most often chosen by the T.I. as the ten leaders they would want if they were responsible for a major project before the community and they were seeking leaders nearly everyone would accept.

The twelve influentials with the highest sociometric choice status are shown in Table 2 for the three cities. In Pacific City and Southern United States business representation predominates among the K.I. A comparison of the proportions of business representation within the T.I. (Table 15-1) and the business representa-

TABLE 15-2. KEY INFLUENTIALS AS SELECTED BY TOP INFLUENTIALS AND RANKED BY STATUS AS INFLUENTIAL POLICY MAKERS

Pacific City	English City	Southern City
1. Manufacturing executive	1. Labor party leader	1. Utilities executive
2. Wholesale owner and investor	2. University president	2. Transport executive
3. Mercantile executive	3. Manufacturing executive	3. Lawyer
4. Real estate owner —executive	4. Bishop, Church of England	4. Mayor
5. Business executive (woman)	5. Manufacturing executive	5. Manufacturing executive
6. College president	6. Citizen party leader	6. Utilities executive
7. Investment executive	7. University official	7. Manufacturer owner
8. Investment executive	8. Manufacturer owner	8. Mercantile executive
9. Bank executive— investor	9. Labor leader	9. Investment executive
10. Episcopalian bishop	10. Civic leader (woman)	10. Lawyer
11. Mayor (lawyer)	11. Lawyer	11. Mercantile executive
12. Lawyer	12. Society leader	12. Mercantile owner
Business representation: 67 per cent	Business representation: 25 per cent	Business representation: 75 per cent

tion within the K.I. (Table 15-2) reveals that the T.I. chose business men more frequently as K.I., in the two American cities.[10] In con-

[10] A test of the significance of the difference between the proportions of business representation in Pacific City showed that the difference was significant at the .02 level. No statistically significant difference was found for Southern City, although the direction toward increased business representation among its key influentials is indicated. If the two corporation lawyers were classified as business, the business representation would be 92 per cent, and a significant upward difference.

trast, English City retains a representation of business among its K.I. (25 per cent) that corresponds closely to the business representation among its T.I. (34 per cent). Moreover, English City reveals a more even representation from the various institutional sectors of the community among its K.I.

This marked difference between the American cities and English City raises questions about community organization. Why should two labor leaders be among the outstanding leaders in Eng-

TABLE 15-3. SPEARMAN RANK ORDER CORRELATIONS DERIVED FROM POLICY COMMITTEE CHOICE RANKINGS OF TOP INFLUENTIALS AND RANKING ON VARIOUS MEASURES OF COMMUNITY BEHAVIOR

Policy Committee Choice Rank Compared With:	Pacific City (N=44)	English City (N=32)
Committee appointments accepted during past two years, as shown by newspaper reports	.51	.43
Committee participation for two year period, as designated by T.I. on the interview schedule	.84	.67
Newspaper mentions of community activities and statements	.15	−.31
Participation in other businesses as owner or director	.53	.33
Participation in social clubs	.51	.47
Participation in civic organizations	.58	.43
Participation in professional organizations	.45	.34
Total social participation in business, social, civic, and professional organizations	.59	.48

lish City while not one labor leader appears among the key influentials of the two American cities? These and other questions will be explored later when the findings of further analysis have been presented.

Evidence for the influence of the K.I. was sought by establishing measures of actual behavior for all the T.I. These measures included the activity of T.I. in committee work as reported in the newspapers over a two year period, and by their own statements of committee participation. Likewise, we sought evidence of their activity as spokesmen in community life as reported by the newspapers. Participation scores were derived from adapted Chapin Social Participation scales for social, civic, professional, and other business affiliations.

Table 15-3 shows the Spearman rank-order correlations of the top influentials for these various forms of community behavior in Pacific City and English City. These correlations indicate that there is a definite correspondence between the policy committee choices designating K.I. and actual behavior patterns in both Pacific City and English City. The highest correlation is shown to be that between policy committee choice rank and the committee participation for a two year period as designated by the T.I. on the interview schedule. K.I. are very active in community affairs. However, this activity may not be reflected in newspaper accounts. There is no significant correlation in Pacific City between committee choice status and newspaper mentions of community activities; in English City there is a low negative correlation indicating that K.I. have received less newspaper publicity than T.I. This lack of publicity is in keeping with two features of civic activity as engaged in by K.I.: (1) much of their activity is policy making and is carried on quietly, and (2) there is a social convention that "key" leaders do not seek publicity. In England, a deliberate effort is made by some K.I. to keep their names from the newspaper as a role requirement of their social class. The similarities exhibited by K.I. in the two cities suggest that there are many common role patterns. The influentials participate widely in social, civic, and professional organizations. Based on his research contacts, the writer believes that key community leaders develop skills and influence that enable them to originate action for others. It would appear that such leaders could exchange positions with comparable influentials in other American or English cities and soon come to function effectively as K.I. in another community. However, marked differences may be discerned between Pacific City and English City. In general, there is more participation of all kinds by Pacific City K.I., and especially in other businesses. This is because the K.I. in Pacific City have a much higher business composition and because they rely more heavily on voluntary organizations for influence in community decision making.

CONCLUSION

Validity of the K.I. as identified is now assumed to be demonstrated with sufficient confidence to validate the hypothesis for Pacific City. Business men do exert a predominant influence in community decision making in Pacific City and Southern City. However, in English City the hypothesis is rejected. The K.I. come from a broad representation of the institutional sectors of community life. Why should this difference exist between the two American cities and the English city? Two major factors seem to explain much of this difference. The first is the difference in occupational prestige values between the United States and England. In contrast to the United States "the social status of industry in England, and so of its captains is low by comparison with the law, medicine, and the universities."[11] Top business managers are recruited from the universities (and upper-class families) where the tradition of a liberal education predominates, and this kind of education emphasizes humanistic values and minimizes the business orientation that characterizes the social climate of the typical American university campus. Many top business leaders, educated at Oxford and Cambridge, reported during interviews that they regarded business life as a very useful activity but did not view it as occupying the whole man. They expressed a respect for scholarly pursuits. Indeed, specialized courses in business administration in the University are very few, and the tradition continues that business management is learned by experience within the firm. This value system plays a role in the selection of community leaders in English City just as the larger emphasis and prestige of business leadership influences the selection of community leaders in the two American cities.

A second major factor is the structure of city government. In Pacific City the city council is composed of nine members elected at large on a non-partisan ballot. These nine members have the following occupational affiliations:

Newspaper owner-editor	Business
Merchant	Business
Merchant	Business
Newspaper owner-editor	Business
Merchant	Business
Merchant	Business
Housewife (formerly teacher)	Professional
Jeweler (and labor officer)	Skilled worker
Bus operator	Semi-skilled worker

A background of small business predominates. None of the council members was chosen as a top influential by our panel raters or by top influentials. There is every indication that the top community leaders do not regard the council as a strong center of community power. The council tends to make decisions on community issues after a relatively long period of debate and after power mobilization has taken place in the community. During this period such groups as the Chamber of Commerce, the Labor Council,

---

[11] Bosworth Monck, "How to Make a Captain of Industry," *The Listener*, p. 57 (January 13, 1955). Cf. C. J. Adcock and L. B. Brown, "Social Class and the Ranking of Occupations," *British Journal of Sociology*, 8:26–32 (March, 1957).

Municipal League, Parent-Teachers Association, and Council of Churches take stands. Council members may be approached and appeals made to them. Newspaper editors write articles. K.I. may make open declarations for or against the current issues and use their influence with the "right persons or groups." The mayor as administrative head and an elective official is both relatively powerful as patronage dispenser, and, at the same time, exposed to pressure from citizens to whom he may be indebted for his position either in the past or in the future.

In contrast to this pattern, English City has a city council composed of 112 members drawn from 28 wards. Each ward elects four members. When the council is organized, members are appointed to committees that meet once or twice a week. Issues that arise in any part of the community are quickly brought to the Council's attention. The city clerk is the administrative head of the city government. He is a civil servant appointed by the council on the basis of his administrative ability and serves under a requirement of impartiality as elections come and political parties change in power. The members of the Council are released by their employers from work at the time of meetings. They are paid a stipend by the local government for time lost from work and for any personal expenses incurred in attending meetings within or outside the city. Table 15-4 shows the occupational composition of 110 members (2 vacant seats) of English City Council in 1955.

TABLE 15-4. OCCUPATIONAL COMPOSITION OF ENGLISH CITY COUNCIL IN 1955

32 Per Cent Trade Union Members N=37	30 Per Cent Business Group Members N=33	37 Per Cent Other Community Sectors N=40
2 Foremen	4 Manufacturers	2 Solicitors
16 Skilled workers	7 Wholesale and	1 Doctor
5 Semi-skilled	retail owners	1 Dentist
workers	1 Cinema owner	1 Engineer
8 Clerical workers	4 Contractors	1 Accountant
4 Trade union	8 Company directors	1 Auctioneer
officials	and secretaries	1 Teacher
2 Unskilled workers	1 Bank official	2 Ministers
	8 Insurance officials	3 Political party organizing secretaries
		3 National government officials
		12 Housewives
		12 Retired workers

The council is composed of three major groups, trade union members (32 per cent), business members (30 per cent), and other community members (37 per cent). Five of the twelve K.I. of the community are members and play major roles in their respective parties. The council is the major arena of community decision. Issues reach it directly, are investigated by Council committees, and are decided upon by a vote taken in the full council. Community organizations play important roles in debating the issues, but these are definitely secondary or supplementary activities. The community value system condemns any pressure tactics on the Council as "bad taste." However, in the council a caucus of elected party leaders is held before any important vote and a position is taken by the leaders for the party. The "whip" is applied and members are expected to vote as instructed. Such action is rationalized as necessary for responsible party government.

Two factors, a different occupational prestige system and a different council-community power complex, seem to explain the variation in the composition of key influentials who come to power in Pacific City and English City.

The Significance of Membership in Associations

BASIL G. ZIMMER
Brown University
and
AMOS H. HAWLEY
University of North Carolina, Chapel Hill

Most studies of voluntary associations in American society have been limited to the frequency of memberships and the demographic characteristics of members.[1] Important as such studies are, they neglect suburbanization and its effect on membership as well as the social implications of membership.

Of the many questions posed by the deconcentration of the urban community, one of considerable importance concerns the effect of this increasingly widespread settlement on the participation of residents in community activities. One dimension of this is membership in formal associations.[2] In the absence of specific measures of distance, the question may be phrased as follows: Is there a substantial difference in the frequency of memberships in voluntary associations among residents of the central city and of fringe areas? If fringe residents have a significantly lower membership rate, it might be inferred that the continued spread of population beyond central-city limits will lead to a progressive anomie in community life. On the other hand, if fringe residents have a

Reprinted by permission of publisher and authors from *The American Journal of Sociology*, Vol. LXV, No. 2, pp. 196–201 (September, 1959). Copyright © 1959 by the University of Chicago.
[1] For a comprehensive review of the literature on formal organizations by demographic and other variables, see J. C. Scott, Jr., "Membership and Participation in Voluntary Associations," *American Sociological Review*, 22:315–326 (June, 1957).
[2] Differential participation in informal groups between central-city and fringe residents is not considered here, since the authors are concerned only with formal community structures. A low membership rate does not mean that residents live in isolation but only that they do not participate in the formal community structure.

higher frequency, it may mean that leadership in the civil life of the community is shifting or has shifted from the center to the outskirts. Some support for this is found in the study by Wright and Hyman, who report that "voluntary association participants are more involved civically than the nonmembers."[3]

A difference in membership rates between central-city and fringe residents might be expected. A higher-than-average rate could occur in the fringe as a consequence of its selectivity of young adults with education and income above those prevailing in the central city, since, as many studies have shown, these are the persons who have high membership rates. But membership rates may be lower in the fringe than in the central city. That could be a result of the recent rapid growth of suburbs and the lack of sufficient time for associations to have taken form; and, given the immature state of fringe settlement, distance may impose an effective barrier to participation in associations based in the central city. Further, it may be that the fringe is populated with young families whose adult members are preoccupied with domestic responsibilities and may seek relief in household-centered production and recreation.

If there is, indeed, an important difference in the behavior of central-city and fringe residents, this raises the question of what meaning, if any, does the difference have for the cohesiveness of the community as a whole? Cohesiveness, of course, may have many meanings. One of the most problematic forms of cohesiveness in the contemporary urban community resides in the governmental or political sphere. Governmental disunity is the last major obstacle to the establishment of an integrated, or at least a unified, community in the urbanized area in and about a large city. The persistence of that disunity in the face of all rational arguments to the contrary suggests that it has its roots in the local social structure or structures.

The formal associations of a community are one manifestation of social structure; thus these might well be probed for their bearing on governmental disunity. Is there a significant difference between central city and fringe in the frequencies with which residents of the respective areas are members of formal associations? Second, is membership in such associations systematically related to participation in other activities and to measures of resistance to governmental unification?

Concerning the first question, previous studies either fail to distinguish central-city and fringe populations relative to member-

[3] Charles R. Wright and Herbert H. Hyman, "Voluntary Association Memberships of American Adults: Evidence from National Sample Surveys," *American Sociological Review*, 23:293 (1958).

ship in associations or provide information on one segment of the total population without comparable information on the other.[4] A partial exception to this state of affairs appears in a recent paper reporting on a sample of the total national population[5]; but here, unfortunately, the part of the total sample that fell into fringe zones (rural non-farm in metropolitan counties) is so small that it probably is not representative. Similarly, on the second question the literature has little to say: there is, rather, a tacit assumption that membership has some kind of derivative importance.

This study treats the questions raised with data pertaining to a single urbanized area, that of Flint, Michigan. Flint offers a fairly severe test of the differential influence of place of residence on membership in associations. The area is relatively small and compact; hence distance is not a barrier of any great consequence. From the outer edge of the area to the city's center is not over six miles. Moreover, the local population is unusually homogeneous. While there are differences in the composition of the population as between central city and fringe, they are in no instance large. But these features, particularly the latter, also cast some doubt on the general applicability of the findings.

The Flint urban area is not unlike other large urban areas in the United States in the pattern of its growth and in respect to its political disunity. During the last intercensal period the central city increased by some 7 percent, while the four adjoining townships increased by 55 percent. Political disunity is evidenced by the fact that there are, in addition to the central city, four townships, two small municipalities, seventeen school districts, two special-service districts, and, of course, the county involved in the government of the area. This situation has remained relatively constant since 1920, despite the rapid spread over the outlying area of people and institutions whose activities are centered in the city. The question of governmental unification and the bearing that association membership has on it, therefore, is not an idle one.

The data were obtained from two surveys based on area samples. The first was conducted in the fringe area in the spring of 1957 and involved interviews with 413 heads of households; the second was completed in the fall of the same year in the central city and included interviews with 295 heads of households. The fringe survey was undertaken initially to investigate attitudes toward annexation. Many of the findings, however, proved difficult to interpret without comparative data. Consequently, the second survey

[4] Walter T. Martin, *The Rural-Urban Fringe: A Study of Adjustment to Residence Location* (Eugene, Ore.: Oregon University Press, 1953); Morris Axelrod, "Urban Structure and Social Participation," *American Sociological Review*, 21:13–18 (1956).
[5] Wright and Hyman, *op. cit.*, pp. 284–294.

was launched in the central city. For purposes of this research, formal association is defined as a formally constituted group that elects officers, holds regular meetings, and has an expressly stated program of activities. In applying the definition, certain exclusions were made, in order to secure data about only those with more or less voluntary membership. Thus the term "formal associations" will denote fraternal, veteran, business, professional, civic, service, and charitable organizations; excluded are labor unions, religious bodies, church-related groups, and parent-teacher associations.[6]

The first and most important finding is that place of residence in the urbanized area of Flint clearly differentiates the population relative to association membership. As may be observed in Table 16-1, more than two-fifths (43.1 percent) of the central-city respondents belong to formal associations, whereas less than one-fourth (24.7 per cent) of the fringe sample held such memberships: the difference has a chance occurrence of less than one in one million trials. It may be noted in passing that neither of the membership frequencies approximate the 63 percent frequency reported by Axelrod for the Detroit urbanized area as a whole.[7] The Flint percentages are also well below those reported by Wright and Hyman.[8] The explanation probably lies in the more restricted definition of associations employed in the present study. From the latter were excluded all casual and occasional associations, but these were included in the two other studies. Zimmer, however, employed a similar definition of formal associations in a study of a small urban area.[9] His finding of 41.0 percent for the area involved in his study, which extended beyond the city limits but did not include the whole urbanized area, exceeds the average for central city and fringe in the present study (32.4 percent). The disparity in this case may be an effect of differences in size and in the spread of socioeconomic variation in the representative populations, as well as of differences in the area covered.

The control of various demographic characteristics leaves the difference between central city and fringe relatively unaffected. One reversal of the difference may be noted in Table 16-2. That occurs in the skilled-worker class: skilled workers in the fringe have a higher frequency of membership than do their counterparts in the central city. The difference, however, is not significant.

[6] In a separate analysis on church participation by place of residence, a much lower participation rate was observed in the fringe area than in the central city. This difference was found not to be due to distance or demographic composition of the population. This is reported in Social Forces, 37:348–354 (1959).
[7] Axelrod, op. cit., p. 15.
[8] Wright and Hyman, op. cit., p. 290.
[9] Basil G. Zimmer, "Participation of Migrants in Urban Structures," American Sociological Review, 20:218–224 (1955).

TABLE 16-1. NUMBER AND PERCENT DISTRIBUTION OF MEMBERSHIP
IN ASSOCIATIONS BY PLACE OF RESIDENCE

Membership	Central City		Fringe	
	No.	Percent	No.	Percent
Belong	127	43.1	102	24.7
Not belong	165	55.9	296	71.7
No answer	3	1.0	15	3.6
Total	295	100.0	413	100.0

It is of interest to note that membership varies directly with
age in the central city but has no such relationship in the fringe. In
both areas, on the other hand, membership frequencies increase
with the number of years of education. Household heads with some
college education exceed all other fringe categories in their frequency of membership, though they rise above the central-city
average by a very small amount. The direct relationship is repeated
with income in the fringe, but not in the central city. However, in
the latter area the top-income group also has the highest membership. We cannot speak of the direction of relationship of associa-

TABLE 16-2. PROPORTIONS BELONGING TO ASSOCIATIONS BY DEMO-
GRAPHIC CHARACTERISTICS AND PLACE OF RESIDENCE

Demographic Characteristics	Central City	Fringe
Average*	43.1	24.7
Age:		
Under 35 years	35.8	26.8
35–49 years*	40.8	24.6
50 years and over*	51.9	26.4
Education:		
8 years or less	27.9	17.5
9–12 years*	38.0	29.3
13 years and over*	76.3	45.8
Income per week:		
Under $75	36.4	11.0
$75–$99	31.0	24.4
$100 and over*	54.7	35.1
Occupation:		
Proprietor and manager*	70.4	32.6
Clerical-sales*	60.0	29.0
Skilled	34.6	38.0
Other*	26.8	16.4
Not working*	53.1	29.2
Family composition:		
With children of school age*	43.3	23.5
Without children of school age	44.2	29.6

* Percent difference significant at .05 level.

tion memberships with occupation, since the principle involved in the conventional occupational classification is not clear. Still, a strong tendency for membership to decline through the white-collar classes and again through the blue-collar classes in both areas is to be noted. The high frequencies among heads of households who were not working are perhaps a function of their leisure time. Memberships are also more numerous in households without school-age children, especially in the fringe.

The close similarity in the patterns of variation of membership frequencies with demographic characteristics makes unlikely the possibility that radical differences in population composition may be responsible for the large difference between the average proportions of members in the central city and the fringe area. The application of a standardization procedure confirms that inference. Assuming that the fringe population had the same distribution by age, education, income, occupation, and family composition as the central-city population and that the specific membership rates observed in the fringe remained unchanged, the adjusted rates are as follows: age, 25.6; education, 29.8; income, 25.3; occupation, 26.4; family composition, 26.4. As previously noted, the actual membership rate in the fringe is 24.7. Thus, while in general the demographic composition of the fringe is slightly unfavorable to association membership, no one of the adjusted rates differs appreciably from the actual rate. The strongest effect is exerted by education, with which, it will be recalled, membership in associations is most closely associated. But the rate adjusted for differences in education distribution still differs significantly from the central-city rate.

TABLE 16-3. PERCENT OF HOUSEHOLD HEADS BELONGING TO ASSOCIATIONS BY RESIDENTIAL EXPERIENCE AND PLACE OF RESIDENCE

Residential Experience	Central City	Fringe
Average	43.1	24.7
Nativity status:		
Born in county: native	44.9	37.0†
Born elsewhere: migrant*	43.0	22.7†
Length of residence of migrants:		
10 years or less*	39.0	19.5
Over 10 years*	44.8	24.2
Local residential experience:		
Has lived in opposite place*	41.3	24.5
Has not lived in opposite place*	44.7	25.9

* City-fringe difference significant at .05 level.
† Within-area difference significant at .05 level.

There remains the possibility that the differential in frequency of membership in associations may depend upon familiarity with, or accommodation to, the local community. To permit a test of this, we have assumed that these qualities can be adequately represented by certain measures of residential experience, such as place of birth, length of residence in the county, and the experience of having lived in the opposite part of the urban area before settling in the present place of residence. The percentages of the sample who are members are shown, with these factors controlled (Table 16-3); the most notable finding is the relatively high incidence of membership among fringe residents born in the county. Place of residence, i.e., central city or fringe, appears to have little or no effect on association membership of persons born and raised in the locality. The numbers of such persons, however, are small, not exceeding one-fifth of the total. Among heads of households who were born elsewhere, frequency increases with years of residence in the county. But the differences between length of residence categories are too small for statistical significance. The effect of having moved or not having moved from city to fringe or from fringe to city is also too small to be dependable.

Life in the fringe is clearly not conducive to membership in formal associations, at least not to anything like the extent that obtains in the central city. An explanation of this is not at hand, though it has been observed not to be a consequence of population composition or differences in residential experience. We can inquire, however, into the importance of association membership. Does it have any bearing on other forms of participation in community affairs?

It is apparent that labor-union membership (Table 16-4) is not an encouragement to participation in formal associations in either the central city or the fringe. In both, the proportions among union members who belong to formal associations are below the average proportions for the respective samples. The possibility that association membership affects union membership has fewer degrees of freedom, of course, for the latter is governed largely by occupation and the closed shop. Needless to say, union membership is held mainly by persons whose social-economic characteristics fall in the middle and lower ranges of the scales (Table 16-2).

Weekly church attendance coincides with an above-average membership rate, particularly in the central city. In the other two church attendance categories, membership appears to be distributed in approximately the same way as in the population as a whole. Thus the relationship between the two variables is tenuous, especially in the suburbs.

Membership in associations is more closely related to election registration and to voting in either of the last two elections than would be expected on the basis of chance. Conversely, members are comparatively rare among persons who have not registered or voted recently. But non-voters in the central city are members about as frequently as are voters in the fringe.

In view of the evidence pointing toward a somewhat greater involvement in community affairs on the part of heads of house-

TABLE 16-4. PERCENT OF PARTICIPANTS IN VARIOUS FORMS OF COMMUNITY ACTIVITY WHO ARE MEMBERS OF ASSOCIATIONS BY PLACE OF RESIDENCE

Type of Community Participation	Central City	Fringe
Average	43.1	24.7
Labor-union membership:		
Belong	34.2†	24.2
Do not belong*	52.0†	28.8
Church attendance:		
Weekly*	51.7	27.8
Three or less times per month*	38.8	23.9
Seldom or never*	36.8	23.6
Election registration:		
Registered*	47.3†	28.6†
Not registered*	26.9†	10.9†
Voted in either of last two elections:		
Voted*	50.7†	28.6†
Not voted	26.2†	19.5†

* City-fringe difference significant at .05 level.
† Within-area difference significant at .05 level.

holds who belong to formal associations, does it follow that such people are more inclined to favor political or governmental unification than are nonmembers? The answer appears to be negative (Table 16-5). Association membership is considerably more frequent among respondents who believe that the size of government affects its operation than among those who do not. Central-city and fringe residents are similar in this respect. Nor are members numerous among those who think that a plurality of administrative units makes for inefficiency; the difference between percentages who are members among those giving "Yes" and "No" in answer is not statistically significant, however. Members in both residential areas are more disposed toward the opposite view.

A similar finding is yielded by this question: Have conditions in the fringe area reached a stage at which an expansion of governmental functions is needed? Willingness to pay higher taxes for improved public services shows the same pattern in the fringe, but a reversal in the central city. In the latter, those willing to pay higher taxes have a significantly higher frequency of membership than those opposed. It is of interest to note that, among residents opposed to a tax increase, membership does not differ by place of residence. Members of associations are relatively content with the status quo and relatively unaware of any compelling reason for making changes in the existing local government. The responses to a possible proposal for annexation are especially interesting: in the central city, membership does not affect opinion. Not so in the fringe, however: there only 14 per cent of the heads of households who favor annexation are members, while over 29 percent of those opposed belong to one or more associations.

In the Flint area and particulary in the fringe, it appears that formal associations recruit a membership which is unsympathetic to governmental unification, in application, if not in principle. There is even a suggestion that associations are the vehicles of

TABLE 16-5. PERCENT OF RESPONDENTS TO SELECTED QUESTIONS BEARING ON GOVERNMENTAL UNIFICATION WHO ARE MEMBERS OF ASSOCIATIONS, BY PLACE OF RESIDENCE

Attitudes Pertaining to Political Unification of Area	Central City	Fringe
Average	43.1	24.7
Does size of government adversely affect its operation?		
Yes	49.7*	32.2*
No	34.0*	14.8*
Is a number of government units less efficient than a single centralized authority?		
Yes	43.0	24.0
No	49.6	29.3
Have conditions reached a stage at which expansion of governmental functions is needed?		
Yes	43.0	24.2
No	46.8	29.1
Willingness to pay higher taxes for improved services		
Yes	53.0*	24.3
No	33.3*	29.8
Do you favor annexation of fringe to central city?		
Yes	43.1	14.2*
No	44.0	29.4*

* Within-area difference significant at .05 level.

opposition to that kind of cohesion in the community. In contrast, those who perceive important changes at work in the community and who are willing to adapt to them are comparatively inarticulate. At least, they have not availed themselves of organizations for voicing their opinions to the same extent as have the opponents of governmental change.

In any event, it is clear that in the Flint urbanized area there is an important difference as between the residents of central city and of fringe in the frequency with which they belong to one or more formal associations. Membership in formal associations, moreover, is of some consequence in the affairs of the community, particularly those having to do with the political unification of the area. Whether membership has a broader significance is open to conjecture, though the finding in this study is presumptive evidence that it has. It would seem advisable to pursue this type of investigation much further, not only into various aspects of community life but also into the possible effect of membership in different kinds of associations.

The Voluntary Associations of Negroes

NICHOLAS BABCHUK
University of Nebraska
and
RALPH V. THOMPSON
Donaldson Technical Institute,
Port of Spain, Trinidad

This report is concerned with the voluntary associations of Negroes.[1] It focuses on (a) the extent to which Negroes affiliate with formal voluntary associations and on (b) selected situational determinants and personal attributes (e.g., length of residence, family status, sex of subject, etc.) as these affect affiliation among Negroes.

Information in the literature dealing with the voluntary associations of Negroes appears contradictory. Myrdal suggests that Negroes have a relatively larger number of associations than whites and are more likely to belong to such associations. Furthermore, he notes, "This characteristic of the Negro community becomes even more striking when it is realized that generally upper- and middle-class people belong to more associations than do lower-class people. Thus, despite the fact that they are predominantly lower class, Negroes are more inclined to join associations than are whites; in this respect . . . , Negroes are 'exaggerated' Americans."[2] Drake and Cayton agree that Negroes organize large

From *American Sociological Review*, Vol. 27, No. 5, pp. 647–655 (October, 1962). Reprinted by permission of the authors and the American Sociological Association.
[1] For aid in drawing the sample, we are indebted to Richard Videbeck. Both he and Jerry Behringer of the University of Nebraska were most helpful in clarifying the present discussion.
[2] Gunnar Myrdal, Richard Sterner, and Arnold Rose, *An American Dilemma,* p. 952 (New York: Harper, 1944). As a part of a study on leisure, Lundberg, Komarovsky, and McInery found that Negroes residing in a poor suburban village were more likely to be affiliated with voluntary associations than whites. The investigators reported that the Negroes living in an adjacent wealthy suburban village were domestic servants who were not permitted to affiliate with any of the indigenous voluntary associations. However, these persons often were members of groups situated in the poor suburb. (The social-class background of the Negro participants was not treated in this study.) Thus, Myrdal's findings support this position. See George A. Lundberg, Mirra Komarovsky, and Mary A. McInery, *Leisure: A Suburban Study,* pp. 131–140 (New York: Columbia University Press, 1934).

numbers of formal voluntary associations but find that such asso-
citions are primarily middle-class and, to a lesser extent, upper-
class organizations.[3] They state that Negroes in the lower class
participate in very few formally organized activities (except those
of the church).[4] In their words: "Middle-class individuals are great
'joiners' and 'belongers,' and these [formal] organizations assume
a special importance in a community where family background is
not too important. ... At the lower-class level the church is almost
the only element of stable, organized life; but this is not true of the
middle class."[5] On the other hand, the positions of both Myrdal and
of Drake and Cayton are contradicted by information presented in
a study by Wright and Hyman, who, reporting from national
survey data, note that less than 50 per cent of the white families
and 63 per cent of the white adult respondents questioned belonged
to no associations compared with 60 per cent of the Negro families
and 73 per cent of the Negro adults.[6] These figures take on a special significance because they are derived from samples based on a
probability design.

The figures from the Wright and Hyman report require clarification. The data on families was from a 1953 National Opinion
Research Center Survey in which the memberships of all persons in
the family were included in the enumeration and in which union
membership was included as constituting membership in voluntary associations. On the other hand, the percentages reported on
individuals were from a 1955 NORC Survey in which only the associations of adults were taken into account and in which union membership was not counted. Wright and Hyman did not include
church membership as constituting membership in voluntary association and neither did Myrdal nor Drake and Cayton. However, it
is unclear whether Myrdal or Drake and Cayton took union membership into account. In the present inquiry, we excluded both
church and union affiliations.

On the grounds that the sampling procedure in the Wright and
Hyman report was the most rigorous and least likely to contain
bias, we expected to find that Negroes as a subgroup in our society
would be less likely to be affiliated with voluntary associations than
whites. Such an expectation seemed highly plausible because
Negroes tend to be over-represented in the lower social classes as
indicated by educational achievement, income, and occupational

[3] St. Clair Drake and Horace R. Cayton, *Black Metropolis*, pp. 526–715 *passim*
(New York: Harcourt, Brace, 1945).
[4] *Ibid.*, pp. 606–607.
[5] *Ibid.*, p. 669.
[6] Charles R. Wright and Herbert H. Hyman, "Voluntary Association Memberships of American Adults: Evidence from National Sample Surveys," *American Sociological Review*, 23:287 (June, 1958).

rank.[7] At the same time, however, we expected that the pattern of affiliation as it related to social class (i.e., the higher the social-class background the more likely that the person will be a member of a formal voluntary association) would be the same for Negroes as whites.

We assumed that selected situational determinants and correlates of membership found to be directly related to affiliation with associations would not reveal any systematic differences between Negroes and whites in the present inquiry. Specifically, we expected: (1) married persons more likely to be affiliated with associations than single persons; (2) persons who had resided in the community for the longest period of time more likely to be affiliated with associations; (3) home ownership to be positively associated with membership in formal voluntary groups; (4) religious affiliation to be positively associated with membership; (5) persons having a greater number of friends more likely to be members of voluntary associations than those having fewer friends; and (6) men more likely to be members of associations than women.[8]

[7] Extensive research has been carried out corroborating the relationship between social class and membership in voluntary associations. Several representative studies are: W. Lloyd Warner and Paul S. Lunt, *The Social Life of a Modern Community* (New Haven: Yale University Press, 1941); John M. Foskett, "Social Structure and Social Participation," *American Sociological Review*, 20:431–438 (August, 1955); John Scott, Jr., "Membership and Participation in Voluntary Associations," *American Sociological Review*, 22:315–326 (June, 1957); and Howard Freeman, Edwin Novak, and Leo Reeder, "Correlates of Membership in Voluntary Associations," *American Sociological Review*, 22:528–533 (October, 1957).

[8] We drew from numerous sources in proposing these hypotheses. In this respect, we were especially guided by the following studies: Walfred A. Anderson, "The Membership of Farmers in New York Organizations," *Agricultural Extension Service Bulletin 695* (Ithaca: Cornell University Press, 1938); Morris Axelrod, "Urban Structure and Social Participation," *American Sociological Review*, 21:13–18 (February, 1956); Wendell Bell and Maryanne T. Force, "Social Structure and Participation in Different Types of Formal Associations," *Social Forces*, 34:345–350 (May, 1956); Wendell Bell and Marion Boat, "Urban Neighborhoods and Informal Social Relations," *American Journal of Sociology*, 62:391–398 (January, 1957); Frederick A. Bushee, "Social Organization in a Small City," *American Journal of Sociology*, 51:217–226 (November, 1945); Howard E. Freeman, Edwin Novak, and Leo G. Reeder, *op. cit.*; Harold F. Kaufman, "Participation in Organized Activities in Selected Kentucky Locations," *Kentucky Agricultural Extension Service Bulletin 528* (Lexington: University of Kentucky Press, 1949); Mirra Komarovsky, "The Voluntary Associations of Urban Dwellers," *American Sociological Review*, 11:686–698 (December, 1946); William G. Mather, "Income and Social Participation," *American Sociological Review*, 6:380–384 (June, 1941); John Scott, Jr., *op. cit.*; Irving L. Webber, "The Organized Social Life of the Retired in Two Florida Communities," *American Journal of Sociology*, 59:340–346 (January, 1954); Charles R. Wright and Herbert H. Hyman, *op. cit.*; and Basil G. Zimmer, "Participation of Migrants in Urban Structures," *American Sociological Review*, 20:218–224 (April, 1955).

For the most part, studies on participation in voluntary associations (including both whites and Negroes) in which generalizations are derived from samples selected on a probability-design basis have tended to be in high agreement on factors associated with affiliation. The figures on extent of affiliation reported by Wright and Hyman (64 per cent of the respondents belonged to no associations), however, are somewhat lower than those reported in other studies. To illustrate, the Michigan Survey Research Center found that 37 per cent of all Detroit Area residents (1952) had no membership in any organization other than a church. Furthermore, apart from both churches and labor unions, 45 per cent of the population belonged to no organization.[9] Scott's figures for Bennington, Vermont (1947) showed 35.8 per cent of the persons in the sample held no membership other than a church.[10] The lower rate of affiliation in the Wright and Hyman study is probably explained by the inclusion in their sample of persons living in rural areas. The large amount of non-joining of rural inhabitants has been documented extensively.[11] Since the Wright and Hyman report is based on data derived from two national surveys, rural persons were presumably included in the samples. This fact might then account for part of the variance in the affiliation rate in their study as compared with the Michigan Survey Research Center's report on Detroit and Scott's report on Bennington.

METHOD AND DATA

The data for our study were collected from a universe of adult Negroes, 20 years and older, in Lincoln, Nebraska (population, 130,000) during February and March, 1960. A structured schedule was used. The community has five relatively distinct Negro areas. In addition there are many Negro families living at the Lincoln Air Force Base. A predetermined sample of 120 persons was selected from these areas on a prorated basis.[12] A survey was made of the areas from which the sample was to be drawn; in this survey an enumeration was made of all of the dwelling units and

[9] *A Social Profile of Detroit,* Report of the Detroit Area Study (Ann Arbor: University of Michigan Press, 1952).

[10] John Scott, Jr., *op cit.*

[11] Various studies by Anderson are especially pertinent. See, for example, Walfred A. Anderson, "The Family and Individual Social Participation," *American Sociological Review,* 18:420–424 (August, 1953).

[12] A fuller description of the community and other related data are presented in a separate study supervised by the senior author. They are summarized in: Ralph V. Thompson, "Voluntary Associations Among Negroes in Lincoln, Nebraska" (unpublished M.A. thesis, University of Nebraska, 1961).

households and such information was utilized in drawing the sample. The largest enclave of Negro population was found concentrated in a twelve square block area situated close to the central business district. We estimated that there were somewhat less than 3,000 Negroes living in the community. The sample design called for a random selection of blocks and a random selection of dwelling units within the blocks. Specific persons in the sample were chosen as follows: In those residences where both spouses were present, the husband was interviewed. On other occasions, the schedule was administered to any adult found to be in the household when there by himself. In cases where two or more couples were found residing in the same dwelling unit, the schedule was administered to the person (husband taking precedence over the wife) who owned or was responsible for renting the unit. We gave precedence to the male because many interviews were conducted during the day, a time which would unduly result in weighing our sample in the direction of women. Fortuitously, both sexes were equally represented in the final number.

The schedule was pretested prior to its use in the field. Refusal rates among persons contacted in the course of the survey were low; several persons refused to be interviewed and in several cases the respondents did not provide adequate information on all items on the schedule. All told, ten substitutes were used in arriving at the final total of the 120 persons who constituted the sample. Thus the response rate was over 92 per cent. This is high, especially in view of the generally depressed socio-economic status of the group.[13]

FINDINGS

Extent of Membership

Three out of every four persons interviewed were affiliated with one or more formal voluntary associations and were, in addition, members of a church. Eighty-seven and a half per cent of the

[13] In a study of participation in voluntary associations in four neighborhoods in San Francisco, Bell and Force had a response rate of 90.8 per cent in the high family and high economic status neighborhood and a response rate of 83.9 per cent in their low family and low-income status neighborhood. Greer, in a study of voluntary associations, had a response rate of about 85 per cent in two Los Angeles census tracts. See Wendell Bell and Maryanne T. Force, "Urban Neighborhood Types and Participation in Formal Associations," *American Sociological Review*, 21:27 (February, 1956); Scott Greer, "Urbanism Reconsidered: A Comparative Study of Local Areas in a Metropolis," *American Sociological Review*, 21:20 (February, 1956).

sample was affiliated with a church. These figures are higher than those reported in most previous studies. The 25 per cent Negroes in our study found to be nonaffiliated compares with other research (pertaining both to Negroes and whites) as follows: Wright and Hyman, 47 per cent of the families and 64 per cent of the respondents; the Detroit Area Study, 37 per cent; and Scott's study, 35.8 per cent. The hypothesis that Negroes belong to fewer associations than whites was not supported by the data. Indeed, the converse proved to be the case.

As noted, Wright and Hyman may have found a lower rate of affiliation because of their inclusion of rural inhabitants who are less likely to affiliate with organizations. The fact that Negro respondents were drawn as a part of two national samples and were widely dispersed in space and that they represented communities substantially different in racial and ethnic composition and in size may also have had a bearing on the conclusions reached.[14] Similar "group compositional effects" might be in operation in surveys limited to a city population when generalizations are made regarding members of a minority population.[15] Myrdal and Drake and Cayton, on the other hand, based their conclusions on the responses of persons representing a homogeneous racial population isolated in space. Thus, their sampling procedure and "group compositional effects" may both have contributed to the higher rate of affiliation they report.[16] These same conditions bear, of course, on the rate of affiliation we found in this study.

Social-Class Background

Three measures of social-class background were used: occupation, education, and family income. Occupations were classified into three categories, namely, non-manual, skilled, and unskilled. The non-manual category included persons in the professions, the business community, as well as those in clerical work. Thirty-six persons, or 30 per cent of the sample were in this group. Forty-four

[14] This has to do with the statistical principles involving individual correlations and ecological correlation. W. S. Robinson, "Ecological Correlations and the Behavior of Individuals," *American Sociological Review*, 15:351–357 (June, 1950).

[15] The rate of affiliation reported by Negroes living in Negro areas could differ substantially from the rates reported by Negroes living in mixed neighborhoods or as isolates in predominantly white areas. The effects of group composition are discussed in James A. Davis, Joe L. Spaeth, and Carolyn Huson, "Analysing Effects of Group Composition," *American Sociological Review*, 26:215–225 (April, 1961).

[16] Differential opportunity to affiliate is underscored in the study of Lundberg, Komarovsky, and McInery cited in footnote 2.

respondents, or 36.7 per cent of the sample, were skilled workers, and 40 respondents, or 33.3 per cent, were in the unskilled category. Married women (whether they were employed for wages or worked only in the home) were classified according to the occupations of their husbands. Eighty-one per cent in the non-manual category, 80 per cent of the skilled workers and 65 per cent of the unskilled were affiliated with one or more associations. There was a direct but slight relationship between occupational rank and multiple memberships. While the general direction of our finding was expected, the extent of affiliation of persons in the blue-collar occupations was much higher than we would have predicted. Both Komarovsky and Dodson, for example, found that only 40 per cent of the blue-collar white workers were affiliated with one or more associations.[17] This figure is also similar to one reported by Bell and Force for blue-collar workers when union membership is not counted as constituting membership in a voluntary group.[18]

Essentially the relationship revealed between occupation and membership in voluntary associations prevailed also for educational achievement and for family income. For example, 80 per cent of those with more than a high school education were affiliated with a voluntary group compared with 77 per cent of those with ten through twelve years of formal schooling and 67 per cent of those with less than ten years of formal school work. In summary, there was a direct positive relationship between occupational rank and educational achievement and family income and membership in voluntary groups.

Other Factors

Data for our Negro sample pertaining to factors suggested by other studies as being related to membership in associations included the relationship between membership in voluntary associations and (1) marital status, (2) residential mobility, (3) home ownership, (4) religious affiliation, (5) friendships, and (6) sex.

1. *Marital Status.* There were 96 married and 24 non-married persons in our sample. Seventy-six persons, or 79 per cent, of the married, but only 14 persons, or 58 per cent, of the non-married (the non-married included the divorced and widowed as well as single persons) were members of one or more associations. And while it was true that the married were more likely to be members of groups, we found that among those who were affiliated,

[17] Mirra Komarovsky, *op. cit.*, and Floyd Dodson, "Patterns of Voluntary Associations Among Urban Working-Class Families," *American Sociological Review*, 16:687–693 (October, 1951).
[18] Wendell Bell and Maryanne Force, *op. cit.*

a greater proportion (25 per cent) of the non-married belonged to four or more associations than the married (15 per cent). The longer the person had been married, the more likely it was that he would be affiliated with a group.

2. *Residential Mobility.* We divided one sample into three resident time periods: those who had lived in the community less than a year, those who had lived there one year but less than ten, and those who had lived in the community ten years or longer. On the basis of this division, the non-affiliated were respectively 10 out of 30 (33 per cent), 13 out of 50 (26 per cent), and 7 out of 40 (17.5 per cent). Only 7 per cent of those who had been in the community less than one year belonged to four or more groups. This compares with 20 per cent with four or more memberships for those who had been in the community for more than one year.

3. *Home Ownership.* Sixty per cent, or 72 respondents, were home owners. Holding socio-economic status constant, we did not find any appreciable difference between home owners and non-home owners in the matter of affiliation or non-affiliation. We found, however, that those who owned their homes were more likely to belong to four or more associations (21 per cent) than those who rented (10 per cent).

4. *Religious Affiliation.* One hundred and five persons in our sample were formally affiliated with religious organizations. We found, without exception, that every person in our sample affiliated with one or more associations was also affiliated with a church. Had affiliation with a church been counted as constituting membership in a voluntary organization, extent and number of affiliations for our sample would have been greatly expanded. The 12.5 per cent of our sample who were not religiously affiliated were also not members of any voluntary association.

5. *Friendships.* The evidence indicates that persons with many friends are more likely to be members of voluntary groups.[19] In our study, persons who claimed that they had six or more close friends were not only more likely to be members of voluntary groups but were more likely to have multiple memberships.

[19] Cf. Morris Axelrod, *op. cit.* In a study of informal relations in a homogeneous community, the investigators found that an extension of the social circle involved a net increase in social interaction. As number of families known increased, average intimacy reported increased; furthermore, there did not appear to be any "fund" or "lump" of sociability to be exhausted by expanding the number with whom one was intimate. See Theodore Caplow and Robert Forman, "Neighborhood Interaction in a Homogeneous Community," *American Sociological Review*, 15:357–366 (June, 1950). It is highly credible that persons with many friends would be more likely not only to be affiliated with associations but also to be affiliated with these same friends in common organizations. This point is supported in the study by Scott Greer, *op. cit.*

TABLE 17-1. DISTRIBUTION OF 120 NEGROES IN SAMPLE BY SELECTED
CHARACTERISTICS AND BY SPECIFIED NUMBER OF MEMBERSHIPS
IN VOLUNTARY ASSOCIATIONS

	Number of Memberships in Voluntary Associations			
	0	1–3	4 or more	Total
1. Marital Status				
Married	20	62	14	96
Not married	10	8	6	24
2. Residence in community				
Less than 1 year	10	18	2	30
1 year but less than 10	13	27	10	50
10 years or more	7	25	8	40
3. Home ownership				
Yes	18	39	15	72
No	12	31	5	48
4. Religious affiliation				
Affiliated	15	70	20	105
Not affiliated	15	0	0	15
5. Sex				
Male	12	36	12	60
Female	18	34	8	60
6. Number of intimate friends				
1–3	18	32	4	54
4 or 5	8	26	8	42
6 or more	4	12	8	24

Indeed, number of close personal friends, and marital status were the two variables found to be most closely associated with membership in voluntary groups. Forty-five per cent of those with fewer than four close personal friends, 19 per cent with four to six close personal friends, and 17 per cent of those having six or more close friends were not members of a single voluntary association. On the other hand, only 7 per cent of those with fewer than four close personal friends but 33 per cent of those with six close friends were associated with four or more voluntary groups.

6. *Sex.* As expected, more Negro males were affiliated with associations than females.[20] Also Negro males held more multiple

[20] Drake and Cayton suggest that women's clubs predominate in the Negro middle-class "society." Also, Lundberg, Komarovsky, and McInery suggest that Negro women may be as active in associations as men because they often play a central economic role in the structure of the Negro family. These two studies are among the few that imply that women might be members of organizations as frequently as or even more frequently than men. St. Clair Drake and Horace R. Cayton, *op. cit.*, p. 688, and George A. Lundberg, Mirra Komarovsky, and Mary A. McInery, *op. cit.*, p. 140.

memberships than females; 36 males and 34 females were members of one to three associations, and 12 males but only 8 females were members of four or more associations. In all, 80 per cent of the males and 70 per cent of the females were members of one or more voluntary associations. Data on the factors discussed above are presented in greater detail in Table 17-1.

SUMMARY AND DISCUSSION

Our findings strongly support Myrdal's thesis that American Negroes belong to a far greater number of formal voluntary associations than whites. We found this was true for Negroes at all social class levels when compared to their white counterparts, but it was especially true of lower-class Negroes. Indeed, two-thirds of the lower-class Negroes in our sample belonged to one or more voluntary associations. An even greater proportion of Negroes in the higher social classes were found to be affiliated. The proportions take on special importance because they do not include either church or union affiliation as constituting membership in voluntary organizations.

An analysis of the characteristics of the Negroes who are affiliated with voluntary associations showed them to be much like whites who are affiliated. A measure of difference, however, was the tendency of Negroes also to be affiliated with formal religious organizations to a far greater extent than is probably characteristic of the adult population as a whole. This will be discussed presently. The reasons for the widespread affiliative tendency of Negroes will be considered first.

Myrdal contends that the wide-spread participation of Negroes in voluntary associations is mainly pathological. He states that extent of participation, type of organization, and organizational achievement are all to be understood within this framework. First, Negroes create and are active in associations because they are not allowed to be active in much of the other organized life of American society. Second, the type of organization and the content of meetings that are popular in Negro circles follow a pattern which is a generation behind the general American pattern; the focus reveals the lag of the Negro adaptation to modern society. And third, (most) Negro associations accomplish so little in comparison to what their members set out to achieve by means of them.[21] To be sure, the Negro's position in American society has improved since Myrdal first proposed his framework. It might even be argued

[21] Gunnar Myrdal, *op. cit.*, pp. 952–954.

that Myrdal's thesis no longer applies, since the Negro has recently participated more directly in improving his lot through his own actions and organizations. But the evidence in our study would indicate that Myrdal's analysis is still applicable. For, while persons in our sample belonged to groups such as the National Association for the Advancement of Colored People, they were far more likely to belong to expressive associations (e.g., Birthday Club, North Side Squires, Saturday Nighters Society, Singspirational Male Chorus, Bowling Club, etc.) which, according to Myrdal's three qualifications, would be considered pathological and accomplish little. Expressive groups are, of course, non-utilitarian in nature. They exist to provide immediate gratification for the individual; as organizations they have little bearing on the normative order and are not likely to have much of an impact on nonmembers. Nor did the members join associations to achieve personal success. It seemed questionable that any significant proportion of Negroes joined the associations as a means of achieving business, political, or social success, although such motivation may have been characteristic of some of the middle-class Negroes in our sample.

A major current running through much of the literature on lower-class Negroes indicates that the extended kin group does not constitute much of a resource for fulfilling interpersonal satisfaction.[22] Yet, this resource is probably the major one for the lower-class white adult. Dodson, in this respect, found that although lower-class whites were not likely to affiliate with formal voluntary groups, they met with their kinsmen regularly.[23] On the other hand, ties among kin are looser in the lower-class Negro family, and visiting among members is probably irregular.[24] Consequently the structure of the Negro family (which does not provide a good resource for interpersonal satisfactions) may help to account for the greater affiliation and participation by Negroes in voluntary associations (and, quite possibly too, with formally organized religion). Even the pattern of friendships within the two racial groups lends support to such a thesis. Lower-class white

---

[22] This position is maintained by St. Clair Drake and Horace R. Cayton, op. cit., and is also voiced by Davis, Gardner, and Gardner. See Allison Davis, Burleigh B. Gardner, and Mary R. Gardner, Deep South, pp. 208–251 passim (Chicago: University of Chicago Press, 1941).

[23] Floyd Dodson, op. cit. Support for this view is also found in the work of Komarovsky, op. cit., Wendell Bell and Marion D. Boat, op. cit., and Scott Greer, op. cit.

[24] Marital instability, frequent common-law marriages, maternal family organization in the lower-class family, illegitimacy, desertion, overcrowded housing, etc., are all more characteristic of Negroes and bear directly on the structure of interpersonal relations in the Negro family. See St. Clair Drake and Horace R. Cayton, op. cit., pp. 564–599.

adults are more given to limiting associations to kinsmen, but the lower-class Negro adult enters freely into friendship and clique relations with non-kin.[25] Since there exists a general tendency for persons with friends to participate in voluntary organizations, this factor provides support for the proposition that lower-class Negroes will show higher rates of affiliation than lower-class whites.

Regarding participation, the rank and file Negro adult finds in his formal voluntary associations, in the same way that he finds in his church, release from his restrictive social environment. Negro individuals do not typically enjoy a degree of status recognition that is proportionate to their objective characteristics or achievement. Status recognition tends to be lacking for the Negro in general, but especially the lower-class Negro outside of the segregated setting. In contrast, the lower-class white has greater access to status claims afforded in the impersonal marketplace and also has higher class status and class-related attitudes that support him in the larger society. Such considerations help to explain why so much larger a proportion of lower-class Negroes affiliate with associations than lower-class whites.

There is no readily apparent explanation for the low rate of affiliation reported by Drake and Cayton for lower-class Negroes as compared with the rates in the Myrdal report or with our own findings. In fact, at one point in *Black Metropolis* Drake and Cayton present the social characteristics of 133 members of 13 typical female social clubs and in this particular presentation it is difficult to see where there is any difference in affiliation between women representing extremes in socio-economic status.[26] A factor, however, that may warrant closer examination regarding affiliation is migration. Migration appears to limit participation. To be sure, participation differences decrease in time as the migrant becomes familiar with the urban environment; low rates of affiliation are especially characteristic of farm migrants. (High status, however, tends to transcend even farm background in connection with joining groups.) Consequently in a given community rates of affiliation might vary considerably, depending upon the extent to which migrants (and especially farm migrants) are represented in a sample at a given time.[27] Such a factor as migration may have played a role in the conclusions reached by Drake and Cayton.

[25] This is brought out, for example, by Davis, Gardner, and Gardner, *op. cit.*, pp. 208–227.
[26] Drake and Cayton, *op. cit.*, p. 704.
[27] This discussion is suggested to us by the work of Basil G. Zimmer, *op. cit.*; also see Basil G. Zimmer, "Farm Background and Urban Participation," *American Journal of Sociology*, 6:470–475 (March, 1956).

The voluntary association functions in much the same way as the church to provide the Negro not only with an opportunity for self-expression and status recognition but also with an avenue to compete for prestige, to hold office, to exercise power and control, to win applause and acclaim.[28] The importance of the church for the Negro is reflected in the widespread membership that characterizes this subgroup. While it is estimated that about half of the Negro population of the United States are members of some church (usually segregated churches), it seems safe to assume that an even higher proportion of the Negro population feels a strong bond to a church as reflected by church attendance.[29] Lenski, reporting from a sample of the adult Negro population in Detroit, notes that nearly 40 per cent of his sample attended worship services every Sunday, and more than three quarters attended at least once a month. Few Negroes had completely divorced themselves from religious associations; only five per cent never went to church.[30] Furthermore, Lenski found that active churchgoers were also much more likely to be active in voluntary associations, although he found a lower rate of affiliation with associations for persons in his sample than we found in ours.[31] In our group, every person who was a member of a voluntary organization was also affiliated with a church. While it might be that the church and the voluntary association provide comparable avenues for achievement and satisfaction for the Negro, it would certainly be spurious to equate the church with other formal voluntary organizations.[32] It is hard to deny, however, that the recognition that the Negro is able to obtain from his church and voluntary associations is almost impossible for him to obtain in any other sphere. It is possible that for the whites the church serves a very different function from that of the voluntary association.

Our findings strongly support the thesis that affiliation patterns differ substantially between the two races. Our conclusions, however, require qualification. Other variables over which we were not able to exercise control may well have played a part in the con-

[28] Drake and Cayton, op cit., pp. 422–424.

[29] These estimates are reported by George E. Simpson and J. Milton Yinger, Racial and Cultural Minorities, revised edition, p. 574 (New York: Harpers, 1958).

[30] Gerhard Lenski, The Religious Factor, p. 37 (Garden City, New York: Doubleday and Company, 1961).

[31] Ibid., p. 226.

[32] Increasingly, sociologists who have been studying voluntary associations rightly have been reluctant to count religious organizations (church affiliation) as voluntary groups. Lenski presents an incisive rationale for the position that religious organizations are different from other voluntary formal organizations. Lenski, op. cit., pp. 17–19.

clusions we reached. Those that come to mind include size of community, region, ratio of Negroes to whites living in the community, and the residential stability of the Negro subgroup. To illustrate, only a small proportion of the population in the community studied was Negro, and this proportion has remained relatively stable over the past few years. Factors such as these might also help to account for the discrepancy that exists between our findings and those reported in other investigations.

Geographic Mobility and Extended Family Cohesion

EUGENE LITWAK
University of Michigan

This is the second of two companion papers,[1] both of which seek to demonstrate that *modified* extended family relations are consistent with democratic industrial society.[2] These papers, then, attempt to modify Parson's hypothesis that the isolated nuclear family is the only type which is functional for such a society.[3] Because Parsons so clearly relates his hypothesis to a more general theory of class and business organization there is considerable value in keeping his point of view in the forefront of discussion, for its modification under such circumstances provides rich intellectual dividends.

Parsons assumes only one kind of extended family relational pattern, the "classical" type exemplified in the Polish and Irish peasant families.[4] There is some evidence, however, for the exist-

From *American Sociological Review*, Vol. 25, No. 3, pp. 385–394 (June, 1960). Reprinted by permission of the author and the American Sociological Association.

[1] The author wishes to express his thanks to Glenn H. Beyer, Director of the Cornell Housing Research Center, for permitting use of the data in this study, and to Paul F. Lazarsfeld, Arthur R. Cohen, and Bernard Barber for their helpful comments, although they are not necessarily in agreement with the author's point of view.

[2] The first paper is Eugene Litwak, "Occupational Mobility and Extended Family Cohesion," *American Sociological Review*, 25:9–21 (February, 1960).

[3] Talcott Parsons, "The Social Structure of the Family," in Ruth N. Anshen (ed.), *The Family: Its Function and Destiny*, pp. 191–192 (New York: Harper, 1949).

[4] These families were marked by geographical propinquity, occupational integration, strict authority of extended family over nuclear family, and stress on extended rather than nuclear family relations.

ence of a modified[5] extended family that is theoretically more relevant and empirically more predictive than either of the two alternatives posed by Parsons' hypothesis—the isolated nuclear family and the classical extended family.[6] The present inquiry supplements the earlier paper by demonstrating that modified extended family relations can be maintained despite differential geographical mobility. The first part of this paper examines the assumptions underlying Parsons' point of view as well as the modification suggested herein. In the second part empirical evidence is presented to show that extended family identification can be maintained despite geographical mobility.

GEOGRAPHICAL MOBILITY AND EXTENDED FAMILY ANOMY

There are at least three arguments which support the view that extended family relations are not consistent with geographical mobility: (1) individuals who are strongly attached to their extended families will be reluctant to move even if better jobs are available elsewhere; (2) it is unlikely that identification with extended family will be retained where only one nuclear family moves while the rest of the extended family remains behind; and (3) it is financially more difficult to move a large family and locate jobs for many individuals simultaneously.

The first and third of these propositions suggest that individuals with extended family ties are unlikely to move. The second proposition suggests that if they do move individuals are unlikely to retain their extended family identification with those who remain behind. These arguments can be buttressed by the more general analysis of Homans, who points out that contact is one of the four major prerequisites for primary group cohesion.[7] Since these are familiar arguments they need not be elaborated.

---

[5] The modified extended family differs from past extended families in that it does not require geographical propinquity, occupational nepotism, or integration, and there are no strict authority relations, but equalitarian ones. Family relations differ from those of the isolated nuclear family in that significant aid is provided to nuclear families, although this aid has to do with standard of living (housing, illness, leisure pursuits) rather than occupational appointments or promotions.

[6] The counter hypothesis advanced in this paper is a modification of Parsons' position in that it accepts his analysis that the classical extended family is disfunctional for contemporary society, but it rejects his view that the isolated nuclear family is the only theoretically meaningful alternative.

[7] George C. Homans, *The Human Group*, p. 36 (New York: Harcourt, Brace, 1950).

GEOGRAPHICAL MOBILITY AND EXTENDED FAMILY COHESION

In this analysis, major attention is given to propositions which are contrary to those stated above, namely, the following: (1) individuals who are part of a modified extended family grouping are in a better position to move because the latter legitimizes such moves, and as a consequence provides economic, social, and psychological support; (2) extended family relations can be maintained over great geographical distances because modern advances in communication techniques have minimized the socially disruptive effects of geographic distance; and (3) financial difficulties of moving extended families in a bureaucratic industrialized society are minimized because family coalescence takes place when the family is at its peak earning capacity and when it is least likely to disrupt the industrial organization.

Modified Extended Families Aid Geographical Mobility

Implicit in the argument that extended family relations lead to a reluctance to move is the view that extended families cannot legitimize geographical mobility. If it can be demonstrated that in current society the contrary is the case, then it can also be shown that such families have far greater facilities than the isolated nuclear family for encouraging spatial movement.

Past instances of legitimation of such movement by the extended family help to clarify the point. In situations of economic or political catastrophe (the Irish potato famine or the Russian pogroms), the extended family encouraged mobility. Given this type of situation, the extended family had at least two advantages over the isolated nuclear family. First, its greater numbers permitted easier accumulation of capital to finance the trip of any given nuclear family. This led to a push-and-pull kind of migration, with the migrant sending money to help those who had remained behind. Secondly, because of its close ties and size the extended family had superior lines of communication. Thus the migrant became a communciation outpost for those who remained behind, providing information on jobs, housing, local social customs, and language. Those who had migrated earlier also could aid the newcomer at the most difficult point of migration.[8]

In a mature industrial society there is great institutional pressure on the extended family to legitimate differential geographical

Of the large literature on this point, see, e.g., Walter Firey, *Land Use in Central Boston*, pp. 184–186 (Cambridge: Harvard University Press, 1947).

mobility among its nuclear family members. This pressure derives from the fact that the extended family can never fully control the economic destiny of its nuclear sub-parts. Although the extended family provides important aid, the major source of economic support for the nuclear family must come from its own occupational success, which is based much more on merit than nepotism. As a consequence, if the extended family wants to see its member nuclear families become successful, it must accept one of the chief prerequisites to occupational success—geographical mobility.[9]

In other words, it is postulated that a semi-independent relation links the nuclear family to the extended family. Because the extended family cannot offer a complete guarantee of occupational success, it legitimates the moves of nuclear family members. On the other hand, receiving as it does significant aid in achieving many of its goals, the nuclear family retains its extended family connections despite geographical distance.

Extended Family Identification is Retained Despite Breaks in Face-to-Face Contact

There are two reasons why extended families can provide important supplements to nuclear family goal achievement despite geographical distance and therefore two reasons why extended family identification can be maintained despite breaks in face-to-face contact.[10] As noted above, the rapid development of techniques of communication has made it relatively easy for family members to keep contact despite great distances. Nor does distance, in a money economy, prevent or seriously hinder such aids to family members as help in times of illness, emergency loans or gifts, home purchase, and the like—all at long range.

[9] C. Wright Mills, C. Senior, and R. K. Goldsen, in the *Puerto Rican Journey*, p. 51 (New York: Harper, 1950), provide some indirect evidence on legitimation when they point out that the Puerto Rican migrant rarely moves out of a sense of economic necessity but because of a desire for economic betterment. They also show that these migrants rely on extended family communications before migrating (pp. 53–55). These facts illustrate that for the lowest income strata of migrants there has been a legitimation of geographical mobility for maximizing goals. This would seem to be doubly true of the middle-class migrant since he is economically better off to start with.

[10] In addition to these assumptions, two more general ones should be made. First, it is assumed (in counterdistinction to W. F. Ogburn, for example, in "The Changing Functions of the Family," *Selected Studies in Marriage and the Family*, pp. 74-75 [New York: Henry Holt, 1953],) that extended families have not lost their functions. See Litwak, *op. cit.* Secondly, it is assumed that extensive family activity does not lead to occupational nepotism (*ibid.*); but Parsons' hypothesis states that extended family structures will collapse, or nepotism will destroy the industrial order.

Geographical Coalescence Takes Place at Peaks
of Earning Power

Although the extended family encourages mobility when it is occupationally rewarding, it does not do so when such moves no longer bring rewards. Given the character of large-scale organizations, there are regular occasions when geographical mobility is not linked to occupational rewards, for example, when the individual is at the peak of his career. The career in the large organization is one in which the individual moves up until he retires. Careers of bureaucrats are rarely downward. Two aspects of this situation are particularly important in the present context: (1) once a person has advanced as far as he can occupationally his working efficiency is no longer tied to geographic moves; and (2) it is at this point that the nuclear family is in the best economic position to support moves of extended family. At this period of his life, the careerist can seek a position near his extended family if he can find a job which matches his present one. Or he can encourage retired parents to settle near him. In short, it is suggested that when the extended family does coalesce it does not lead to undue financial strain (trying to locate jobs for many people simultaneously), nor is it likely to mean an irrational distribution of labor since it involves either retired people or job exchanges between people on the same occupational level.

FINDINGS

In order to test alternative propositions about the relationship between family structure and geographical mobility, data from a survey of 920 white married women living in the Buffalo, New York, urban area were analyzed. The sample is biased in the direction of white, younger, middle-class, native-born individuals and as such is not representative of the total population.[11] However, the

[11] The field study was conducted in the Buffalo area between June and October, 1952. For details of the study and the sampling, see Glenn H. Beyer, Thomas W. Mackesey, and James E. Montgomery, *Houses are for People: A Study of Home Buyer Motivations* (Ithaca: Cornell University Housing Research Center, 1955). Some special features of the sample should be noted here. The sample cannot be considered to be a random one. Being a study designed to investigate housing, five or six different sampling procedures based on neighborhood and housing design were used. The varied nature of the sample complicates the problem of the appropriate statistical test. Therefore the argument must rest heavily on its theoretical plausibility and its consistency with other relevant studies. However, if the assumptions of a random area sample are made, and the sign and Wilcoxon signed-ranks tests are used, then all major findings are significant at the .05 level and beyond. The signs for these tests were always taken from the most complex table in which the given variables appeared.

bias is a useful one since this is the very group which should most likely illustrate Parsons' hypothesis.[12] If it can be shown that his hypothesis does not hold for this group, then it is unlikely to hold for any division of the society.

Mobility Reduces Extended Family Face-to-Face Contact

The common basis for the opposing views—that geographical mobility is or is not antithetical to extended family relations—should be made explicit so that it is not mistaken for the main issue. Both positions are in agreement that geographical mobility generally reduces extended family face-to-face contact. Of the respondents in this study, 52 per cent with relatives living in the city received one or more family visits a week. In contrast, only four per cent of those with no such nearby relatives received visits this frequently.

Breaks in Face-to-Face Contact Do Not Reduce Extended Family Identification

Central to the argument advanced in this paper is the view that geographical distance between relatives does not necessarily lead to a loss of extended family identification. In order to measure family orientation, all individuals were asked to respond to the following statements: (1) "Generally I like the whole family to spend evenings together." (2) "I want a house where family members can spend time together." (3) "I want a location which would make it easy for relatives to get together." (4) "I want a house with enough room for our parents to feel free to move in." These items formed a Guttman scale pattern.[13] Individuals who answered items 3 or 4 positively[14] were considered to be oriented toward the extended family. Those who answered items 1 or 2, but not 3 or 4, positively were considered to be nuclear family oriented. Those who

[12] Parsons, op. cit., pp. 180–181.
[13] Although these items were dichotomized to form a Guttman scale pattern, it is not argued that they meet all of the requirements for such a scale. See Eugene Litwak, *Primary Group Instruments of Social Control in Industrial Society: The Extended Family and the Neighborhood*, pp. 43–47 (unpublished Ph.D. thesis, Columbia University, 1958).
[14] The fact that only four per cent of the population answered item 4 positively means that item 3 defines extended family orientation for most of the population. In this connection, no assumption is made that this operational definition exhausts the meaning of extended family orientation; it is only assumed that it will correlate highly with any other measures of extended family orientation.

answered none[15] of the questions positively were classified as non-family oriented.

In order to measure the effects of distance between relatives on family identification, all respondents were divided into two categories, those who had relatives living in town and those who did not. The data presented in Table 18-1 indicate that geographical distance does not mean a loss of identity. Those who are geographically distant from their relatives are as likely as those who live nearby to retain their extended family identification (22 and 20 per cent, respectively).

Table 18-1 very likely underestimates the relationship between mobility and extended family identification, since there may have been many individuals who either moved to the community because their relatives lived there or encouraged relatives to come later. In such cases family identification would have been maintained ini-

TABLE 18-1. GEOGRAPHICAL DISTANCE DOES NOT LEAD TO A LOSS OF EXTENDED FAMILY IDENTIFICATION

	Percentage Extended Family Oriented	Percentage Nuclear Family Oriented	Percentage Non-Family Oriented	Total
Relatives living in town	20	52	28	100 (648)*
Relatives living out of town	22	58	20	100 (272)

* In this and the following tables the figures in parentheses indicate the population base for a given percentage. For tests of significance in these tables, see Footnote 11.

tially despite geographical distance. To deal with this question, all respondents again were divided, this time between those who spent their first 20 years in the city under study and those who were raised elsewhere. If the latter are considered to be migrants, it can be seen from Table 18-2 that the migrants (23 per cent) are more likely than the non-migrants (18 per cent) to be identified with their extended families.

[15] Because some people may have interpreted "family" to mean only extended family, it is possible that in this non-family oriented group there are some people who are nuclear family oriented. This, plus the fact that the items were dichotomized to maximize their scaling properties, suggests that little reliance should be placed on the absolute percentage of people exhibiting each value position but only on their differential distribution in various groups.

*Close Identification with Extended Family Does Not Prevent
Nuclear Families from Moving Away*

Are people who are close to their extended families likely to leave
them in order to advance themselves occupationally? To measure
the likelihood of persons moving from the community for occupational reasons, the respondents were asked the following question:
"Is there a good chance that your husband might take a job out of
town?" Those who answered "yes" were classified as potential
migrants. To test the likelihood of leaving their relatives, only respondents with relatives in town were examined. It can be seen
from table 18-3 that those individuals more closely identified with
the extended family also were more likely to leave the city and pre-
scmably their nearly relatives (23 and 14 per cent, respectively).
The same point can be made for the general population if the figures
from Tables 18-1 and 2 are calculated to show how likely family
oriented persons are to be migrants. Table 18-4 presents results
which are consistent with Table 18-3. People are likely to move,
then, even when they are strongly identified with their families,
and once having moved away from them, they are likely to retain
their family identity.

Bureaucratic Career and Extended Family Mobility

The analysis is thus far consistent with the view that in modern
bureaucratic society extended family relations can retain their viability despite differential rates of geographic mobility. To be fully
consistent, however, it should be shown that extended family movement is related to career development in the way anticipated by the
foregoing discussion. For it was pointed out that it is only when
the individual is on the upswing of his career that mobility will be
encouraged, while it will be discouraged when he reaches the peak.
   In order to measure career stages individuals were asked:
"Within the next ten years, do you expect the head of the household
will be making: a. a great deal more than now; b. somewhat more
than now; c. same as now; d. other, e.g., retired, don't know, etc."
Those who said that they expected to earn "a great deal more"
income were assumed to be on the upswing of their careers, those
who named "somewhat more" were assumed to be fast approaching
the peak, while all others were assumed to have reached the peak or
plateau of their careers.[16] Table 18-5 confirms the view that bureau-

[16] Since 95 per cent of the sample subjects were 45 or younger, and since the
study was conducted during a period of great prosperity, virtually no one
said he expected to earn less than now.

TABLE 18-2. MIGRANTS ARE NOT LESS EXTENDED FAMILY IDENTIFIED
THAN NON-MIGRANTS

	Percentage Extended Family Oriented	Percentage Nuclear Family Oriented	Percentage Non-Family Oriented	Total
Spent major part of first 20 years in city	18	51	31	100 (504)
Spent major part of first 20 years out of the city	23	56	21	100 (416)

cratic development is congenial to family movement when people are upwardly mobile: 39 per cent of those on the upswing were migrants.

Two additional bits of evidence supplement this point. First, if the hypothesis advanced in this paper is correct, the individuals who are both extended family oriented and rising in their careers should be most mobile because they have the advantage of aid from their extended families. Comparatively speaking, extended family identity should not lead to mobility when individuals have reached the career plateau. Table 18-6 suggests that this is the case. When individuals are moving ahead occupationally, those who are psychologically close to their families are much more mobile than those who dissociate themselves from their families (47 and 22 per cent, respectively, are mobile). In contrast, among people at the career peak, the extended family oriented are no more mobile than the non-family oriented (12 and 11 per cent, respectively).

The second bit of evidence which supports the view that extended family aid encourages mobility on the upswing of the career and discourages it otherwise involves the direction of the move. Individuals who have reached the career plateau *might possibly* still move if such moves meant bringing them closer to their extended family. To investigate this possibility, respondents were asked: "Compared to your last house is your present house closer, the same, or farther away from your family?" Table 18-7 shows that where individuals are climbing the ladder they are as likely, if not more likely, to move away from their relatives when they are identified with their extended families as when they are not (53 per cent as compared to 37 and 48 per cent). However, where individuals have reached the occupational plateau, those who are identified with their extended families are less likely to move away from them (38 per cent as compared to 62 and 53 per cent).

TABLE 18-3. STRONG IDENTIFICATION WITH RELATIVES DOES NOT
PREVENT PEOPLE FROM TAKING JOBS ELSEWHERE

	Among Those with Relatives in the City the Percentage Saying Good Chance Husband Will Take Job Out of Town
Extended family orientation	23 (128)
Nuclear family orientation	18 (336)
Non-family orientation	14 (184)

TABLE 18-4. PEOPLE IDENTIFIED WITH EXTENDED FAMILY ARE AS
LIKELY OR MORE LIKELY TO BE MIGRANTS THAN OTHERS

	Percentage Raised Out of Town	Percentage Having No Relatives in the City
Extended family oriented	51 (187)	32 (187)
Nuclear family oriented	47 (493)	31 (493)
Non-family oriented	37 (240)	23 (240)

In short, the evidence presented here indicates that the career strongly influences the extent and the direction of geographical mobility in a manner consistent with the view that extended family relations are viable in contemporary bureaucratic society.

Bureaucratic and Non-Bureaucratic Careers

This index of career, however, does not necessarily imply a *bureaucratic* career. Earlier discussions often assume that careers take place in a bureaucratic context. Therefore, the findings of this study should be further differentiated in terms of bureaucratic and non-bureaucratic occupations. In order to isolate the non-

TABLE 18-5. THOSE ON THE UPSWING OF THEIR CAREER ARE LIKELY
TO BE MIGRANTS

	Within the Next Ten Years	Percentage Without Relatives Living in the City
Upswing of career	Expect to make a great deal more than now	39 (183)
Medium point	Expect to make somewhat more than now	29 (603)
Peak of career or plateau	Expect to make the same or somewhat less than now	16 (134)

bureaucratic career, working-class persons whose fathers were also from a working-class occupational group were segregated from the rest of the population. Non-manual middle-class and upper-class individuals are more likely to follow bureaucratic careers, involving standard promotional steps associated with geographical mobility.[17]

TABLE 18-6. EXTENDED FAMILY IDENTIFICATION IS LIKELY TO ENCOURAGE GEOGRAPHICAL MOBILITY WHEN INDIVIDUALS ARE ON THE UPSWING OF THEIR CAREERS

| Within the Next Ten Years | | Percentage Having no Relatives in the City | | |
		Extended Family Oriented	Nuclear Family Oriented	Non-Family Oriented
Upswing of career	Expect to make a great deal more than now	47 (49)*	40 (107)	22 (27)
Medium point of career	Expect to make somewhat more than now	30 (112)	31 (322)	27 (169)
Peak or plateau of career	Expect to make the same or less than now	12 (26)	22 (63)	11 (45)

* This cell reads as follows: 47 per cent of the 49 people who are extended family oriented and who expect to make a great deal more in the future have no relatives in the city.

[17] On the basis of the U.S. Census's occupational categories, the husband and the husband's father were classified into: (1) professional, technical, and kindred, and managers, officials, and proprietors; (2) clerical and kindred workers, and sales workers; or (3) all others except farmers or farm help. Husbands' and husbands' fathers' occupations were cross-classified to provide four occupational categories: (1) upper-class husbands whose parents were upper-class; (2) husbands whose parents were from a higher occupational group; (3) husbands whose parents were from a lower occupational group; (4) working-class husbands whose parents were working-class. Two groups were eliminated: all individuals of farm background, and middle-class individuals of middle-class parentage (excluded because of the small number of cases). The stationary upper-class group is considered to approximate most closely the bureaucratic occupations, while the stationary manual groups are assumed to be the polar opposite. Here "upper-class" does not refer to an old-line "aristocracy" but to a professional-managerial occupational grouping. By definition, all people in administrative positions in large-scale organizations and professionals are included in the upper-class or upwardly mobile occupational groups. There remains the question of whether or not they constitute a sufficiently large number within the overall classification to give a distinct direction. Gold and Slater in a study based upon a random sample of the Detroit area point out that in the one category roughly similar in age and occupation to the "upper-class" in this investigation, 74 per cent of the individuals were members of a bureaucratic organization. Martin Gold and Carol Slater, "Office, Factory, Store—and Family: A Study of Integration Setting," *American Sociological Review*, 23:66,69 (February, 1958).

In contrast, these features do not necessarily mark occupational advancement among manual workers. In this group occupational success may mean the achievement of plant seniority or the opening of a small business.[18] In such cases success is negatively

TABLE 18-7. EXTENDED FAMILY IDENTIFICATION IS LIKELY TO ENCOURAGE MOVES* AWAY FROM THE EXTENDED FAMILY WHEN PEOPLE ARE ON THE UPSWING OF THEIR CAREERS

| | Percentage Whose Last Move Carried Them Farther from Their Families | | |
	Extended Family Oriented	Nuclear Family Oriented	Non-Family Oriented
Expect to make a great deal more in 10 years	53 (49)**	37 (67)	48 (27)
Expect to make somewhat more	52 (112)	56 (322)	59 (169)
Expect to make the same or less	38 (26)	62 (63)	53 (45)

* Those with relatives in the city were classified together with those without relatives, since the same statistical pattern occurred in each case.
** This figure reads 53 per cent of 49 people who were extended family oriented and who expected to earn a great deal more in the next ten years moved farther away from their families.

TABLE 18-8. ONLY AMONG UPPER- AND MIDDLE-CLASS BUREAUCRATIC OCCUPATIONS DO CAREER LINES PLAY A ROLE

| | | Percentage Having No Relatives in the City | | | |
Within the Next Ten Years		Stationary Upper-Class *	Upwardly Mobile	Downwardly Mobile	Stationary Manual Workers
Upswing of career	Expect to make a great deal more than now	43 (76)**	39 (72)	40 (25)	10 (10)
Medium point of career	Expect to make somewhat more than now	42 (146)	39 (183)	26 (99)	11 (176)
Peak or plateau of career	Expect to make the same or less than now	23 (26)	13 (32)	28 (18)	12 (58)

* For a definition of occupational classification, see footnote 18.
** This cell should read as follows: 43 percent of the 76 people who were stationary upper-class and who had high expectations of future economic improvement had no relatives in the city.

[18] See, e.g., Seymour Martin Lipset and Reinhard Bendix, "Social Mobility and Occupational Career Patterns," in Bendix and Lipset, ed., Class, Status and Power, pp. 457–459 (Glencoe, Ill.: Free Press, 1953).

related to future geographic mobility. As a consequence, a manual worker who envisions an upswing in his career may encourage family members to settle nearby because future success is closely linked to present location. Thus, it is expected that occupational advance has far different meanings for members of the working class and for the middle- and upper-class persons.

In Table 18-8 it can be seen that the only instances of upswings in careers leading to geographic mobility occur among members of the upper class (43 per cent of those who are on the upswing have no relatives in the community compared to 23 per cent of those who have achieved a plateau). For members of the stationary working class, occupational advancement is least likely, comparatively speaking, to result in geographical mobility (10 per cent of those on the upswing and 12 per cent of those on the plateau have relatives in the city).

Table 18-8 more than any other should indicate the limitations of the present hypothesis. The latter cannot claim to explain any major features of current American society but only the behavior of members of that group which is often thought to be prototypical of future American society—those belonging to bureaucratic occupations. It is assumed here that future societies will in fact become increasingly bureaucratized. Since Parsons' analysis is largely concerned with this same group,[19] it is maintained that this study provides evidence contrary to his hypothesis.

The Extended Family and Emotional, Social, and Economic Aid

Extended families have a unique function in providing aid to those who are moving. This is based partly on the fact that family membership is defined in terms of blood ties and therefore is least pervious to changes in social contact, and partly on the fact that the individual receives his earliest and crucial socialization with people who eventually become extended family members. The individual might find voluntary associations of lesser help than family aid because new personal contacts must be established when one moves, and old contacts tend to have no continuing meaning when geographical contact is broken. Aid from neighbors has somewhat the same character. This point emerges clearly when newcomers to a neighborhood are compared with long-term residents in terms of the average amount of social participation in various areas of life. Table 18-9 shows that family contacts are as likely, if not more likely, to occur among newcomers than among long-term residents. In contrast, neighborhood and club affiliations are likely to increase

[19] Parsons, op. cit., pp. 180–181.

the longer individuals live in the neighborhood.[20] This suggests the unique function of the extended family during the moving crisis.

TABLE 18-9. THE EXTENDED FAMILY MEETS THE NEEDS OF RECENT MOVERS[a]

	Percentage Receiving Frequent Family Visits [b]	Percentage Belonging to More Than One Club [c]	Percentage Knowing Five or More Neighbors [d]	Total Population
	Respondents Having No Relatives in the City			
Newcomers	22	25	38	110
Long-term residents	16	51	63	166
Difference	06	—26	—25	
	Respondents Having Relatives in the City			
Newcomers	54	44	41	163
Long-term residents	49	43	60	485
Difference	05	01	—19	

[a] The respondents were divided between the newcomers, or those people who had lived in their houses nine months or less, and the long-term residents, or all others.
[b] When no relatives in the city a frequent visit is defined as one or more family visits a month—either invited or noninvited. When relatives live in the city a frequent visit is defined as one or more family visits a week.
[c] This is the closest approximation to the average number of clubs to which the population belonged.
[d] This is the closest approximation to the average number of neighbors the respondents knew well enough to call on.

SECONDARY EVIDENCE

The evidence presented above consistently documents the position that extended family relations are not antithetical to geographical mobility in bureaucratic industrialized society. In fact, at times such relationships actually encourage mobility. The limits of the sample, however, place severe restrictions on the general application of these data. It is of some importance, therefore, to seek in other researches supportive evidence for extended family viability.

First, as a necessary but not sufficient condition, it should be shown that extended family relations are fairly extensive in Ameri-

[20] The striking differences between respondents with relatives living in the city and those without nearby relatives, shown in Table 9, are discussed in an unpublished paper, Eugene Litwak, "Voluntary Associations and Primary Group Development in Industrial Society."

can society today. In recent years, four studies that provide data on extended family visiting have been carried out, respectively, in Los Angeles, Detroit, San Francisco, and Buffalo. Three of these indicate that close to 50 per cent of the residents make one or more such visits a week. And three of the four investigations, on the basis of comparisons of family, neighbors, friends, and voluntary associations, conclude that the family relationships were either the most frequent or the most vital. These findings, as limited as they are, strongly suggest that extended family relations are extensive.[21]

What is of even greater interest is that these studies indicate that middle-class white persons share this viability with others and that these relations are highly important ones. Thus Sussman, in a study of middle-class white Protestant families, shows that 80 per cent of the family relationships studied involved giving aid, and in 70 per cent of the cases respondents felt that the recipients would suffer loss of status if the aid were not continued. Moreover, this aid had much more to do with standard of living than with locating jobs or helping people to advance in them through nepotism.[22] This investigation was supplemented by a study by Bell and Boat which indicates that 76 per cent of the low-income and 84 per cent of the high-income subjects could count on extended family aid in cases of illness lasting a month or longer; they also report that 90 per cent of the respondents indicated that at least one member of the extended family was a close friend.[23] Studies on working-class families,[24] Puerto Rican families,[25] Negro families,[26] and Italian families[27] indicate that extended family relations in these cases are viable and warm.

Although these relations are of a far different character from the middle-class family contacts discussed in this paper,[28] the studies of working-class and ethnic groups do provide insight into the

[21] Morris Axelrod, "Urban Structure and Social Participation," *American Sociological Review*, 21:13–18 (February, 1956); Wendell Bell and Marion D. Boat, "Urban Neighborhoods and Informal Social Relations," *American Journal of Sociology*, 62:391–398 (January, 1957); Scott Greer, "Urbanism Reconsidered," *American Sociological Review*, 21:22 (February, 1956); Litwak, *Primary Group Instruments . . .* , *op. cit.*, p. 82.

[22] Marvin B. Sussman, "The Help Pattern in Middle Class Family," *American Sociological Review*, 18:22–28 *passim* (February, 1953).

[23] Bell and Boat, *op. cit.*, p. 396.

[24] Michael Young and Peter Willmott, *Family and Kinship in East London*, pp. 159–166 (London: Routledge and Kegan Paul, 1957).

[25] Mills, Senior, and Goldsen, *op. cit.*, pp. 115, 117.

[26] E. Franklin Frazier, "The Impact of Urban Civilization upon Negro Family Life," P. K. Hatt and A. S. Reiss, Jr. (ed.), *Cities and Societies: The Revised Reader in Urban Sociology*, pp. 495–496 (Glencoe, Ill.: Free Press, 1957).

[27] Firey, *op. cit.*, pp. 184–186.

[28] Cf. Litwak, "Occupational Mobility and Extended Family Cohesion," *op. cit.*

extension and warmth of extended family relations in all strata of contemporary society. They do not by themselves refute Parsons' formulation, because he assumes that extended family relations are declining, not that they have disappeared. However, they buttress the alternative hypothesis advanced here, because they do suggest a basic prerequisite of that hypothesis, namely, that extended family relations are viable in contemporary urban society.

CONCLUSIONS

It is argued, then, that these relations can retain their social significance under industrial bureaucratic pressures for geographical mobility. Evidence has been presented that is inconsistent with Parsons' hypothesis. Two theoretical points support this contrary view: first, that the extended family relationship which does not demand geographical propinquity (not examined by Parsons) is a significant form of social behavior; second, that theoretically the most efficient organization combines the ability of large-scale bureaucracy to handle uniform situations with the primary group's ability to deal with idiosyncratic situations. These two theoretical points suggest that there is both a need and a capacity for extended families to exist in modern society.

The data presented here (and in the earlier companion paper) demonstrate that persons separated from their families retained their extended family orientation; those with close family identification were as likely, if not more likely, to leave their family for occupational reasons; those on the upswing of their careers were apt to move away from their families and to receive family support; those on the career plateau were not likely to move or to move toward their family; that considerations of this kind hold only for bureaucratic occupations; and that the modified extended family seems to be uniquely suited to provide succor during periods of movement. These findings suggest interesting questions for future research. With respect to the family system, there is a need to isolate the mechanisms by which the nuclear family retains its semi-independence while receiving aid from the extended family.[29] It is also important to specify in greater detail the limits of the modified extended family organization in terms of time (does it extend over two or three generations?) and social distance (is it limited, for example, to parents and married children or siblings?). Concerning

[29] Cf. Eugene Litwak, "The Use of Extended Family Groups in the Achievement of Social Goals: Some Policy Implications," *Social Problems* (forthcoming).

the occupational system, it is important to identify the type of bureaucratic structure which permits the family to be linked with occupations without affecting productivity.[30] For the analysis of class structure, the question arises as to how likely it is that extended family relations become significant factors blurring class identification without reducing occupational mobility.

[30] Cf. Litwak, "Occupational Mobility and Extended Family Cohesion," *op. cit.;* and *Primary Group Instruments* . . . , *op. cit.,* pp. 6–30.

Urbanism, Ethnicity, and Extended Familism

ROBERT F. WINCH
SCOTT A. GREER
Northwestern University

FAMILISM AND THE URBAN-RURAL CONTINUUM

There was a time when it seemed that everyone knew—or at least we sociologists knew—that there were in our country a rural family form and an urban family form. According to that view the rural family was large, highly functional, and had much interaction with extended kin. We also knew that the urban family was small, showed few, if any, functions, and was adrift in a sea of urban anonymity with the result that it was thought to have no contact with kinsmen and thus to be a detached social system. Furthermore, since we also knew that our society was rapidly becoming urban, it followed that the family was rapidly becoming small, detached, and functionless.

The general explanation for rural-urban differences in familial form was, simply, the better fit between a small nuclear family and a society that was mobile and individually oriented. In such a society, so the argument ran, commitment to extended kin restricted mobility; at the same time, the increasing development of formal, commercial enterprises for various goods and services replaced the kin group as a source of exchange and security. And with the increasing socioeconomic status of the population, particularly increasing disposable income (which has more than doubled in the last 60 years), the cash nexus could easily substitute for the older exchange system. To telescope the argument: the nature of large-scale society encouraged, and indeed demanded, spatial and social mobility; extended kinship hindered mobility; market organi-

From *Journal of Marriage and the Family*, Vol. 30, No. 1, pp. 40–45 (February, 1968). Reprinted by permission of the authors and the National Council on Family Relations.

zation of goods and services substituted for the positive functions of kin and thus allowed the mobility to occur with displacement of functions of both the nuclear and the extended family.

More recently, beginning in the 1950's, some sociologists, who were following our tribal custom of disbelieving and criticizing our elders, began studies of the family in urban settings. From these studies it developed that the nuclear family was not usually detached from its kin but interacted with them and exchanged services with them.

To some it seemed that this spate of studies showed the earlier writers to have been generally wrong in their view of the difference between the rural and the urban family in America. To us it seems the time has come to examine the question by the simple device of cross-tabulating measures of extended familism and an index of urbanism-ruralism.[1]

Our data come from a survey based on a state-wide probability sample, carried out in Wisconsin in the fall of 1964.[2]

[1] The authors are happy to acknowledge the financial support of this study provided by the Center for Metropolitan Studies of Northwestern University. Data for the paper come from a survey carried out in the fall of 1964. The authors also wish to thank Joyce Sween for programming the statistical analysis and Rae Lesser Blumberg for a critical review of the statistical analysis.
[2] This survey is based upon a multistage area probability sample design that gives each housing unit in the state an equal chance of being selected for interviewing. The procedure begins with a sample of the state's counties and moves to a sample of U.S. Census enumeration districts within counties. From the enumeration district is made a sample of chunks (geographical areas containing approximately 30 housing units each). From each chunk is drawn a sampling segment (a small geographical area containing approximately four housing units). This procedure identifies for the interviewer the housing unit within which he or she is to make the call. Finally, there is a random procedure for selecting the person to be interviewed among the persons in the household who have passed their twenty-first birthdays. In the two largest cities of Wisconsin—Milwaukee and Madison—a somewhat different procedure is followed: a sample of addresses is drawn from the annually revised city directory and coverage of addresses not appearing in the directories is obtained through the use of area samples of city blocks. No substitutes are permitted for sample housing units or for respondents. Four or more calls are made by the interviewers, if necessary, in order to interview the randomly specified respondent. A sample of 702 people was interviewed—322 men and 380 women. As of 1960, about 48 percent of the population of Wisconsin over the age of 19 was male; in the sample the proportion male was 46 percent. We wish to thank Harry Sharp, Director, and the Wisconsin Sample Survey Laboratory for making these data available to us.

Because of our interest in having a standard basis for estimating the opportunity of a household to engage in familistic behavior, we based our study on married couples. (It is reasonable to assume that the number of households of kin available to a married couple is different from the number available to a single person.) Accordingly, we eliminated from the sample all respondents who were not either married male heads of households or wives of heads. Presently it will be seen that we were also interested in the religious affiliation of respondents. Because they represented categories too differentiated from others to be combined with them and too small for separate analysis, Jews and Eastern rite Catholics were omitted. The number of nonwhites was

We have four measures of extended familism, that we call *extensity* of the presence of kin, *intensity* of the presence of kin, *interaction* with kin, and the *functionality* of the interaction with kin. Extensity of presence is based on the respondent's answer to the question: how many households of kin do you and your spouse have in this community? Intensity has to do with degree of kin of both respondent and respondent's spouse. A distinction is drawn between those of the respondent's kin who have been or are now in his family of orientation and of procreation—parents, siblings, and offspring, spoken of as "nuclear" kin—and all other relatives, characterized as "extended" kin. "High" intensity signifies that the respondent reports having in the community households of both nuclear and extended kin and that the respondent also reports that his or her spouse has households of both nuclear and extended kin in the community. "None" denotes that neither spouse has a household of kin of any degree in the community; "other" indicates the presence of one or more households of kin of respondent and/or spouse but not enough of the appropriate degrees on both sides of the house to qualify as "high." Interaction has to do with the number of categories of households of kin with which some member of the respondent's household interacts at least monthly.[3] Functionality concerns the instrumental value of the interaction as revealed in the giving and/or receiving of goods and services.

To get the purest possible measure of urbanism, we classify Milwaukee, Madison, Wauwatosa, and West Allis as urban; our rural category consists of all unincorporated territory not in any SMSA. The remaining area is labelled "other" and is regarded as of intermediate urbanism-ruralism.

Table 19-1 shows that two of our four measures of extended familism—interaction and functionality—are significantly and monotonically related to urbanism-ruralism with ruralism at the highly familistic end. Neither extensity nor intensity of presence correlates significantly with urbanism-ruralism. We conclude, therefore, that although there is little variation in the number of households of kin as we move from the country through the small towns and suburbs to the city, there is appreciable variation in both inter-

---

also too small for statistical analysis. After these exclusions were made, the sample of 702 shrank to 513. Of these there was an absence of information with respect to migratory status on nine individuals, with respect to religious affiliation on one.

[3] The measure of interaction in this study differs from that in our suburban study (cf. footnote 8, below). In this study it is based on the number of categories of kin households with which someone in the respondent's household has at least monthly contact. The categories are respondent's (1) siblings, (2) parents, and (3) other kin, as well as (4–6) the same categories of the respondent's spouse's kin.

TABLE 19-1. PERCENTAGE DISTRIBUTION OF RESPONDENTS BY ECOLOGICAL TYPE AND BY LEVEL OF EXTENDED FAMILISM, FOR FOUR MEASURES OF EXTENDED FAMILISM

Measure and Level of Extended Familism	Ecology*				Gamma
	Metropolitan	Other	Rural	Total	
Extensity of Presence[a]	N=115	N=286	N=112	N=513	
None	17.4	14.0	10.7	14.0	
Some	40.0	48.6	38.4	44.4	.10
High	42.6	37.4	50.9	41.5	
Intensity of Presence[b]	N=115	N=286	N=112	N=513	
None	17.4	14.0	10.7	14.0	
Some	60.9	64.0	64.3	63.4	.09
High	21.7	22.0	25.0	22.6	
Interaction[c]	N=115	N=286	N=112	N=513	
None	7.8	7.7	7.1	7.6	
Some	55.7	49.7	35.7	48.0	.20**
High	36.5	42.7	57.1	44.4	
Functionality[d]	N=115	N=286	N=112	N=513	
None	20.0	12.6	7.1	13.1	
Some	59.1	52.8	47.3	53.0	.30**
High	20.9	34.6	45.5	33.9	

[a] *Extensity of presence* refers to the number of households of kin in the community: "some" =1–8; "high" =9+.

[b] *Intensity of presence* refers to the degree of kin present in the community. In the following categories, a nuclear kinsman is a member of the respondent's family of orientation or of procreation. "None" means neither the respondent nor spouse reports any household of kin in the community; "high" means both respondent and spouse report having households of both nuclear and extended kin in the community; and "some" signifies the presence of kin but not satisfying the conditions of the "high" category.

[c] *Interaction* refers to the number of categories of households of kin with which some member of the respondent's household has been in contact (face to face, phone, or mail) at least monthly. "Some" =1–3; "high" =4–6.

[d] *Functionality* refers to the number of categories of service to and/or received from some kinsman. "Some" =1–2; "high" =3+.

* The three ecological types are:
  Metropolitan: Milwaukee, Madison, West Allis, and Wauwatosa
  Rural: unincorporated territory outside any SMSA
  Other: residual territory—small cities, suburbs, etc.

** The gammas so marked are significant at the .01 level; the others are not significant at the .05 level. Although the data in this and subsequent tables are reported as percentages, the measures of association and tests of significance have been conducted on the frequencies.

action and functionality. To state it more fully, on the average, rural households interact more with their kin than do urban households and that interaction tends to be more functional.

Having found some degree of association between ruralism-urbanism and certain measures of extended familism, one is entitled to inquire about third variables that might account for the association. Socioeconomic status and migratory status are two that seem especially to warrant our attention. It turns out that, when socioeconomic status is used as a control variable, the correlations between the rural-urban dimension and extended familism (as measured by interaction and functionality) remain generally unaffected.[4]

When migratory status was used as a control variable, the correlations between ecology and the two measures of familism disappeared where neither spouse was a migrant but held up otherwise.[5] In other words, in couples where one or both spouses are migrants, there is more interaction and more functional interaction with kin among rural families than among urban. An understanding of how migratory status is associated with extended familism can be obtained from Table 19-2, where it is seen that only where both spouses are migrants is there any appreciable proportion with no kin in the local community.

EXTENDED FAMILISM AND ETHNICITY

In earlier studies we have found separately and jointly that in our American samples Jewish families are more familistic than are Christian families.[6] A more recent paper has investigated a pro-

[4] Family income and education of head of household were the two indexes used for socioeconomic status. Each was dichotomized as near the median as possible, and gammas were computed between the ecological (rural-urban) variable and the two familistic variables showing significant gammas in Table 19-1. Of the eight resulting gammas, only one became nonsignificant: in the low-income category the correlation between ecology and interaction was of the same sign as before but dipped below the significance level.

Generally speaking, extended familism is not correlated with membership in voluntary organizations. Only at the lower level of SES and in the rural ecological category do significant correlations appear. Indeed, in the low-SES-rural category the more familistic are the greater joiners as is reflected by a gamma of .60, $P < .01$.

[5] A person was classed as a non-migrant if he or she had been born in the community where interviewed or if brought there before turning 18. Migratory status was trichotomized: both migrants, one spouse migrant, and neither spouse migrant. The interaction-ecology correlation for the both-migrant category was .20, very slightly below the two-sided .05 level of significance; for the one-migrant category, it was .29, significant at the .05 level. The functionality-ecology gammas were .30 and .49 respectively, both significant at the .01 level.

[6] Scott Greer, unpublished tabulation from the Metropolitan St. Louis Survey (1957); Robert F. Winch, *Identification and Its Familial Determinants*, Table 7, p. 122 (Indianapolis: Bobbs-Merrill, 1962); Robert F. Winch and Scott A. Greer, "The Uncertain Relation Between Early Marriage and Marital Stability: A Quest for Relevant Data," *Acta Sociologica*, 8:83–97 (1964).

TABLE 19-2. PERCENTAGE DISTRIBUTION OF MIGRATORY STATUSES, BY INTENSITY OF PRESENCE OF KIN

Intensity of Presence of Kinship	Both Migrants N=230	One Migrant N=150	Neither Migrant N=124	Total N=504	Gamma
None*	29.1	1.3	1.6	14.1	
Some	60.4	76.0	51.6	62.9	.67**
High	10.4	22.7	46.8	23.0	

Migratory Status

* These categories are explained in footnote b to Table 19-1.
** Significant at the .01 level.

posed explanation of Jewish familism. This involved the idea that Jews were more concentrated in less migratory occupations than non-Jews and that Jews were more familistic because their lower migration permitted them to be. The data were interpreted, however, as indicating that the Jews were less migratory because they were more familistic rather than the other way about. Among the Christians the Catholics were a bit more familistic than the Protestants, a bit less so than the Jews.[7]

Since the data underlying the above-stated conclusions came from an upper-middle-class suburb, the authors were interested in determining whether or not similar relationships would obtain in the broader social space afforded by the state-wide probability sample of Wisconsin. This sample offered a considerably broader range with respect to socioeconomic status and urban-rural residence, but it lacked the full ethnic spectrum represented in the United States, and in particular it had too few Jews and Negroes to permit their being used as statistical categories.

In the earlier study we regarded the classification of respondents into Jewish and non-Jewish as a dimension of ethnicity rather than of religion, because we were interested in values and behavior pertaining to the family rather than in theology. In the present study the same reasoning led us to look for what we thought of as ethnicity in our data on religious affiliation. Two large denominations, accounting for slightly more than two-thirds of the sample, were Roman Catholic and Lutheran. We decided to use these two categories and, anticipating that Lutherans would be more familistic than most other Protestant denominations, we decided to add a

[7] Robert F. Winch, Scott Greer, and Rae Lesser Blumberg, "Ethnicity and Extended Familism in an Upper-Middle-Class Suburb," *American Sociological Review*, 32:265–272 (1967).

TABLE 19-3. PERCENTAGE DISTRIBUTION OF RESPONDENTS BY ETHNIC CATEGORY AND BY LEVEL OF EXTENDED FAMILISM, FOR FOUR MEASURES OF EXTENDED FAMILISM

Measure and Level of Extended Familism*	Ethnicity				Gamma
	Catholic	Lutheran	Other Protestant	Total	
Extensity of					
Presence	N=197	N=177	N=138	N=512	
None	9.1	13.0	21.7	13.9	
Some	40.6	45.8	48.6	44.5	—.26**
High	50.3	41.2	29.7	41.6	
Intensity of					
Presence	N=197	N=177	N=138	N=512	
None	9.1	13.0	21.7	13.9	
Some	64.0	62.1	64.5	63.5	—.25**
High	26.9	24.9	13.8	22.7	
Interaction	N=197	N=177	N=138	N=512	
None	4.1	6.2	13.8	7.4	
Some	49.7	42.4	52.9	48.0	—.17**
High	46.2	51.4	33.3	44.5	
Functionality	N=197	N=177	N=138	N=512	
None	15.2	9.0	15.2	13.1	
Some	49.2	58.2	51.4	52.9	—.02
High	35.5	32.8	33.3	34.0	

* These indexes and categories are explained in footnotes a-d to Table 19-1.
** Significant at the .01 level.

third category of "other Protestants" that would also include the "none" and "don't know" responses to the query about religious affiliation.[8]

We were intrigued to see whether, with our highly familistic Jews absent from the analysis, we should still find that ethnicity correlated with extended familism. Table 19-3 shows a pattern that is similar to, but markedly weaker than, that found in the suburban

[8] An ethnic category is an aggregate of people sharing, and therefore participating in, a common culture. Since our interest is in culture rather than attitudes toward or beliefs about a supernatural being, we speak of this variable as ethnicity rather than religion. It is realized that within each of the three foregoing categories there is considerable variation in national origins and that for this reason the reader may decline to attribute cultural homogeneity to them. A study is now under way to investigate the cultural homogeneity of the Lutheran category. The present authors believe there is some homogeneity within each category with respect to attitudes about the family, but no harm will be done if the reader disagrees and simply prefers to regard these as categories of religious affiliation. Because we expected that Lutherans would be intermediate between other Protestants and Catholics with respect to familism, we chose the ordinal measure of association, gamma.

study—the interaction and two presence measures producing larger relationships than functionality.[9] With respect to extensity and intensity of presence, Catholics are most familistic, Lutherans intermediate, and other Protestants least. In the case of interaction, Lutherans are a bit more familistic than Catholics, and the measure would be larger if these two categories were reversed.

When the two indexes of socioeconomic status were employed as control variables, it was found that at the high level of SES all six correlations between ethnicity and the three measures of extended familism (with which it correlated significantly) remained significant and in the same direction. At the lower socioeconomic level, however, the four following correlations became nonsignificant: with income as the index, the correlations with interaction and extensity;[10] with education as the index, the correlations with interaction and intensity. These results indicate that the order of ethnic categories with respect to extended familism—Catholics most familistic, Lutherans intermediate, and other Protestants least familistic—is operative at the upper socioeconomic level, but at the lower level, especially with respect to interaction, there is some tendency for ethnic differences to wash out.

When migratory status is introduced as a control variable, the correlation between ethnicity and extended familism remains for the "both migrant" category but disappears for the other two migratory statuses. When one or both spouses are non-migrants, then the data indicate that Catholics and Lutherans are not significantly more familistic than other Protestants.

Since both socioeconomic status and migratory status affect the correlation between ethnicity and extended familism, it is of interest to see what happens when they are introduced simultaneously as control variables. The result is that most of the correlations between ethnicity and extended familism shrink to nonsignificance. Of the 36 computations only six remained significant.[11] Of these six, three combined the both-migrant status with high socioeconomic status; of the other three, two combined the both-migrant and

---

[9] In the suburban study the gammas between ethnicity (Jewish, Catholic, Protestant) and extended familism (extensity, intensity, interaction, functionality) were .81, .68, .74, and .29, respectively, all significant at the .01 level. See *ibid.*

[10] This correlation was marginal, however, the pattern of association being the same and the gamma being just slightly below that required for the .05 level of significance.

[11] The 36 gammas represent three indexes of extended familism (extensity, intensity, interaction), three levels of migration, two indexes of socioeconomic status, each at two levels; and 3 X 3 X 2 X 2 = 36.

262   Urban Sociology

low socioeconomic statuses, and the sixth combined one-spouse migrant with high SES.

If the foregoing reasoning is correct, it should follow that the correlations between the three categories of ethnicity and the three measures of extended familism with which it correlates significantly are higher in metropolitan areas, where the proportion of migrants and the average SES are relatively high, than in rural areas, where they are low. As Table 19-4 indicates, such a relationship is supported by the data, which also show the relationship in small towns and suburbs (the "other" ecological level) to be much like that in metropolitan areas.

TABLE 19-4. MEASURES OF ASSOCIATION (GAMMAS) BETWEEN ETHNICITY AND THREE MEASURES OF EXTENDED FAMILISM, WITHIN ECOLOGICAL LEVEL

Measure of Extended Familism	Ecology			Total
	Metropolitan	Other	Rural	
	N=115	N=286	N=112	N=513
Extensity of Presence	—.31*	—.30**	—.14	—.26**
Intensity of Presence	—.35*	—.26**	—.15	—.25*
Interaction	—.24	—.23**	—.07	—.17*

* Significant at the .05 level.
** Significant at the .01 level.

Taking into account that there is an ethnic gradient of migration such that the proportion of migrants is lowest among Catholics and highest among other Protestants,[12] these results seem to indicate that for the most part the correlation between ethnicity and extended familism prevails where both spouses are migrants and their socioeconomic status is relatively high and that this familism consists in interacting with more households of kin and, to some extent, having more households of kin to interact with. In other words, when neither spouse is a migrant, there is no significant difference among ethnic categories with respect to extended familism, but when both spouses are migrants, the correlation of ethnicity with familism prevails.

SUMMARY AND CONCLUSIONS

This paper has sought to illuminate the dependent variable of extended familism, which has been operationalized by means of four indexes: extensity (number of households of kin in the local community), intensity (degree of kinship of these households on both husband's and wife's sides), interaction (number of categories

[12] Gamma = .21, significant at the .01 level.

of households of kin interacted with), and functionality (instrumental value of that interaction).

No matter how we operationalize extended familism—whether as extensity or intensity of presence of kin, as categories of kin interacted with, or as the functionality of that interaction—the overwhelming majority of our respondents report involvement with kin. Indeed, this is the case with even the least familistic subcategories of our respondents.

Ruralism correlates significantly with extended familism as indexed by functionality and interaction, but there is little difference between rural and urban couples in the number of households of kin or the degree of kinship of these households.

The ruralism-familism correlation is not related to socioeconomic status, but it is to migratory status. That is, the correlation stands up where one or both spouses are migrants and disappears where neither is a migrant. Stated differently, non-migrant urban couples are as familistic, on the average, as non-migrant rural couples, but migrant urban couples are less familistic than migrant rural couples. (It should be kept in mind, of course, that the dimension of ruralism-urbanism is being investigated within Wisconsin.)

Ethnicity—represented here as Catholic, Lutheran, and other Protestants—correlates significantly with extended familism in that Catholics and Lutherans are more familistic than other Protestants with respect to extensity, intensity, and interaction, but there is little difference among ethnic categories with respect to functionality. With respect to our control variables, this correlation tends to hold up for migratory couples of relatively high SES and those in urban areas; conversely, there is little correlation between ethnicity and familism in couples of low SES, where one or both spouses are non-migrants, and in rural areas.

In this sample, then, the extended familism associated with ruralism consists largely of functionality and of interaction, and this familism tends to occur differentially in ecological categories where one or both spouses are migrants. The extended familism associated with the levels of ethnicity considered here consists largely of the presence and degree of households of kin (extensity and intensity), and to some extent it consists of interaction with these households; the interethnic difference is most evident in both-migrant couples of high socioeconomic status and those of urban residence.

Thus the argument stated in brief at the beginning of this paper gains some plausibility. Non-migration is associated with the maintenance of extended kin networks, and part of the greater familism of rural areas is due to the greater stability of the population. But part of it is associated with the greater familism of migrants in rural areas. Perhaps the rural, and, to a less extent, small-town and suburban, areas are more conducive, culturally or ecologically, to using whatever kin system is present. In this case we have an interaction of individual attributes (migratory status) and situational attributes (the general level of kin interaction and functionality in the community).[13]

With respect to ethnicity, we note that it makes a difference in interaction but not in functionality. Furthermore, it holds only for migrant couples of higher status. Thus one suspects it is most important for "phatic" interaction[14] rather than mutual aid and, conceivably, is related to the greater resources for visiting in general, and therefore visiting of relatives, among those with more money, time, and education.

[13] Peter Blau, "Structural Effects," *American Sociological Review*, 25:178–193 (1960); and James A. Davis, Joe L. Spaeth, and Carolyn Huson, "A Technique for Analyzing the Effects of Group Composition," *American Sociological Review* 26:215–225 (1961).
[14] In phatic discourse the words mean "nothing excepting as a device to avoid silence and signify social solidarity." Gordon W. Allport, *The Nature of Prejudice*, p. 273 (Garden City, New York: Doubleday Anchor Books, 1958).

Chapter 6

THE NEIGHBORHOOD AS A
CONTINUING ENTITY IN
URBAN LIFE

Cooley listed the neighborhood, along with the family, and the childhood play group, as one of his three classic examples of the primary group. Cooley had in mind, of course, not the "neighborhood" of the ecologist, but the "neighborhood" composed of people who had lived in proximity to each other for a long time and had become bound to each other through strong ties of intimacy and mutual obligations. This kind of neighborhood clearly would exist in rural areas and in small towns and cities. The view of rural and urban settings as polar types led to the tendency, then, to allocate the neighborhood, implying a network of close social relationships, to the rural end of the continuum. Such relationships were viewed as atypical of urban dwellers.

It is true, of course, that the term "neighborhood," in the vocabulary of the urban resident, is often a label designating a particular, more or less definitely delimited, section of the city, perhaps centered around a shopping center, a park, or some other identifying landmark. Such an area may have a large population, and certainly the residents may have little sense of being neighbors.

However, the tendency to assume a lack of "neighboring" in the life of the city dweller clearly was erroneous. To be sure, conditions of urban life do often make it possible for the individual to minimize any degree of involvement with those persons living close to him. In many sections of the city it is probably a great deal easier to maintain such social distance, such anonymity, than is ordinarily true in the small community. Some sections of the city may be characterized by a low incidence of meaningful contacts or ties between neighbors. Even so, it is a long way from such statements as these to an assumption that a meaningful sense of neighborhood is incompatible with, or unlikely in, the metropolitan setting.

Literature upon suburbia, of course, has stressed—as we have already seen, perhaps has overstressed—that type of metropolitan setting as being characteristically given to a high frequency of interaction with neighbors. Insofar as the central city, the inner city itself, is concerned, a meaningful identification with neighborhood, and meaningful ties among the residents of such a neighborhood, may provide a redeeming factor, going far to offset characteristics which might otherwise be considered (by a middle-class outsider, at least) as undesirable.

Jane Jacobs, with conviction and eloquence, has argued that neighborhood meeting points—the shops and stores—are important. The bustling life of the streets, observed by the persons living in the flats along it, is deeply missed when the slum neighborhood is destroyed in urban renewal, to be replaced by the perhaps more comfortable but impersonal towers of a vast housing project.[1] Gans, in his study of Italian-Americans in a section of Boston destined for urban renewal, similarly emphasized the manner in which the "urban villagers" maintained a way of life in which the primary relationships of family and of neighborhood were focal.[2]

In the selection from Heberle, the author draws upon his knowledge of rural and urban patterns of living in Europe and America to call attention to a basic and often neglected point. The relationship between neighbors, he notes, may be less essentially a relationship of friendship or liking or sociability than one of mutual dependence. Obligations toward each other, thoroughly understood and relied upon, are often quite explicit in European rural settings. Such obligations become less precisely prescribed in urban areas and in America but, nonetheless, expectations of being able to depend upon neighbors continue to be important. Among very poor people—to whom such expectations are of greatest urgency— obligations of this type may be felt even among people who are defined as inappropriate for visiting or for friendship; Heberle cites mutual aid between neighboring white and Negro families in such cities as Baton Rouge and New Orleans to make his point that

[1] See Jane Jacobs, *The Death and Life of Great American Cities* (New York: Random House, 1961).
[2] Herbert Gans, *The Urban Villagers* (New York: The Free Press of Glencoe, 1962).

the commitment to assist one's neighbor does not imply sociability in the usual sense. The norms of obligation toward the neighbor, in short, seem to Heberle to have been understated, for we too often have viewed the relation of neighbor to neighbor essentially in terms of interaction based upon liking.

Gans interprets the importance in the suburban setting of propinquity as compared with homogeneity as a basis for the establishment of friendship bonds within the neighborhood. He notes that the matters considered in urban planning, which may encourage or discourage contacts based on propinquity, are less basic in establishing friendship ties than might be surmised on the basis of some interpretations. Friendship grows from common interests, from "homogeneity."

The excerpts from Bracey's comparison-contrast of subdivision life in an English and an American metropolitan area present both similarities and contrasts. In both countries, recognition was general that one's relationships with neighbors was an important part of subdivision life. The ability to rely upon neighbors for help in case of need was expressed by residents in both countries, but the English residents were much more likely to view the neighbor as a source of help. Americans were more often caught up in a round of neighborhood activities. They were much more likely than were the English to be church-oriented; in both countries the residents, while valuing the presence of their neighbors, also sought to maintain privacy.

Urban life offers a wide range of associations and activities in which the city resident may participate. Many of these involve impersonal relationships of the secondary-group type. Primary relations continue to be important in the urban setting, however, and one form which such relationships may take is the establishment of meaningful interaction with one's neighbors.

The Normative Element in Neighborhood Relations

RUDOLF HEBERLE

Louisiana State University

In the vast literature on the neighborhood, analysis is, as a rule, confined to the levels of behavior (interaction) and attitudes, while the *normative* aspect of the relationship, i.e., the presence or absence of *obligation*, is usually overlooked. These studies are informative but do not reach an understanding of the specific characteristics of neighborhood as a *social* relationship. For, human relations are *social* relationships in the strict sense if and insofar as they contain a normative element, a sense of mutual obligation.

Mere physical interaction—e.g., an accidental collision of two human bodies—does not constitute social interaction, as Max Weber has pointed out, although it may become the occasion for the development of a social relationship. Furthermore, emotions, sentiments and attitudes oriented toward another person do not *per se* constitute a social relationship. Their quality may vary and change without necessarily affecting the social relationship under consideration. Husband and wife may express love and hate for each other in the course of a day, but their marital relationship persists as long as they recognize those mutual obligations which this relationship involves.

The differentiation between the psychic aspects and the social aspects of human relations is especially obvious in the case of legal relationships, but it is also important in cases where a social relationship is based on custom only. We shall call a social "norm" any rule of conduct, prohibitive, permissive or mandatory; social norms

From *Pacific Sociological Review*, Vol. 3, No. 1, pp. 3–11 (Spring, 1960). Reprinted by permission of the author and the publisher. This paper is the result of research under the auspices of the Institute of Population Research in the Department of Sociology at Louisiana State University.

assign rights and duties to persons. It will be noted that I do not, as many do, consider the term "norm" to denote a pattern of actual or expected behavior. These patterns may be the result of an awareness of certain rules on the part of the acting persons, as in the case of boys playing a game, but patterns are not rules.

This paper intends to analyze the normative character of the neighborhood relationship and its relation to the non-normative aspects. It will also indicate *changes* in the normative element which may help to explain why this aspect has been so widely ignored.

The term "neighbor" has various meanings. In urban society today it simply means somebody who lives near the reference person; (Mr. Smith is my neighbor, he lives next door to me. Mr. Jones, also a neighbor, lives around the corner, or "down the street"), but in rural communities, at least in those which are well integrated socially, it means a person to whom the reference person is socially related by specific rights and duties established by custom and, in part, by law—because of the proximity of the dwellings.

The word "neighborhood", correspondingly, may denote an *area* within a local community (which may or may not have definite boundaries and a name) or it may mean a specific type of *social relationships*, which make up a real social institution.

The sociological problem is, to what extent do the two aspects of neighborhood coincide in concrete situations, that is to say, to what extent and under what circumstances do persons inhabiting an area called a "neighborhood" interact socially in the specific ways expected of "neighbors" in the institutional sense?

We shall therefore first inquire as to what social conduct is expected of neighbors in this second sense.

NEIGHBORHOOD RELATIONS IN RURAL COMMUNITIES

Max Weber states that "neighborhood" is originally a social relationship of mutual aid in various emergencies and crisis-situations.[1] In European agricultural communities this is still the meaning of "neighborhood", especially in the less urbanized areas. A farmer in a European cluster village expects his neighbors right and left and across the street to come to his aid when the resources of his own household are insufficient to cope with extraordinary situations. When a child is to be born, the women of the neighborhood will assist in the preparations (though today a doctor or a

[1] Max Weber, *Wirtschaft und Gesellschaft*, Tübingen: J. C. B. Mohr, 1922, pp. 197–199.

midwife is likely to perform the delivery) and will help to relieve the housewife of her daily duties; when a death has occurred some neighbor will furnish the wagon for the coffin, others will serve as pall-bearers, still others will ring the church bells, and the wives and daughters will help to prepare the after-funeral meal, and so forth.

It is understood that no immediate compensation will be offered for such services, but certainly the receiver will give the same kind of neighborly aid to any of his neighbors when the need arises. There are, of course, many other occasions for mutual aid, at harvest time or in case of sickness of men or animals and in case of fire or flood.[2] The rigidity of aid expectations seems to vary largely with the urgency of the matter.

The neighbors are also entitled to share the joyous events in the life of a family: when a child is baptized, or married, the neighbors must be invited, and in villages where neighborhood customs are strictly observed, the neighbors will on these occasions have precedence over personal friends of the host. For, the neighborhood relationship is not merely a relationship between individuals but a relationship between households, or more precisely, between homesteads.[3] A German farmer once told me that curiously enough one of his neighbors was a farmer living about a mile outside the village on an "isolated" farmstead. When I asked how long the farm had been there, my informant recalled that about 120 years ago in the course of a re-allocation of land in the village community this farmstead, which had been adjoining his own, had been shifted to its present location. The inference is obvious: the neighborhood relationship had been continued in spite of the spatial separation of the two houses. In this case the neighborhood relationship rested upon the two houses as if it were a mortgage. That rural people think in this way became clear also in the half-joking complaint of a village school teacher, occupant of a former farm house, that he and his wife had to invite their neighbors at many occasions where they would rather invite their personal friends.

---

[2] Willi Latten, "Die Halligen," *Koelner Vierteljahrshefte für Soziologie*, VIII, 4, gives an excellent description of neighborhood relations on the small island off the west coast of Schleswig-Holstein. Here in times of flood or when ice in the shallow waters isolates the islands, mutual aid is absolutely indispensable.

[3] I have pointed this out first in: *Die Heidedörfer Moide und Suroide*, Schriften des geographischen Instituts der Universität Kiel, Band V, Heft 2, Kiel, 1938, p. 55: "From these neighborly relations is to be distinguished the neighborhood as an institution which is attached to the farmsteads rather than to the persons who occupy them. . . . The rule 'neighbor goes before friend' [naber geiht vör fründ (plattdeutsch)] expresses the character of neighborhood as contrasted with personal relationships. . . ." (my translation).

Whenever I asked village people in Germany about these matters, I found them well aware of all the implications of neighborhood relations. One of my informants showed me a typed sheet on which he had written what he knew about neighborhood relations in his village "so that the young people might not forget the customs". In the community of Moide in the Lueneburger Heide one of the farms had been acquired by a businessman from the nearby city of Hamburg and was now managed by a superintendent who had a very high labor turnover. When I asked one of the other farmers whether this condition had any effect on neighborhood relations he said: "You bet it has. For example, do you think we like it if in case of a funeral they send a stranger over here, a man who may even wear a red tie?"[4]

The sociologically important aspects of rural neighborhood relations in Europe are thus that *they are relationships between occupants of certain adjoining farmsteads*, often dating back several generations; that they are not voluntary but obligatory; that they adhere to the farm rather than to its changing occupants; and that they involve mutual aid in needs as well as mutual sharing of pleasant events. The neighborhood relationship is thus reciprocal on two levels: emergency aid and sociability.

How strongly these obligations are felt by the villagers themselves may be illustrated by the following case which I observed in the village of Medelby close to the Danish border during the first years of the Hitler regime. With the exception of one family (who had moved there from Denmark), the entire village was organized in the NSDAP and its affiliated organizations. The Danish family had openly demonstrated their opposition to the regime and the villagers had, for a while, boycotted them. But the village farmers' leader—a functionary of the party—who told me this, added with an apologetic smile: "to-morrow is my wife's birthday and we are going to have a big party; we invited those people, too, for after all they are our neighbors".[5] This case showed also the concept of neighbor is sometimes extended in space: not only immediately adjacent households but also some more distant ones may be considered as neighbors. But the typical social neighbor is the immediate one in the physical sense.

The rural neighborhood relationship functions also—or at least it did in Germany as I knew it—where families of unequal social status are involved: the owner of a full-sized farm would lend his

---

[4] Instead of a black one as custom prescribes.

[5] Significantly, another Nazi farmer who had moved but recently to this community from a distant region of the country commented that, "these people here" were not really true Nazis because, for example, they would associate with "that Danish family."

team to the cottager and the latter would reciprocate by helping his wealthier neighbor when he needed additional labor. As Max Weber points out, any work done by the small farmers and cottagers for the larger farmer was in many regions of Germany regarded as a kind of neighborly help. Even the owner of an estate was in some areas included in these mutual aid relationships.

In the United States where rural communities had to be created out of nothing—at least during the period of rapid westward advance of the "frontier"—such rigidly institutionalized neighborhood relations could not develop everywhere, but the fundamental principle of mutual aid among neighbors was generally accepted and adapted to frontier conditions (e.g., log-rolling, barn-raising, etc.).

There is ample evidence in the accounts of "neighboring" practices in American rural communities that farmers in well-integrated communities regard the services they perform for neighbors as exempt from ordinary business principles. This was brought home to a well-meaning outsider who had persuaded a community of East Frisian farmers in Illinois to keep records of work performed for their neighbors. When the balances were to be settled, the groups, upon the suggestion of an old farmer, decided to tear up the checks "because we are not in business with each other, we are neighbors".[6]

It seems, however, that the neighborhood as a social relationship among farmers in this country has lost some of the definite and obligatory character it had in Europe. This is at least the conclusion which I draw from the numerous sociological studies of rural neighborhoods. Almost invariably the neighborhood is defined as an "area", i.e., as a subdivision, sometimes with a name of its own, of the larger "community", comprising more families than the European farmer's neighborhood.[7] These groups are considered to be

[6] The story is told in: E. T. Hiller, Faye E. Corner, and Wendell L. East, *Rural Community Types*, University of Illinois, Urbana, 1930, p. 30. See also my review of "Rural Community Studies" in *Rural Sociology*, 7 (June, 1942), pp. 212–216.
[7] N. L. Sims, in his *Elements of Rural Sociology*, 1928, p. 563, relates that in certain field studies the question arose whether spatial groupings of only half a dozen families should be called (sic!) neighborhoods. Charles P. Loomis and J. Allan Beegle in their *Rural Social Systems*, New York: Prentice Hall, 1959, treat the neighborhood definitely as an area. They point out that it is "very unrealistic" to expect that all families in a neighborhood area will exchange work or borrow from each other. Groups which do this also engage in "visiting"; these groups our authors call "cliques or friendship groups." Some cliques consist of neighbors-in-space (nigh dwellers); these cliques correspond to the kind of group that constitutes a neighborhood in the European sense. When Loomis shows (p. 165) that in a German village which he studied cliques were formed very largely among people of the same class and among adherents of the same political party, this merely reveals that the village of Rietze was not a purely agricultural place and not a well integrated community.

"active" neighborhoods if the families engage in visiting, borrowing (lending), and other mutual aid and if they maintain a school, a church, and other "institutions". In Europe, the maintenance of these institutions is the function of the local community (*Gemeinde*) or of the state. The local community has definite administrative boundaries.

In view of this difference in the allocation of social functions, it is easy to understand why the term neighborhood among European farmers has a more specific and restricted meaning. The very fact that American rural sociologists are able to distinguish "active" from "inactive" neighborhoods[8] shows that in the U. S. the social relationships among neighbors are no longer considered obligatory to the degree that is the case in Europe. It also seems to me quite significant that in many American rural neighborhood studies, "visiting" is regarded as the most important among the "neighboring" activities, just as or even more important than mutual aid.[9]

All this suggests that the meaning of the term neighborhood has undergone a change in this country precisely because the functions of the neighborhood as a social group have changed.

A recent theoretical paper states clearly that economic prosperity resulting in "a relatively high degree of economic security ... has brought changes in social organizations in locality groups. On the one hand, less need is felt for mutual-aid agreements (sic) or other types of dependence on neighbors".[10] On the other hand, the American farmer depends more on special purpose organizations, on public institutions and on private enterprise.

When formerly at a funeral the neighbors would perform the necessary functions they now "set up a flower fund to send flowers in case of death in the community".[11] Mutual-aid is still provided, but it seems no longer self-understood, or else it would not be

---

[8] J. H. Kolb and D. G. Marshall, "Neighborhood-Community Relations in Rural Society," *University of Wisconsin AES Research* Bulletin 154, 1944. Cf. Lowry Nelson, *Rural Sociology*, New York: American Book Co., 1952, pp. 84–87.
[9] Selz Mayo, in his "Testing Criteria of Rural Locality Groups," *Rural Sociology*, 14 (December, 1949), pp. 317–325, uses certain "behavior characteristics" in rating locality groups, e.g., visiting, mutual aid in emergencies or in work, spontaneous play and recreation (hunting, fishing), and "exchange of personal confidences" etc. No mention is made of a sense of obligation or of the normative element in neighborhood relations. Alvin Boskoff, in his "The Ecological Approach," *Rural Sociology*, 14 (December, 1949), p. 309, likewise neglects the normative character of neighborhood relations.
[10] Alvin L. Bertrand, "Rural Locality Groups: Changing Patterns, Change Factors, and Implications," *Rural Sociology*, 19 (June, 1954), p. 176. See also my discussion of Bryce Ryan, "The Neighborhood As a Unit of Action in Rural Programs," *Rural Sociology*, 9 (March, 1944), pp. 35–36.
[11] From: Inez Lovelace, Eugene Gambill, and Milburn E. Jones, *Projects of Organized Rural Communities*, Agricultural Extension Service, University of Tennessee, No. 332, p. 7.

regarded as a meritorious feature of "community organization" by agricultural extension sociologists.[12]

The general impression gained from the more critical studies made in the United States in recent years[13] is that rural neighborhood relations have become less obligatory, more a matter of choice and individual preference, which means that they have become more like neighborhood relationships in the modern city.

IN TOWNS AND CITIES

In the larger cities of Europe as well as in North America, the neighborhood has assumed a very different meaning, as we shall presently see. But first, let us consider briefly the nature and role of neighborhood relations in medieval or rather in pre-industrial towns and cities. The middle ages were the age of cooperative organizations mostly constructed on the pattern of brotherhoods. This pattern seems to have been adopted also by small local groups more or less formally organized to take care of certain common interests of people living in the vicinity of each other. Some historians suggest that these neighborhood groups were one of the starting points of the revival of municipal government. Thus it seems that in the city of Florence groups of this kind, which originally were formed for the upkeep of streets, bridges, fountains, and for the repair of the parish church, sometimes established joined committees for purposes of common interest. The members of these committees, *boni homines* (good men) later assumed the more glamorous title of *consuls*—an indication that they were regarding themselves as successors to the ancient Roman institution of city government.[14] The reason for their existence was the need for cooperation among spatial neighbors in the maintenance of a well or fountain as well as in firefighting (which of course presupposed care of a water supply). We have the description of one of these associations that existed in the town of Burg on the isle of Fehmarn in North Germany in the beginning of the nineteenth century. "The heads of households sharing the property of a well (*die Sod-Herren*) assembled during the carnival season to consider repairs,

[12] *Ibid.*
[13] For example, Walter L. Slocum and Herman M. Case, "Are Neighborhoods Meaningful Social Groups Throughout Rural America?" *Rural Sociology*, 18 (March, 1953), pp. 52–59.
[14] F. Schevill, *History of Florence*, London: G. Bell and Sons, 1937. Institutionalized neighborhood groups were a common feature of medieval cities in Germany and persisted well into the nineteenth century. In some small cities and towns they have survived to the present day (pp. 26f.).

to collect the fees for well-use from outsiders and to approve the accounts, whereupon they engaged in three days of drinking and feasting".[15]

Similar neighborhood associations were still functioning in small towns in the Rhein-Gau a hundred years ago when W. H. Riehl described them in his "Wanderbuch" as follows:[16]

The origin of the neighborhoods (*Nachbarschaften*) or well-associations (*Brunnengenossenschaften*) lies certainly far back in the middle ages, although it seems that older written statutes than those of the year 1607 have not yet been found. The neighbors on certain streets or in certain quarters (of the town) associate (*verbünden sich*) themselves for the maintenance and clean keeping of a common well, elect annually a "well-master", keep a "well-record" (*Bornbuch*); they bind themselves not only to stand by each other in matters concerning the well, but also to celebrate common festivals and to aid one another in any kind of emergency and danger, especially in burying their dead and in consoling each other in sorrow. Lastly, it is an old custom for the whole neighborhood to help a neighbor carrying his cross and to drink with him a measure of wine for consolation. A neighbor must not even depart without giving advance notice to the neighborhood, indicating the reason for traveling, and asking for leave, by penalty of ½ quart of wine. (Penalties are always assessed in wine.) The hardest penalty is imposed for quarreling and fighting in meetings: the disturber of peace has to pay the drinks for the entire neighborhood for that day, "as in the old days". These corporations had also their banners and drums, even "guns and cannon" are mentioned, "which belong in common to the neighborhood": though it is likely that these were used only to fire *salut* (*Freudenschüsse*).

Of particular interest is the well-book which contains by no means merely a record of well-cleaning but should give account of "all memorable events" that occurred during the year. Thus we find in those excerpts which Schunk[17] has published, that these well-books were virtual chronicles which, like the statutes themselves, tell us of the urbane culture (*Bildung*) of those country-townspeople. At present these neighborhoods are said to be best preserved in the town of Lorch; they occur however even farther down the river and the "well-book" still exists as "neighbor-book." Along with their ancient traditional functions these groups serve now also as a "caucus" for state and municipal elections, etc. . . . .

The last remarks indicate a change in functions which is not at all unusual in institutions of this kind.

A more recent account of neighborhood associations, also in the Rhine Valley, is given by W. Latten in an article on small towns on

[15] George Hanssen, *Historisch—statistische Darstellung der Insel Fehmarn*, Altona, 1832, pp. 318–319.
[16] W. H. Riehl, *Wanderbuch. Die Naturgeschicte des Volkes*, 4 Band, 2 ed., Stuttgart, 1869, pp. 207–209. The Rhein-Gau is the area between Weinheim and Lorch. (Translation by R. Heberle.)
[17] Riehl refers to Schunk, *Beitraege zur Mainzer Geschichte*, date unknown.

the lower Rhine.[18] Besides the old well-fraternities, Latten found still another kind of neighborhood (street) associations without any specific practical purpose. The statutes of well-association which Latten reproduces, reveal various secondary functions of mutual aid and conviviality.

The well-associations in the town of Jever (Ostfriesland), like similar organizations in other towns and cities of North Germany, have evidently developed from the ancient rural neighborhood; the rural neighborhood was, as we pointed out before, more than a well-company. It has a variety of functions. But the urban well-company, while primarily a one-purpose specialized group, also had secondary, especially sociable (*"gesellige"*), functions and it is characteristic that participation in the annual banquet was and still is a major obligation of the members.[19]

It is evident from these studies that the urban institutionalized neighborhood group has a larger membership than the original rural neighborhood; the urban neighborhood tends to extend further than the immediate neighbors "next door and across the street". In the case of well-associations named neighborhoods this larger membership and wider spatial extension is easy to understand.

On the other hand, as soon as the functions of maintaining a water supply and providing fire protection are taken over by the municipal government, the neighborhood tends to shrink again and relationships between neighbors tend to become less obligatory, although they by no means become unimportant.

In large cities of today there is less *need* for mutual aid and cooperation among neighbors since most functions of the old village and town neighborhoods are taken over by public utilities and private enterprises—funeral "parlors", etc. Where formal organizations of residents of a neighborhood area exist ("organized streets", etc.),[20] they are in most cases, though not always, associations for the protection of real estate values. While they sometimes arrange picnics and engage in other forms of sociability, they rarely perform the same kind of essential services which the older street and fountain companies used to give. Certain so-called "Neighborhood Councils" or committees which have been formed in

[18] Willi Latten, "Die Niederrheinische Kleinstadt," *Koelner Vierteljahrshefte für Soziologie*, 1930, p. 316.
[19] Hans Siuts, *Püttnachbarn und Püttbier, Das Jeversche Püttwesen und seine Stellung in der deutschen Volkskunde, Jever*, 1957, contains a wealth of information on neighborhood groups in other parts of Germany.
[20] See for example, Stuart A. Queen and D. F. Carpenter, *The American City*, New York: McGraw-Hill, 1954, pp. 159–166.

Chicago and a few other large cities, comprising areas with a population of 100,000 or more, are only nominally neighborhood organizations.[21] Furthermore, the *mobility* of population in many urban areas impedes the development of strong social ties even among immediate neighbors. There are, of course, even in the largest cities, neighbors who know one another and who help each other, and who share leisure-time activities. But these "neighboring" activities, numerous and diverse as they may be, are entirely voluntary. No city dweller acknowledges an imperative obligation to associate with his neighbors and he will not associate with them unless he likes them or finds them useful. It is therefore, in urban society, often impossible to distinguish between personal friendship and neighborhood relations. It is quite significant that in urban society the very meaning of the term neighborhood changes; no longer does it denote a specific kind of social relationship existing by the force of custom between nearby households; instead it denotes a vaguely defined area which may comprise a city block or two, or even an entire "subdivision" or city district. Louis Wirth was probably the first sociologist to point this out.[22] Thus, if the city dweller speaks of somebody as his neighbor, he means that the person referred to happens to live near him,[23] perhaps within walking distance, but he does not recognize any specific social obligations in relation to this person. There are not any specific neighborhood relations attached to a city-house or dwelling as they are to a farmstead in a tradition-bound village community.

Consequently, we find that actual neighborhood relationships may vary greatly within a given urban community between individuals and also between ecological areas:

First, we find cases of social isolation because persons either are avoided by their neighbors or on their own part avoid contacts with their neighbors. This is rarely possible in villages and small towns (William Faulkner's "A Rose for Emily" notwithstanding) but not at all infrequent in large cities.[24]

Second, we find that where need for mutual aid is greatest neighborhood relations are most similar to those in rural communi-

---

[21] See Wilbur C. Hallenbeck, *American Urban Communities*, New York: Harper and Bros., 1951, pp. 580 ff.

[22] Louis Wirth, "A Bibliography of the Urban Community," in R. E. Park, E. W. Burgess, and R. D. McKenzie, *The City*, Chicago: University of Chicago Press, 1925, p. 190.

[23] Stuart Queen therefore proposes to use the term "nigh-dweller" rather than neighbor.

[24] See the novel *My Brother's Keeper* by George Melville Baker which is based on a real case of two brothers who lived as recluses in New York City.

ties. Intensity of social interaction between neighbors tends to decrease as one moves from working class areas to upper-income bracket residential suburbs.[25] In the tenements of working class people borrowing, exchange of services, and assistance in sickness are a necessity, and gossiping and visiting, at least among housewives, are typically frequent. The children and young people of a tenement or of adjoining houses or of a section of the street will meet and play together, thus inducing relations among the parents—which are by no means always free of conflict. However, even in working class areas one associates only with certain neighbors whom one chooses; and if a neighbor moves, his successor in the flat or house need not enter into the same kind of relationship with the neighbors and he may not even be accepted by them. The better off people are financially, the less dependent they are on their neighbors and the more choosy they will be in establishing more than superficial contacts with neighbors. If some studies made in the United States seem to contradict these statements, it should be remembered that we are referring to mutual aid as the main function of neighborhood relations, rather than with "casual neighboring" or visiting.[26] Among poor people in the South, neighborly mutual aid is sometimes given even between white and Negro families who would never "visit" with one another. This presupposes of course that whites and Negroes live on the same street or in the same block, a fact which is not unusual in cities like Baton Rouge or New Orleans.

Third, children and their mothers are more important as partners in neighborhood relations in the city than are men. This observation of G. Kirch is confirmed by many studies made in this country. The population of suburban areas in U.S. cities often has a very narrow age-range. In a neighborhood composed mainly of married couples with young children, the latter will form informal play groups and induce acquaintances among their mothers. The mothers will take turns to look after the children, to take them to the movies, etc. As the children grow up, they will establish more intimate contacts outside the neighborhood and social relations among the families may then begin to decline.

Fourth, within a given area or vicinity, proximity of dwellings is often less decisive for the establishment of neighborly relations

[25] G. Kirch, "Die Nachbarschaft in der Vorstadt," *Koelner Vierteljahrshefte für Soziologie* VIII, 1, 1929, p. 74; René König, *Die Gemeinde,* Hamburg, Rowohlt, 1958, p. 59.
[26] See for example, Judith T. Shuval, "Class and Ethnic Correlates of Casual Neighboring," *American Sociological Review,* 21 (August, 1956), pp. 453–458, and the literature referred to in that paper.

than occupation and social status. While in the tradition-bound farmer village the members of the family next door *are* one's neighbors in the social sense, whether one likes them or not, and regardless of status, the city dweller can pass by those next door and select people of more equal social status (and congenial personalities) as neighbors in the social sense.[27]

There are, of course, bound to be exceptions to these rules. Thus at the extreme urban fringe, where even people of wealth are occasionally dependent upon their next-door neighbors, the pattern of neighborhood relations may resemble more that of a rural community. Or, a suburb or subdivision may contain cliques of people who have moved there because they wanted to live near certain of their friends and acquaintances. In that case, interaction among neighbors may be very lively in spite of a relatively high socio-economic level.

The sociological insight that among city people the so-called "secondary" or, as I would rather say, utilitarian and contractual relationships tend to be more frequent than "primary" relationships seems to have led some sociologists to believe that the latter kind do not occur at all among urban people. In any case, a study has been made in Lansing, Michigan, in order to dispel this erroneous belief.[28] This study is an excellent case of a fight against sociological windmills. One wonders what the three authors did expect when one reads: "Therefore the data may be interpreted as showing that intimate social relationships are to be found in urban areas and that these relationships may be found both inside and outside the local area of residence."[29]

---

[27] The selective character of neighborhood relations in cities is confirmed by a recent comparative study of suburban housing development (*Siedlungen*) in Germany. According to this study, the very definition of neighborhood is quite "subjective," that is, it depends very largely on the individual as to whom he will consider a neighbor. Furthermore, there is "no recognition of duties, rights and roles (among neighbors) sanctioned by consensus or binding tradition." See Helmut Klages, *Der Nachbarschaftsgedanke und die nachbarliche Wirklichkeit in der Grosstadt*. Forschungsberichte des Wirtschafts- und Verkehrsministeriums Nordrhein-Westfahlen Nr. 566, Sozialforschungsstelle an der Universität Münster zu Dortmund, Abt. Prof. Dr. G. Ipsen. Westdeutscher Verlag, Köln u. Opladen, 1958, pp. 120 ff.

[28] Joel Smith, William H. Form, and Gregory P. Stone, "Local Intimacy in a Middle-Sized City," *American Journal of Sociology*, 60 (November, 1954), pp. 276 ff.

[29] *Ibid.* 278. This discovery is really the main conclusion of the elaborate study. "Thus, urban social integration is contributed to (sic!) by the fact that urbanites derive social satisfaction from informal relationships both within and outside of their local areas of residence. Spatial mobility makes for city-wide ties, stability makes for local area ties, and most urban residents have both." See pp. 283–284.

An interesting result of the study, however, is that people in "high" economic areas seemed to have higher rates of intimacy with their neighbors than residents of "low" economic areas, because this is contrary to expectations.

The authors of the study explain this finding partly by the fact that in the city of Lansing the upper-class residential alternatives are rather limited, and partly by the greater intra-city mobility of the lower-income groups. The first factor would have been modified, I believe, if the town of East Lansing had been included, because that is a major upper-stratum area comprising a fairly mobile element of university personnel. Furthermore, the questionnaire contains at least one question[30] which working class people are likely to answer in the negative because they, or at least their wives, will rarely "spend a whole afternoon or evening" visiting with some neighbor. This is more a middle-class and upper-class custom.

THE NORMATIVE ELEMENT VS. THE SENTIMENTAL

Urban sociologists have been especially inclined to proceed from the fallacious assumption that the neighborhood relationship should, in the ideal case, demand emotional involvement of the partner, that neighbors should be "friends." However, Willi Latten in the island study mentioned above (footnote 2) points out that "a personal, sentimental bond does not seem to exist at all between the inhabitants of a 'Warft' " (i.e., between spatially very close neighbors). Later he says: "Obvious to the observer was the contrast between spatial proximity and psychic distance, which could be observed with almost all the Hallig people. The compulsion of the regulated living together becomes tolerable only on the condition that the individual does not have to be personally devoted to every neighbor with whom he stands in objective relations".[31] One could perhaps rephrase this observation by making a distinction between emotional and categoric relationships. Neighborhood, as a social relationship, is originally indifferent in regard to emotional-affectual attitudes of neighbors to one another. Neighbors will do certain things for each other, whether they like each other or

---

[30] In this study, as in many recent empirical studies in sociology, the statistics do not refer to actually observed facts but to people's statements about their social actions and attitudes. It is quite possible that the poorer people actually "visit" more often than they admit because they want to give the impression of being too busy.

[31] Latten, op. cit., p. 393.

not.[32] To use Max Weber's terms: inter-action in neighborhood relations is typically tradition-oriented, not emotional-affectual.

The reciprocal obligation between neighbors is a consequence of their proximity and their interdependence. Where interdependence ceases because of the availability of services as in the city, proximity no longer constitutes the basis for a categoric social relationship. Neighbors may now choose to what extent they want to associate with each other. Friendship of a more or less intimate nature may thus develop between some neighbors. On the other hand, there are, even in cities, many situations in which neighbors in space will engage in mutual aid without becoming personal friends; one may lend each other garden tools or exchange plants and yet not invite one another for parties. To illustrate the first possibility, I can remember from my suburban childhood in Germany that my parents would make formal calls on our immediate neighbors (right, left and across the street) and even invite them to formal parties, but we would never dream of borrowing anything from any one of them, not even from the one family with whom my parents were really quite intimate socially. At present I am living in a "middle-class" suburban area where every-day relations between neighbors are restricted to the exchange of little favors but do not involve visiting in our homes or invitations to parties. However, I have reasons to assume that in emergencies the women would come to each others' aid (as some have done in certain cases of sickness); in this sense we seem to represent a case of what Ruth Glass has called "latent social neighborhood integration".

There is a tendency in contemporary sociology to focus attention too exclusively on attitudes and to neglect the normative element in

[32] Werner Bar, "Das Winzerdorf an der Ahr als Siedlungsgebilde," *Koelner Vierteljahrshefte für Soziologie*, XII, 1933, pp. 118 f., observes that even those neighborhood customs which might indicate a more sentimental attitude, as for example those connected with weddings, baptisms, or funerals, are mainly determined by tradition. "One acts not because of a psychic urge but because the forefathers used to do it this way." Likewise borrowing-and-lending is done under exclusion of any sympathetic motivations. "Lending (*Bittleihe*) is a completely traditional custom, which obviously no longer has any sentimental foundation." A recently published study by Elizabeth Pfeil of neighborhood relations in working class and white-collar districts of a German city shows that these people had a fairly precise idea of what kind of conduct was expected of inhabitants of the same tenement or apartment house; also, they did not want to become too intimate with neighbors, making a clear distinction between them and their personal friends. (Elizabeth Pfeil, "Nachbarkreis und Verkehrskreis in der Grosstadt," in: R. Mackensen a. o. *Daseinsformen der Grosstadt*, Tübingen, J. C. Mohr, 1959, pp. 158–225. This study, which I had seen in manuscript, was published after completion of my article.) See also René König, *op. cit.*, p. 64, about the general tendency to keep distance from one's neighbors and to differentiate between neighborliness and friendship.

social relationships. By overlooking the latter in the study of neighborhoods we run the risk of not adequately understanding the
structure of this relationship of mutual aid. As such it is regulated
by ancient custom which determines quite rigorously who the
neighbors are, and what neighbors may expect of each other. The
relationships assume the characteristics of a social institution. That
neighbors should harbor particularly sympathetic sentiments
toward each other is by no means implied. Where the institution is
well preserved, neighbors will act as expected even if they do *not*
particularly *like* each other. Only where the institution of neighborhood has been weakened because of a decline in the need for
mutual aid, do personal sentiments and attitudes of neighbors
towards one another tend to determine the amount and quality of
"neighboring" interaction.

HOSTILITY AND CONFLICT

This is not to say that neighborhood relations do not involve psychological problems. On the contrary, there seem to exist specific
patterns of hostility which arise from the peculiar physical and
social qualities of relations between neighbors.

Spatial proximity gives occasion to many conflicts. Among
peasants there is the notorious squabble over boundary lines, especially where, like in most parts of Europe, the holdings of each
farmstead are scattered in small lots all over the village land. In
cities, especially where multiple family dwellings are located close
together, e.g., in tenement and apartment-house districts, the occasions for conflict are numerous: the noises of radio and other gadgets, the nuisances caused by dogs, cats and other pets, the disturbing games of children, and so forth. In slums and blighted areas the
sharing of water-faucets and toilets by several households is a frequent cause of friction.

It seems a sound hypothesis to say that the greater the physical proximity, the more numerous the chances of conflict—other
things being equal.

One of the great advantages of the characteristic American
patterns of rural as well as urban settlement—the single farmstead
and the urban one-family house with garden—appears to be that
they minimize these occasions for conflict.

It also seems warranted by experience to maintain that conflicts between neighbors tend to be particularly bitter and long-
lasting. In rural areas it is not at all unusual that they go on from
one generation to the other; proximity not only makes it impossible

for the alienated parties to avoid one another but, on the contrary, gives occasion to new conflict-generating contacts. Besides, it seems a general rule that animosities which arise out of violations of primary group norms tend to become particularly bitter.[33]

Thus we are, as so frequently in the study of social relationships, confronted with a paradox: the relationship which on the one hand involves cooperation and mutual aid is at the same time, by its very nature, a seat of potential friction and hostility. It is the awareness of this ambivalence which keeps the wise peasant and the experienced city dweller from becoming too involved emotionally with his neighbors and induces him to preserve "social distance" in spite of nearness in space.

THE LAW AND NEIGHBORHOOD RELATIONS

The kind of conflicts which typically arise between neighbors are reflected in the vast body of law concerning the rights and duties of neighbors in relation to one another. This body of law has grown largely from custom through court decisions and is therefore to a large extent of local or regional nature.

Curiously enough, these legal aspects are almost completely ignored by sociologists as if custom (folkways and mores) alone could regulate the relations between neighbors. Even in a relatively static society this would be impossible; the very fact that immediate neighbors own or occupy adjoining pieces of land makes it necessary to protect property rights against interferences from neighbors and to impose restrictions on property rights in favor of neighbors. In a changing society and under conditions of a rapidly changing technology there arise constantly new problems, new types of conflict, which can be solved or alleviated only by legislative law or local ordinances.

The confusing variety of neighborhood law prevents us from dealing here with its substance in detail. We can only give examples of the kind of legal questions that arise out of neighborhood-relations and point out some of the general problems of neighborhood law.

In rural areas of Europe, where one farmer may own many very small fields that are sandwiched in between other farmers' fields, the right to walk or even drive over the neighbor's land is often indispensable for effective cultivation. Or, in an urban com-

---

[33] Simmel refers to this phenomenon repeatedly. See *The Sociology of Georg Simmel*, translated and edited by Kurt H. Wolff, Glencoe, Illinois: The Free Press, 1950.

munity one may have to go on the neighbor's lot in order to trim a hedge or to do some repair work on one's house. Does the neighbor have to tolerate such trespassing? The keeping of cattle, pigs, chickens and other animals may be prohibited on city lots; incorporation of fringe areas may lead to a change in the legal situation in these and other respects. There are specific restrictions in cities on such uses of property which result in molestation of one's neighbor by noise, smell, fumes or by interference with his radio, phonograph or TV equipment. While a great deal of neighborhood law has developed out of custom, many of the problems arising from rapid urbanization or from technological innovations have to be met by enactment of statutory legal rules.

The beginnings of legislation on neighborhood relations seems to coincide with the rise of the modern state. The enlightened absolutism of eighteenth century monarchs has been responsible for a great many enactments in this field. In some cases legislation was deemed necessary where tradition was no longer strong enough to maintain what had so far been useful institutions. The *Brunnenordnung* of Jever of 1756, regulating the functions of well-associations, may have been issued for this reason.[34]

Sociologically it is very significant that modern neighbor-law, as a rule, deals almost exclusively with property and does not concern itself with mutual aid. Neighborhood-law is essentially a body of legal norms by which compromises are reached between the conflicting interests of owners of adjoining pieces of real estate.[35] Like the mutual obligations in the original rural neighborhood, these restrictions of property rights often assume the form of servitudes resting upon certain fields or town lots rather than pertaining to the proprietor as a person.

CONCLUSION

We started from the observation that the word neighborhood may mean either an area or a social relationship. Neighborhoods in the first sense may be small in area as well as in the number of people comprised or they may be quite large in both respects, as is often the case in cities.

Neighborhood in the second sense means originally a small number of people *whose dwellings are adjoining* and who by the

[34] H. Siuts, *op. cit.*, pp. 3, 13.
[35] Meisner-Stern-Hodes, *Nachbarrecht*, 2nd. edition, Berlin, 1955, p. 2. The Norwegian Law, however, recognizes neighborly mutual aid (*dugnad*) as "a strong legal obligation" according to Edv. *Bull, Vergleichende Studien über die Kulturverhaeltnisse des Bauerntums*, Oslo, 1930, p. 19.

nature of things are dependent on each other for mutual aid in emergencies. Custom prescribes what kind of aid may be expected and assigns definite roles to the occupants of the various dwelling places involved. But mutual aid obligations are not the only content of the relationship; neighbors are also entitled to share certain joyous or festive events in each other's lives. In this sense, neighborhood is an institution. The institutional character of neighborhood is not abolished but rather re-enforced when the group is extended beyond the immediately adjoining households, as is the case particularly in preindustrial cities. As the need for mutual aid declines in the modern city and also in modern rural communities, the functions of the neighborhood tend to become less important; the sociability aspects tend to predominate. At the same time, as a consequence of this change, association with one's neighbors becomes essentially a matter of choice.

The latter development has led sociologists to focus on attitudes and behavior and to neglect the normative element in neighborhood relations, and to ignore completely the legal aspects.

The question whether the term "neighborhood" should be used to designate an area or a type of social relationship is not merely a semantic problem. We do not advocate change in terminology. What matters is the distinction between a social order in which occupants of an area, that is "neighbors in space," are related to each other in a specific way by mutual rights and duties attaching to their dwelling places (and where they act accordingly) and another type of social order in which it is a matter of choice whether and in what ways one associates and interacts with one's spatial neighbors. There are, of course, empirically many transitions from one type to the other and it is especially interesting to observe that the normative element never quite disappears, that even in the city a minimum of neighborhood custom survives along with legal regulations.

Planning and Social Life:
Friendship and Neighbor Relations
in Suburban Communities

HERBERT J. GANS
Columbia University

. . . Although propinquity initiates many social relationships and maintains less intensive ones, such as "being neighborly," it is not sufficient by itself to create intensive relationships. Friendship requires homogeneity. . . .

Propinquity leads to visual contact between neighbors and is likely to produce face-to-face social contact. This is true only if the distance between neighbors is small enough to encourage one or the other to transform the visual contact into a social one.[1] Thus, physical distance between neighbors is important. So is the relationship of the dwellings—especially their front and rear doors—and the circulation system.[2] For example, if doors of adjacent houses face each other or if residents must share driveways, visual contact is inevitable.

The opportunity for visual and social contact is greater at high densities than at low ones, but only if neighbors are adjacent hori-

From the *Journal of the American Institute of Planners*, Vol. 27, No. 2, pp. 135–139 (May, 1961). Reprinted by permission of the author and of the *Journal of the American Institute of Planners*.

[1] If the physical distance is negligible, as between next-door neighbors, social contact is likely to take place quickly. When neighbors are not immediately adjacent, however, one or the other must take the initiative, and this requires either some visible sign of a shared background characteristic, or interest, or the willingness to be socially aggressive. This is not as prevalent as sometimes imagined. Although the new suburbs are often thought to exhibit an inordinate amount of intrablock visiting, I found that on the block on which I lived in Levittown, New Jersey, some of the men who lived three to five houses away from each other did not meet for over a year after initial occupancy. The wives met more quickly, of course.

[2] L. Festinger, S. Schachter, and K. Back call this "functional distance." *Social Pressures in Informal Groups*, pp. 34–35 (New York: Harper & Bros., 1950).

zontally. In apartment buildings, residents who share a common hallway will meet, but those who live on different floors are less likely to do so, because there is little occasion for visual contact.[3] Consequently, propinquity operates most efficiently in single-family and row-house areas, especially if these are laid out as courts, narrow loops, or cul-de-sacs.

Initial social contacts can develop into relationships of varying intensity, from polite chats about the weather to close friendship. (Negative relationships, varying from avoidance to open enmity, are also possible.) Propinquity not only initiates relationships, but it also plays an important role in maintaining the less intensive ones, for the mere fact of living together encourages neighbors to make sure that the relationship between them remains positive. Propinquity cannot determine the intensity of the relationship, however; this is a function of the characteristics of the people involved. If neighbors are homogeneous and feel themselves to be compatible, there is some likelihood that the relationship will be more intensive than an exchange of greetings. If neighbors are heterogeneous, the relationship is not likely to be intensive, regardless of the degree of propinquity. *Propinquity may thus be the initial cause of an intensive positive relationship, but it cannot be the final or sufficient cause.*

This is best illustrated in a newly settled subdivision. When people first move in, they do not know each other, or anything about each other, except that they have all chosen to live in this community—and can probably afford to do so.[4] As a result, they will begin to make social contacts based purely on propinquity, and because they share the characteristics of being strangers and pioneers, they will do so with almost every neighbor within physical and functional distance. As these social contacts continue, participants begin to discover each other's backgrounds, values, and interests, so that similarities and differences become apparent. Homogeneous neighbors may become friends, whereas heterogeneous ones soon reduce the amount of visiting, and eventually limit themselves

[3] L. Festinger, "Architecture and Group Membership," *Journal of Social Issues*, Vol. 7, p. 157 (1951). See also A. Wallace, *Housing and Social Structure* (Philadelphia: Philadelphia Housing Authority, 1952). In urban tenement areas, where neighbors are often related or from the same ethnic background, there may be considerable visiting between floors. A high degree of homogeneity can thus overcome physical obstacles.

[4] Home buyers do not, however, move into a new area without some assurance that neighbors are likely to be compatible. They derive this assurance from the house price (which bears some correlation to purchasers' income level), from the kinds of people whom they see inspecting the model homes, and from the previous class and ethnic image of the area within which the subdivision is located.

to being neighborly. (This process is usually completed after about three months of social contact, especially if people have occupied their homes in spring or summer, when climate and garden chores lead to early visual contact.) The resulting pattern of social relationships cannot be explained by propinquity alone. An analysis of the characteristics of the people will show that homogeneity and heterogeneity explain the existence *and the absence* of social relationships more adequately than does the site plan or the architectural design. Needless to say, the initial social pattern is not immutable; it is changed by population turnover and by a gradual tendency to find other friends outside the immediate area.[5]

If neighbors are compatible, however, they may not look elsewhere for companionship, so that propinquity—as well as the migration patterns and housing market conditions which bring homogeneous people together—plays an important role. Most of the communities studied so far have been settled by homogeneous populations. For example, Festinger, Schachter, and Back studied two student housing projects whose residents were of similar age, marital status, and economic level. Moreover, they were all sharing a common educational experience and had little time for entertaining. Under these conditions, the importance of propinquity in explaining visiting patterns and friendship is not surprising. The fact that they were impermanent residents is also relevant, although if a considerable degree of homogeneity exists among more permanent residents, similar patterns develop.

PROPINQUITY, HOMOGENEITY, AND NEIGHBOR RELATIONS

Although propinquity brings neighbors into social contact, a certain degree of homogeneity is required to maintain this contact on a positive basis. If neighors are too diverse, differences of behavior or attitude may develop which can lead to coolness or even conflict. For example, when children who are being reared by different methods come into conflict, disciplinary measures by their parents will reveal differences in ways of rewarding and punishing. If one child is punished for a digression and his playmate is not, misunderstandings and arguments can develop between the parents. Differences about house and yard maintenance or about political issues can have similar consequences.

The need for homogeneity is probably greatest among neighbors with children of equal age and among immediately adjacent neighbors. Children, especially young ones, choose playmates on a purely

[5] See W. Form, "Stratification in Low and Middle Income Housing Areas," *Journal of Social Issues*, Vol. 7, pp. 116–117 (1951).

propinquitous basis. Thus, positive relations among neighbors with children of similar age are best maintained if the neighbors are comparatively homogeneous with respect to child-rearing methods. Immediately adjacent neighbors are likely to have frequent visual contact, and if there is to be social contact, they must be relatively compatible. Some people minimize social contact with immediately adjacent neighbors on principle, in order to prevent possible differences from creating disagreement. Since such neighbors live in involuntary propinquity, conflict might result in permanently impaired relationships which might force one or the other to move out.

Generally speaking, conflicts between neighbors seem to be rare. In the new suburbs, current building and marketing practices combine to bring together people of relatively similar age and income, thus creating sufficient homogeneity to enable strangers to live together peaceably. In the communities which I have studied, many people say that they have never had such friendly neighbors. Where chance assembles a group of heterogeneous neighbors, unwritten and often unrecognized pacts are developed which bring standards of house and yard maintenance into alignment and which eliminate from the conversation topics that might result in conflict.

THE MEANING OF HOMOGENEITY

I have been stressing the importance of resident characteristics without defining the terms homogeneity and heterogeneity. This omission has been intentional, for little is known about what characteristics must be shared before people feel themselves to be compatible with others. We do not know for certain if they must have common backgrounds, or similar interests, or shared values—or combinations of these. Nor do we know precisely which background characteristics, behavior patterns, and interests are most and least important, or about what issues values must be shared. Also, we do not know what similarities are needed for relationships of different intensities or, for any given characteristics, how large a difference can exist before incompatibility sets in. For example, it is known that income differences can create incompatibility between neighbors, but it is not known how large these differences must become before incompatibility is felt.

Demographers may conclude that one community is more homogeneous than another with respect to such characteristics as age or income, but this information is too general and superficial to predict the pattern of social life. Social relationships are not based on census data, but on subjectively experienced definitions of homogeneity and heterogeneity which terminate in judgments of compatibility or incompatibility. These definitions and judgments have received little study.

Sociologists generally agree that behavior patterns, values, and interests—what people think and do—are more important criteria for homogeneity than background factors.[6] My observations suggest that in the new suburbs, values with respect to child rearing, leisure-time interests, taste level, general cultural preferences, and temperament seem to be most important in judging compatibility or incompatibility.

Such interests and values *do* reflect differences in background characteristics, since a person's beliefs and actions are shaped in part by his age, income, occupation, and the like. These characteristics can, therefore, be used as clues to understanding the pattern of social relationships. *Life-cycle stage* (which summarizes such characteristics as age of adults, marital status, and age of children) and *class* (especially income and education) are probably the two most significant characteristics. Education is especially important, because it affects occupational choice, child-rearing patterns, leisure-time preferences, and taste level. *Race* is also an important criterion, primarily because it is a highly visible—although not necessarily accurate—symbol of class position.[7]

Background characteristics provide crude measures that explain only in part the actual evaluations and choices made by neighbors on a block. Until these evaluations themselves are studied—and then related to background data—it is impossible to define homogeneity or heterogeneity operationally. Since considerable criticism has been leveled at the new suburbs for being overly homogeneous—at least by demographic criteria—such research is of considerable importance for the planner's evaluation of these communities and for the planning of future residential areas.

VARIATIONS IN HOMOGENEITY

The degree of population homogeneity varies from suburb to suburb. Moreover, since residents usually become neighbors by a

[6] For one study which deals with this problem, see Lazarsfeld and Merton, *op. cit.* They concluded that the sharing of values is more important than the sharing of backgrounds.

[7] Studies such as M. Deutsch and M. Collins, *Interracial Housing* (Minneapolis: University of Minnesota Press, 1951) and E. and G. Grier, *Privately Developed Interracial Housing* (Berkeley: University of California Press, 1960) suggest that where people are relatively homogeneous in class and age, race differences are no obstacle to social relationships, and race is no longer a criterion of heterogeneity. This is especially true in middle-class residential areas occupied by professional people.

fairly random process—for example, by signing deeds at the same time—many combinations of homogeneity and heterogeneity can be found among the blocks of a single subdivision.[8] In some blocks, neighbors are so compatible that they spend a significant amount of their free time with each other and even set up informal clubs to cement the pattern. In other blocks, circumstances bring together very diverse people, and relationships between them may be only polite, or even cool.

Whyte's studies in Park Forest led him to attribute these variations to site planning features. He found that the small "courts" were friendly and happy; the larger ones, less friendly and sometimes unhappy. He also found that the residents of the smaller courts were so busy exchanging visits that, unlike those of the larger ones, they did not become active in the wider community.[9] My observations in Park Forest and in Levittown, New Jersey, suggest, however, that homogeneity and heterogeneity explain these phenomena more effectively.[10] When neighbors are especially homogeneous, blocks can become friendly, regardless of their size, although the larger blocks usually divide themselves into several social groupings. Block size is significant only insofar as a small block may *feel* itself to be more cohesive because all sociability takes place within one group. In the larger blocks, the fact that there are several groups prevents such a feeling, even though each of the groups may be as friendly as the one in the smaller block.

Community participation patterns can be explained in a similar fashion. If the block population is heterogeneous, and residents must look elsewhere for friends, they inevitably turn to community-wide clubs, church organizations, and even civic groups in order to meet compatible people. If participation in these organizations is based solely on the need to find friends, however, it is likely to be minimal, and may even cease, once friendships are established. This type of membership differs considerably from civic or organizational participation proper. The distinction between the two types is important. Whyte recommends that site planners encourage par-

[8] This is true of the larger subdivisions. Smaller ones are sometimes not settled randomly, but are occupied by groups, for example related households or members of an ethnic group moving *en masse* from another area.

[9] Whyte, *The Organization Man*, pp. 333–334 (New York: Simon and Schuster, 1957).

[10] These comments are based on observations, however, rather than on systematic studies. Macris studied visiting patterns in Park Forest in 1957 and found considerably less intrablock visiting than did Whyte. He also found that there was almost no visiting at all between tenants and homeowners, even though they were living in physical propinquity in the area he studied. This suggests the importance of neighbor homogeneity. D. Macris, "Social Relationships Among Residents of Various House Types in a Planned Community," unpublished master's thesis (University of Illinois, 1958).

ticipation by making blocks large enough to discourage excessive on-the-block social life. While this might increase the first type of participation, it cannot affect the second type. People who are inclined to be really active in community-wide organizations are a self-selected minority who will desert the social life of the block, regardless of the block's layout or of the neighbors' compatibility. They are usually attracted to community participation by pressing community problems and by interest, ambition, or the hope of personal gain. Site planning techniques cannot bring about their participation.

THE ROLE OF PROPINQUITY

Given the importance of homogeneity in social relationships, what role remains for propinquity? Since propinquity results in visual contact, whether voluntary, or involuntary, it produces social contact among neighbors, although homogeneity will determine how intensive the relationships will be and whether they will be positive or not. Propinquity also supports relationships based on homogeneity by making frequent contact convenient. Finally, among people who are comparatively homogeneous and move into an area as strangers, propinquity may determine friendship formation among neighbors.

In addition, some types of people gravitate to propinquitous relationships more than others. Age is an important factor. As already noted, children choose their playmates strictly on a propinquitous basis, though decreasingly so as they get older. This is why parents who want their young children to associate with playmates of similar status and cultural background must move to areas where such playmates are close at hand.

Among adults, the importance of propinquity seems to vary with sex and class. Women generally find their female friends nearby, especially if they are mothers and are restricted in their movements. In fact, young mothers must usually be able to find compatible people—and therefore, homogeneous neighbors—within a relatively small radius. Should they fail to do so, they may become the unhappy isolated suburban housewives about whom so much has been written. My observations suggest that most women are able to find the female companionship they seek, however. In addition, the increase in two-car families and women's greater willingness to drive are gradually reducing the traditional immobility of the housewife.

The relationship between propinquity and class has received little study. Generally speaking, the "higher" the class, the greater the physical mobility for visiting and entertaining. Thus, working-class people seem to be least mobile and most likely to pick their friends on a propinquitous basis. However, since they visit primarily with relatives, they may travel considerable distances if relatives are not available nearby.[11] Upper-middle-class people seem to go farther afield for their social life than do lower-middle-class ones, in part because they may have specialized interests which are hard to satisfy on the block.

Propinquity is also more important for some types of social activities than others. In America, and probably everywhere in the Western world, adolescents and adults socialize either in peer groups—people of similar age and sex—or in sets of couples. Peer groups are more likely to form on the basis of propinquity. For example, the members of that well-known suburban peer group, the women's "coffee klatsch," are usually recruited in the immediate vicinity. Since the participants indulge primarily in shop talk—children, husbands, and home—the fact that they are all wives and mothers provides sufficient homogeneity to allow propinquity to function.[12] For couples, homogeneity is a more urgent requirement than propinquity, since the two people in a couple must accept both members of all other couples. The amount of compatibility that is required probably cannot be satisfied so easily among the supply of neighbors within propinquitous distance.

The role of propinquity also varies with the size of the group, and with the activities pursued. The larger the group, the less intensive are the relationships between participants, and the less homogeneity is required. If the group meets for a specific activity, such as to celebrate a major holiday or to play cards, the behavior that takes place is sufficiently specialized and habitual that the participants' other characteristics are less relevant. If the group meets for conversation, more homogeneity of values and interests is required. . . .[13]

LIMITATIONS OF THESE OBSERVATIONS

The foregoing comments are based largely on observations and studies in new suburban communities. Little is known about the

[1] M. Young and P. Willmott, *Family and Kinship in East London* (London: Routledge and Kegan Paul, 1957).

[2] There must, however, be general agreement about methods of housekeeping, getting along with husbands, and child rearing. Since these methods vary with education and socio-economic level, some homogeneity of class is necessary even for the coffee klatsch.

[3] The kinds of gatherings which Whyte studied so ingeniously in Park Forest were mainly those of peer groups indulging in single-purpose activities. This may explain why he found propinquity to be so important.

role of propinquity and homogeneity in established communities, although there is no reason to expect any major differences.[14] Whatever differences exist are probably due to the reduction of much of the initial homogeneity in established communities through population turnover. The same process is likely to take place in new communities. Moveouts create a gap in established social groupings. Newcomers may be able to fill this gap—provided they are not too different from those they have replaced. Even so, it is hard for a newcomer to break into an established coffee klatsch or card party, and only people with a little extra social aggressiveness are likely to do so. In addition, there is the previously noted tendency of the original residents to find new friends outside the immediate area and to spend less time with neighbors. As a result of these processes, patterns of social life in new communities will eventually resemble those in established areas.

[14] See I. Rostow, "The Social Effects of the Physical Environment," *Journal of the American Institute of Planners*, Vol. 27, p. 131 (1961).

Neighbours in England and the United States

H. E. BRACEY
University of Bristol

The following pages derive from a survey begun on new housing estates near Bristol, England, in 1957 and continued on a number of new subdivisions[1] near Columbus, Ohio, in 1958 and 1959. The inquiry was designed to study the adjustment of (mainly) urban families to life in new rural-urban fringe neighbourhoods. As far as we know, it is the first household survey of its kind to attempt a comparison of the way of life of such families in the two countries, which are separated by three thousand miles of sea yet speak the same language, almost, and think of themselves, often, as being so alike but are in fact, as we shall see, frequently, so different.

■ ■ ■

An interview outline was devised and interviews were taken in the homes of a sample of householders selected on a random basis. It was later decided to increase the number of interviews to 120, and, if possible, to carry out the same number in new neighbourhoods around Columbus, Ohio, choosing subdivisions where the residents were, as near as possible, comparable by income and social status. . . .

■ ■ ■

From H. E. Bracey, *Neighbors: Subdivision Life in England and the United States*, pp. ix–x, 74–81, and 181–183 (Baton Rouge: Louisiana State University Press, 1964). Reprinted by permission of the Louisiana State University Press.
[1] The word "subdivision" is used here to describe a new American, and the word "estate" a new English, housing development.

A quarter of all householders interviewed, both English and American, gave as one of the reasons for their satisfaction with their new neighbourhood the friendliness of the people. Analysing the interview reports it was found that somewhere or another during the interview 66 percent of all American families and 26 percent of all English families mentioned the general friendliness of their neighbours as being important to them. It was quite clear, however, that friendliness meant different things to different individuals, on different estates (subdivisions), with different income groups: in fact, it varied noticeably with the background of the individual. But the common denominator of friendliness in neighbours, on both sides of the Atlantic, appeared as "... being easy to talk with," "... speaks to you in the yard" (garden), both American; or "... speaks to you all the time. Has no moods," English. This need for *conversation* with neighbors was mentioned in England by 9 per cent, and in America by 8 per cent, of all householders, proportions which did not vary noticeably from one subdivision or estate to another. The neatest and most telling expression of this need came from a housewife on one of the high-cost American subdivisions who described a good neighbour as one who was "... friendly, happy to see you." Men seemed less bothered about this, but the thought was clearly in the mind of the English husband who said, "They never let you pass without passing the time of day." But nobody wanted the "real gabby type," as an American housewife described the neighbour who did not know when to stop talking.

What do they talk about? Two American women gave interesting answers to this question, which, incidentally, was not asked by the interviewer. The first explained, "You are out in the yard (garden) and you see someone working and you say, 'Isn't it a lovely day?' and pretty soon you are saying 'Isn't your boy in my son's class?' or 'Has the boy delivered your papers yet?' and the first thing you know you have found things in common. . . . You just like people, that's all." The second said, "Most of us gossip in a friendly way. For example, we say, 'Oh! That's the dress you bought at such-and-such a store. Somebody was telling me about that.' That's the innocent kind of gossiping." This homemaker (housewife) recognized the existence of another kind of gossiping, but she was far too friendly a person herself to do more than hint at it. Others were less inhibited as we shall see later.

The early offer of friendliness is extremely important to the new arrival. "If it was not for the neighbours here, I would go back to Frenchay," i.e., to the neighbourhood from whence she had come, said an English housewife (homemaker).

An English husband was not so sure about neighbours gossiping. He disliked seeing three or four women "with aprons on talking and gossiping in the street while the children are making a noise and enjoying themselves." His wife's rejoinder was brief and to the point: "You're a man!" The wife saw only the friendliness she shared with her neighbours. This was a new council housing estate and subsequent questions showed that the sight of women talking in the street conjured up for the husband a picture of life in the near-slum which he had left behind him. Already, he was jealous of the fair appearance and good name of the new neighbourhood, with which he sought to identify himself.

Linked with the appreciation of conversational friendliness was the feeling that it was an advantage if you shared a common interest with your neighbours; some 8 per cent of American families mentioned this. Most of these were from intermediate-priced subdivisions where the people were younger. In general, common interests were not looked for in neighbours by those who lived on estates or subdivisions which were occupied, predominantly, by people drawn from the lowest or from the highest income bracket. In England, only 3 percent mentioned sharing common interest with neighbours, as a reason for liking the neighbourhood, and these referred to the experience which most shared, that of bringing up children. Help with the children, however, was mentioned by many more parents in other contexts.

HELP IN AN EMERGENCY

One quarter in the United States, and 70 percent in England, looked for *help* from their neighbour in some shape or form: help which varied noticeably with the income bracket and the composition of the household. In general, it was "help in an emergency." One or two carried it farther: for example, "A person who would help you in trouble or who would recognize that you were in trouble." The young mother usually thought of help with the children in sickness. An English housewife (homemaker) added, expressively, "You *need* help with the children." Aged 33 years, she had four children whose ages ranged from 3 to 10 years. She did not instance examples but had clearly found her neighbours helpful in this direction.

At the lowest level, help with children comprised advice as to simple childish ailments, but much evidence was given of help, sometimes continued over long periods, which must have involved

the neighbours in a very considerable amount of effort and, sometimes money. Two English examples illustrate this. In the first,
when the mother was severely ill in hospital, the husband lost only
the first two days from work because housewives (homemakers) on
each side came in and assumed responsibility for the two children,
both under five years of age. The second, a husband, speaking of
the time when his wife was ill, said, "Our neighbor gave up her job
for a week to nurse the wife." Similar neighbourly actions were met
in America: "Last winter when I was ill my two neighbors came in
and took my children (6 and 3 years old), one each, to their homes.
My husband was out of town and they prepared food for me." Quite
clearly the severe illness of the mother is one of the most difficult
problems to deal with if you have a young family.

The second problem which seems to bring neighbours together
in mutual self-help is bereavement or serious illness of a near relative, especially one who lives a fair distance away. For one American homemaker, the most important act of neighbourliness had been
provided by a near neighbour who, at a moment's notice, took her
son into her own home (she already had two small children of her
own) to allow her to journey to Georgia, a thousand miles away, to
be with her dying father; because of her own husband's irregular
hours some form of temporary adoption was necessary. A neighbour
round the corner whom we interviewed was equally grateful, but
less articulate, about the help she had received from neighbours
when she lost her baby. All she could repeat, over and over again,
with tears in her eyes, was, "They're fabulous, I'll say! They're
fabulous!" Similar sentiments were expressed by the English
housewife whose husband had very recently gone off with another
woman and left her with two children. Of her neighbours she said,
"I have found out what a good neighbour is, these last two weeks,
since my husband left me." Neighbourly help in this instance
included lending money, for the poor woman was left with no
income, until the county welfare department came on the scene;
this was a council estate where incomes rarely exceeded £10 ($28)
or £12 ($34) a week and the real meaning of the neighbour's help
may be imagined.

On the whole, however, the lending of money to neighbours
was an obligation which English council householders seemed
rather afraid of, and partly explained why some did not want to
get too friendly with their neighbours. It was usually linked as follows with the definition of a good neighbour: "One who keeps herself to herself and doesn't borrow." Another put it rather bluntly
as, "A lot try to be good neighbours but are on the scrounge all the

time." This kind of remark came only from council houses and never from house-owners in England and never in America. This is not to say that other forms of borrowing between neighbours do not take place; in fact, many seemed to welcome the opportunity to show their friendliness by lending tools, especially gardening tools; it did not worry anybody sufficiently to put it forward as an adverse criticism of their neighbours.

The apprehension of council tenants that neighbours might wish to borrow money may be due to the fact that they were living much nearer the subsistence line than other families we interviewed, and that their recent house removal, with its attendant expenses, had sharpened their awareness of the dangers of neighbours wishing to borrow money from them. In areas of close living, from which many had just moved, borrowing money "to finish the week out" had been an accepted practice amongst neighbours who had known each other for long periods. These new neighbours were unknown or, at least, untried, and, therefore, one had to be careful.

"Settling in" provides opportunities for the display of neighbourly spirit. On one council estate in England several families moved into their new home in the middle of a very cold spell of weather and "When we came out here first, people were running round helping one another with buckets of coal." This emergency clearly broke down even an Englishman's reserve. The traditional way to show your neighbourliness in America at times like these is to bring across a pie for the newcomers on their day of arrival. This experience was enjoyed by several families met, but perhaps the finest example of neighbourliness was given us by a stonemason who has moved into a new neighbourhood where three-quarters or more of the residents were from the professional classes. While building his house he injured his back and had to spend several weeks in hospital. When he was able to get about again he still had to wear a brace support and was unable to "grade" the garden. This expression, for English readers, means clearing up the rubbish and levelling the lot (plot) so that it could be seeded with grass and subsequently cut with the minimum of effort with a wide-cut motor mower—an essential in the hot humid summer, especially when your lot measures an acre, as in this case. This man watched with envy as his neighbours laid out their yards (gardens) and he needed little imagination to visualize the "jungle" he would have by June: this was early April. But, one Saturday morning at 8 a.m., without previous warning, a knock came to his front door and "There was all my neighbours, nine or ten of them, and they done all my landscaping for me. They brought tractors, wheelbarrows and rakes. . . . They worked hard from 8:30 to 5 o'clock without a stop. . . . They sowed the grass and planted the plants. It gave us a nice feeling." This last was clearly an understatement.

A wistful comment from a rather lonely housewife makes a suitable tailpiece to this section: "It's nice to be thought of even if you don't need help."

PRESERVING PRIVACY

My greatest surprise, as an Englishman, came from the limitations which so many Americans put to the desirable activities of a good neighbour, and the stress laid on preserving privacy. And remember, the word "privacy" was not mentioned by the interviewer; nor was any phrase suggesting privacy. The question put was, "What do you understand by a 'good neighbour'?" or "How would you describe a 'good neighbour'?" But let us look first at how the English householders regard their neighbours.

I had felt for a long time that the average Englishman considered that the proper place for a neighbour was on his own side of the fence and that most conversations between neighbours were conducted across the fence or hedge or whatever served to mark the boundary of the adjoining property. I was not therefore surprised to learn that many English definitions of a "good neighbour" included reservations as to the degree of friendliness which would be welcomed by our informants. Thus, one housewife on an English council estate expected her neighbour to be "friendly without being pushing; kind without being nosey." In other words, offers of help would be welcomed in an emergency but would be examined carefully for snags or implications at other times. Another, an English husband, after his wife had described her idea of a good neighbour as "one you can rely on," cut in quickly with, "Yes, but one you talk to over the fence, but no further than that." His wife still would not agree: "I like to invite them in and go to their house," she said. After a pause, upbringing proved too strong and she also felt obliged to insert a limiting clause, "but not to get intimate with."

English householders clearly recognized that neighbours constitute a threat to privacy. In old-established English neighbourhoods, the garden fence effectively marks the physical limits to neighbouring activities and there was much less emphasis on maintaining privacy. Indeed, it became apparent that few had actually suffered from excessive intrusion from neighbours, in the past. Although, in their new homes, the physical barriers were slender in the extreme—in most cases two strands of wire running the length of the garden (yard)—in most people the mental barrier which they had grown up with remained as robust as ever. They tended to keep some newcomers farther apart from their neighbours than they really wanted to be in their new surroundings. Others saw the boundary wire as far too weak a line of defence if the neighbour became "difficult." This fear was particularly noticeable amongst the group of working-class people who found themselves on an open-plan council estate, straight from city congestion where close living had helped to make their mental reservations and physical barriers of prime importance. Thus, "I like being friendly but not too friendly. I don't go into anybody else's home." This housewife, aged 38 years, had spent all her life in one working-class neighbourhood.

Did these English householders really believe that the maintenance of a formal or semi-formal barrier of reserve between neighbours was absolutely necessary? Most did, we gathered, but many had put up the barrier on hearsay evidence alone or, more commonly, were continuing the practice of their parents. Very frequently the definition of a good neighbour, who was to be kept to her own side of the fence, was followed by qualifications which suggested that there might be something in having more to do with neighbours, after all. One housewife, aged 31 years with two children, occupying a house (owned) for the first time in her married life, first of all defined a good neighbour as " . . . a person who is not inquisitive about other people's affairs. . . . People who are ready to take you at face value." This was the stereotyped reply but, after a pause, she added, rather wistfully, "Someone who would help—but we have never done this much—but it would be nice to have a give-and-take arrangement." She had lived in three furnished apartments in her seven years of married life where neighbours were too close for comfort at times. After two years in her present house she still had not been able to establish a "give-and-take arrangement," as she called it, with her neighbours.

American homemakers seemed to possess to a still more marked degree the fear that neighbours might seriously threaten their privacy. Eighteen per cent wanted neighbours to mind their own business and another 14 per cent, making 33 per cent in all, put it a little more mildly and felt that neighbours should not be allowed to get too familiar. These figures are higher than for England and are undoubtedly related to the greater ease of, and the existing pattern for, neighbouring in the United States, an ease which is due as much to physical differences between the two countries as to contrasts in human values, in tradition, outlook and the general way of life.

Over much of the United States, the lowest-cost houses occupied by the lowest-paid workers are set as close as, and often closer than, houses occupied by their opposite numbers on a council housing estate in England. . . .

■ ■ ■

Undoubtedly, the most noticeable contrast between the two countries to emerge from the enquiry is the greater neighbourliness existing on American subdivisions contrasted with the aloofness, if not actual chilliness, which passes for neighbourliness on English estates, both council and private-enterprise. Yet, surprisingly, in both countries there was general agreement that neighbours are best kept at arm's length: only rarely should you make real friends of your neighbours.

In both countries, the great majority, some 80 percent, were very content with the house and neighbourhood they had chosen. But for many Americans this was recognized to be only a short-time satisfaction: it was accepted that in a few years the family would be moving on.

In the choice of a new neighbourhood both groups of nationals rated highly its accessibility relative to the husband's place of work. English householders, council and private-enterprise, rated more highly the nearness of open country, a feature which weighed with Americans not at all. The latter sought a good school system: this was not mentioned by English people.

Many women on English estates experienced loneliness. They missed the friends from whom their move to the new neighbourhood had separated them. No loneliness was evident on American subdivisions. All families were able to keep in touch with friends and relatives in other parts of the city with little difficulty. Many kept in close, frequent, contact with friends in other towns, some at a great distance by English standards.

On all English neighbourhoods there were complaints of too few organizations for adults and, especially, too few for children. No English organization, religious or secular, appeared to be adequately equipped to welcome newcomers or to recruit them to their membership. In America, there were many formal and informal organizations whose activities, consciously or unconsciously, helped to make newcomers feel at home in their new neighbourhood.

In both countries, children proved to be very important in bringing parents, especially mothers, together for neighbourly intercourse. In America, this applied particularly to extracurricular school activities and youth organizations like the Scouts and 4-H club. In England, these organizations were relatively unimportant.

American Churches provide a wealth of social club facilities for all ages—for children, teenagers and adults of both sexes—as well as programmes for religious instruction and observance. English Churches concentrate on the religious aspects of their faith and few arrange purely social functions for their members. In America, churchgoing was especially important on higher-priced subdivisions and relatively unimportant on low-cost subdivisions. In England, only a small minority of the families interviewed were churchgoers.

Englishmen of all income levels appeared more educated to an appreciation of the need to conserve natural beauty in the countryside. They were also most alert to the concomitant danger of uncontrolled development. Most Americans, on the other hand, appeared to be living cosily in the belief that both natural beauty and land suitable for development were inexhaustible and expendable. It is true, of course, that they have more land to spread themselves over, but the Americans we met showed little awareness of the unpleasant corollaries of longer daily journeys to work and recession of the natural environment from daily living which are applicable however much land you have to build on. For most, a new motor road and another and a bigger, faster automobile were complete solutions to bigger and bigger towns. We met little more than half a dozen, during the whole of our stay in America, who appeared to have given serious thought to this problem. These few lived near the more congested eastern seaboard. . . .

Chapter 7

SOCIAL PATHOLOGY IN THE METROPOLIS

The contemporary urban crisis has many dimensions—political, eco-logical, engineering, and others—but certainly it is the concentra-tion in our great cities of perplexing social problems which has received the greatest popular emphasis. In the United States, rising rates of crime and racial upheavals have become of particular con-cern. The sense of helplessness, of powerlessness, experienced by the individual urban resident when a breakdown occurs in the meshing of normal institutional activity contributes to the wide-spread demand that means be sought to ameliorate the socially unhealthy aspects of metropolitan existence.

Critics of Louis Wirth have sometimes maintained that he gave too much emphasis, in his theory of urbanism, to pathological aspects of the modern city. Today, however, it seems likely that the average American would agree with Wirth and not with his critics. Many persons, indeed, may find little justification for the study of the social structure of the city except in the expectation that some alleviation of pathology may result. In any event, Wirth himself did give much consideration to problems of urban life.

This is hardly surprising. Wirth resided in Chicago during the time when the city became an international symbol of organized crime, gangster domination, and machine rule. He wrote his article toward the end of the depression, which had inflicted terrible suffering upon the urban unemployed. Moreover, the Department of Sociology of the University of Chicago, of which Wirth was a leading member, made the city its sociological laboratory. The origins of sociological theory in respect to urban areas may in some respects be traced back to Simmel, Durkheim, and Weber, but the emergence of urban sociology as a field of empirical research took place at the University of Chicago during the period of Wirth's tenure there.

Social problems of compelling urgency are by no means new to urban existence. In the earliest phases of the Industrial Revolution, for example, as all readers of Dickens will recall, urban suffering was acute. Our concern today with such problems indicates that contemporary Western man, with his affluence and his technological skills, does not accept the undesirable aspects of his great cities fatalistically, but holds instead that the detrimental features of urban communities should be reduced or eliminated.

In America, many of the problems of the great cities are linked with the continued existence of slums in these cities and with the continued location in such slums of large numbers of persons who live in poverty. With all her affluence, America has lagged behind a number of other Western nations in the removal of slums and in combating poverty on the most desperate levels. In America, many of the problems of the great cities also are perceived as racial. The migration of millions of black Americans to the great population centers has made this people—once among the most rural of America's groups—more urban, more metropolitan, and more centered by far in the inner city than is the population as a whole. The movement of whites to the suburbs obviously combines with the movement of blacks to the central city to create the contrast in racial composition between city and suburb. Growth of the Negro population of the great cities will no doubt continue, both because the urbanward direction of migration presumably will continue and because of natural increase within that population. The Negro population remaining within the rural South, however, is no longer large enough, when compared with the base population of metropolitan America, to maintain migration as momentous as that of the period between 1915 and 1960.

In a manner similar to that of the immigrants before them, black migrants to the great cities of the nation became concentrated in the occupations of lower skill and in the residential areas of lowest rentals—in short, in the slums. Unlike the previous migrants, however, the Negro American has been handicapped in his adaptation to the city by the racial barriers which have existed. Every major city in America, whether its black population be enormous or quite small in proportion to the total, has maintained segregation; as Karl Taeuber has put it, "There is no need for cities to vie with each other for the title of 'most segregated city'; there is room at the top for all of them."[1]

Some of the results of metropolitan residential segregation are well-known. There are slums and slums, but because of the continued influx of migrants and the resistance to expansion of the boundaries of the racial ghettos, black slums have become more congested, and are more expensive for the facilities offered, than are comparable areas inhabited by poor persons of other origins. Moreover, the successful Negro who otherwise might seek housing in a different section of the city may be quite unable to locate such housing. The walls of segregation have kept the black middle- and lower-classes in close contact, at least spatially. Segregated schools and segregated institutions of other kinds develop and are maintained because of the segregation of housing. The "open-housing" provisions included in the federal legislation of 1968 represent the most emphatic frontal attack upon the underlying residential basis of segregation which has been made by American society, but many observers believe that the actual implementation of the goals of the legislation may be a long, slow process.

What is most relevant at this point, perhaps, is that in America metropolitanization has not yielded "an" urban man, but two urban men, separated, unequal, residing and working in one great metropolitan setting but in many respects living out their respective lives in separate social worlds. Many of the indications of social pathology in our great cities reflect the racial cleavages of our society.

Clinard presents a concise summary of rural-urban variations, and of the variations within the city, in various forms of social disorganization. In so doing, he also provides a brief description of the famous concentric circle ecological view of the city.

Weinberg deals with rural-urban variations in respect to mental illness. He notes particularly the variations between communities and between different sections of a metropolis in rates of diagnosed schizophrenia, which is much the most serious form of psychosis in terms of the number of persons hospitalized at any given time. Both Clinard and Weinberg mention the "drift" hypothesis, which suggests that high rates of commitment come from certain disadvantaged areas because persons undergoing disorganization, as a part of their progressive loss of effectiveness, end up in those areas. Weinberg does not find this explanation adequate in accounting for the existing variations in respect to the rates of psychotic commitments. Sociologists lean toward explanations which see stress-inducing factors in the sociocultural setting

[1] Karl Taeuber, "Negro Residential Segregation: Trends and Measurement," *Social Problems,* Vol. 12, p. 48 (Summer, 1964).

as contributing toward the high incidence of psychological break-downs in some sections of the community. Migration may often induce such stress. Weinberg notes these and other possible explanations for the variations which exist.

Violence as a part of intergroup relations is not new. More specifically, that particular type of violent behavior which we call riots is not new. Riots have been directed, at one time or another, against Irish, Italian, Mexican, Oriental, and other ethnic groups, but most numerous by far have been riots which involved black people.

Until recent years, most such riots had involved actual physical conflicts between white crowds and black crowds, or at least, between raiding bands of whites and of blacks. In such assaults, the aggressors very often—more often than not, apparently—were bands of white youths seeking black victims. Damage to property sometimes occurred but was often more or less incidental and, when it occurred, was frequently caused by white rioters destroying property they considered to be Negro property.

Since 1964, most rioting has been of a different kind. Particularly since the Watts riot of August, 1965, the rioters have nearly all been Negroes. Bands of white youths have been involved very little in assaults upon black rioters. These riots have been struggles between black rioters and law enforcement personnel of one kind or another, and the target of much of the activity of the rioters has been property, usually property owned by whites. The profound distrust between residents of the black community and the police force of the city has been illustrated over and over during the riots since 1964. Oberschall discusses these and related topics in his analysis of the Watts riot of 1965.

Following the particularly damaging riots, with the loss of 85 lives, during the summer of 1967, former President Johnson appointed a commission to investigate the conditions leading to civil disorders and to make recommendations for corrective actions. The National Advisory Commission on Civil Disorders, often called the Kerner Commission, submitted its report on March 1, 1968. The underlying factors identified by this Commission resembled those described by Oberschall in Los Angeles. The basic cause was identified as white racism. Precipitating incidents, most typically involving police, preceded the eruption of violence; no indication of an undercover conspiracy manipulating the course of events was found. The grievances over police treatment, unemployment, and housing were the most often cited complaints leading to bitterness on the part of ghetto residents. The report described conditions of life in the urban ghetto in a short selection which is reproduced here.

Urbanization, Urbanism, and Deviant Behavior

MARSHALL B. CLINARD

University of Wisconsin

COMPARISONS OF CERTAIN FORMS OF DEVIANT BEHAVIOR IN RURAL AND URBAN AREAS

For centuries writers have been concerned about the debauchery and moral conditions of the cities and have generally praised rural life.[1] Hesiod, for example, wrote about the corrupt justice of the cities. The Greeks and Romans compared the city with agricultural areas, noting the greater evils and sources of criminality in the cities. One of the first systematic comparisons of rural and urban peoples was made by Ibn Khaldun in the fourteenth century. This famed Arab historian compared life in the city with that among the nomadic tribes. He found that the nomads had good behavior, whereas evil and corruption were abundant in the city; that honesty and courage were characteristic of the nomads, whereas lying and cowardice were prevalent in the city; and that the city caused decay, stultified initiative, and made men depraved and wicked. In general, rural life has been, and still largely is, a world of close personal relationships which Burgess has thus described:

> But the main characteristics of small-town life stand out in clear perspective: close acquaintanceship of everyone with everyone else, the dominance of personal relations, and the subjection of the individual to

From Chapter Three, "Urbanization, Urbanism, and Deviant Behavior," from *Sociology of Deviant Behavior*, Third Edition, by Marshall B. Clinard. Copyright © 1957 by Marshall B. Clinard. Copyright © 1963, 1968 by Holt, Rinehart and Winston, Inc. Reprinted by permission of Holt, Rinehart and Winston, Inc.

[1] See Pitirim Sorokin, Carle Zimmerman, and Charles Galpin, *A Systematic Sourcebook in Rural Sociology*, pp. 27–52, 54–68 (Minneapolis: University of Minnesota Press, 1930).

continuous observation and control by the community.... This fund of concrete knowledge which everyone has of everyone else in the small town naturally emphasizes and accentuates the role of the personal in all relationships and activities of community life. Approval and disapproval of conduct, likes and dislikes of persons, play correspondingly a tremendous part in social life, in business, in politics, and in the administration of justice.[2]

Delinquency and Crime

The types, incidence, and reactions to rural crime, as with urban crime, are a function of the type of life and the various norms and values of the communities. Delinquency and crime rates today are generally much lower in rural areas than in urban. A study of crime in France and Belgium has shown similar major differences between rural and urban areas.[3] In Japan it is reported that the rate of urban crime is higher than that of rural areas, and that the general increase in crime is particularly noticeable in the largest cities.[4] In India an official report of the Intelligence Bureau observed that "it was found that juvenile crime in an acute form is confined to the cities, particularly the cities of India, and to some of the larger towns which have suffered from economic distress. It is not a problem of the rural areas."[5] Pronounced differences have been found in the incidence of delinquency and crime in the urban and rural areas of Latin-American and African countries.[6]

In general, the differences between rural and urban property crimes are greater than the differences in crimes against the person. Some delinquent and criminal acts committed in rural areas are dealt with informally and not officially reported, and there are undoubtedly more opportunities to commit offenses in urban as compared with rural areas. The differences between rural and urban rates, however, are so great that differential reporting or

[2] Ernest W. Burgess, in Albert Blumenthal, *Small-Town Stuff*, pp. xi–xiii (Chicago: the University of Chicago Press, 1932).
[3] Denis Szabo, *Crimes et Villes* (Louvain: Catholic University of Louvain, 1960).
[4] Quoted in *Urbanization in Asia and the Far East*, Proceedings of the Joint UN/UNESCO Seminar, Bangkok, August 8–18, 1956, Chap. IX, p. 232 (UNESCO, 1958—SS.57.V7A).
[5] *Urbanization in Asia and the Far East*, p. 233. Also see *A Report on Juvenile Delinquency in India*, p. 8 (Bombay: The Children's Aid Society, 1956).
[6] Philip M. Hauser (ed.), *Urbanization in Latin America* (New York: International Documents Service, Columbia University Press, 1961) and *Social Implications of Industrialization and Urbanization in Africa South of the Sahara* (Lausanne: Imprimerie Centrale Lausanne S. A., 1956).

opportunity could, at most, account for only a small part.[7] Also, there is little evidence to support the theory held by some that the city attracts deviants from rural areas.[8]

As Table 23-1 shows, burglary rates in the United States, as a whole, are generally two and a half times as great in urban areas as in rural, larceny is over three times as great, and robbery over ten times.[9] The rates for burglaries known to the police per 100,000 population in 1966 were, for example, 855.3 in urban areas and 335.1 in rural areas. Crimes such as murder, which are relatively infrequent as compared with property crimes, are about the same, with a somewhat higher rate in urban areas, where the rate is 6.0 as compared with 4.7 in rural. Rape rates are much higher in urban areas: 14.2 in urban as contrasted with 8.9 in rural.

TABLE 23-1. RATES PER 100,000 POPULATION FOR CRIMES KNOWN TO THE POLICE IN RURAL AND URBAN AREAS, UNITED STATES, 1956

| | Rate | |
Offense	Urban	Rural
Murder and nonnegligent manslaughter	6.0	4.7
Forcible rape	14.2	8.9
Robbery	115.0	10.0
Aggravated assault	142.8	60.9
Burglary—breaking or entering	855.3	335.1
Larceny—theft ($50 and over)	573.7	188.2
Automobile theft	394.3	60.7

SOURCE: Derived from Federal Bureau of Investigation, "Crime in the United States." *Uniform Crime Reports 1966*, pp. 96–97 (Washington, D.C.: Government Printing Office, 1967). The population figures used were based on the estimated 1966 census. Rates for the above are based on estimated 1966 census data. "Urban areas" include Standard Metropolitan Areas.

[7] See, for example, Marshall B. Clinard, "Rural Criminal Offenders," *American Journal of Sociology*, 50:38–45 (1944); William P. Lentz, "Rural-Urban Differentials in Juvenile Delinquency," *Journal of Criminal Law and Criminology*, 47:311–339 (1956); and Marshall B. Clinard, "A Cross-Cultural Replication of the Relation of Urbanism to Criminal Behavior," *American Sociological Review*, 25:253–257 (1960).
[8] See page 111. [Not reproduced here].
[9] In such countries as France, Belgium, Switzerland, Holland, Germany, Sweden, Finland, Denmark, and Italy, the incidence of urban offenses, crimes known, and convictions per population has been reported as generally higher than among rural areas. Hans H. Burchardt, "Kriminalität in Stadt und Land," *Abhandlungen des Kriminalistischen Instituts an der Universität Berlin*, 4. Folge, 4 Bd., 1. Heft (1936). Louis Wirth and Marshall B. Clinard, "Public Safety," in *Urban Government*, Supplementary Report of the Urbanism Committee to the National Resources Committee, I, pp. 247–303 (Washington, D. C.: Government Printing Office, 1939). Denis Szabo, *Criminologie*, pp. 204–239 (Montreal: University of Montreal Press, 1965).

Specific studies, rather than statistical comparisons, also seem to support the thesis that the urbanization of rural areas and an increase in crime go hand in hand. A study of the southern mountain villages showed that as the hill country was opened to outside contacts criminal activities increased.[10] The most important factor associated with this increase was the growing lack of community identification on the part of individuals as the villages became more urbanized. A study of rural inmates in an Iowa reformatory revealed that characteristics associated with an urban way of life played a significant role in their criminal behavior.[11]

Mental Disorders

Most contemporary data on mental disorders, but not all, show that the rates are generally higher in urban than in rural areas. As with crime, many writers feel that the expansion of urbanism is significant in the production of mental illness in our society. After a study of the prevalence of mental disorder among the urban and rural populations of New York State, Malzberg concluded that the rural regions of the state had less mental disorder than the urban.[12] In another study, Texas rates for all persons who became psychotic for the first time were found to be two and a half times greater in urban areas than in rural, a difference which was statistically significant.[13] The same differential held for the sexes and age-specific psychoses rates. The large rate differentials between urban and rural areas were not due to differences in the accessibility of psychiatric treatment facilities or to the type of psychiatric facilities available in the two areas.[14]

Not all the evidence supports the conclusion that the incidence of mental illness is much less in rural areas. The differences may actually be smaller than they now appear to be because of the likelihood that rural families may keep mentally disturbed members at home rather than have them treated in clinics or have them hospitalized. For this reason it is possible that mental deviants in urban

[10] M. Taylor Mathews, *Experience Worlds of the Mountain Peoples* (New York: Columbia University Press, 1937).

[11] Marshall B. Clinard, "The Process of Urbanization and Criminal Behavior," *American Journal of Sociology*, 48:202–213 (1942). Also see his "Rural Criminal Offenders," and "A Cross-Cultural Replication of the Relation of Urbanism to Criminal Behavior." Also see Harold D. Eastman, "The Process of Urbanization and Criminal Behavior: A Restudy of Culture Conflict," unpublished doctoral thesis (University of Iowa, 1954).

[12] Benjamin Malzberg, "The Prevalence of Mental Disease among the Urban and Rural Populations of New York State," Psychiatric Quarterly, 9:55–88 (1935).

[13] E. Gartly Jaco, *The Social Epidemiology of Mental Diseases* (New York: Russell Sage Foundation, 1960). Also see Leacock, p. 314.

[14] Jaco, *op. cit.*

society may be somewhat more socially visible, and that both unofficial and official tolerance of the deviation will be less.

Alcoholism

The chances that rural persons will become chronic alcoholics are less than half as great as those for urban dwellers.[15] Urban commitments for alcoholic psychoses are reported to be three and a half times the rate for rural areas.[16] The principal reasons for this lower rate of alcoholism in rural areas are the social norms and the amount of social control at the personal level over drinking or excessive drinking. Farm people in the United States are much less likely to drink alcoholic beverages than are city dwellers. Both farm rearing and farm residence are associated with lower proportions of heavy drinkers. An Iowa study showed that 58 percent of drinkers in the city were either moderate or heavy drinkers as compared with 43 percent of the farm drinkers.[17] Moreover, the extent of drinking increased among the farm-reared who had migrated to the city, but this increase was in moderate rather than heavy drinking.

Suicide

On the whole, persons living on farms and villages are less likely to take their lives than persons living in cities. In London the standardized rate, expressed as a percentage of that for the whole of England and Wales, is 115, for the county boroughs 106, for other urban districts 97, and for rural districts 88.[18] In Sweden, Denmark, and Finland wide differences in the suicide rates exist between farm and city. A detailed study of suicide in France showed that the chances that farm people and persons living in places of less than 2,000 population would take their lives were considerably less than for city people.[19]

The differential in rural and urban suicide rates in the United States appears to be declining because of the tendency for an urban way of life to characterize rural areas. Fifty years ago the rural rate per 100,000 population was about two-thirds of the urban

[15] E. M. Jellinek, "Recent Trends in Alcoholism and Alcohol Consumption," *Quarterly Journal of Studies on Alcohol*, 8:23 (1947).

[16] Carney Landis and James D. Page, *Modern Society and Mental Disease* (New York: Holt, Rinehart and Winston, 1938).

[17] Harold A. Mulford and Donald E. Miller, "Drinking in Iowa. II. The Extent of Drinking and Selected Socio-cultural Categories," *Quarterly Journal of Studies on Alcohol*, 21:34–35 (1960).

[18] Figures cited in Peter Sainsbury, *Suicide in London: An Ecological Study* (New York: Basic Books, Inc., 1956).

[19] M. Halbwachs, *Les Causes du Suicide* (Paris: Librairie Félix Alcan, 1930).

rate; in 1960 the rates were about the same, the rural being slightly higher: 10.5 in the urban and 10.8 in the rural.[20] An analysis of 3081 cases of suicide in Michigan between 1945 and 1949 revealed that rural males exhibited higher suicide rates than urban males.[21] Although "farmers and farm managers" had a high suicide rate in Michigan, the majority of "rural" males who committed suicide were engaged in urban occupation and resided in urbanized fringe areas. It is possible that the high rural rate in this sample was due to two factors: as urban values become more widely disseminated in rural areas they create an intense personal conflict because of the disparity between urban and rural values as they affect behavioral alternatives; and the occupations of rural males who committed suicide are characteristic occupations of urban groups, thus suggesting exposure to conflicting values and norms. Although they lived in the country, these people were oriented to an urban way of life.

DISTRIBUTION OF DEVIANT BEHAVIOR WITHIN A CITY

According to the most generally accepted theory, the characteristic spatial pattern of cities in developed, industrial societies is a series of concentric circles, with each circle having certain distinctive characteristics moving out from the central business district into increasingly better areas of housing.[22] The ecological pattern of the city in terms of concentric zones leading out from the first circle are Zone I, the central business district; Zone II, an area known variously by a number of names, such as the slum, zone in

---

[20] W. Widick Schroeder and J. Allan Beegle, "Suicide: An Instance of High Rural Rates," *Rural Sociology*, 18:45–52 (1953).

[21] See Jack P. Gibbs, "Suicide," in Robert K. Merton and Robert A. Nisbet, *Contemporary Social Problems*, rev. ed., p. 302 (New York: Harcourt, Brace & World, Inc., 1966).

[22] Ernest W. Burgess, "The Growth of the City," in Robert E. Park and Ernest W. Burgess, *The City* (Chicago: The University of Chicago Press, 1925). This theory has been criticized particularly because it does not apply to the spatial pattern of cities of less-developed countries. See Leo F. Schnore, "On the Spatial Structure of Cities in the Two Americas," in Hauser and Schnore, pp. 347–398; George A. Theodorson, *Studies in Human Ecology* (New York: Harper & Row, Publishers, 1961); and Sjoberg. Another theory based on city growth is that cities have a pattern of sectors like pieces of a pie. According to this theory, industrial areas follow river valleys, water courses, and railroad lines out from the city and become surrounded by workingmen's housing, with factories tending to locate even along the outer fringe of the city. According to the sector view, the best housing then does not fringe the entire city but only parts of it. The main industrial areas of the future may well be located on the outskirts of cities in new industrial towns and suburbs as is now taking place. —Homer Hoyt, *The Structure and Growth of Residential Neighborhoods in American Cities*, pp. 75–77 (Washington, D.C.: Federal Housing Administration, 1939), and his "The Structure of American Cities in the Post-War Era," *American Journal of Sociology*, 48:475–481 (1943).

transition, blighted area, "gray area," or "inner core" area; Zone III, an area of two- and three-family flats or dwellings; Zone IV, an area of single-family dwellings; and Zone V, the suburban or commutation area. These circles can be thought of as undergoing constant movement in the form of expansion outward, much like the movement taking place on the surface of water when a pebble is dropped into it. The central business district is constantly expanding, depending on how many persons living in each successive zone eventually move outward to another area. Although this theory implies equal expansion in all directions, few cities ever completely approximate a series of concentric circles. Rivers, mountains—or a lake, as in Chicago—interfere with this natural growth. Even so, there are some cities, such as Rochester in New York, which closely resemble this pattern. This abstraction of concentric circles is no different from the law of falling bodies in which the principle of an equal rate of fall between an iron ball and a feather is valid only if both are in a vacuum.

In each section of the city there are wide variations in age, sex, nationality and racial origin, occupation, social class, home-ownership, condition of housing, literacy, and education. Differences in social class are one of the most important characteristics of various areas of a city. The shifting of persons under *ecological* pressures brings about an association of like with like and a tendency for population specialization in certain areas.[23]

The population of both the central business district and the slum is heterogeneous; the residents are chiefly unskilled workers and their families, and include migrants from rural and other areas, and various nationality and racial groups. Zone III has a more stable population, more skilled workers, and fewer foreign-born or racial groups. Second-generation immigrant groups moving out of the slum generally move here first. Zones IV and V largely consist of apartment houses, single-family dwellings, and commuters' houses, which means that they are chiefly upper-middle and upper class.

Over a century ago a few studies were made of the distribution of deviant behavior within a city,[24] but most of this type of

---

[23] For many years botanists and geologists have been interested in studying the pattern of distribution and movement in space of plant and animal life, which they call plant and animal ecology. Following this, interest grew in human ecology, or the study of the distribution of man and his institutions in space, which includes the study of rural-urban differences as well as differences in city size and within cities. The study of the ecology or distribution of deviant behavior has largely developed in the past forty years.

[24] Yale Levin and Alfred Lindesmith, "English Ecology and Criminology of the Past Century," *Journal of Criminal Law and Criminology*, 27:801–816 (1937); and Alfred Lindesmith and Yale Levin, "The Lombrosian Myth in Criminology," *American Journal of Sociology*, 42:653–679 (1937).

research began with the stimulation of sociological studies by Park, Burgess, and their students of the Chicago community in the 1920s. The spot-mapping of labeled deviants in larger cities by place of residence has revealed that, on the whole, certain types of social deviation tend to be concentrated in specific areas.[25] For example, conventional crime, delinquency, mental illness in general and schizophrenia in particular, suicide, prostitution, vagrancy, dependency, illegitimacy, infant mortality, as well as associated problems, such as high death and disease rates, have been found to vary with the areas of the city. The highest rates are in Zones I and II, and become successively lower out from this area. The evidence on alcoholism and the manic-depressive psychoses does not show quite this pronounced pattern for, although there are probably higher rates in Zones I and II, the differences are not as marked from one part of the city to another. White-collar crime, on the other hand, is greater in Zones IV and V of the city. Gambling and prostitution are prevalent not only in Zone II but sometimes beyond the suburban fringe of the city.[26]

Delinquent gangs were found by Thrasher to be largely concentrated in the slum areas.[27] The spot-mapping of some 60,000 cases of delinquency, truancy, and crime by Shaw and McKay showed a close correlation among the rates of all three groups, with wide variation in their distribution among the local communities of the city.[28] The slum area near the centers of commerce and industry had the highest rates, whereas those in outlying residential communities of higher economic status were uniformly low. In a later study of some 25,000 juvenile court delinquents, distributed over 33 years, Shaw and McKay reported additional evidence of the consistency of high rates of delinquency in Zone II.[29]

Findings similar to those in Chicago have been reported for eight other large metropolitan cities and eleven other cities, all widely separated geographically, including Boston, Philadelphia,

[25] For a discussion of the patterns in a smaller city see, for example, Lyle W. Shannon, "Types and Patterns of Delinquency in a Middle-sized City," *Journal of Research in Crime and Delinquency*, 1:53–66 (1964).

[26] Walter C. Reckless, *Vice in Chicago* (Chicago: University of Chicago Press, 1933).

[27] Frederic M. Thrasher, *The Gang* (Chicago: University of Chicago Press, 1927).

[28] Clifford R. Shaw and Henry D. McKay, *Delinquent Areas* (Chicago: University of Chicago Press, 1929). Jonassen has criticized the limitations of data, the methodology, and the internal consistencies of the data. Christen T. Jonassen, "A Re-Evaluation and Critique of the Logic and Some Methods of Shaw and McKay," *American Sociological Review*, 14:608–614, (1949).

[29] Clifford R. Shaw, Henry D. McKay, *et al.*, *Juvenile Delinquency and Urban Areas* (Chicago: University of Chicago Press, 1942).

Cleveland, Richmond, Birmingham, Omaha, and Seattle.[30] Higher rates of delinquency were found in the inner zones and lower rates in the outer zones, and in all nineteen cities, except for Boston, Birmingham, and Omaha, the rates also declined from innermost to outermost zones. Even in these cities where rates in the outermost zones were somewhat higher than in the intermediate, as in Boston, the explanation may possibly be not only that the industrial areas are near the periphery, but that differences exist in the policies of the courts in the various areas. Similar findings have been reported in more recent studies in Baltimore, Detroit, and Indianapolis.[31] A study of Croyden, a large English city near London, revealed that the highest rates for delinquency were concentrated in areas of the city populated by unskilled and semiskilled workers' families.[32] Studies of Kanpur and Lucknow in India showed that juvenile delinquency and crime are primarily associated with slum areas.[33]

The correlation of delinquency rates with economic factors should not be interpreted as indicating any direct relation to poverty or bad housing, as Shaw and McKay have indicated. They point out that in rural areas, there may be poverty but little delinquency. Poverty, moreover, does not produce a tradition of delinquency because of a lack of money in itself; rather, it may interfere with the realization of status or prestige. The explanation of delinquency, they believe, is to be found in the general social situations in delinquency areas.

The rate of arrests of adults per 10,000 population 17 years of age and over was more than ten times as great in the central area of Chicago as in the outlying areas of the city.[34] The rates for nearly all 29 types of crimes known to the police in Seattle, and arrests for these crimes during the period 1949-1951, showed a decline as one moved out in six one-mile concentric zones from the

[30] Shaw, McKay, et al. Automobile theft may often be somewhat of an exception to the generalization that delinquency tends to be concentrated in areas such as these.

[31] Roland J. Chilton, "Continuity in Delinquency Area Research: A Comparison of Studies for Baltimore, Detroit, and Indianapolis," American Sociological Review, 29:71–83 (1964); Bernard Lander, Towards an Understanding of Juvenile Delinquency: A Study of 8464 Cases of Juvenile Delinquency in Baltimore (New York: Columbia University Press, 1954); and David J. Pordua, "Juvenile Delinquency and 'Anomie': An Attempt at Replication," Social Problems, 6:230–238 (1958–1959).

[32] Terence Morris, The Criminal Area, A Study in Social Ecology (London: Routledge and Kegan Paul, Ltd., 1958).

[33] Shankar S. Srivastava, Juvenile Vagrancy: A Socioecological Study of Juvenile Vagrants in the Cities of Kanpur and Lucknow (New York: Asia Publishing House, 1963).

[34] Ernest R. Mowrer, Disorganization, Personal and Social, p. 143 (Philadelphia: J. B. Lippincott Company, 1942).

highest land value in the central business district.[35] There was a tendency for 23 out of the 29 types of crime known to the police to decrease more or less in direct proportion from the center of the city, in particular shoplifting, theft, arson, rape, sodomy, and burglary. Bicycle theft was the only crime known to the police which had a higher rate in Zone VI (149.5) than in Zone I (65.3). The differentials between inner and outer zones were relatively small for Peeping Toms, obscene telephone calls, indecent liberties, and carnal knowledge. Not a single category in the arrest series showed a high rate in the peripheral zones. Arrest rates for fraud, rape, prostitution, lewdness, robbery, gambling, and common drunkenness showed the greatest difference, while auto theft and indecent exposure showed the least.

White-collar crime, as one might expect, follows a reverse pattern, with concentration in Zones IV and V of the city. In a study of wartime black-market offenders in the wholesale meat industry in Detroit, Hartung found that more than 80 percent of them lived in the most desirable areas of the city.[36] Of the ten who lived in the least desirable areas (4 and 5), three lived in good downtown hotels.

[35] Calvin F. Schmid, "Urban Crime Areas: Part II," *American Sociological Review*, 25:655–678 (1960). There also appears to be a remarkable constancy and uniformity in the spatial patterning of crime by gradients. A comparison of two series of offenses known to the police in Seattle, 1939–1941 and 1949–1951, shows a close correspondence with high correlations for burglary and robbery.—Schmid, p. 669.

[36] Frank E. Hartung, "White-Collar Offenses in the Wholesale Meat Industry in Detroit," *American Journal of Sociology*, 56:25–35 (1950).

Urban Areas and Hospitalized Psychotics

S. KIRSON WEINBERG

Roosevelt University

Although few studies have been made of the residential distributions of neurotics in the urban community, many inquiries have traced the residential patterns of hospitalized psychotics, particularly of schizophrenics and manic-depressives. These inquiries have demonstrated a relationship between the residential distribution of hospitalized psychoses generally and of schizophrenia particularly and the organization and growth of the urban community. Faris and Dunham initiated ecological studies of these psychotic types mainly for Chicago and for Providence, Rhode Island.[1] They have had their pioneer conclusions corroborated, with slight variations, by other studies of St. Louis, Cleveland, Omaha, Kansas City, Milwaukee, and Peoria.[2] Since these ecological patterns of residential distribution in the urban community prevailed before the extensive rehabilitation of deteriorated areas around the center of the city and before the building of high-rise, low-cost housing throughout the city, the relative decline of the neighborhood, and the movement to the suburbs, their inquiries characterized the patterned distribu-

Reprinted from S. Kirson Weinberg (ed.), *The Sociology of Mental Disorders: Analyses and Readings in Psychiatric Sociology*, pp. 22–26 (Chicago: Aldine Publishing Company, 1967); Copyright © 1967 by S. Kirson Weinberg.
[1] Robert E. L. Faris and H. Warren Dunham, *Mental Disorders in Urban Areas* (Chicago: University of Chicago Press, 1938).
[2] Stuart A. Queen, "The Ecological Study of Mental Disorder," *American Sociological Review*, V, pp. 201–209 (April, 1940); Howard W. Green, *Persons Admitted to the Cleveland State Hospital, 1928–1937* (Cleveland: Cleveland Health Council, 1939); Clarence W. Schroeder, "Mental Disorders in Cities," *American Journal of Sociology*, XLVIII, pp. 40–47 (July, 1942); Ernest W. Mowrer, *Disorganization: Personal and Social*, chapters 15 and 16 (New York: J. B. Lippincott, 1942; and E. E. Hadley et al., "Military Psychiatry: An Ecological Note," *Psychiatry*, VII, pp. 379–407 (Nov., 1944).

tion for an urban community of a past era. In addition, the ethnic composition of the city has changed with the rising influx of Negroes, Southern whites, and Puerto Ricans as first settlers into the city.

Despite these changes, the enduring features of these studies pertain to their determination of the positive relationships between low rental and disorganized urban areas and rates of schizophrenia, and of the randomly distributed urban residential pattern for manic-depression. In their ecological study Dunham and Faris analyzed 28,763 cases from four state mental hospitals; these cases represented all persons committed to these institutions between 1922 and 1934. Their findings confirmed the hypothesis that the residential distributions of hospitalized psychoses, like other detected social deviants, fit the conventional pattern of distribution in the unplanned urban community. These rates of disorders are highest near the center of the city and tend to decline toward the circumference of the city.

Schizophrenia, the first of the psychoses to be analyzed ecologically, is characterized by blunt mood, by delusion and at times hallucinatory behavior, by emotional and social withdrawal, by impaired judgment in the area of personal conflict, and generally by the substitution of private for shared versions of social reality.

The ecological findings concerning the residential distributions of schizophrenics in the urban community include:

(1) The rates for hospitalized schizophrenics in the different zones of the urban community are consistent with the rates for all mental disorders: highest near the center of the city and declining as one moves toward the periphery of the city.

(2) The highest rates for schizophrenia are concentrated in very disorganized, lower-income communities, but most communities have low rates of schizophrenics except for the few with high rates.

(3) The rates for male and female schizophrenics separately reveal similar residential concentrations.

(4) The rates for schizophrenia for the foreign born by total number and by sex in the urban community indicate that differences between rates result from other factors than varying proportions of foreign born.

(5) The upper quartile of the communities contained 40 percent of the cases but only 24 percent of the population.

(6) The rates of schizophrenia by race and nativity in different areas of the city showed consistently high rates in the extremely disorganized parts of the city.

(7) The rates of schizophrenia for whites are highest in areas where Negroes are in the majority, although the rates of

schizophrenia for Negroes in all-Negro areas tend to be lower than in racially mixed areas.

Manic-depressives, characterized by an extremely elated mood or an extremely depressed mood, or a circulation of moods, in contrast with the residential distribution of schizophrenics, have a random residential distribution in the city. Although the highest rates are in the first zone, the rates do not decline with the distance from the center of the city. In all other zones, the difference between rates is so small that it lacks statistical significance.

Therefore, we may conclude:

(1)   The rates of urban residential distribution for manic-depressives are neither high nor low in any systematic way.

(2)   The distributions of rates for male and female manic-depressives separately show similar random patterns.

(3)   The distributions of rates of cases from private and state hospitals reveal a similar randomness.

(4)   The rates for manic and depressed types separately are distributed randomly.

(5)   The manic-depressive rates show that approximately similar numbers of communities had high and low rates.

(6)   Since the percentages in each quartile are similar for manics and for depressives, no definite concentration of cases exists.

(7)   The rates for manic-depression distributed according to nativity and race by housing areas lack a residential distribution pattern.

From comparing the residential distributions of schizophrenics and manic-depressives, we may conclude as follows:

(1)   Distributions of rates of schizophrenics and manic-depressives differ in almost every way.

(2)   The schizophrenic rates which have this conventional distributive pattern are concentrated in the disorganized and poverty-ridden urban areas.

(3)   Seemingly, manic-depressives come from a higher socioeconomic stratum than do schizophrenics.

(4)   The rates for manic-depressives according to race and nativity in different areas of the city lack consistency but rates for schizophrenics for a given nativity group increase in areas which are not populated primarily by members of that group.

These findings have been supported by Schroeder for five midwestern cities. Dee reported that in St. Louis no correlation exists between distributions of schizophrenia and of manic-depression. Ruess found that in Milwaukee distributions of manic-depression, although more random than distributions of schizophrenia, concentrate in areas in the downtown and river valley sections. Mowrer found from his studies in Chicago that distributions of manic-depression, while not random, had little in common with distributions of other psychoses. Mowrer claimed too that "the same concentric pattern exists for manic-depression as for schizophrenia but with a break in the upper four-fifths of the range," and that this diagnostic type did not necessarily come from a relatively high socioeconomic status.[3]

These results have a similarity to the findings of Hollingshead and Redlich, who studied the prevalence of treated mental disorders in New Haven, Connecticut. Using the criteria of occupation, education, and place of residence for class stratification, they reported that schizophrenia had a frequency in the lowest social class stratum almost ten times that of the highest two social classes.[4]

INTERPRETATION OF THE DISTRIBUTIONS

These findings can be viewed as reflecting the results of urban ecological processes and as indices of the influences affecting the etiology of these disorders.[5] Our concern is with the latter problem.

We can say at the outset that these ecological distributions as epidemiological indicators of presumed social or biogenetic processes of etiological significance have not been demonstrated. At best the ecological distributions provide clues for further and more definitive inquiry. The interpretations of these distributions when made from the biogenetic viewpoint would emphasize the genetic predisposition and constitutional vulnerability of those who have incurred schizophrenic or manic-depressive disorders. Despite the works of Kallman and others concerning the influence of heredity on schizophrenia and other disorders, these findings have not been related to the ecological distributions. Furthermore even assuming greater genetic vulnerability in this social selection process among the lower socioeconomic strata to schizophrenia, we would still have to assume a certain constancy of the social environment because

---

[3] Schroeder, op. cit., pp. 40–47, and Mowrer, op. cit.

[4] August B. Hollingshead and Fredrick C. Redlich, "Social Stratification and Psychiatric Disorders," American Sociological Review, 18:163–169 (April, 1953).

[5] There have been some criticisms of the validity of these findings. One criticism has been that the number of cases initially used for the manic-depressive group were too few. The second criticism is that the differences between the rates in the communities were due to chance and were not significant.

Melvin L. Kohn and John A. Clausen, "The Ecological Approach in Social Psychiatry," American Journal of Sociology, 60:140–151 (September, 1954).

persons in the lower strata seem to experience a more stressful social reality than do persons in the middle classes. We would also have to assume that persons genetically predisposed to manic-depression are randomly distributed in the class structure.[6]

Krout, from a psychoanalytic viewpoint, has read into these distributions differences of childhood training.[7] The schizophrenics, who predominated in the lower socioeconomic levels, had an arrested development at the oral stage of infancy because of feeding difficulties. But the manic-depressives, who more frequently come from the higher socioeconomic levels, had an arrested development in the anal stage of growth because of defective toilet training. First, it has not been ascertained empirically that these respective differences in feeding and toilet training hold for the lower and higher socioeconomic levels, respectively. Second, there is no definite evidence that frustrations in these different erogenous zones of the body are causally correlated with schizophrenia and manic-depression, respectively. In short, as stated in this specific psychoanalytic manner, this contention may seem untenable. But early emotional deprivation may affect the subsequent adaptation of the individual in his competitive process and in his bid for occupational success and hence may contribute to his immobility within the communities with low rentals. This kind of interpretation would be relevant for the interpretations of the distributions of schizophrenia. Since many persons in the lowest stratum have not drifted downward, they may have been impeded in their early personality development because of the excessively high rates of schizophrenia among this socioeconomic category.

The other interpretation is that some schizophrenics drift or remain in or near the center of the city and thus are a selected group. This interpretation implied at the time of the study that foreign-born white and Negro groups would have a greater tendency to schizophrenic disorders than native groups. Faris and Dunham, however, found that the rates for the foreign-born populations divided by the total foreign-born population are distributed similarly to the rates for all cases.[8] Rates for Negroes are high in areas not populated entirely by Negroes but low in areas inhabited pre-

[6] For an analysis of the status of the ecological approach to personal disorders, see H. Warren Dunham, "Current Status of Ecological Research in Mental Disorder," *Social Forces*, XXV (3), pp. 321–326 (March, 1947).

Franz J. Kallman, *Heredity in Health and Mental Disorder* (New York: W. W. Norton, 1953).

[7] Maurice H. Krout, "A Note on Dunham's Contribution to the Ecology of the Psychoses," *American Sociological Review, III*, pp. 209–212 (April, 1938).

[8] Robert E. L. Faris and H. Warren Dunham, *Mental Disorders in Urban Areas*, p. 169.

dominantly or entirely by Negroes.[9] Although this evidence is not sufficient to invalidate the drift hypothesis, it makes the validity of the hypothesis unlikely.

The other problem concerns the downward mobility of some schizophrenics and the upward mobility of some manic-depressives, particularly manics.[10] As we have pointed out, the schizophrenics most likely to drift would be the paranoids and hebephrenics who inhabit the "hobohemian" sections of the city. But these "hobohemian" areas comprise only a small proportion of the total cases. In addition, some schizophrenics have been born and reared in family slum areas adjacent to the central business district and may possibly have been influenced by the local neighborhood and class subculture. The "drift" hypothesis does not explain the allocation of schizophrenia only by a social selective process resulting from personal and economic maladjustment. This has been affirmed by H. Warren Dunham in his study of "Social Class and Schizophrenia."

The other side of the coin emphasizes the influences inherent within the community. There are those who claim that communities with high rates of mobility tend to have high rates of disordered persons.[11] This may mean that the downwardly mobile persons are more likely predisposed to psychotic disorders than are the immobile. It can be argued that excessive personal mobility may create personal instability which may contribute to an eventual breakdown. On the other hand, it may be contended that, in areas of very marked mobility, the anonymity and isolation among the residents would deprive each person of those intimate social relations that are necessary for sustaining an ordered condition and may contribute to the precipitation of schizophrenia. The function of the anomic condition of the community may be an essential influence on the onset of disordered behavior. Lander found from his factorial analysis of community criteria affecting delinquency that the

[9] *Ibid.,* pp. 164–169. Faris and Dunham studied catatonics and paranoids separately between 15 and 29 and those 30 and over. They found that the younger cases of paranoids, who did not have time to drift ,were concentrated in central areas, as were the older cases. The younger catatonic cases had a slightly different distribution than the other cases. Seemingly, the catatonics showed a tendency to drift from the slum residential areas to the hobo areas. See Robert E. L. Faris, *Social Disorganization*, p. 231, footnote (New York: Ronald Press, 1948).

[10] See Morris S. Schwartz, "The Economic and Spatial Mobility of Paranoid Schizophrenics and Manic Depressives" (University of Chicago: unpublished master's thesis, August, 1946).

[11] Christopher Tietze, Paul Lemkau, and Marcia Cooper, "Personal Disorders and Spatial Mobility," *American Journal of Sociology,* XLIII, pp. 29–39 (July, 1942).

Bruce P. Dohrenwend, "Social Status and Psychological Disorder: An Issue of Substance and An Issue of Method," *American Sociological Review,* 31 (1), pp. 14–34 (February, 1966).

anomic condition rather than the low income was instrumental to the rise of delinquency. Perhaps there is a generic quality of social disorganization that may contribute to the deviant or the delinquent as it does to the onset of schizophrenia.[12]

In "family" slum neighborhoods, relationships are claimed to be harsh. Since social difficulties are presumably more harsh than in middle-class areas, the individual resident adjusts with difficulty. But it is not known whether this factor is crucial. Indeed, before they break down, prepsychotic persons from lower-income groups have experiences in different groups through their jobs. Hence, a psychotic breakdown cannot be attributed merely to the social relationships within the community, at least not for all cases. Catatonics who are committed at a relatively early age may be influenced by a manipulating mother rather than by the play patterns and the modes of relationships with juvenile and adolescent groups who may contribute to the onset of their personal disorders.[13] Nonetheless, despite these relationships among lower-income groups, these groups do not practice exclusion as intensely as the same age groups do in upper-middle socioeconomic levels.

The different value judgments and the reasons for committing disordered persons to mental institutions in different communities may also affect the ecological distributions. Are there uniform criteria in this commitment process in all types of communities? Owen maintains that certain types of disorders may lead to commitment in one community but not in another.[14] Faris contends that the persons committed to mental hospitals are so "extremely insane" that few families would be wealthy enough to care for them outside the hospital.[15] Very likely most schizophrenics and manic-depressives may be committed to mental hospitals, but it is also known that some cases are reported long after the breakdown has occurred, or they may not be reported at all.[16]

Lemkau, Tietze, and Cooper, in a survey of a Baltimore community, found that 367 psychotics were hospitalized and that 73 psychotics were not hospitalized. Age and sex seemed to influence the commitment of psychotics in this community. Nonhospitalized

[12] Bernard Lander, *Towards An Understanding of Juvenile Delinquency* (New York: Columbia University Press, 1954).

[13] H. Warren Dunham, "The Social Personality of the Catatonic-Schizophrenic," *American Journal of Sociology*, 49:508–518 (May, 1944).

[14] Mary Bess Owen, "Alternative Hypotheses for the Explanation of Some of Faris' and Dunham's Results," *American Journal of Sociology*, 47:48–51 (July, 1941).

[15] Robert E. Faris, *Social Disorganization*, pp. 230–231 (New York: Ronald Press, 1948).

[16] Robert White, *The Abnormal Personality*, pp. 564–565 (New York: Ronald Press, 1948).

patients were somewhat older that the hospitalized—median age, 51 against 43—and were more often females—59 per cent against 46 per cent. The racial distribution was the same for both groups.[17]

In general, ecological distributions are significant in showing the communities where the varied disorders are concentrated and where the disorders are sparse. From these facts, we can analyze more intensively the social influences upon the persons within these communities. The disparate concentrations of these disorders in different communities, however, are only indices to the whole universe of personal relationships which disordered persons experienced until they broke down and were then committed by others to mental hospitals.

The circular nature of the variables is such that the geneticists and biological determinists claim that preexisting predisposition to disorder influences socioeconomic position of residence as it would socioeconomic status. On the other hand, the sociologists claim that the stresses within the varied communities would exert a contributing causal influence upon the onset of disordered behavior. Srole and his associates in their study of Midtown Manhattan found an inverse relationship between their subjects' symptoms or degree of mental health and the socioeconomic status of the subjects' parents. From this they infer that emotional deprivation in childhood and downward intergenerational mobility may have contributed to this inverse relationship. But this relationship had not as yet been demonstrated for schizophrenia and manic-depression. Perhaps there is no single general inference to be made concerning the influence of the community on disorders, especially schizophrenia. Perhaps some predisposed individuals may gravitate to certain areas. Other persons may be affected markedly by the local community which represents a network of stressful influences and which in turn can contribute markedly to the onset of schizophrenia.[18]

[17] Paul Lemkau, Christopher Tietze, and Marcia Cooper, "Mental Hygiene Problems in an Urban District," *Mental Hygiene*, 26:275–288 (1942).
[18] See H. Warren Dunham, "Social Structures and Mental Disorders: Competing Hypotheses of Explanation," *Causes of Mental Disorders: A Review of Epidemiological Knowledge, 1959*, pp. 227–265 (New York: Milbank Memorial Fund, 1961).

The Los Angeles Riot of August 1965

ANTHONY OBERSCHALL
Yale University

While the Watts-Los Angeles[1] riot is now more than two years past, it has not yet received the scholarly attention it deserves.[2] Most newspapers and national magazines reported it at some length since it was an eminently newsworthy event. Four months after the riot, the Commission which Governor Brown appointed to make an objective and dispassionate study of the riot handed in the report of its findings.[3] The *McCone Report* was a mere 88 pages in length, and in it the actual description of riot events received no more than 15 pages of space. The Report concentrated mainly on cataloguing the social, economic, and psychological conditions which prevailed in the South Los Angeles area prior to the riot (which were well known to students of the Negro, poverty, and urban problems), and on suggesting changes designed to prevent a future riot. No attempt was made to provide anything but a superficial explanation of the motivation of the rioters and the patterns of their actions. In this paper, an attempt will be made to use existing social science knowledge on collective behavior and riots to provide

Reprinted from *Social Problems*, Vol. 15, No. 3, pp. 322–341 (Winter, 1968). Reprinted by permission of the author and of The Society for the Study of Social Problems.
[1] I wish to thank Mr. Borden Olive for helpful comments and assistance in locating some of the data on which this account is based.
[2] While the riot engulfed a far wider area of South Los Angeles than the Watts district, it has come to be known as the Los Angeles or the Watts riot, and I use both these terms interchangeably. The question of whether the events that took place are best characterized as a "riot" or something else will be dealt with below.
[3] Governor's Commission on the Los Angeles Riots, *Violence in the City—An End or a Beginning* (December 2, 1965), popularly known as the *McCone Report* after the Commission chairman's name.

a fuller explanation for the riot. Because the socioeconomic conditions which acted as a backdrop to the riot are generally well-known they will receive only limited attention in this paper. An account of the natural history of the riot and other statistics on the duration, number of victims, extent of the property damage, and magnitude of the law enforcement effort will not be provided here since they have been widely publicized and are readily available.[4]

The sociological analysis of the riot undertaken below relies on Smelser's analytic framework in accounting for the cause of collective behavior and the forms which it takes.[5] The strength of this approach consists in the emphasis on a number of determinants of social action which must all be present at the same time for a riot to occur. In addition to socioeconomic factors, such as high unemployment, low income, well defined racial cleavages, and authorities inaccessible and unsympathetic to grievances, this approach emphasizes the importance of a generalized belief in the population as a necessary determinant of collective action. It refers to a state of mind, formed over a period of time, which provides a shared explanation for the undesirable state of affairs and pinpoints blame upon specific agents or groups who become the targets of hostility. Incidents, such as the police arrest or shooting of a suspect, that normally receive but passing attention and are considered the private business of the parties involved, can become the precipitants of a riot when that state of mind is present and when it provides a symbolic interpretation of the incident in terms of shared cleavages, grievances, and hostilities. Another useful feature of the scheme is the emphasis on the operation of social control as a crucial variable in explaining the magnitude and course which the collective outburst takes.

A methodological difficulty in applying the scheme should, however, be pointed out and is indeed typical of many instances where the social scientist is confronted with an event whose causes have to be reconstructed after it has already occurred. Evidence for the amount of deprivation in the population and for the presence of a generalized belief prior to the collective outbreak is usually hard to come by. There is the temptation to take the outbreak itself as an indication of the prior presence of a state of mind conducive to the outbreak. Yet if this is done, there does not exist the possibility of disproving the view that an outbreak might have occurred even in the absence of such a state of mind. Evidence for the existence and

[4] For the relevant statistics, see the *McCone Report*, p. 1 and pp. 23–25; for a natural history of events, see Jerry Cohen and William S. Murphy, *Burn, Baby, Burn* (New York: Dutton, 1966); and *McCone Report*, pp. 10–23.
[5] Neil J. Smelser, *Theory of Collective Behavior*, Chapter 8 (New York: Free Press, 1962).

extent of the generalized belief has to be established independently of the subsequent events upon which it is meant to shed some light. Fortunately, in the case of the Los Angeles riot, there exists some information on the state of police-Negro relations and Negro grievances prior to the riot itself. But before a sociological explanation of the riot is presented, it will be useful to review briefly the views about the riot which have been propagated in the press and by official circles.

POPULAR AND OFFICIAL VIEWS OF THE RIOT AND THE EVIDENCE

Important questions about the riot need be answered before one can explain what the riot was all about. How many individuals actually participated in the looting, the burning, fighting the police, obstructing the firemen? Who were they? Was the riot spontaneous or planned, and if spontaneous, did certain groups subsequently provide the riot with leadership and organization? To what extent were youth gangs and adult criminal groups involved in the riot and the looting? Just what did the rioters and inhabitants do during the riot week? What levels of participation were there, and by whom? How widespread was the use of firearms and where did these weapons come from? How did the ecology of the area and the riot events themselves establish covert or tacit communication links among the rioters? Did the news media coverages of the riot contribute to its intensity and duration? Was the aggression of the rioters directed at the police and the white absentee owners as such, or were they conveniently available targets symbolizing the white man and white domination in general? Was the riot an irrational outburst directed against all authority, stemming from the life-long accumulation of frustration which found release in generalized aggression and violence? Is there evidence for norms operating among the rioters? Were specific targets selected and bounds to action recognized? Because of lack of information, or inaccurate and biased information, definitive answers cannot be given to all of these questions. Nevertheless, enough information is now available from many sources to rule out some characterizations of the riot, and to permit a plausible reconstruction of the character of the 1965 Los Angeles riot.

Immediate public reaction was a mixture of shock, fear, and belief that the riots were organized and led by some radical and disaffected groups in league with gangs and hoodlums; that quite possibly a conspiracy was at work; that it was a typical manifestation of irrational crowd behavior, unpredictable and similar to an animal stampede; that the rioters were well armed after they had systematically looted gun stores, hardware stores and pawn shops and that the riot consequently was an armed uprising by Negroes against the police, the political authorities, and the white man in general.

This initial climate of opinion was a result of the news coverage and the pronouncements of officials. They focused selective attention upon those events that did in fact fit the above loose conception of what the riot was all about. The irrational aspect of the riot was highlighted in Police Chief Parker's widely quoted phrase describing the rioters as behaving like "monkeys in the zoo." The insurrectionary aspect was stressed by *Time* and by the *Los Angeles Times* coverage, both of which reported extensively on the weapons allegedly used by the rioters and seized from them.[6] The conspiratorial and organized aspects of the riot, after its start, were stressed by Mayor Yorty[7] and other officials such as Police Chief Parker in his testimony on the use of bullhorns during the riot and the "expertly made" Molotov cocktails used by the rioters.[8] Indirect evidence for police belief in riot organization is the August 18th police siege, storming and subsequent destructive search of a Black Muslim Temple which was "deliberately provoked by false telephone calls to police that Negroes were carrying guns into the building."[9] The police did not question the veracity of the anonymous callers because the information fitted their belief of some formal riot leadership and organization. The reaction of fear by the white population of Los Angeles is illustrated by the run on gun stores, which took place far beyond the residential areas adjoining the curfew area.[10]

While the conspiracy theory was popular with some officials and could be used as a political alibi, the McCone Commission found no evidence for a conspiracy in setting off the Los Angeles riot. The Commission wrote that "There is no reliable evidence of outside or pre-established plans for rioting", although it pointed to

[6] *Time*, p. 16 (August 20, 1965): "After looting pawn shops, hardware and war supply stores for weapons, the Negroes brandished thousands of rifles shotguns, pistols, and machetes." See also the *Los Angeles Times* (August 17 and 18, 1965).
[7] *Los Angeles Times* (August 15, 1965).
[8] *Ibid.* (September 20, 1965).
[9] *Ibid.* (September 16, 1965).
[10] While the immediate reaction about what the riot was all about is to my mind distorted, the news media, statements by many officials, especially Negroes, as well as the later *McCone Report*, did reveal at least a moderate amount of sophistication and acceptance of ideas current in social science when it came to a description of the broader social and economic conditions that made the riot possible and even likely.

ome evidence of the promotion of the riot by gangs and other groups within the curfew area after the riot had started, such as he "sudden appearance of Molotov cocktails in quantity" and of 'inflammatory handbills".[11] The Commission did not elaborate a comprehensive theory of its own, yet it nevertheless hinted at another theory that has often been invoked in the explanation of violent collective outbursts, namely the "criminal riff-raff" theory of rioting. According to this view, every large urban ghetto contains a disproportionate number of criminals, delinquents, unemployed, school dropouts, and other social misfits who on the slightest pretext are ready to riot, loot, and exploit an explosive social situation for their private gain and for satisfying their aggressive anti-social instincts.[12] Thus the Commission emphasized that many Negroes were caught in a frustrating "spiral of failure", that they had been encouraged "to take the worst extreme and even illegal remedies to right a wide variety of wrongs, real and supposed", that nonetheless only a small minority of Negroes were involved in the disorder, and that a majority of those arrested had a prior criminal record.[13]

But as Blauner has pointed out in a perceptive analysis, the Report is, in the main, silent about who the participants were and what their motivations were. It did not attempt to explain how in the absence of planning and formal leadership a collective action on the scale and duration of the riot could be sustained in the face of a major show of force by over 1000 police and eventually 13,000 National Guardsmen.[14] Indeed, if the Commission's figure of a maximum of 10,000 Negroes taking to the streets is accepted,[15] this represents about 10 percent of the age cohorts 15 to 44, male and female, of the Negro population living in the South Los Angeles area, which roughly corresponds to the curfew area. Moreover, one should distinguish between several levels or degrees of participation. There are some who participated to the extent of physically fighting the police, of obstructing the firemen, of beating white motorists, and of breaking into stores and setting them on fire, in short, the

[11] *McCone Report*, pp. 22–23.
[12] On how both the conspiracy and criminal riff-raff explanations have been traditionally invoked by contemporaries to explain riots and rebellions in the 18th and 19th centuries see Georges Rudé, *The Crowd in History*, esp. Chapter 14 (New York: Wiley, 1964).
[13] *McCone Report*, pp. 1, 4–6, 24.
[14] Robert Blauner, "Whitewash over Watts," *Transaction*, 3 (March/April, 1966). Blauner himself concluded from published statements of Negro leaders and the reports of his informants that the McCone Commission had underestimated the widespread support for and participation in the riot, and explicitly rejects the view that the riot was primarily a rising of the lawless.
[15] *McCone Report*, p. 1: "perhaps as many as 10,000 Negroes took to the streets in marauding bands."

activists. There are others who helped themselves to the merchan
dise in the stores already broken into. Still others, far more numer
ous, simply milled about in the streets, jeered at police, and openly
encouraged the activists. Finally there were those who were no
involved beyond being curious observers, or just went about the
business of survival at a time of disaster. Among active partici
pants in a riot, adolescents and young adult males can be expected
to predominate. But if a substantial proportion of the remaining
population overtly manifests sympathy and support for the active
participants, the riot can only be interpreted as a broad group
response to shared grievances, and not as the expression of an
unrepresentative, lawless minority. An examination of the charac
teristics of those arrested during the riot can bring us a step closer
to resolving this controversy.

Almost 4,000 people were arrested on riot-related charges
during the Los Angeles riot, and a considerable amount of informa
tion about many of them has been collected and tabulated in two
separate studies conducted by government agencies. The first of
these, entitled *Riot Participation Study*,[16] concerns juvenile
arrests only and rests ultimately on information assembled by
Deputy Probation Officers from questioning the arrested youths
and other family members, and consulting the police and other
official records, for the purpose of presenting the Juvenile Court
with a "social report" on each youth. The second of these reports
entitled *Watts Riot Arrests*,[17] is ultimately based on police and
court records, and for a large sub-set, on data secured by the Los
Angeles Probation Department during a pre-sentence investigation
demanded by the courts. These data should therefore be treated
with caution, but in my opinion can lead to fairly definite conclu
sions on whether the riot participants were disproportionately com
posed of criminals, school dropouts, hoodlums, youths from broken
homes, the unemployed, recent migrants, in short the rootless and
drifting element which according to some is a characteristic of all
the large urban ghettos in the United States.

A question that has to be answered first, however, is whether
those arrested can reasonably be considered a typical cross-section
of the unknown total of persons who participated in some way in
the riot. It could well be that those arrested are more likely to be
representative of the groups which were milling about or looting
than of the activists.

[16] Los Angeles County Probation Department, *Riot Participation Study*, Re
search Report No. 26 (November, 1965), hereafter referred to as RPS.
[17] Bureau of Criminal Records, Department of Justice, State of California
Watts Riot Arrests (June 30, 1966), Sacramento, California, hereafter referred to as WRA.

Several facts suggest that this may indeed be the case. Available eye-witness reports indicate that on the first three days and nights, Wednesday to Saturday morning before the National Guard was fully deployed, police officers were seldom in a position to make arrests among the rioters who were physically fighting them, assaulting white motorists, preventing the effective operation of firemen, and breaking into stores and looting. Many arrests were of course made, but the bulk of them took place after the curfew had been declared, and the police and National Guard had begun to control the riot. For the juveniles 30 percent were arrested on Wednesday, Thursday, and Friday, and the rest on Saturday and later.[18] The figures for adults probably do not differ much but are unfortunately not available. Thus the bulk of those arrested were arrested at a time when the pattern of rioting had shifted from mass confrontation to small scale looting and more isolated incidents of confrontation with the authorities. Furthermore, since roughly 8 percent of the adults arrested were later released by the police, and another 32 percent not convicted by the courts, it is evident that a substantial proportion of the arrests were in fact of people who were not riot participants in the legal sense. It remains, therefore, an open question whether the activists of the first three nights differed significantly from those arrested for whom data are available.

A total of 3,371 adults and 556 juveniles were arrested, of whom about 60 percent were convicted. The most common booking offense for adults was for burglary, yet the most common conviction was for trespassing. It would seem that many individuals who happened to be in or near stores that were broken into were arrested without positive proof that they had stolen any merchandise. The booking offenses in most cases are more serious than the final dispositions, which resulted primarily in misdemeanors, ranging from simple assault and petty theft to trespassing, curfew violation, disturbing the peace, drunkenness and drunken driving, and the like. All in all, only 63 cases, or less than 3 percent of those arrested, received sentences of 6 months or more.[19]

Examining the prior criminal record of adults arrested—and the distribution is the same for those not convicted and those convicted—one finds that 26 percent had no prior record whatsoever, 2 percent had an arrest record but no conviction, 7 percent had convictions of less than 90 days, 18 percent had one or two convictions of 90 days and over, 4 percent had 3 or more convictions of 90 days and over, and 11 percent had a prior prison record, with no infor-

[18] R⬛S, p. 21.
[19] WRA, Tables 25 and 2.

mation available on the remaining 5 percent.[20] These facts abou¹
convictions and prior criminal record prompted the following con
cluding comment by the compilers of these statistics:

> The relatively minor types of offenses for which the great majority
> of riot participants were convicted would seem to indicate that this group
> of individuals was not the same type of persons usually booked on similar
> felony charges. A review of their prior criminal history fails to show a
> record as serious as that generally present in many of the nonriot felony
> bookings usually handled in urban areas by the police and courts.[21]

The criminal riff-raff and hoodlum theory of riot participation does
not receive any support from these data.

It is difficult to establish to what extent those arrested were
representative of the South Los Angeles population, because census
categories and breaking points often differ from those reported in
the riot statistics, and the potential reservoir for riot participants is
mainly the male 14 to 50 year old group. Nevertheless, since 41 percent of those arrested were in the 25 to 39 age category, and a further 17 percent 40 years old and over, it is inaccurate to describe
the rioters as mainly composed of irresponsible youth and young
hoodlums. Unlike gang incidents and other outbursts that are confined to a particular age cohort, the Los Angeles riot drew its participants from young and old alike.

Socioeconomic information about adults arrested is available
for the 1057 convicted cases that were referred to the Los Angeles
Probation Department for a pre-sentence investigation and report.
This figure is 31 percent of all adults originally arrested in the riot
and 52 percent of the adults convicted. These cases therefore represent slightly over a half of those arrested against whom proof of
criminal participation was sustained in the courts. Of these, 75 percent have lived in Los Angeles County 5 or more years, and only 6
percent less than a year. The rioters were therefore not "recent
migrants" to Los Angeles. Furthermore their educational achievements compare favorably with that of the population. The median
years of education of the 1,057 convicted adult participants is
slightly over ten completed years, which is about the same as that
of the South Los Angeles area. The information on labor force
characteristics of the rioters is unfortunately not comparable to the
census breakdowns for Watts and the South Los Angeles area.
Among the arrested rioters, only about 10 percent were in the non-
manual category, and of the remaining proportion only 9.4 percent
are classified as skilled workers. Moreover, 22.6 percent of the

[20] WRA, Table 6.
[21] WRA, p. 37.

arrested rioters were unemployed, compared with 13.2 percent for the Watts labor force in November 1965, and 10.1 percent for South Los Angeles.[22] The lower-class character of riot participation clearly emerges from these figures.

The detailed information on the juveniles arrested during the riot, incomplete as it is, confirms the picture which emerges from the adult data. There were 556 juvenile arrests, resulting in 338 cases referred to formal probation supervision. The vast majority of them were placed under probation supervision in their own homes. 82.5 percent of the youths were in school, as opposed to 14.8 percent who were dropouts, not a high figure in an area where two-thirds of the students do not finish high school. The youths arrested can not accurately be called "dropouts." They appear to have come in disproportionate numbers from the poor and broken homes of the ghetto, but were not typical "delinquents." Thus, 81 percent of the cases are described as having "acceptable" to "good" relations with their families, 57 percent have never been on probation before, and a further 26 percent only once. On the other hand 34 percent of their families were currently receiving their major economic contribution from the Bureau of Public Assistance (compared to 24 percent for the Watts population), only 26 percent were living in homes with both parents present (compared to 53 percent of persons under 18 years old in Watts living with both parents, and 62 percent for the South Los Angeles Area), and a little over 50 percent lived in families classified as having a "major family problem" by the Probation Department, the most frequent one being a major economic problem such as unemployment and poverty.[23]

All in all, piecing together the above information for adults and juveniles, what strikes one is the extent to which the riot drew participants from all social strata within the predominantly lower-class Negro area in which it took place. The riot cannot be attributed to the lawless and rootless minority which inhabits the ghetto, though, no doubt, these were active in it as well. The riot is best seen as a large-scale collective action, with a wide, representative base in the lower-class Negro communities, which, however much it gained the sympathy of the more economically well-off Negroes, remained a violent lower-class outburst throughout. If there were numerous jobless among the participants and many

[22] Figures above taken from or recalculated from WRA, RPS, *McCone Report*, and "Special Census Survey of the South and East Los Angeles Areas: November 1965," *Current Population Report*, Technical Studies, Series P-23, 17 (March 23, 1967).
[23] Figures cited above were taken from or recalculated from WRA, RPS, "Special Census Survey . . ." *op. cit.*, and the *McCone Report*.

youths from families with problems, it is precisely because such cases abound in the neighborhoods in which the riot occurred.

POLICE-NEGRO RELATIONS

The conspiracy and criminal riff-raff theories of the riot are not supported by the evidence on arrests. The key to a sociological explanation is the state of police-Negro relations before the riot, for it was a major source of Negro frustrations and accounts for the presence of a generalized belief which is a necessary ingredient in producing collective action. The objective factors producing strain among Negroes in the South Los Angeles area, such as a high unemployment rate and stationary (even declining) incomes at a time of increasing prosperity in the rest of Los Angeles and the country at large, have been well documented and noted.[24] The increases in racial tensions due to other than economic factors have also received the attention they deserve. In the November 1964 election, California voters repealed the Rumford Fair Housing Act in a constitutional referendum by a 2:1 margin. Repeal was particularly high in Southern California and even higher among the white population surrounding the Negro neighborhoods in Los Angeles County. White areas there were in favor of the repeal in the 80 percent to the 90 percent range, whereas Negro precincts voted against it in the 90 percent range. The vote was widely interpreted as a hardening of white public opinion with respect to integrated housing. While most major U.S. cities had come up with acceptable organizational structures within the War on Poverty Program by the summer of 1965, events took a different turn in Los Angeles:

> Advance billing with respect to federal programs had created the false impression that more job opportunities would be available than actually developed. The endless bickering between city, state and federal government officials over the administration of the authorized programs—most particularly the Poverty Program—has disappointed many.[25]

There were no compensating factors in Los Angeles such that Negroes would be conscious of progress in some matters directly affecting them. The civil rights movement has not been very active in Los Angeles, and its crowning achievement, the passage of the

[24] See "Special Census Survey . . ." op. cit., which contains up to date figures and allows a comparison to be made between the separate districts making up the South Los Angeles area. Other pertinent information is contained in the McCone Report.
[25] McCone Report, p. 40.

Civil Rights Act of 1964, has not had any impact on the city's Negro population since segregation did not exist in Los Angeles, and California has had, for many years, laws against discrimination in employment, political participation, and other activities. The charge of police malpractice and of police "brutality" is of course not confined to Los Angeles, but has been a problem in most large U.S. cities and a precipitant in the 1964 and later riots in the U.S. The situation in Los Angeles had been the subject of hearings held in Los Angeles in September 1962 by the California Advisory Committee of the U.S. Commission on Civil Rights, headed by Bishop Pike of San Francisco. The purpose of the hearings was to ascertain the state of police-minority group relations after an April 1962 incident involving Los Angeles police officers and Black Muslims became a focal point of organized Negro protest against alleged discriminatory treatment by Los Angeles police.[26]

■ ■ ■

The whole matter of police-Negro relations in Los Angeles is a complicated one. Police brutality refers to more than the excessive use of physical force during an arrest, the man-handling of suspects in the police station and in jail, and other physical acts usually associated with the term brutality. It means arrests, questionings and searches of Negroes by police without apparent provocation, the use of abusive and derogatory language in addressing Negroes, such as the word "nigger," and a general attitude toward the minority groups which represents an affront to their sense of dignity.[27] Police brutality in this sense is a reality to be reckoned with in the Negro ghetto, no matter how exaggerated some incidents turn out to be and regardless of whether political or criminal groups try to exploit the issue. The presence of the police in the South Los Angeles area was a constant source of irritation and left behind a legacy of bitterness and hostility. Two years before the riot, a study conducted by the Youth Opportunities Board with 220 people in Watts, Avalon, and Willowbrook on their attitudes toward several agencies operating in the community found that a majority of both adults and children felt that "the behavior of the

[26] U.S. Commission on Civil Rights, California Advisory Committee, *Police Minority Group Relations in Los Angeles and the San Francisco Bay Area* (hereafter referred to as the *Pike Report*), p. 1 (August, 1963).
[27] On these points, see Ray Murphy and Howard Elinson (ed.), *Problems and Prospects of the Negro Movement*, p. 232 (Belmont, Calif.: Wadsworth Co., 1966); Robert Blauner, "Whitewash over Watts," *Transaction*, 3:8 (March/April 1966); and Jerry Cohen and William S. Murphy, *Burn, Baby, Burn*, p. 210 (New York: Dutton, 1966).

police aggravated the problems of growing up in the Negro community rather than contributed to their solution" in marked contrast to the respondents' attitudes towards schools, probation officers, and health agencies.[28] It is important to note, however, that the tension-filled relations between police and Negroes have a structural and situational as well as a personal origin. The police as the daily visible representative of a white-dominated world bear the full brunt of the accumulated frustrations and hostility of the ghetto. Negro attitudes towards the police are not merely a reaction to police behavior and attitudes, but to their total situation in the society. The role of the police in this situation is as unrewarding as it is dangerous.

■ ■ ■

THE PRECIPITATING INCIDENT AND MOBILIZATION FOR ACTION

Prior to the start of the riot, therefore, Negroes in South Los Angeles were subjected to considerable strain due to unemployment, low income, police-Negro relations, frustrated hopes about the war on poverty, and similar factors. The normal channels for voicing Negro grievances had been ineffective in bringing about a change in the conditions producing these strains. A widespread belief in police brutality had existed for some time and was coupled with deep hostility against police. The Frye arrest on the evening of August 11 provided the spark which ignited the accumulated frustrations of the South Los Angeles population. In order to explain how a simple traffic arrest could escalate in a short time into a full-fledged riot of the magnitude and duration of the subsequent events, one has to examine the characteristics of the precipitating incident, the communications processes within the riot-prone population, the ecology of the South Los Angeles area, and the nature of the police effort to control it.

Marquette Frye, a 21-year-old Negro, driving his mother's car, with his brother as a passenger, was stopped by a California Highway Patrolman after he failed to stop at a red light, about 7 p.m. near, but not in Watts. Marquette Frye had been drinking and was unable to produce a driver's license. The officer, soon joined by two more, was getting ready to arrest him. The evening this occurred was the hottest one so far of the summer, a lot of people were simply hanging about on the sidewalks outside their homes. A small crowd quickly gathered to observe the arrest. Everything went

[28] Blauner, op. cit., p. 6.

without incident until Frye's mother, living nearby, arrived on the
scene. What happened after that is still not clear since the police, the
Fryes, and witnesses have sworn to contradictory testimony.[29]
Apparently, while at first Mrs. Frye turned against her son to discipline him, eventually the three Fryes, with encouragement from
the onlookers, turned upon the policemen and had to be forcefully
subdued and arrested. Meanwhile the Highway Patrolmen had
radioed for reinforcements, and Los Angeles police officers arrived
for help. By 7:25 p.m. the patrol car with the Fryes under arrest
and a tow truck pulling the Frye car left the scene.[30] As the patrolmen were about to leave, a woman in the menacing crowd spat on
one of them, and an officer did go into the hostile crowd to arrest
her. She was wearing a shirt outside her skirt. The rumor immediately spread that the police were beating and arresting a "pregnant"
woman—which she was not—just as the crowd had earlier "seen"
the policemen use excessive force to subdue the Fryes. By the time
the last police car left the arrest location, it was stoned by the
crowd and the riot had begun.[31]

Regardless of what actually happened, the events surrounding
the arrest fitted in with preconceptions and the generalized belief
about police brutality. In a confusing context such as an arrest in
the evening with lots of people milling about and a high noise level,
it is plausible that apart from a few Negroes who actually eye-
witnessed most of the arrest-events, many others pieced out an
incomplete perceptual record of these events according to their preconceptions and predispositions. . . .[32]

■ ■ ■

During the entire riot a common thread was the aggression against
the police. Yet from the start the riot was more than just a police
riot. The Los Angeles riot did not exhibit the character of the classic race-riot in which crowds of one race systematically seek out
and assault isolated individuals and small groups of another race.
Nevertheless the first two nights witnessed many incidents which
fit the classic pattern as unsuspecting (and later curious) white
motorists driving through the riot area were pelted with bricks and
bottles, pulled out of their cars and beaten up, and news reporters
and TV crews were assaulted. It is difficult to document how the

[29] The most plausible reconstruction of the incident is presented in great detail in Chaps. 2–4 of Jerry Cohen and William S. Murphy in *Burn, Baby, Burn.*
[30] *McCone Report*, p. 11.
[31] *Ibid.*, p. 12.
[32] Evidence for these psychological processes can be found in Bernard Berelson
and Gary Steiner, *Human Behavior*, pp. 101, 115 (New York: Harcourt, Brace
and World, 1964).

subsequent major pattern of breaking into stores, looting, and burning them down became established. . . .

■ ■ ■

RIOT BEHAVIOR AND MOTIVATION

No one would deny the extensive property damage perpetrated by the rioters in looting and burning the stores, the physical assault upon police, white motorists, firemen, and others. One can, however, question whether this behavior is essentially an irrational stampede and orgy of destruction, and hence void of collective social significance and personal meaning. Nothing is gained by defining riot behavior as irrational *a priori*. There is considerable evidence that the rioters observed certain *bounds*, that they directed their aggression at *specific targets*, and that they selected *appropriate means* for the ends they intended to obtain.

The fact that no deaths resulted from the direct action of the rioters is evidence that they observed certain bounds and limits. The first two nights when white motorists were dragged out of their cars and beaten, and when newsmen were severely roughed up, none were beaten to death or killed as might easily have happened since the police were unable to offer protection at the time. Furthermore, the sniper fire directed at police and firemen did not result in any fatalities either, despite reports that it was widespread and lasted throughout the riot week and the fact that police and firemen were easy targets. It seems that sniping was aimed towards obstructing law enforcement and fire fighting and not toward killing officials.

The riot crowds gave evidence of being able to pick specific targets for their aggression. Negro business establishments, many of them carrying signs such as "Blood Brother" or "Soul Brother" were for the most part spared. Private houses, post offices, churches, schools, libraries, and other public buildings in the riot area were not broken into and burned down, vandalized, or otherwise purposely damaged. Some white-owned stores also were spared. While the McCone Commission states that "Our study of the patterns of burning and looting does not indicate any significant correlation between alleged consumer exploitation and the destruction [of stores],"[33] insufficient evidence is cited to back up this conclusion, which would require a careful and controlled study of all stores and their practices in the riot area. Some informed observers have disagreed with the Commission's conclusions on this point. Moreover, the Los Angeles Police, the main target of pre-riot hos-

[33] *McCone Report*, p. 62.

tility, was also the main target of riot aggression. Only ten National Guardsmen out of a maximum of 13,900 were reported injured, as compared to 90 Los Angeles policemen out of a combined total of 1,653 police at the time of maximum deployment.[34] The evidence, meager as it is, supports the view that there was a systematic relationship between the specific targets of aggression and the sources of the rioters' grievances.

The destructive and violent behavior of the rioters was confined to specific kinds of events within the riot situation. Eyewitnesses reported that rioters and looters in cars were observing traffic laws in the riot area—stopping for red lights, stopping for pedestrians at cross walks—even when carrying away stolen goods. Firemen were obstructed in putting out fires set to business establishments, yet one incident is reported where "people beseeched firemen to save a house which had caught fire when embers skipped to it from a torched commercial building,"[35] and during which firemen were not hindered in any way from carrying out their job. These and similar incidents testify to the ability of riot participants to choose appropriate means for their ends. While riot behavior cannot be called "rational" in the everyday common meaning of that term, it did contain normative and rational elements and was much more situationally determined than the popular view would have it.

Looting is furthermore quite common in disaster situations other than riots and need not be interpreted as an expression of specifically racial hostility. Its attraction to people lacking the consumer goods others take for granted needs no complex explanation beyond the simple desire to obtain them when the opportunity to do so involves a low risk of apprehension by the police. Such action is facilitated by low commitment to the norms of private property expressed in the prosperity of "the poor to seek a degree of elementary social justice at the expense of the rich",[36] the fact that others were doing the same thing, and the fact that the stores sacked in this case belonged to "Whitey." . . .

■ ■ ■

Looting was a predominantly neighborhood activity, often uncoordinated, and carried out by small groups. Between 50 and 65 percent of the minors were arrested less than a mile from their home, and a little over 63 percent were arrested in the company of others, mainly for "burglary", that is they were apprehended in or

---

[34] *Ibid.,* p. 20.
[35] Cohen and Murphy, *op. cit.,* p. 157.
[36] See Rudé, *op. cit.,* p. 244, and *passim* for historical instances of this.

near stores broken into. . . .[37] While the actions of some looters were described in some accounts as that of a savage mob bent on plunder and fighting each other for the spoils, other descriptions and material, such as a photograph showing two women and one man rolling a fully loaded shopping cart past firemen, suggest a much more relaxed and calm mood.

Looting as well as other riot activity were essentially group activities during which participants and onlookers experienced a sense of solidarity, pride, and exhilaration. They were bound together by shared emotions, symbols, and experiences which a black man inevitably acquires in white America and which makes him address another one as "Brother".[38] They were also bound together by the common enemy, "Whitey", and struck out against Whitey's representatives in the flesh, the police, the firemen, the merchants, the news reporters, and the motorists, and they felt good about striking out. Bystanders were swept along in this tide of we-feeling. . . .

The rioters did not form an amorphous mass, a collection of individuals acting out private frustrations and hostility. Rioting was a group activity in the course of which strangers were bound together by common sentiments, activities, and goals, and supported each other in the manner typical of primary groups. The riot was a collective celebration in the manner of a carnival, during which about 40 liquor stores were broken into and much liquor consumed. It was also a collective contest similar to that between two high school or college athletic teams, with the supporters cheering and egging on the contestants. One could settle old scores with the police, show them who really controlled the territory, humiliate them and teach them a lesson. . . .

In assaulting the police and breaking into business establishments, some rioters were not only responding to the long standing frustrations and humiliations suffered at the hands of the police and the exploitative practices of merchants, but were reacting along racial lines which can only be understood in the wider social context of the Negro in the U.S. Rioters were pelting motorists and firemen with rocks while shouting: "This is for Bogalusa! This is for Selma!" The riot situation became defined in global, dichotomous, we-they terms, where we and they stood for the two races and the long history of conflict associated with them. In such a situ-

[37] RPS, pp. 16, 18. Comparable data on adults arrested are not available.
[38] A Negro student recalls driving his rundown automobile during the riot outside of the curfew area, and stopping at a red light next to a late-model car driven by a middle-aged, prosperous looking Negro. The other driver, a total stranger and probably mistaking the student for one of the active rioters, smiled broadly and asked him before driving off: "Where are you going to strike next, Brother?"

ation, when one status (racial membership) becomes predominant and one's other statuses and role obligations irrelevant, mediation becomes impossible because one cannot remain sitting on a fence. When Negro Assemblyman Marvin Dymally tried to calm some rioters a boy asked him: "Who you with?" Dymally answered: "I'm with you, man," to which the boy retorted: "Then here's a rock, baby, throw it!"[39] Those who bridge the dichotomy by siding with the opponent are perceived as traitors, and will be singled out for special abuse as was the case with a Negro National Guardsman who was called a "white nigger" by the crowd.[40]

CONCLUSION

These considerations about the actions and motivations of the rioters enable one to come closer to a characterization of the Watts riot. Was it a police riot, a race riot, an insurrection, a revolt, a rebellion, a nationalist uprising, or a revolution? A lot depends upon how these terms are defined, and they are often used loosely and interchangeably. There is no point engaging in a definitional exercise with which many will take issue. It can however be pointed out that in all of the above manifestations of collective behavior, common grievances, sentiments, emotions, and we-feeling bind the actors together, common targets become the object of aggression, and violent physical means are used by the participants. These cannot therefore be used to distinguish a riot from a revolt or a rebellion. One must examine what collective goals and demands are voiced by the actors. If their actions are directed at overthrowing the constituted authorities, if political demands are voiced such as the resignation of certain leaders and officials, if an attempt is made to achieve physical control in an area or territory by forcing out the existing authorities and substituting for them other authorities, then one is dealing with a revolt, rebellion, insurrection, or uprising. If, on the other hand, the main purpose of the action is to inflict damage and/or injury upon certain groups or a category of persons, such as police, merchants, or whites in general, then one is dealing with a riot.[41] The Los Angeles events therefore constituted a riot rather than anything else.

[39] Cohen and Murphy, op. cit., p. 119.
[40] *Ibid.*, p. 195.
[41] "A riot is an outbreak of temporary but violent mass disorder. It may be directed at a particular individual as well as against public authorities. But it involves no intention to overthrow the government itself. In this respect riot stops short of insurrection or rebellion, although it may often be only a preliminary to the latter" is the definition of Smellie in the *Encyclopedia of the Social Sciences.*

The riot was remarkable for the lack of any leadership and organized effort to express collective demands of the rioters and the Negro population in South Los Angeles. However many persons in that area may have wished to see the resignation of Police Chief Parker, or the establishment of a Civilian Police Review Board, no banners proclaiming these demands were raised.[42] No attempts were made to address the crowds to spell out collective aims. No spokesmen emerged from the ranks of the rioters to make a statement to the authorities or the press.[43] No effort was made to hold an area after the police were forced out of it and to coordinate action designed to prevent its comeback. No barricades were thrown up. Single individuals sniped at police and firemen from different locations and on numerous occasions, but there was no attempt to create a more organized form of armed resistance. While the precipitating incident touched off a police riot, which soon thereafter widened into a riot during which the targets of aggression became other whites besides police, subsequent days and nights produced a repetition of the same sort of behavior over an ever wider area and involving greater numbers of participants, but did not produce a change towards a more insurrectionary or revolutionary pattern of action.

It is the magnitude of the Los Angeles riot, both in duration, participation, amount of damage and casualties, and the forces needed to control it, which led many to characterize it as more than just a riot. But aside from magnitude, the Los Angeles riot was structurally and behaviorally similar to the Negro riots in other cities during the Summers of 1964, 1965, and 1966. The collective significance of these events, however, is that the civil rights gains made by the Negro movement in the last few years, which have benefited the Southern Negro and middle-class Negroes, have not altered the situation of the lower-class urban Negroes outside of the South and have not removed the fundamental sources of grievances of a large proportion of the Negro population in the U.S.

[42] Although some handbills from an unidentified source denouncing Parker were passed out during the riot.

[43] Negro leaders and influentials did of course speak out during the riot on television and through other means. They expressed Negro demands such as Assemblyman Dymally's call for Parker's removal. But the leaders were reiterating views that they had long held and publicly voiced. They were not asked by the rioters to be spokesmen for riot goals or terms of negotiation with the authorities.

Conditions of Life In the Racial Ghetto

The conditions of life in the racial ghetto are strikingly different from those to which most Americans are accustomed—especially white, middle-class Americans. We believe it important to describe these conditions and their effect on the lives of people who cannot escape from the ghetto.[1]

CRIME AND INSECURITY

Nothing is more fundamental to the quality of life in any area than the sense of personal security of its residents, and nothing affects this more than crime.

In general, crime rates in large cities are much higher than in other areas of our country. Within such cities, crime rates are higher in disadvantaged Negro areas than anywhere else.

The most widely used measure of crime is the number of "index crimes" (homicide, forcible rape, aggravated assault, robbery, burglary, grand larceny, and auto theft) in relation to population. In 1966, 1,754 such crimes were reported to police for every 100,000 Americans. In cities over 250,000, the rate was 3,153, and in cities over 1 million, it was 3,630—or more than double the national average. In suburban areas alone, including suburban

From *Report of the National Advisory Commission on Civil Disorders*, March 1, 1968, pp. 133–141 (Washington: Government Printing Office, 1968).
[1] We have not attempted here to describe conditions relating to the fundamental problems of housing, education, and welfare, which are treated in detail in later chapters.

cities, the rate was only 1,300, or just over one-third the rate in the largest cities.

Within larger cities, personal and property insecurity has consistently been highest in the older neighborhoods encircling the downtown business district. In most cities, crime rates for many decades have been higher in these inner areas than anywhere, except in downtown areas themselves, where they are inflated by the small number of residents.

High crime rates have persisted in these inner areas even though the ethnic character of their residents continually changed. Poor immigrants used these areas as "entry ports," then usually moved on to more desirable neighborhoods as soon as they acquired enough resources. Many "entry port" areas have now become racial ghettos.

The difference between crime rates in these disadvantaged neighborhoods and in other parts of the city is usually startling, as a comparison of crime rates in five police districts in Chicago for 1965 illustrates. These five include one high-income, all-white district at the periphery of the city, two very low-income, virtually all-Negro districts near the city core with numerous public housing projects, and two predominantly white districts, one with mainly lower middle-income families, the other containing a mixture of very high-income and relatively low-income households. The table shows crime rates against persons and against property in these five districts, plus the number of patrolmen assigned to them per 100,000 residents, as follows:

TABLE 26-1. INCIDENCE OF INDEX CRIMES AND PATROLMEN ASSIGNMENTS PER 100,000 RESIDENTS IN 5 CHICAGO POLICE DISTRICTS, 1965

Number	High-income white district	Low-middle income white district	Mixed high- and low-income white district	Very low-income Negro district No. 1	Very low-income Negro district No. 2
Index crimes against persons	80	440	338	1,615	2,820
Index crimes against property	1,038	1,750	2,080	2,508	2,630
Patrolmen assigned	93	133	115	243	291

These data indicate that:

Variations in the crime rate against persons within the city are extremely large. One very low-income Negro district had 35 times as many serious crimes against persons per 100,000 residents as did the high-income white district.

Variations in the crime rate against property are much smaller. The highest rate was only 2.5 times larger than the lowest.

The lower the income in an area, the higher the crime rate there. Yet low-income Negro areas have significantly higher crime rates than low-income white areas. This reflects the high degree of social disorganization in Negro areas described in the previous chapter, as well as the fact that poor Negroes as a group have lower incomes than poor whites as a group.

The presence of more police patrolmen per 100,000 residents does not necessarily offset high crime in certain parts of the city. Although the Chicago Police Department had assigned over three times as many patrolmen per 100,000 residents to the highest crime areas shown as to the lowest, crime rates in the highest crime area for offenses against both persons and property combined were 4.9 times as high as in the lowest crime area.

Because most middle-class Americans live in neighborhoods similar to the more crime-free district described above, they have little comprehension of the sense of insecurity that characterizes the ghetto resident. Moreover, official statistics normally greatly understate actual crime rates because the vast majority of crimes are not reported to the police. For example, studies conducted for the President's Crime Commission in Washington, D.C., Boston, and Chicago, showed that three to six times as many crimes were actually committed against persons and homes as were reported to the police.

Two facts are crucial to an understanding of the effects of high crime rates in racial ghettos; most of these crimes are committed by a small minority of the residents, and the principal victims are the residents themselves. Throughout the United States, the great majority of crimes committed by Negroes involve other Negroes as victims. A special tabulation made by the Chicago Police Department for the President's Crime Commission indicated that over 85 percent of the crimes committed against persons by Negroes between September, 1965, and March, 1966, involved Negro victims.

As a result, the majority of law-abiding citizens who live in disadvantaged Negro areas face much higher probabilities of being victimized than residents of most higher income areas, including almost all suburbs. For nonwhites, the probability of suffering from any index crime except larceny is 78 percent higher than for whites. The probability of being raped is 3.7 times higher among nonwhite women, and the probability of being robbed is 3.5 times higher for nonwhites in general.

The problems associated with high crime rates generate widespread hostility toward the police in these neighborhoods for reasons described elsewhere in this Report. Thus, crime not only creates an atmosphere of insecurity and fear throughout Negro neighborhoods but also causes continuing attrition of the relationship between Negro residents and police. This bears a direct relationship to civil disorder.

There are reasons to expect the crime situation in these areas to become worse in the future. First, crime rates throughout the United States have been rising rapidly in recent years. The rate of index crimes against persons rose 37 percent from 1960 to 1966, and the rate of index crimes against property rose 50 percent. In the first 9 months of 1967, the number of index crimes was up 16 percent over the same period in 1966, whereas the U.S. population rose about 1 percent. In cities of 250,000 to 1 million, index crime rose by over 20 percent, whereas it increased 4 percent in cities of over 1 million.[2]

Second, the number of police available to combat crime is rising much more slowly than the amount of crime. In 1966, there were about 20 percent more police employees in the United States than in 1960, and per capita expenditures for police rose from $15.29 in 1960 to $20.99 in 1966, a gain of 37 percent. But over the 6-year period, the number of reported index crimes had jumped 62 percent. In spite of significant improvements in police efficiency, it is clear that police will be unable to cope with their expanding workload unless there is a dramatic increase in the resources allocated by society to this task.

Third, in the next decade, the number of young Negroes aged 14 to 24 will increase rapidly, particularly in central cities. This group is responsible for a disproportionately high share of crimes in all parts of the Nation. In 1966, persons under 25 years of age comprised the following proportions of those arrested for various major crimes: murder, 37 percent; forcible rape, 64 percent; robbery, 71 percent; burglary, 81 percent; larceny, about 77 percent; and auto theft, 89 percent. For all index crimes together, the arrest rate for Negroes is about four times higher than that for whites.

[2] The problem of interpreting and evaluating "rising" crime rates is complicated by the changing age distribution of the population, improvements in reporting methods, and the increasing willingness of victims to report crimes. Despite these complications, there is general agreement on the serious increase in the incidence of crime in the United States.

Yet the number of young Negroes aged 14 to 24 in central cities will rise about 63 percent from 1966 to 1975, as compared to only 32 percent for the total Negro population of central cities.[3]

HEALTH AND SANITATION CONDITIONS

The residents of the racial ghetto are significantly less healthy than most other Americans. They suffer from higher mortality rates, higher incidence of major diseases, and lower availablility and utilization of medical services. They also experience higher admission rates to mental hospitals.

These conditions result from a number of factors.

Poverty

From the standpoint of health, poverty means deficient diets, lack of medical care, inadequate shelter and clothing and often lack of awareness of potential health needs. As a result, almost 30 percent of all persons with family incomes less than $2,000 per year suffer from chronic health conditions that adversely affect their employment—as compared with less than 8 percent of the families with incomes of $7,000 or more.

Poor families have the greatest need for financial assistance in meeting medical expenses. Only about 34 percent of families with incomes of less than $2,000 per year use health insurance benefits, as compared to nearly 90 percent of those with incomes of $7,000 or more.[4]

These factors are aggravated for Negroes when compared to whites for the simple reason that the proportion of persons in the

[3] Assuming those cities will experience the same proportion of total United States Negro population growth that they did from 1960 to 1966. The calculations are derived from population projections in Bureau of the Census, *Population Estimates*, Current Population Reports, Series P–25, No. 381, p. 63 (Dec. 18, 1967).

[4] Public programs of various kinds have been providing significant financial assistance for medical care in recent years. In 1964, over $1.1 billion was paid out by various governments for such aid. About 52 percent of medical vendor payments came from Federal Government agencies, 33 percent from states, and 12 percent from local governments. The biggest contributions were made by the Old Age Assistance Program and the Medical Assistance for the Aged Program. The enactment of Medicare in 1965 has significantly added to this flow of public assistance for medical aid. However, it is too early to evaluate the results upon health conditions among the poor.

United States who are poor is 3.5 times as high among Negroes (41 percent in 1966) as among whites (12 percent in 1966).

Maternal Mortality

Mortality rates for nonwhite mothers are four times as high as those for white mothers. There has been a sharp decline in such rates since 1940, when 774 nonwhite and 320 white mothers died for each 100,000 live births. In 1965, only 84 nonwhite and 21 white mothers died per 100,000 live births—but the gap between non-whites and whites actually increased.

Infant Mortality

Mortality rates among nonwhite babies are 58 percent higher than among whites for those under 1 month old and almost three times as high among those from 1 month to 1 year old. This is true in spite of a large drop in infant mortality rates in both groups since 1940.

TABLE 26-2. NUMBER OF INFANTS WHO DIED PER 1,000 LIVE BIRTHS

Year	Less than 1 month old		1 month to 1 year old	
	White	Nonwhite	White	Nonwhite
1940	27.2	39.7	16.0	34.1
1950	19.4	27.5	7.4	17.0
1960	17.2	26.9	5.7	16.4
1965	16.1	25.4	5.4	14.9

Life Expectancy

To some extent because of infant mortality rates, life expectancy at birth was 6.9 years longer for whites (71.0) than for nonwhites (64.1 years) in 1965. Even in the prime working ages, life expectancy is significantly lower among nonwhites than among whites. In 1965, white persons 25 years old could expect to live an average of 48.6 more years, whereas nonwhites 25 years old could expect to live another 43.3 years, or 11 percent less. Similar but smaller discrepancies existed at all ages from 25 through 55; some actually increased slightly between 1960 and 1965.

Lower Utilization of Health Services

A fact that also contributes to poorer health conditions in the ghetto is that Negro families with incomes similar to those of whites spend less on medical services and visit medical specialists less often.

TABLE 26-3. PERCENT OF FAMILY EXPENDITURES SPENT FOR MEDICAL CARE, 1960–61

Income group	White	Nonwhite	Ratio, white to nonwhite
Under $3,000	9	5	1.8:1
$3,000 to $7,499	7	5	1.4:1
$7,500 and over	6	4	1.5:1

Since the lowest income group contains a much larger proportion of nonwhite families than white families, the overall discrepancy in medical care spending between these two groups is very significant, as shown by the following table:

TABLE 26-4. HEALTH EXPENSES PER PERSON PER YEAR FOR THE PERIOD FROM JULY TO DECEMBER 1962

Income by racial group	Total medical	Expenses Hospital	Doctor	Dental	Medicine	Other
Under $2,000 per family per year:						
White	$130	$33	$41	$11	$32	$13
Nonwhite	63	15	23	5	16	5
$10,000 and more per family per year:						
White	179	34	61	37	31	16
Nonwhite	133	34	50	19	23	8

These data indicate that nonwhite families in the lower income group spent less than half as much per person on medical services as white families with similar incomes. This discrepancy sharply declines but is still significant in the higher income group, where total nonwhite medical expenditures per person equal, on the average, 74.3 percent of white expenditures.

Negroes spend less on medical care for several reasons. Negro households generally are larger, requiring greater nonmedical expenses for each household and leaving less money for meeting medical expenses. Thus, lower expenditures per person would result even if expenditures per household were the same. Negroes also often pay more for other basic necessities such as food and consumer durables, as discussed in the next part of this chapter. In addition, fewer doctors, dentists, and medical facilities are conveniently available to Negroes than to most whites—a result both of geographic concentration of doctors in higher income areas in large cities and of discrimination against Negroes by doctors and hospitals. A survey in Cleveland indicated that there were 0.45 physicians per 1,000 people in poor neighborhoods, compared to 1.13 per 1,000 in nonpoverty areas. The result nationally is fewer visits to physicians and dentists.

TABLE 26-5. PERCENT OF POPULATION MAKING ONE OR MORE VISITS TO INDICATED TYPE OF MEDICAL SPECIALIST FROM JULY 1963 TO JUNE 1964

Type of Medical Specialist	Family incomes of $2,000-$3,999		Family incomes of $7,000-$9,999	
	White	Nonwhite	White	Nonwhite
Physician	64	56	70	64
Dentist	31	20	52	33

Although widespread use of health insurance has led many hospitals to adopt nondiscriminatory policies, some private hospitals still refuse to admit Negro patients or to accept doctors with Negro patients. As a result, Negroes are more likely to be treated in hospital clinics than whites and they are less likely to receive personalized service. This conclusion is confirmed by the following data:

TABLE 26-6. PERCENT OF ALL VISITS TO PHYSICIANS FROM JULY, 1963 TO JUNE, 1964, MADE IN INDICATED WAYS

Type of visit to physician	Family-incomes of $2,000-$3,999		Family incomes of $7,000-$9,999	
	White	Nonwhite	White	Nonwhite
In physician's office	68	56	73	66
Hospital clinic	17	35	7	16
Other (mainly telephone)	15	9	20	18
Total	100	100	100	100

Environmental Factors

Environmental conditions in disadvantaged Negro neighborhoods create further reasons for poor health conditions there. The level of sanitation is strikingly below that which is prevalent in most higher income areas. One simple reason is that residents often lack proper storage facilities for food—adequate refrigerators, freezers, even garbage cans, which are sometimes stolen as fast as landlords can replace them.

In areas where garbage collection and other sanitation services are grossly inadequate—commonly in the poorer parts of our large cities—rats proliferate. It is estimated that in 1965, there were over 14,000 cases of ratbite in the United States, mostly in such neighborhoods.

The importance of these conditions was outlined for the Commission as follows:[5]

Sanitation Commissioners of New York City and Chicago both feel this [sanitation] to be an important community problem and report themselves as being under substantial pressure to improve conditions. *It must be concluded that slum sanitation is a serious problem in the minds of the urban poor and well merits, at least on that ground, the attention of the Commission.* A related problem, according to one Sanitation Commissioner, is the fact that residents of areas bordering on slums feel that sanitation and neighborhood cleanliness is a crucial issue, relating to the stability of their blocks and constituting an important psychological index of "how far gone" their area is.

* * * There is no known study comparing sanitation services between slum and non-slum areas. The experts agree, however, that there are more services in the slums on a quantitative basis, although perhaps not a per capita basis. In New York, for example, garbage pickups are supposedly scheduled for about six times a week in slums, compared to three times a week in other areas of the city; the comparable figures in Chicago are two to three times a week versus once a week.

The point, therefore, is not the relative quantitative level of services but the peculiarly intense needs of ghetto areas for sanitation services. This high demand is the product of numerous factors including: (1) higher population density; (2) lack of well managed buildings and adequate garbage services provided by landlords, number of receptacles, carrying to curbside, number of electric garbage disposals; (3) high relocation rates of tenants and businesses, producing heavy volume of bulk refuse left on streets and in buildings; (4) different uses of the streets—as outdoor living rooms in summer, recreation areas—producing high visibility and sensitivity to garbage problems; (5) large numbers of abandoned cars; (6) severe rodent and pest problems; (7) traffic congestion blocking garbage collection; and (8) obstructed street cleaning and snow removal on crowded, car-choked streets. Each of these elements adds to the problem and suggests a different possible line of attack.

[5] Memorandum to the Commission dated Nov. 16, 1967, from Robert Patricelli, minority counsel, Subcommittee on Employment Manpower and Poverty, U.S. Senate.

EXPLOITATION OF DISADVANTAGED CONSUMERS BY RETAIL MERCHANTS

Much of the violence in recent civil disorders has been directed at stores and other commercial establishments in disadvantaged Negro areas. In some cases, rioters focused on stores operated by white merchants who, they apparently believed, had been charging exorbitant prices or selling inferior goods. Not all the violence against these stores can be attributed to "revenge" for such practices. Yet it is clear that many residents of disadvantaged Negro neighborhoods believe they suffer constant abuses by local merchants.

Significant grievances concerning unfair commercial practices affecting Negro consumers were found in 11 of the 20 cities studied by the Commission. The fact that most of the merchants who operate stores in Negro areas are white undoubtedly contributes to the conclusion among Negroes that they are exploited by white society.

It is difficult to assess the precise degree and extent of exploitation. No systematic and reliable survey comparing consumer pricing and credit practices in all-Negro and other neighborhoods has ever been conducted on a nationwide basis. Differences in prices and credit practices between white middle-income areas and Negro low-income areas to some extent reflect differences in the real costs of serving these two markets (such as differential losses from pilferage in supermarkets), but the exact extent of these cost differences has never been estimated accurately. Finally, an examination of exploitative consumer practices must consider the particular structure and functions of the low-income consumer durables market.

Installment Buying

This complex situation can best be understood by first considering certain basic facts:

Various cultural factors generate constant pressure on low-income families to buy many relatively expensive durable goods and display them in their homes. This pressure comes in part from continuous exposure to commercial advertising, especially on television. In January, 1967, over 88 percent of all Negro households had TV sets. A 1961 study of 464 low-income families in New York City showed that 95 percent of these relatively poor families had TV sets.

Many poor families have extremely low incomes, bad previous credit records, unstable sources of income, or other attributes which make it virtually impossible for them to buy merchandise from established large national or local retail firms. These families lack enough savings to pay cash, and they cannot meet the standard credit requirements of established general merchants because they are too likely to fall behind in their payments.

Poor families in urban areas are far less mobile than others. A 1967 Chicago study of low-income Negro households indicated their low automobile ownership compelled them to patronize neighborhood merchants. These merchants typically provided smaller selection, poorer services, and higher prices than big national outlets. The 1961 New York study also indicated that families who shopped outside their own neighborhoods were far less likely to pay exorbitant prices.

Most low-income families are uneducated concerning the nature of credit purchase contracts, the legal rights and obligations of both buyers and sellers, sources of advice for consumers who are having difficulties with merchants, and the operation of the courts concerned with these matters. In contrast, merchants engaged in selling goods to them are very well informed.

In most states, the laws governing relations between consumers and merchants in effect offer protection only to informed, sophisticated parties with understanding of each other's rights and obligations. Consequently, these laws are little suited to protect the rights of most low-income consumers.

In this situation, exploitative practices flourish. Ghetto residents who want to buy relatively expensive goods cannot do so from standard retail outlets and are thus restricted to local stores. Forced to use credit, they have little understanding of the pitfalls of credit buying. But because they have unstable incomes and frequently fail to make payments, the cost to the merchants of serving them is significantly above that of serving middle-income consumers. Consequently, a special kind of merchant appears to sell them goods on terms designed to cover the high cost of doing business in ghetto neighborhoods.

Whether they actually gain higher profits, these merchants charge higher prices than those in other parts of the city to cover the greater credit risks and other higher operating costs inherent in neighborhood outlets. A recent study conducted by the Federal Trade Commission in Washington, D.C., illustrates this conclusion dramatically. The FTC identified a number of stores specializing in selling furniture and appliances to low-income households. About

92 percent of the sales of these stores were credit sales involving installment purchases, as compared to 27 percent of the sales in general retail outlets handling the same merchandise. The median income annually of a sample of 486 customers of these stores was about $4,200, but one-third had annual incomes below $3,600, about 6 percent were receiving welfare payments, and another 76 percent were employed in the lowest-paying occupations (service workers, operatives, laborers and domestics), as compared to 36 percent of the total labor force in Washington in those occupations.

Definitely catering to a low-income group, these stores charged significantly higher prices than general merchandise outlets in the Washington area. According to testimony by Paul Rand Dixon, Chairman of the FTC, an item selling wholesale at $100 would retail on the average for $165 in a general merchandise store and for $250 in a low-income specialty store. Thus, the customers of these outlets were paying an average price premium of about 52 percent.

While higher prices are not necessarily exploitative in themselves, many merchants in ghetto neighborhoods take advantage of their superior knowledge of credit buying by engaging in various exploitative tactics—high-pressure salesmanship, "bait advertising," misrepresentation of prices, substitution of used goods for promised new ones, failure to notify consumers of legal actions against them, refusal to repair or replace substandard goods, exorbitant prices or credit charges, and use of shoddy merchandise. Such tactics affect a great many low-income consumers. In the New York study, 60 percent of all households had suffered from consumer problems (some of which were purely their own fault). About 23 percent had experienced serious exploitation. Another 20 percent, many of whom were also exploited, had experienced repossession, garnishment, or threat of garnishment.

Garnishment

Garnishment practices in many states allow creditors to deprive individuals of their wages through court action, without hearing or trial. In about 20 states, the wages of an employee can be diverted to a creditor merely upon the latter's deposition, with no advance hearing where the employee can defend himself. He often receives no prior notice of such action and is usually unaware of the law's operation and too poor to hire legal defense. Moreover, consumers may find themselves still owing money on a sales contract even after the creditor has repossessed the goods. The New York study cited earlier in this chapter indicated that 20 percent of a sample of low-income families had been subjected to legal action regarding consumer purchases. And the Federal Trade Commission study in Washington, D.C., showed that, on the average, retailers specializing in credit sales of furniture and appliances to low-income consumers resorted to court action once for every $2,200 of sales. Since their average sale was for $207, this amounted to using the courts to collect from one of every 11 customers. In contrast, department stores in the same area used court action against approximately one of every 14,500 customers.[6]

Variations in Food Prices

Residents of low-income Negro neighborhoods frequently claim that they pay higher prices for food in local markets than wealthier white suburbanites and receive inferior quality meat and produce. Statistically reliable information comparing prices and quality in these two kinds of areas is generally unavailable. The U.S. Bureau of Labor Statistics, studying food prices in six cities in 1966, compared prices of a standard list of 18 items in low-income areas and higher income areas in each city. In a total of 180 stores, including independent and chain stores, and for items of the same type sold in the same types of stores, there were no significant differences in prices between low-income and high-income areas. However, stores in low-income areas were more likely to be small independents (which had somewhat higher prices), to sell low-quality produce and meat at any given price, and to be patronized by people who typically bought smaller sized packages which are more expensive per unit of measure. In other words, many low-income consumers in fact pay higher prices, although the situation varies greatly from place to place.

Although these findings must be considered inconclusive, there are significant reasons to believe that poor households generally pay higher prices for the food they buy and receive lower quality food. Low-income consumers buy more food at local groceries because they are less mobile. Prices in these small stores are significantly higher than in major supermarkets because they cannot achieve economies of scale and because real operating costs are higher in low-income Negro areas than in outlying suburbs. For instance, inventory "shrinkage" from pilfering and other causes is

[6] Assuming their sales also averaged $207 per customer.

normally under 2 percent of sales but can run twice as much in high-crime areas. Managers seek to make up for these added costs by charging higher prices for food or by substituting lower grades.

These practices do not necessarily involve exploitation, but they are often perceived as exploitative and unfair by those who are aware of the price and quality differences involved but unaware of operating costs. In addition, it is probable that genuinely exploitative pricing practices exist in some areas. In either case, differential food prices constitute another factor convincing urban Negroes in low-income neighborhoods that whites discriminate against them.

Chapter 8

SOCIAL ASPECTS OF PLANNING
AND URBAN RENEWAL

More and more of the social processes of the contemporary world, as Petersen points out, are planned. The necessity of planning in order to meet the problems of the twentieth-century metropolis is seldom questioned. The difficult matter is not building the case for the need to plan, but establishing the procedures by which such planning can most effectively be implemented.

The planning function involves on the most basic level some consensus of goals. The desire to build for an urban life in which aesthetic and social needs may be fulfilled in terms of high humanistic standards has led to sweeping condemnation of the contemporary city as a setting for the "good life." There are many such critics; perhaps Mumford is the best known and the most eloquent of them all. Inescapable, in any event, is the fact that the planner does, by his decisions, make judgments on the character of urban life he foresees. The planner himself may or may not be consciously aware of this, but much of the difficulty in achieving consensus in urban planning derives precisely from the different models which exist in the minds of those who seek to create more desirable conditions for urban man.

On less subjective levels, the difficulty of implementing planning derives in part from the wide variety of professional skills involved. The contemporary metropolis is, beyond doubt, the most intricately complex setting in which man has ever sought to live. If

the metropolis is to function at all adequately, precision coordina
tion of the various components of the entity is demanded. To plai
for such functioning on an enduring basis requires meeting basi
problems of water supply, air cleanliness, waste disposal; of trans
portation into and within the metropolis; of specialized educationa
and medical and welfare services; of public finance and publi
administration; and so on. Metropolitan planning requires th
skills of the sociologist, but it also requires the skills of the engi
neer, the architect, the economist, the geographer, the politica
scientist, and many others.

Metropolitan planning is rendered all the more difficult, o
course, by the fragmentation of political responsibility for the larg
urbanized areas. As has been repeatedly stated, most central citie
are either stationary or actually declining in population. Increas
ingly the inner city is becoming the home of "refugees" from a
declining rural economy, and these are typically persons of lov
skills. In addition, they are often black or Spanish-American, anc
meet the additional handicaps of discrimination. The needs of the
metropolis as a whole can only be met by coordinated planning. The
problems, of course, are most intense in the inner city—the very
area from which segments of the suburban population have only
recently "escaped." Involving the residents of both city and suburb
in common enterprises is an extremely difficult challenge, but is one
which somehow must be met. To help take steps toward meeting
the needs for interdisciplinary planning on a basis which cai
involve more than just the central city, Congress authorized the
establishment of a new Cabinet position with the formation in 196!
of the Department of Housing and Urban Development. (Robert C
Weaver, first Secretary of Housing and Urban Development, is the
author of one of the selections which follow.)

Petersen maintains that what is needed is not "city planning"
this is on far too limited a scale. The need is for a broader concept
of planning which can refer to proposals of national or even inter
national scope, but which can also focus regionally or locally upor
metropolitan needs. He suggests the term "urbanization planning'
to designate planning of this scope and flexibility. He also states a
warning: some who have attempted to plan for cities have reflectec
a dislike of cities and a hope that urbanization may be minimized

Peter Marris, a British sociologist who has studied problem
of urban needs in West Africa, in North America, and in his owr
nation—which is the most urbanized of all societies—is able to bring
his comparative perspective to bear upon the problems facing pro
grams of urban development in American cities. He is well aware
that basic gains are unlikely to be achieved through any planning

of urban redevelopment which fails to be realistic in terms of the subcultural traditions of the persons most affected. Weaver summarizes social class and racial factors affecting urban renewal programs in the United States. Much which is considered racial, as he notes, is essentially class-linked. However, racial barriers become particularly limiting to members of the rapidly growing Negro middle-class, who in all respects except racial membership are eligible for entry into different neighborhoods. (The "open housing" legislation of 1968, as previously noted, may aid in this respect in the future.) Weaver's discussion may also be read meaningfully in connection with the materials in the preceding chapter dealing with social pathology in the metropolis.

The school is typically considered by urban planners to be a "service," of necessity provided to residents in much the same manner that any other essential service is made available. Glazer contends that the school can do much more than this. The school, he is convinced, can be utilized in a far more imaginative manner in effective urban planning. He sees the school system as a means of anchoring a "heterogeneous" population within the city.

Underlying the approach is the assumption that parents representing some traditions and reflecting some status levels tend to move out of the city because of their perception of the inadequacy of the school system. (The effort to have schools become meaningfully responsive to the needs of the residents of the neighborhood, on the one hand, and the effort to adhere to system-wide standards of quality and of personnel procedures on the other, is a basic dilemma of schools in any large and heterogeneous city.) Through a combination of the neighborhood principle and through the establishment of specialized programs available for qualified children in the various areas of the city, Glazer believes that the retention of more segments of the total population within the central city may be facilitated.

On the Concept of Urbanization Planning

WILLIAM PETERSEN
Lazarus Professor of Social Demography,
Ohio State University

One need have only a casual acquaintance with the 20th-century world to know that more and more of its social processes are, in one sense or another, planned.[1] Five-year plans, once restricted to the Soviet Union, have now spread not only to other Communist states but to such diverse countries as, for example, India and Brazil. In the United States, which is featured in Communist propaganda as the last capitalist redoubt, the whole social-economic structure was altered by the government's response to the depression of the 1930's and to World War II. As part of this trend policy-makers have become increasingly concerned with a congeries of social problems concerning cities. This effort, as yet so indefinite it does not even have a name, is here called "urbanization planning."

Urbanization planning constitutes all schemes of whatever sort relating to the urban sector of a nation's population, especially policies of national governments but also those of regional bodies or international agencies. Cities have been built as part of industrialization programs, as grandiose capitals, as sites of this or that government function. Urban populations have been moved to areas less subject to military attack. Some of those living in metropolitan areas have been dispersed to satellite towns. Efforts have been made to inhibit urban growth—for example, by fostering rural industry. While such measures have varied, of course, between democratic and totalitarian states and between developed and

From *Population Review*, Vol. 6, No. 2, pp. 100–104 (July, 1962). Reprinted by permission of the author and of *Population Review*, published by the Indian Institute for Population Studies.
[1] This is part of a larger study sponsored by International Population and Urban Research, University of California, Berkeley.

underdeveloped economies, policies of these types have been proposed or put into effect all over the world.

Urbanization planning is both different from city planning and in some ways derivative from it. Until recently city planners have typically tried to cope with each urban aggregate as an isolated unit. To the degree that they can, they control the physical environment of a particular city, both by eliminating such hazards to health and happiness as slums or traffic congestion and by adjusting future growth to a master plan. This control is established and maintained, moreover, mainly through the city's own legal system—through zoning laws, ordinances regulating transportation facilities, laws to "renew" blighted areas or to create parks and civic centers. However, since the city is in fact an integral part of a larger unit, these aims generally cannot be wholly realized within the municipal framework. It is often not possible, thus, to plan facilities effectively if no account is taken of in-migrants and commuters, or to lay out a suitable street plan without considering how it is to be connected with the intercity roads, or to provide even such basic needs as water except by relating the city to its region, or to find the tax money for improvements without establishing a minimum co-operation among the dozen independent municipalities that may be affected. In many cases, what is called regional planning is no more than old-style city planning with some attention given to such programs of integration. But attempts to deal with them have induced some of the men in the profession to look over the city wall and think more about their relation to the larger society.

In this extension of their traditional function, city planners have sometimes encountered planners of the national economy, who until recently also often neglected the intermediate area of urbanization. Of the three main factors in production—capital, labor, and land—the first two are invariably included in national plans. The focus of the planners' work is always on how scarce capital shall be allocated among alternative investment possibilities; and a good deal of attention is given, at the very least in propaganda, to improving the people's homes, health, education, and welfare generally. But the third factor is often neglected. "In the economic development plans of such countries as Indonesia, the Philippines, India, Mexico, and Puerto Rico, almost no consideration is given to where development should occur."[2] This omission is related, obviously, to the background of the planners. Location theory is not a highly

[2] Charles Haar, Benjamin Higgins, and Lloyd Rodwin, "Economic and Physical Planning: Coordination in Developing Areas," *News Sheet of the International Federation for Housing and Planning*, 52 (June, 1959), 15–19.

developed field in economics, and undoubtedly most practicing economists know little more than its elements. The other professionals involved in national planning—administrators, agronomists,
social-welfare workers, and so on—by and large know even less of
the determinants of urbanization and the criteria by which good
policy might be judged. But they are becoming more aware that the
neglect of such factors can greatly affect the attainment of other
social and economic goals.

From two sides, thus, the attention of policy-makers has been
converging on urbanization planning. Sometimes, as in efforts of a
national government to alleviate urban housing shortages, the same
objectives are sought as in city planning, but in such cases much
more is usually changed than the sponsoring agency. And national
governments have also set urban policies that transgress entirely
the scope of either economic or city planning. Implicit in urbanization planning, though not necessarily consciously thought out or
precisely stated, are norms about what proportion of the population
should live in towns, the ideal size of cities, the optimum ratio of
primate to other cities, how industrialization and urbanization
should be related, and so on. Sometimes, however, the only value
specified is the approbation of "planning" itself. Indeed, the seeming omnipresence of this kind of social regulation is to some extent
spurious, the consequence of the fact that quite different processes
and philosophies have been identified with an omnibus term.

ON THE MEANING OF PLANNING

Before continuing to expound the concept of urbanization planning,
thus, it would be well to clarify the broader term. Planning is of at
least three types, which can conveniently be identified as "ideological," "deductive," and "inductive." As planning of any type is ordinarily understood, it connotes the injection of rationality into a
particular area of human life, and in this sense it may be said to be
scientific. A scientific proposition is one, first of all, that can be
proved fallacious by comparing it with the empirical world, and a
scientist constantly shuttles between his hypothesis and his data,
between the model he constructs and the pattern he observes. The
analogous process, evaluation, is usually a less routine characteristic of social planning, and it differs somewhat among the three
types.

With respect to utopian or *ideological* plans, first of all, evaluation has little or no meaning. If the purpose of the plan is one or
another paraphrase of David Riesman's "substantial gains in

human happiness,"[3] or Erich Fromm's "self-realization for the masses of the people,"[4] it will never be possible to determine in any precise sense whether this has been achieved. A utopian goal keeps receding as we approach it, and it cannot be used to measure progress along the road toward it. Sometimes it is asserted that a consciously unrealistic social purpose is useful as a goal. Only "overbold" plans, in Lewis Mumford's words, will "awaken the popular imagination: such success as totalitarian states have shown in their collective planning has perhaps been due to their willingness to cleave at a blow the Gordian knot of historic resistances."[5] This supposed proximate value of a utopia has never been more than supposed; how could anyone test the proposition that a visionary purpose is an aid in achieving realistic goals? Frequently, perhaps even usually, the utopia is less an incentive than an alternative to social reform. For in the eyes of the true utopian, anything that can be achieved is not worth attempting; every revolutionary party, for instance, has always devoted much effort to fighting reformists.

The evaluation of ideological plans, then, is ruled out as impossible or meaningless, and one must remember that many non-ideological plans contain a utopian element.

Most persons, perhaps, are likely to understand planning in the *deductive* sense, following what is still the only dictionary definition. The planner draws up a blueprint on a flat surface (or, in Latin, *planum*); and the design is completed before the first steps are taken toward its realization. In this case, one might think evaluation is easy, almost automatic. But consider a specific example—say, the deconcentration of Britain's metropolitan population. The assignment of the Barlow Commission was—

to inquire into the causes which have influenced the present geographical distribution of the industrial population of Great Britain and the probable direction of any change in that distribution in the future; to consider what social, economic or strategical disadvantages arise from the concentration of industries or the industrial population in large towns or in particular areas of the country; and to report what remedial measures, if any, should be taken in the national interest.[6]

The Commission inquired, considered, and recommended; and the policy was a success in the minimal sense that the New Towns

[3] David Riesman, *Individualism Reconsidered, and Other Essays* (Glencoe, Ill.: Free Press, 1954), p. 73.
[4] Erich Fromm, *Escape from Freedom* (New York: Rinehart, 1941), p. 272.
[5] Lewis Mumford, *The Culture of Cities* (New York: Harcourt, Brace, 1938), p. 380.
[6] Quoted in Lloyd Rodwin, *The British New Towns Policy: Problems and Implications* (Cambridge: Harvard University Press, 1956), p. 17.

exist. But have "the social, economic, or strategical disadvantages" of industrial concentration been mitigated? In particular, has London stopped growing, or has it even grown less than it would have without the plan? To answer such a question fully would require another analysis on the same scale as the one the Commission used to support its recommendations. But "all available evidence suggests that the drawbacks to the indefinite growth of the conurbations, and particularly of London, are in fact much greater" than before the Commission made its study.[7]

Or take another example: Several years ago the Venezuelan government housing agency supervised the construction of apartments in Caracas to accommodate an estimated 180,000 persons. In mechanical terms the project was successfully completed: almost a hundred 15-story buildings were erected at a total cost of some $200 million. But 4,000 families invaded the apartments and lived there illegally, while others squatted in the community facilities or in shacks they built on the project site; unpaid rent totaled $5 million; losses in damage to property amounted to $500,000 monthly; delinquency and crime rose appreciably; tenant associations, headed by agitators, impeded control measures and built up a potentially explosive atmosphere. An international interprofessional team, called in to study the situation, recommended that "the government should suspend all construction of superblocks until there exists a defined housing policy related to the economic and social development of the country and within a process of national planning and co-ordination. It was found that the massive construction programs in Caracas had served to attract heavy migration to the city from rural areas and, therefore, severely intensified the housing problem in the capital."[8]

The two examples illustrate a recurrent type of unsuccessful social reform. A vigorous, concentrated attack on the most visible of social ills may cope only with symptoms and in some cases actually aggravates the disease. When an architect's blueprints are transformed into a building, one can say with full justice that his plan has been realized. But to transfer this kind of simplistic evaluation to more complex matters, as architects who have become city planners typically do, is less warranted. If the master plan of a city has been realized in the physical sense, the most important questions are still to be answered: have slums disappeared; have neighbourhoods been reinforced, or shattered; has traffic congestion been

[7] Peter Self, *Cities in Flood: The Problems of Urban Growth* (London: Faber and Faber, 1957), p. 27.
[8] Eric Carlson, "High-Rise Management," *Journal of Housing*, 16:9 (October, 1959), 311–314.

nitigated, or made worse? And in the still more complex world of national urban policies, it is still more difficult to state precisely what one means by evaluation.

The third type, *inductive planning*, is defined as the continual coordination of public policies in several overlapping economic and social areas. "Coordination leads to planning or, rather, it *is* planning as this term has come to be understood in the Western world." Planning in this sense is "pragmatic and piecemeal and never comprehensive and complete"; plans usually constitute "compromise solutions of pressing political issues."⁹ What is here identified as 'planning," in short, is very close to "muddling through," or the opposite of traditional planning. Evaluation of inductive plans is obviously extremely difficult, since the measuring stick and the entity to be measured constantly interact. Yet apart from the simplest cases virtually all real (that is, more than ideological) plans are at least partly inductive, for in the complex social world one cannot foresee every important contingency. If the "plan" is less a blueprint than a guideline, "success" has to be defined before it can be measured.

Inductive urbanization planning can be exemplified by the complex of federal housing legislation in the United States. In some cases, it is true, whatever effect these laws had on the nation's cities was twice removed from their main purpose; the first New Deal housing acts, for example, were intended first of all to prime the pump of the lagging economy, only secondarily to alleviate housing shortages, and hardly at all to restructure metropolitan areas. The vast, complicated, in part contradictory, totality of housing legislation, established over several changes of administration, nevertheless shows a certain consistency. Its two main goals were to help heads of families purchase a new home of their own, and to raze city slums and replace them with more healthful public housing. While these two types of programs were obviously applied to different social classes, they both helped reinforce the trend already under way toward a particular type of decentralization. Low-rent public apartments have generally been available only to families with incomes no greater than a stipulated maximum, so that not only the projects themselves but the whole neighborhoods that they dominate have in fact become restricted to lower-class residents. At the same time, middle-class and lower middle-class families were helped to purchase a one-family house; and this low-density

Gunnar Myrdal, *Beyond the Welfare State: Economic Planning and Its International Implications* (New Haven: Yale University Press, 1960), pp. 63, 23. For a longer paraphrase see Robert A. Dahl and Charles E. Lindblom, *Politics, Economics, and Welfare* (New York: Harper, 1953), pp. 38–39.

construction, which had to be on the periphery of the city, contrib
uted greatly to what has since come to be called "scatteration" or
"urban sprawl."

A generation ago most experts saw great crowded cities as a de
structive anachronism, to be drastically altered by some form of decen
tralization. But suburban sprawl is clearly no solution, and the big centers
have survived despite decay and mounting congestion. Now the new
generation of experts and critics tends to glorify the economic and cultura
virtues of the Great City, scorning decentralization in any form.[10]

It would be an exaggeration, but one with more than a germ of
truth, to say that the plan of one generation has become the social
problem of the next. To evaluate this inductive "plan," one must
determine whether the federal government's shift contributed more
to the plan or to the subsequent problem.

■ ■ ■

[10] Catherine Bauer Wurster, "Framework for an Urban Society," in American
Assembly, *Goals for Americans* (New York: Prentice-Hall, 1960).

The Social Implications
of Urban Redevelopment

PETER MARRIS
Institute of Community Studies, London

By midsummer 1960,[1] urban renewal projects undertaken under the Housing Act of 1949 had displaced about 85,000 families in just under 200 American cities.[2] In scale it is not yet a very large program; but in the range of problems to be resolved, it is one of the most searching issues of domestic policy, and reflects some of the most characteristic dilemmas of contemporary American society. A plan of action which was conceived as the replacement of dilapidated buildings has become deeply involved in fundamental social problems.

These social commitments of urban renewal have to be worked out in their metropolitan context, and the future of American cities is itself problematical. In every age and country, people as they grow prosperous have wished to buy themselves more space. As prosperity spreads downward, everyone seeks his acre, half-acre, quarter-acre of private domain, while cars and telephones enormously increase the social pace in which everyday relationships are conducted. We do not yet know in what form cities will accommodate this expanded scale of human life: nearly every existing city has grown around a center built when people were poorer, and

From the *Journal of the American Institute of Planners*, Vol. 28, No. 3 (August, 1962), pp. 180–186. Reprinted by permission of the author and of the *Journal of the American Institute of Planners*.

[1] The author acknowledges the generous support and encouragement of the Ford Foundation, who enabled him to make the visit, and the kindness of all the administrators, planners, social workers, and sociologists who shared their ideas and experience, and provided the material on which this article is based.

[2] *Relocation from Urban Renewal Project Areas, through June 1960*, Bulletin of Housing and Home Finance Agency, Urban Renewal Administration (Washington, D.C., 1960).

walked. Meanwhile, we have to plan either to facilitate or frustrate
this dispersion of the traditional city, and here too, urban redevelopment projects become involved in a far-ranging discussion of social
ideals.

THE DECLINE OF THE CENTRAL CITY

The central city includes, typically, a business district; a rail-
way and bus station; a university; Skid Row; a "hill"—which
though it may be flat, has remained socially elevated amidst the
surrounding decay, an island of gracious town houses for the
sophisticated and well-to-do; a museum housing a superb collection
of pictures from every age and country except that in which the
museum itself was built; and a park. Around these features, and
extending far beyond them, miles of seedy tenements and row
houses peel and flake, amiable or grim in their degenerate old age.
Here, waves of immigration have left behind the least buoyant of
their numbers, as the mainstream moves on to flood the surrounding countryside with suburban tracts. Over, under, and through it
all, the expressways loop, tunnel, and carve their way with the con-
temptuous indifference of a new order. The metropolis of which the
central city is the heart grows continually, but in the city itself
there are sinister portents of decline. Department stores stand
empty; buildings are pulled down and turned into parking lots,
waiting for better times; offices follow their employees to the
suburb. On placards in Detroit buses a wide-eyed child reaches out
exclaiming, "There is more of everything downtown"—but every
year there is less.

This decay of the city center is not new, and seems indeed to
be a characteristic consequence of its growth. As the center
becomes congested, the more prosperous move farther out, aban-
doning their town houses to successively more ruthless exploitation.
In this they are eagerly encouraged by real estate interests, who
hope to realize a handsome return on land acquired on the city's
fringes, and at the same time make a killing in the older property
from which, sub-divided and indifferently maintained, satisfactory
profits can be squeezed long after it deserves to be pulled down.

This pattern of expansion at the fringe, and decay at the
center, would still recur even if suburban life held no particular
appeal. When the social status of a neighborhood is threatened by
the newcomers who impinge on its boundaries, the old residents
begin to take flight. And once the flight begins, the more hesitant
follow, fearing for the value of their property, the safety of their

laughters in the street, the manners of their children in school, and the effect on their social standing of an address no longer fashionable. The newcomers push out all who can afford to escape, until, as in Detroit, the proportion of native-born residents increases directly with the distance from the city center.

Since the war, two influences in particular have accelerated this familiar cycle. Firstly, the newcomers have been predominantly colored. In the central cities of the twelve largest metropolitan areas, the non-white population has increased much more rapidly than the white, and now accounts for over 20 per cent of the residents. Between 1950 and 1960, these twelve central cities lost over two million whites, and gained just under two million non-white residents. Meanwhile the suburbs have added only marginally to their very small colored populations.[3] So the social status of neighborhoods is now drawn more sharply than ever in terms of race, and by playing on prejudice, city blocks change their character more quickly and completely.

This net loss of population from the central city has raised alarm, especially set beside the natural increase of the population as a whole. But for the first time, a new and more disturbing trend has been noticed: the central city is losing not merely population, but its functions. The suburban shopping centers now rival in range and quality the downtown stores; businesses have begun to relocate their offices away from the central district; art galleries and theatres are being established in the suburbs—Philadelphia has five downtown theatres in the winter, but thirty peripheral summer theatres. As fewer people enter the city center to work, shop, to be entertained, it could become merely another suburb of the metropolis, distinguished only by its greater poverty, dilapidation, and perhaps the color of its inhabitants.

THE AIMS OF URBAN RENEWAL

The decline of the central city concerns, most immediately, the political and commercial interests which cannot recoup their loss of revenue or custom. A city can seldom collect taxes from those who have overtipped its boundaries, even though it may still have to

[3] Harry Sharp, "Race as a Factor in Metropolitan Growth, 1930–1960" (University of Michigan Survey Research Center, 1961), paper presented at the 1961 meetings of the Population Association of America. Morton Grodzins, in *The Metropolitan Area as a Racial Problem* (Pittsburgh: University of Pittsburgh Press, 1958), p. 3, comments, "all evidence makes it highly probable that within 30 years Negroes will constitute from 25 to 50 per cent of the total population in at least 10 of the 14 largest central cities."

provide services for their use. The more it taxes those who remain the sooner they, too, will place themselves under a less exacting excise: and so the city faces a losing battle to maintain its functions. To meet the needs of city government and commerce, urban renewal has to attract back into the city those who will provide the highest revenue and the best custom, and revive the prestige of urban life.

Besides the political and commercial interests vested in the city center, the culture of the densely-populated, diverse heart of a metropolis has been credited with all the intellectual vigor of modern life—its tolerance, flexibility, radicalism, wit, taste, sophis tication, and artistic endeavor. In the no man's land between ideol ogy and architecture where utopias are made, no suburbs have even been allowed to enfeeble the stimulating intensity of human inter course. Among the most enthusiastic advocates of urban renewa are those who see it, rightly used, as a strategy to call back the straying sheep from their suburban pastures, and lay the prophetic ghost of Frank Lloyd Wright.

The central city could lose not only its cultural diversity, but the diversity of its population. If present trends continue, the Negro residents of the central cities of the largest metropolitar areas will eventually predominate. If the suburbs continue to balk the entry of Negro households, there could grow up a form of polit ical and residential apartheid. The central city becomes an enor mous ghetto: "A black neck in a white noose." The intermingling of races in the city center is a logical corollary of the campaign for integration in the suburbs. To this end, it is important that urban renewal should maintain a racially-mixed population in the city.

Finally, urban renewal can be seen as an opportunity to tackle the social problems of slum areas. In so far as mean housing demoralizes its inhabitants, and the spirit of the ghetto undermines ambition, relocation offers the chance to introduce people to a more hopeful environment.

These four arguments—economic, cultural, integrationist, and social—provide the main justifications for urban renewal, and set its aims. But it is important to recognize at the outset that these aims are neither the same, nor necessarily compatible. For the reconstruction of the tax base, the fate of the people relocated is not important; while for the social worker, their rehabilitation is the principal object of redevelopment. The most profitable use of cleared land may be tall blocks of luxury apartments, socially and culturally isolated from their surroundings and alien to the tradi tional spirit of urban culture, while the people moved are unlikely

:o enjoy any part of the brave new world erected over their former
homes.

As yet, urban redevelopment projects have pulled down more
than they have rebuilt, and it is too soon to know whether the new
buildings will establish the urban communities for which they are
designed. Meanwhile, whatever new communities urban renewal
creates, its consequences for the families displaced follow a fairly
consistent pattern.

RELOCATION

The households cleared by urban renewal have included many of
the poorest in the city, and they have been mostly Negro. Apart
from the West End of Boston—a characteristically Italian neighborhood—the proportion of non-white families varies from about 62
per cent in New York to nearly 100 per cent in Baltimore, Washington, and Chicago. As a whole, about 80 per cent of the families
relocated are non-white, and the remainder includes many families,
such as immigrants from the Appalachian Mountains, who belong
to a distinctive minority culture.[4] Few, if any, of the families relocated could afford the private housing planned to replace their old
homes.

Information about families relocated is not complete, and
sometimes conflicting. Relocation authorities publish reports, but a
proportion of families, varying from a few per cent to as many as
half, do not use the relocation services, and their fate is unknown.
Estimates of the success of relocation vary according to the
assumptions made about the group who have not reported their
new circumstances: relocation authorities tend to be more optimis-

[4] The percentages given in this section derive from the following reports and
articles; they are not comprehensive or all very recent, but discussions with
relocation authorities suggest that the experience they report is representative:
"Relocation in Philadelphia," Philadelphia Housing Association (Novem-
ber, 1958). (Some figures for 16 cities are given on p. 79.).
"Rehousing Residents Displaced from Public Housing Clearance Sites in
Chicago 1957–1958," special report to the Chicago Housing Authority from the
Department of City Planning.
"Ten Years of Relocation Experience in Baltimore," Baltimore Urban
Renewal and Housing Agency (June 1961).
Dorothy Heltz, "Report on the Relocation of Residents and Certain
Institutions from the Gateway Center Project Area," Housing and Redevelop-
ment Authority, Minneapolis (June, 1961).
Wallace F. Smith, "Relocation in San Francisco," *Bay Area Real Estate
Report*, 4th Quarter (1960).
Nathaniel Lichfield, "Relocation: The Impact on Housing Welfare,"
Journal of the American Institute of Planners, 27:199–203 (1961).

tic than independent inquirers. Again, in assessing the improvement in housing standards, different criteria may be used. The law requires the authorities to ensure that "decent, safe, and sanitary" housing is available to the families relocated, at a reasonable rent. It does not stipulate that the housing should be in a decent, safe, and sanitary neighborhood, nor that the new housing need necessarily be better than the old. Some of the housing in the cleared area will have been up to standard. So a family moved from a decent, safe, and sanitary house in the cleared area to a similar house in a similar neighborhood, and perhaps paying a higher rent, could still be considered to have been satisfactorily relocated. But from their own point of view, they are worse off.

With these qualifications, the consequences of relocation are fairly well known. Most families moved to neighborhoods similar to those from which they were cleared, usually on the fringes of the renewal project. Between 15 per cent and 50 per cent were still in substandard housing, and more than this were still in blighted areas (in Philadelphia, on some assumptions, the figure could be as high as 78 per cent). In most cities, less than 10 per cent were relocated in public housing.[5] On the average, contract rents went up by $12 to $20, and the proportion of income spent on rent probably increased from around 17 per cent to 25 per cent. The number of people to a room did not change, or was slightly reduced; but the families do not seem on the whole to have been very overcrowded in the first place.

These estimates suggest that the families relocated often achieved an only marginal improvement in their housing, at the cost of higher rents. Some are still living in slums, and many more have moved to nearby areas which may rapidly deteriorate into new slums. The director of one Redevelopment Agency, Justin Herman, has stated unequivocally, "San Francisco need not be proud of its record on how it has rehoused its displaced families— four out of five of which are non-white. Look at the relocation map showing where these families have gone and you find the greatest concentration of them just over the borders of the project area, in the very slums that were designated as such by the Board of Supervisors as blighted—and they have not improved—a decade ago."[6] He also affirmed that the housing to be erected in the renewal projects would be out of reach of many families displaced, who often could

[5] A much higher proportion would have been eligible for public housing, but the evidence suggests a widespread prejudice against accepting relocation in public housing projects.
[6] M. Justin Herman, "The Realities of Urban Renewal for Minority Groups," statement before the Council for Civic Unity of San Francisco (March, 1960).

not afford any of the existing housing in San Francisco of minimum quality. Other cities have been no more successful. In these circumstances, urban renewal is unlikely to provide a more helpful setting for social welfare. Some families may well have been encouraged by a better house to face the world with more pride, but for the most part, relocation has probably made the major problems more difficult to tackle.[7] It must disrupt the work of established agencies, and worse, destroy the informal pattern of mutual help and tolerance which had grown up in the old communities. Neurotics and psychotics whose eccentricities were harbored, if not loved, in the slum streets find themselves rejected in primmer neighborhoods. Adolescents whose fear of the wider society was protected by the subculture of the slums become lost and unhappy. In the years after the West End of Boston was pulled down, teen-agers revisited nostalgically the rubble of their former homes. Skid Row has simply moved elsewhere. It may be that in the long run, this exposure to a more demanding society will force the slum dwellers to assimilate its standards; even if this were all to the good, it is harsh medicine. Meanwhile, urban renewal disperses people in need where they may be more difficult to reach.

On the whole then, it seems fair to say that relocation has provided only marginally better housing, in very similar neighborhoods, at higher rents, and has done as much to worsen as to solve the social problems of the families displaced. The dispossessed enjoy as their reward a distant view of luxury apartments rising over their old homes.

Whether or not the welfare of slum dwellers is held to be the most important aim of urban renewal—and to city authorities, it clearly is not—no program of renewal can succeed if it relegates their welfare to second place. Housing degenerates into slums through the inability of its inhabitants to afford anything better. Clearance merely moves the slum—extending the blighted area in a new direction as its boundaries are pushed back elsewhere. Even for those whose primary concern is the reconstruction of the tax base, or the commerce of the city, the crucial issue is the housing of the slum dwellers themselves.

THE CULTURE OF SLUMS

The slum dwellers are characteristically the most recent in-migrants to the city. They include Negroes from the South,

[7] For the experience of one social welfare agency, see Jane Dale, "Families and Children in Urban Development: A View from a Settlement House," *Children*, 6:203–207 (1959).

country people from the Southern Appalachians, Puerto Ricans, Mexicans, American Indians, and a few French-Canadians. Their labor is very valuable to the city, since they are ready to do the worst-paid work, on which important industries depend. It has been estimated, for instance, that three million people in New York depend directly or indirectly on the needle trades, which depend in turn on Puerto Rican labor.[8] In-migration fluctuates with the jobs available: if the work is not there, people do not come. The in-migrants, therefore, come to the city because the city needs them: it cannot repudiate responsibility for their welfare.

Once they reach the city, they seem to settle there as permanently as most Americans. It is sometimes suggested that they are transients, moving house annually, and returning to country districts in bad times. Instances are cited of Negro schools where there has been a complete changeover of pupils in a year. Yet, though some may follow such a restless course, figures I collated do not suggest that the families displaced by urban renewal are especially migratory. In Philadelphia, 17 per cent of families had been living in the homes demolished less than a year, 40 per cent for more than ten years; half had lived in the city more than 20 years. In one cleared area of Baltimore, 18 per cent had been there less than a year, a third more than ten years; in a Chicago program, only 7 per cent had been less than a year in the houses from which they were cleared, and the median length of residence was 8 years; of a group of mostly single men cleared from Skid Row in Minneapolis, 8 per cent had lived less than one year and two-thirds more than ten years at the same address.[9] Since about 17 per cent of American families move each year, these figures suggest that the slum dwellers are if anything less mobile than most people.

Since most of the slum dwellers are not, after all, such newcomers to the city, their failure to make good cannot altogether be explained by their unfamiliarity with urban society. It is, I think, a mistake to conceive the assimilation of immigrants in terms of two cultures: the dominant culture of America, represented by city life, and the culture of the rural society from which they came. The city contains subcultures as stable and viable as the conventional norms, and it is to one of these subcultures that the newcomer is first introduced. The more successfully he becomes integrated in it, the more difficult it becomes to interest him in the values of the dominant culture.

These subcultures, of course, differ among themselves: each has grown out of the experience of an ethnic group with its own

---

[8] Clarence Senior, *Strangers—Then Neighbors*, pp. 64–65 (New York: Freedom Books, 1961).

[9] Figures derived from the sources in note 4 above.

religious and family traditions. But they are likely to share common characteristics arising from their economic and social status. These immigrants are generally the poorest, least educated, and lowest in status of the city's population. Society at large is competitive, and maintains (when convenient) that everyone enjoys an equal opportunity. Some immigrants accept the challenge—especially Jewish newcomers—but for most, the chances of success are remote, and now heavily weighted against them by racial discrimination. So they can protect themselves against a sense of failure and inferiority only by denying that the opportunity is open, and by decrying the rewards for which the more hopeful compete.

Characteristically, the subculture divides the world into "we" and "they".[10] "They" are all the agents of the dominant culture, official or unofficial, benevolent or persecutory—police, government, school, social workers, and indeed anyone who carries the stigmata of the successful middle-class. All these are held to discriminate against the people of the subculture, and to exploit them: even the apparently benevolent must be getting something out of it, a personal advantage which is concealed by the hypocrisy of their avowed intentions. It is thus exceedingly difficult for anyone outside the subculture to be of help, since his motives are immediately suspect. It is even difficult for anyone within it to exercise effective leadership: as soon as he establishes a position where he can act usefully in the wider society on behalf of his people, he is suspected of disloyalty.

In the subculture, people see themselves as poor because they have not lost their pride, and because they despise the mean rewards of a competitive society. Not only does the pretense of a fair chance for them seem fraudulent—a cynical attempt to cloak the realities of power—but even in society at large, those who get on are assumed to have succeeded only by acting contemptibly. However, though they repudiate rewards which can be won only by compromise with the dominant norms, they may admire success achieved in defiance of them. Hence their attitude to crime can be ambivalent: the values of the subculture do not in themselves approve crime, but if the victims belong to the outside world, they

[10] In the description of the slum culture which follows, I have emphasized those aspects of it which will tend to frustrate its assimilation into the wider society. An analysis of any particular slum culture would reveal a greater complexity of social patterns. For this description, I have relied much on the discussions in Herbert J. Gans' forthcoming study of the West End of Boston, *The Urban Villagers* (New York: Free Press of Glencoe), which he kindly lent me in draft. See also William Foote Whyte, *Street Corner Society* (Chicago: University of Chicago Press, 1955); Madeleine Kerr's *The People of Ship Street* (London: Routledge and Kegan Paul, 1958) describes a Liverpool slum community.

may be at least indifferent to it. Quasi-illegal activities, such as gambling, are often more accessible than conventional ways of making money.[11]

It follows that the subculture cannot easily accommodate conventional ambition. Any boy who works hard at school, and qualifies for a good job without losing his integrity, proves that society does not always discriminate against the members of the subculture or exact debasement as the price of its rewards. Hence the ambitious will be discouraged, ridiculed, and finally ostracized; their example is by imputation humiliating to the rest. The subculture exacts close conformity and an overriding loyalty to the group; the deserter travels a lonely road, burdened with a sense of guilt.

If this were all, the subculture would be as dreary as it seems to many conventional observers—apathetic, conformist, leaderless, intolerant, frightened, and quasi-criminal. But its countervailing ethic is free, too, to emphasize the virtues most difficult to reconcile with American norms: it places loyalty above ambition, solidarity above competition, personal relationships above impersonal goals, openhandedness above thrift, and the enjoyment of the present above care for the future. And though it may not interpret the world more honestly than the dominant culture, it is honest about different things.[12] Above all, while the wider society accepts that the interests of a career, even when narrowly conceived as money making or the pursuit of status, may override obligations to family or friends, the subculture does not.

The protective solidarity of the subculture helps to explain an apparent paradox. To the outsider, the community appears very tightly integrated, and yet it has no leaders, few community associations, no means of asserting a common purpose: it may not even be very neighborly, as neighborliness is understood in the suburbs. The functioning groups are much smaller—the circle of close relatives, the age-grades who have grown up together. Hence when such a community is disrupted, people are bereft above all of moral support. They are likely to burrow back as fast as they can into the protective culture of the slums.

---

[11] "In effect, the society at large puts a premium on disloyalty to Cornerville and penalizes those who are best adjusted to the life of the district. At the same time the society holds out attractive rewards in terms of money and material possessions to the 'successful' man. For most Cornerville people these rewards are available only through advancement in the world of rackets and politics." Whyte, op. cit., p. 274.
[12] For a defense of slum culture see John R. Seeley, "The Slum: Its Nature, Use, and Users," Journal of the American Institute of Planners, 25:7–14 (1959).

THE LIMITATIONS OF SOCIAL WELFARE

This very general characterization of low-status groups leaves out of account many other distinctive qualities of their culture. They may differ from the majority in their attitude to children, in the interpretation of sexual relationships, patterns of family structure, or the enjoyment of leisure. But here subcultures may differ as much among themselves as with the conventional norms. It is as a reaction to the threat of humiliation that subcultures raise the most barriers to social reform.

In the first place, if I have understood their function aright, the resistance of subcultures to assimilation does not arise in the origins of the in-migrants. Though it is obviously sensible to forewarn newcomers of the problems they will encounter in the city, and to acquaint them with its institutions, this will not enable them to establish themselves in the city with a high enough status. If they were able to acquire skills before they came to the city which would ensure them a promising job as soon as they arrived, their circumstances would be very different; but, of course, it is just because they lack the opportunities to acquire such skills at home that they migrate to the city.

Secondly, programs of social welfare which plan to work by stimulating local leadership face the difficulty that leadership is suspect. The "natural leaders" whom social workers seek to promote are usually those best able to perform personal services: they can give credit, find jobs, provide information. They are leaders with clients, not organizations, and they need not be disinterested. Their clients are willing to pay a price for their services. Such leadership easily degenerates into exploitation when it is given wider scope.

Thirdly, reformers who appeal to the dominant values of society are likely to drive the slum dwellers further into retreat. Unless slum children qualify for skilled jobs, they will remain poor; but to claim that they *can* qualify if only they take education more seriously is profoundly threatening. It suggests that they have only themselves to blame for their present poverty. A Negro child knows he is handicapped; rather than run the risk of failure, it is safer to cite discrimination to prove that success is out of reach. Even if the brighter children have the courage to attempt a career, they face the ostracism of their peers. They will need much moral support, and hard practical work, to ensure that the promises given them can be made good.

Any social reform directed at the shortcomings of people, rather than of society, is handicapped by the humiliating imputations of its policy. If the remarks administrators make about social reform through urban renewal were addressed, not to respected citizens, but to the slum dwellers themselves, they would amount to something like this:

> Some of you are competent people who can look after yourselves, but we well realize that many of you are drunken, criminal, senile, immoral or mad. We do not, of course, blame you: we are sorry for you. You are probably illiterate peasants from some rural slum, and cannot be expected to know any better. Now, however, eviction from your old homes will provide you with a healthy stimulus to pull yourselves together. And we are ready and eager to help. We are going to get together all the social workers we can find to teach you how to behave properly and keep yourselves clean. Of course, you can't expect respectable citizens to welcome you as neighbors until you have shown that you have lost your nasty habits; it wouldn't be fair to them. So to begin with, quite rightly, you must be grateful for the second-rate. This is how we are discharging our responsibility towards you, and it is an impressive record.

It follows that social welfare agencies, though they provide many useful services, must meet profound resistance when they seek to enlarge their function to include social reform. People need to be very confident of themselves before they can admit their weaknesses as the price of being helped. Besides, the welfare agencies have no powers to reform the injustices and inequalities which have driven the slum dweller into retreat. Even the more comprehensive programs of community development now being worked out in association with urban renewal suffer from the limited resources of voluntary action.

THE REVISION OF URBAN RENEWAL

This discussion has led to three conclusions which are, I think, crucial to the working out of renewal policies:
1) That relocation has achieved little overall improvement in the circumstances of the people displaced. They have tended to move into neighborhoods little different from those pulled down, which may rapidly degenerate.
2) Whether the interests of the people moved, or the revitalization of the city, are put first, urban renewal cannot achieve its ultimate purpose so long as slum communities are merely displaced or scattered. The renovation of one blighted area only accelerates the decay of others, and creates new slums.

) Social welfare programs cannot succeed in integrating slum communities with the wider society. Faced with many handicaps, the slum dwellers retreat into a subculture which, though it increases these handicaps, protects them from humiliation. Hence they are not receptive to the values which welfare workers and social institutions represent as agents of society.

If these conclusions are broadly true, the fundamental need is to dissolve the subculture, in so far as it is a self-frustrating defense against a sense of inferiority. This can be achieved only when the real disadvantages of racial discrimination, low wages, and high rates of unemployment are removed. But meanwhile, anything which raises the status of the community in the eyes of society at large helps to reduce its need to retreat. The cumulative process of low status leading to rejection, and rejection to greater isolation and yet lower status, can be reversed: as people feel less despised, they become more open to the opportunities which society, however grudgingly, extends. Relocation does not greatly help this process, since it either moves people to another low-status neighborhood, or isolates them as a household looked down on by their higher-status neighbors. Much more might be achieved by rehousing the community as a whole, without disrupting it.

Such a policy would require the rebuilding or rehabilitation of slum areas as homes for the slum dwellers themselves, not to a perfunctory minimum standard, but as places in which people can live with pride, and which will enhance the appearance of the city. This would not preclude the clearance of sites for other uses, provided that those displaced were rehoused together in a comprehensively developed community near their place of work. In other words, to get rid of slums, build something better for the slum dwellers—and the higher the standard of rebuilding, the more the city gains. But the rebuilding must be conceived in terms of the whole community, not merely of individual families.

Slum life is inadequate as much in spite of, as because of, its distinct culture: only the defensiveness which sets it against society at large distorts its abundant vitality. Indeed, the humanity of cities depends on this ability to generate a rich variety of communities, each with its distinctive style of life. The metropolitan area is so vast that people need to break it down to a more human scale, to perceive their immediate neighborhood in detachment from the whole. In a highly integrated, populous society, each man and woman is individually impotent, dependent upon anonymous millions to complete his work and satisfy his needs. He needs to be able to retreat into a less intimidating and complex world, where he can feel himself of more account. The corporation vice president with his farm, the professional man with his suburban acre, the Italian immigrant in his close-knit community are all in search of more intimate surroundings, where they can achieve something of themselves, and people are known to each other by name. The sophisticated urbanite is seeking as anxiously a womb to curl up in: agrophobia drives him from the suburban tracts to cultivate a village life in the heart of the city. He is not reassured by the bleak convenience of a downtown apartment block, but searches out the narrow streets of sympathetic old houses—which he reconstructs at fantastic cost, to the derision of his slum neighbors. His social world becomes no wider than another's: friends join him, and his intellectual preoccupations isolate him from such of the original residents who have survived the local boom in real estate. Not that his style of life is to be scorned, but it is as much a flight from the total society of the city as retreat to the suburbs.

Every resident of the city is, then, carving out of it a social space which he can master. It is not geographically integrated, since it extends to his work place and the homes of his relatives and friends, but it usually includes the immediate neighborhood of his home. Here he senses the security of belonging to a society small enough to be comprehended in terms of its individual members. Any sociological study of a city would, I believe, reveal this awareness of distinct neighborhoods, each claiming a particular character, however amorphous the townscape appeared to an outsider. The city exists, as an integrated whole, for certain functions which it must fulfill for its entire population.

To say that the city is dying is only to say that functions which have till now been performed on a metropolitan basis are being subdivided—and this is natural enough as a population grows. City and suburb—center and periphery: can a great metropolis still be understood in these terms? Is not the city rather the superstructure binding together the townships of a conurbation? In this sense the city is not dying, but struggling to be born.

Class, Race, and Urban Renewal

ROBERT C. WEAVER

INTRODUCTION

Urban renewal has opened Pandora's Box in several fields. It has occasioned a fresh look at slums; it has given rise to renewed discussion of racial balance in neighborhoods; it has inspired new thought and approaches relative to the racial and class composition of schools in the central city; and of course it has intensified research in the fields of housing, city planning, and municipal government.

Since one of the principal objectives of urban renewal is to attract more middle-class families back into the central city and slow down the exodus of middle-class families from the inlying areas, much of the current discussion about color and class is oriented around these goals. There is, however, a tendency to treat current problems as though they were unique and devoid of historical precedents. Actually, this is not only untrue but dangerously misleading. As Oscar Handlin has most recently pointed out, the flight of older, middle-class families from proximity to the latest newcomers is as old as immigration. What is unique is not the human behavior but the physical limits of the city and the multiplicity of local governments.[1]

From *Land Economics*, Vol. XXXVI, pp. 235–247 and 250–251 (August, 1960). Copyright, The Regents of the University of Wisconsin. Reprinted by permission of the publisher and author.
[1] Oscar Handlin, *The Newcomers*, pp. 14–16, 30–35 (Cambridge, Massachusetts: Harvard University Press, 1959).

Since in many American cities a principal wave of low-income migrants is composed of readily identifiable members of color minorities, there is a tendency to identify the problem as one of race alone.[2] This is inaccurate and unfortunate. Cities which have few nonwhite migrants are experiencing the same problems[3]—a fact suggesting that this is a class as well as a color phenomenon. Should further proof of this be required, the experiences of Chicago, Cleveland, Detroit, Cincinnati, and a score of other cities with Appalachian Mountain whites will provide convincing documentation.[4]

Identification of the decline of central cities with the encroachment of nonwhites (and in a few places Puerto Ricans) upon established middle-class neighborhoods reflects our consciousness of color. It does more. Such superficial analysis weakens our capacity to deal effectively with the problems of our cities. The color and class aspects of these problems are frequently intertwined, but neither should be ignored. Any workable program must recognize both and learn to deal with each.

On the other hand, it would be sheer sophistry to deny that, under demographic and ecological changes, long-standing racial attitudes, and the current economic forces which operate in the housing market, the arrival of increasing numbers of nonwhite families may, and often does, lead to the departure of previous middle-class whites.[5] This long recognized phenomenon has recently been expressed in terms of a "tipping point" theory, which says that there is in any neighborhood a point at which whites will move out when the proportion of nonwhites reaches a certain size.[6]

Many factors are involved in the desertion of a neighborhood. First there is the economic climate. In a period of general prosperity transition is accelerated; the same occurs in a loose housing

[2] See especially Morton Grodzins, *The Metropolitan Area as a Racial Problem* (Pittsburgh, Pennsylvania: University of Pittsburgh Press, 1958); and "Metropolitan Segregation," *Scientific American*, pp. 33–41 (October, 1957).
[3] Robert C. Weaver, "Non-White Population Movements and Urban Ghettos," *Phylon*, pp. 235–238 (Third Quarter [Fall], 1959).
[4] For an interesting account of the Chicago experience, see Albert N. Votaw, "The Hillbillies Invade Chicago," *Harpers*, pp. 64–67 (February, 1958).
[5] For an excellent account of this process, even when the incoming Negroes were middle-class, see Albert J. Mayer, "Russell Woods: Change Without Conflict," in Nathan Glazer and Davis McEntire (ed.), *Studies in Housing and Minority Groups*, pp. 198–220 (Berkeley, California: University of California Press, 1960). There are, however, in this article and Nathan Glazer's introduction to the volume, unsupported assertions about the absence of racial prejudice on the part of the former Jewish residents.
[6] Morton Grodzins, *op. cit.*, pp. 6–7. While the author of this concept is probably overpessimistic due to his involvement with Chicago's experience, his is a useful idea.

market. The location of the neighborhood involved is important, too. Factors tending to stabilize middle-class occupancy include proximity to, and identification with, institutional facilities, such as in the area around a university or college or around long-established religious facilities.

Access of minority and low-income families to a formerly white middle-class neighborhood is not always a consequence of whites' desertion of an area in the face of the encroachment of new user groups. Often it results from vacancies caused by the movement of earlier residents and failure of other middle-class whites to replace the former occupants. The cause of the desertion of such neighborhoods is usually the attractiveness of other areas: they may be suburban sub-divisions or, as in the case of the East Side of Manhattan, a new prestige location in the central city. Once the vacancy rate becomes high, as it did in New York City's West Side, owners and property managers are happy to substitute new user groups rather than suffer greater losses.

THE IMPACT OF NEWCOMERS ON THE HOUSING MARKET

From early days, middle-class Americans have wanted distance between themselves and the newcomer; that desire has been accentuated by two recent developments—the rise of prestige-laden, single-class, homogeneous suburban areas and the identification of color with a large number of low-income migrants. The recent concern of Americans with the quality of education has, of course, occasioned increasing emphasis upon good schools.

As long as there was ample space within the city limits and no effective modes of rapid transportation, most of the outward movements of middle-class families occurred within the city proper. The streetcar, automobile, and bus changed the situation, opening for housing development large areas of virgin land removed from the central city. The fact that estates of the wealthy were already located on such lands augmented their appeal to medium-income groups intent on upward social mobility. Real estate operators, developers, and land speculators, readily joined the commuting railroad lines in selling the exclusiveness of these developments.[7] This was the stage when the great impetus to Negro migration occurred during World War I. Low income colored Americans from the South poured into many Northern cities, replacing, as the new

[7] For an excellent description of this process, see Charles Abrams, *Forbidden Neighbors*, Chapter XII (New York: Harper and Bros., 1955).

source of unskilled and semiskilled labor, the earlier European immigrants who were no longer available during and after the hostilities. Not only were the newcomers mostly poor and ill-prepared for urban life, but they were also dark skinned. As the readily-identified descendants of slaves, they had the least amount of social prestige of any ethnic group. Race and color joined class in rendering them forbidden neighbors.

Middle-class whites, led by the real estate fraternity, frequently resorted to racial housing covenants and zoning to contain nonwhites in a restricted area. Low-income whites, only slightly less undesirable in the eyes of the middle class, sometimes used intimidation, violence, and threats to assert their Americanism. On the part of the former, this was a manifestation of class as well as racial prejudice; on the part of the latter it was primarily racial. Yet lower-class whites and Negroes frequently shared the same residential areas and faced the same disabilities of poor neighborhoods. Class was often more important than color in neighborhoods which failed to offer prestige or adequate protection and public services to any residents, regardless of race.[8] The early governmental policy of segregation in public housing subsequently served to accentuate color consciousness in low-cost housing at the same time that it reflected the strategic role of authority in establishing racial patterns.

World War II brought in a new stream of Negro, Mexican-American, and Puerto Rican migrants to the urban North and West. It also brought greater residential segregation. This too represented, first, resistance to the expansion of land space available to nonwhites and, most recently, abandonment of segments of the central cities to them. Several factors played an important part in this. The federal government through the Federal Housing Administration had facilitated phenomenal expansion of suburban construction, and low down-payments and a longer period for mortgages had made a large part of this available to middle- and lower middle-income families. At the same time FHA accepted the concept of homogeneous neighborhoods and until 1947 the instrument of the racial restrictive housing covenants.[9] Higher incomes during the war enabled a vast number of families to accumulate down pay-

[8] Findings of recent research challenge the oft-repeated assertion that the source as well as the center of anti-Negro prejudice and discrimination in this country is in the lower socio-economic classes. See Robert K. Merton, "Discrimination and the National Creed," in R. M. MacIver (ed.), *Discrimination and National Welfare*, p. 111 (New York: Harper and Bros., 1949) and National Committee on Segregation in the Nation's Capital, *Segregation in Washington*, p. 38 (Chicago, Illinois: The Committee, 1948).

[9] R. C. Weaver, *The Negro Ghetto*, pp. 71–73, 152–153 (New York: Harcourt, Brace & Co., 1948).

ments and sustained prosperity facilitated their meeting monthly carrying charges. At the same time government housing policy made home ownership more attractive than rental[10] and practically all new construction was in lily-white suburbs. Not only was it possible for the upper-middle class to desert the central city, but many of lesser means—if they were white—could follow suit. Even the low-income white family could hope for homogeneity—either in the suburbs with a little more money or perhaps in the grey areas of the core city if the expansion of nonwhites was contained. Racially homogeneous neighborhoods had achieved a new prestige and this was increasingly apparent in slums and blighted areas where residents sought to emulate dominant racial attitudes.

Rapid movement of whites to the suburbs was but a part of the population trend. For example, over 7,000,000 persons entered the suburbs between 1940 and 1950. While a large volume of long-term residents left the cities, an even larger number of individuals moved from non-urban areas directly to the suburbs. Meanwhile a much smaller number of whites moved into than moved out of central cities while many nonwhites entered the in-lying areas. "The process of losing one net migrant to the suburbs actually was the end result of a larger process whereby for each two nonwhite persons moving into the central city about three white persons moved out."[11]

These movements have brought interesting changes in the housing market. Throughout the North and West, non-whites have acquired a much larger number of housing units and frequently a more diversified and a better quality of housing. In the process they have expanded into many areas which were formerly all white. The Chicago experience of 1940–50 suggests the human components of this development. Those who initiated the movement were long-term rather than newer residents, resulting in no significant changes in socio-economic characteristics,[12] and the first arrivals had had to "pay a premium rental, which they are able to finance only by using residential space very intensively, e.g., by doubling up families in the household or by including relatives or lodgers in the household."[13]

[10] Louis Winnick, *Rental Housing: Opportunities for Private Investment*, Chapter 3 (New York: McGraw-Hill Book Company, 1958).
[11] Donald J. Bogue, *Components of Population Change*, 1940–50, p. 34 (Miami, Ohio: Miami University, 1957).
[12] Otis Dudley Duncan and Beverly Duncan, *The Negro Population of Chicago*, pp. 125, 191, 206, 223, 225 (Chicago, Illinois: The University of Chicago Press, 1957).
[13] *Ibid.*, p. 236.

While it is true that only in a quite general sense has succession in Chicago followed a pattern of racial expansion of the Negro community outward from the center of the city, it is significant that:

"... within both the Negro and the white community, high-status groups tend to share residential areas and to be residentially segregated from low-status groups. Apparently, the selective forces which produce differentiation of residential areas in the urban community operate in somewhat the same way upon the Negro and the white population. This is also in line with the finding that patterns of interarea differentiation with respect to physical characteristics of the area and social and economic characteristics of the residents tend to be maintained under the impact of succession from white to Negro occupancy."[14]

These developments in Chicago, which are fairly typical of larger northern industrial centers, reflect the interaction of many events. Such expansion of housing accommodations for Negroes as took place was facilitated largely by the decline in the white population. It reflected a growing demand for shelter on the part of an expanding nonwhite population in which a significant number were able to pay higher rents and prices for housing, and it enabled some whites to sell profitably and buy new suburban houses. Even where sales were not profitable the availability of Negro purchasers and renters greatly accelerated the liquidation of property in the central city and the acquisition of new homes elsewhere on the part of previous residents in the core areas. To a degree, this greater effective demand for housing on the part of nonwhites sustained property values in many parts of the central city and accelerated the purchase of new homes by whites who were replaced by nonwhites, many of whom paid higher prices than could otherwise have been secured.

Had there been less racial segregation in the suburbs, a larger number of nonwhites would have joined whites in moving from the central cities to the suburbs and going directly to them rather than to the central cities. Even in the face of a most effective color bar, about one-third of a million Negroes did join whites in the 1940–50 trek to the suburbs. Most of those involved were in the South, but there was a pronounced desire of Northern middle-class Negroes to escape from central cities,[15] and there are indications that some of the colored migrants to the North avoided the central city and moved directly to older Negro settlements elsewhere. This seems to

[14] *Ibid.*, p. 298.
[15] Handlin, *op. cit.*, pp. 125–131.

have occurred in the industrial cities of New Jersey and the larger cities in New York's Westchester County.

One upshot of residential segregation has been to contain most Negro middle-class families in the core cities.[16] Another, and much more serious consequence for the cities has been the concentration of demand for housing on the part of the growing middle-class Negroes on certain city areas. This too has often sustained property values but it has tended to accelerate the exodus of middle-class whites. Were middle-class Negroes able to compete freely in the total market, their volume in most neighborhoods would have been so slight as to have occasioned little concern. There would have been much less premium payment incident to initial nonwhite occupancy and white owners would have had less economic incentive to forsake attractive neighborhoods and homes. Even the real estate operators would have had slight impetus to engineer flight of middle-class whites since the principal source of effective demand—the middle-class Negro purchaser—would be more discriminating and less available for any one neighborhood.[17]

For the process described above to have taken place, there would have had to have been a much larger volume of low-priced housing available to nonwhites in metropolitan areas. Without such a supply the sheer pressure of numbers occasioned the growth of nonwhite areas of concentration. In some instances this involved expansion of one or several major Negro ghettos, engulfing surrounding housing regardless of its price or suitability. In other instances it involved the development of new pockets of nonwhite residential concentration. Invariably, it occasioned overcrowding, undesirably high densities, and blight.

However, in a situation where the supply of low-cost housing available to nonwhites is limited, the entrance of middle-income, nonwhite families into a neighborhood and its subsequent desertion

[16] Actually, this is due to factors other than residential segregation, but it is primarily a consequence of the color line: see Weaver, "The Effect of Anti-Discrimination Legislation upon the FHA- and VA-Insured Housing Market in New York State," *Land Economics*, pp. 305–307 (November, 1955).

[17] There can be no better illustration of the confusion between emotion and economics than the implications of this analysis. Without a color line, housing in certain areas of the central city would probably have fallen in value. This would have been accounted for in economic terms—architectural obsolescence, loss of neighborhood prestige, age of structure, competition of more desirable facilities and neighborhood location, and resulting weakness in demand for the affected housing. Under conditions of color concepts the experience in these areas is cited (and rightfully) as evidence that nonwhite occupancy does not necessarily adversely influence property values. See Luigi Laurenti, *Property Values and Race* (Berkeley, California: University of California Press, 1960).

by whites has benefited the mass of colored home-seekers. For, had there been less turnover, there would have been less filtration. This, in turn, would have delayed the improvement in the quality of housing occupied by nonwhites. In the present situation of enforced residential segregation in many segments of the housing market rapid racial transition of desirable housing in parts of the central city has made a larger amount of physically good housing available to nonwhites. It has also resulted in more intensive and often socially undesirable occupancy patterns in the areas recently accessible to nonwhites and it has made it difficult to sustain the middle-class characteristics of the affected areas, even where higher-income nonwhites have attempted to do so. Relatively high vacancy rates, as in Philadelphia and Cleveland, have accelerated racial transition in certain neighborhoods with the result of substantial upgrading in the quality of the occupied housing stock and instability in some middle-class housing areas.

Modern cities can absorb a large supply of low-income migrants without subjecting the newcomers to economic exploitation and greatly augmenting slums and blight only by building more low-rent housing on open sites, solving the problem of rehabilitation without excessive costs and providing a free housing market. The central city has a stake in open occupancy throughout the metropolitan area because it is necessary in order that the market may operate most efficiently. Under conditions of open occupancy a much smaller number of areas of middle-class housing need be threatened by inundation by nonwhites and it is possible to make the most effective use of the existing supply of housing—particularly the low-rent sector.[18]

EFFORTS TO ATTRACT MIDDLE-CLASS FAMILIES TO THE CENTRAL CITY

It is against this background that urban renewal programs' efforts to attract and maintain middle-class families in the central city must operate. Regardless of any social, political, or moral considerations, the economics of the situation require concern for retention

[18] This is the economic rationale for open-occupancy (fair-housing) legislation. As in all nondiscriminatory legislation, enactment of a law is but a first step. To be effective, such laws need implementation—and that involves not only enforcement but also positive action on the part of minority groups. Thus the Philadelphia Commission on Human Relations is encouraging Negroes to seek homes in all-white neighborhoods, saying: "To break the stubborn pattern of segregated housing many Negro citizens must have the courage to live in 'new' neighborhoods." The New York Times, p. 49 (March 6, 1960).

f white middle-class families in central cities because their num-
ers far exceed those among nonwhites.[19] In any given locality the
problem has three manifestations: creation of new areas in which
middle-class families will establish stable communities, rehabilitation or partial renewal of areas which will attract and hold middle-class families, and the arresting or preventing the desertion of
middle-class families from existing areas of residence.

In the larger cities of the South new, segregated middle-class
Negro communities have been developed. This has been possible for
several reasons. In some instances it results from annexation of
new areas by the central city after informal agreements have been
made concerning the color identification of land. Atlanta is a prime
example.[20] New Orleans has had somewhat similar experience.[21]
In cities like Charlotte, Greensboro, and Winston-Salem, North
Carolina, and Austin, Texas, availability of vacant land contiguous
to, or in the path of, existing centers of Negro concentration has
afforded sites for new, segregated FHA-insured housing. In Houston, Texas, where availability of good housing has made the owning
of attractive homes an important source of status among Negroes,
there has been an appreciable amount of new construction and a
significant source of excellent middle-class housing in a good neighborhood available to Negroes during the last decade.

Clearly, by creation of new segregated areas in most of these
cities and restrictions of Negro encroachments upon middle-class
white neighborhoods to a few locations in others, the impact of the
nonwhite market has had but limited effect upon the desertion of

[9] "What the city needs is a core of upper-middle-class people to support its
theatres and museums, its shops and its restaurants—even a Bohemia of sorts
can be of help. For it is the people who like living in the city who make it
an attraction to the visitors who don't. It is the city dwellers who support its
style: without them there is nothing to come downtown to." William H. Whyte,
Jr., "Are Cities Un-American?" Fortune, pp. 124–125 (September, 1957). Despite significant recent improvement in the economic status of nonwhites and
a significant increase in the number of middle-class Negroes in urban areas,
the number of the latter is not now able, nor does it have a potential in the
near future, to provide a large or affluent enough population to perform the
functions outlined above by Whyte.
[0] Robert A. Thompson, Hylan Lewis, and Davis McEntire, "Atlanta and Birmingham: A Comparative Study in Negro Housing," in Glazer and McEntire
(ed.), Studies in Housing and Minority Groups, pp. 22–40 (Berkeley, California: University of California Press, 1960); and "Civil Rights Official Lauds
Atlanta's Gentleman's Agreement," House and Home, p. 91 (May, 1959). For
a discussion of the implications of the use of new, segregated middle-class
Negro housing in the South, see R. C. Weaver, "Southern Comfort: A Possible Misapplication of Federal Funds," Journal of Intergroup Relations (Fall
1960).
[1] Forrest E. LaViolette, "The Negro in New Orleans," in Glazer and McEntire,
op. cit., pp. 124–130; also "Minority Housing," House and Home, pp. 146–147
(April, 1955).

the central city by middle-class whites. In Houston, where ther
seems to have been a rather loose housing market,[22] Negro expar
sion into one good neighborhood served to sustain values an
thereby accelerated movement of the older residents to the suburb:
However, some of those who sold to Negroes may have replace
other central city whites moving to the suburbs and thereby sup
ported property values elsewhere in the central city.

In Northern cities the establishment of all-Negro suburbs i
usually impossible. This is due to the spatial distribution o
nonwhites[23] and rejection of segregated patterns by nonwhites i:
the North.[24] The latter fact is, of course, supported by legislation
a score of northern states and cities have non-discrimination hous
ing laws, and racial discrimination in urban renewal areas i
banned in several states and many cities. In all of these and othe
cities, the capacity and willingness of Negroes to pay for bette
housing in middle-class neighborhoods has increased significantl
during the last decade at the same time that the low-income non
white population has grown appreciably. Indeed, the growth o
nonwhite urban populations has been much greater in border an
northern cities than in their southern counterparts. Thus the pres
sure of Negroes for more housing has had greater impact in th
North than in the South. Also, it has had less outlet via expansio:
into new, vacant areas. The consequence is that Negroes hav
expanded to a much greater degree into areas formerly occupied b
whites in northern than in southern cities.

[22] Jack E. Dodson, "Minority Group Housing in Two Texas Cities," in Glaze
and McEntire, op. cit., pp. 101–109.
[23] See R. C. Weaver, The Negro Ghetto, pp. 91, 138, 154–156.
[24] "In certain ways, the North presents more problems for upper-income Ne
groes than the South, for here the problem is not only to get good housing—
and if Atlanta can supply a Negro market for extensive Negro subdivision:
unquestionably this can also be done in northern cities—but to get goo
unsegregated housing." Glazer, "Introduction," Glazer and McEntire, op. cit
p. 6. Of course, where there is the base of a Negro settlement which originall:
housed domestics, as on the North Shore of Chicago's suburbs or in citie
and towns of Westchester County and Long Island or clusters of industri
workers in suburban towns and cities, growing Negro populations—mostl
in ghettos—are developing in northern suburbs. Also, a small number of uppe
middle-income Negroes have bought homes outside areas of nonwhite concer
tration. Current developments suggest that, were the suburbs open to Negroe:
they would attract a large segment of the still relatively small number o
middle-income nonwhites. At the same time, concentration of industry in fring
areas has already attracted a significant number of nonwhite workers. Man
are now commuting from the core areas, but there are indications of a desir
for, and a trend to, suburban living on their part. Competent studies sugges
that there will be an outward movement of Negroes and Puerto Ricans in th
New York City Metropolitan area in response to job opportunities. See Edga
M. Hoover and Raymond Vernon, Anatomy of a Metropolis, pp. 212–213 (Cam
bridge, Massachusetts: Harvard University Press, 1959).

Efforts to attract and retain middle-class families in the central urban centers of the North and border states must recognize he pressure for housing occasioned by a growing Negro population. Some of these cities also face the arrival of large numbers of Appalachian Mountain whites, Puerto Ricans, and Mexicans. Since he Negro presents problems of class as well as color, concentration upon his impact is fruitful. Glazer, while minimizing the problem of the dark-skinned Puerto Ricans and Mexican-Americans, has set orth the peculiar disabilities of the Negro in American society:

. . . . it may seem far-fetched to consider the implications of a social situation in which Mexicans, Puerto Ricans, and Negroes show roughly he same social constitution as the rest of us. However, in the case of the Negroes such large middle-class groups are already developing. They will hange greatly the whole character of anti-Negro prejudice in America. But—and this is the point of the last observation—the Negroes will still be a long way from taking up the status in American society of assimilated European ethnic groups. The Mexicans and Puerto Ricans, because of their physical characteristics, will find it easier to achieve this status."[25]

Survival of healthy, central cities requires recognition and solution of this problem. First, there needs to be an acceleration of he size of the middle class among nonwhites. Second, this will be achieved in large measure in proportion to the degree that the middle-class Negro is accepted as his immigrant prototype was accepted.[26] Third, unless the achievement of American norms of success on the part of Negroes is rewarded, as it has been among others who started at the bottom of the economic and social scale, here will be a loss of motivation (already apparent among Negroes) with consequences which are inimical to the economic, political, and cultural health of the central city. Fourth, such results would be tragic for the nation—and western democracy—in the world of the cold war and the emergence of Asian and African nationalism.

Northern cities, if they are to maintain a sound economic base, must strive to adjust to continuing in-migration of low-income Negroes, Puerto Ricans, Appalachian whites, and Mexicans. A first step in this direction is to understand the nature of cities and the historical precedents. A second step is to face up to the unique problems of the present migrant groups. These can be summarized in a single statement: All of certain ethnic groups, because of their

[25] Nathan Glazer, op. cit., pp. 11–12. For a more realistic discussion of the Puerto Rican, see Handlin, op. cit., pp. 59–60.
[26] Oscar Handlin, op. cit., pp. 78–80, 100, 103, 117–119.

physical identification, are assumed to be a threat to a middle-class neighborhood, regardless of the individual's or the family's income education, or behavior. Centuries of slavery, generations of color discrimination, repeated instances of economic disadvantage vi perpetuation of a color line, and a liberal amount of guilt have per petuated color concepts. These are most apparent and effective i: situations involving areas of living and schools.

Most liberals and many social scientists advocate heteroge neous neighborhoods. The majority of them would favor a commu nity of homes in which low-, medium-, and upper-income group lived; as a minimum, they would mix low- and medium-incom people. Some have equally strong feelings about racial heteroge neity, affirming that in the modern world it behooves us in th United States to learn and demonstrate how a multi-racial societ; can live together under democracy. Recently an outstanding lan economist has dissented, questioning the innate superiority of mul ti-income neighborhoods.[27] In this paper no attempt will be mad to pass moral, social, or political judgments on this issue; rather the problem will be treated from the point of view of the surviva of central cities. Our orientation will be primarily economic, recog nizing that enforced racial residential segregation is under attacl and in the process of change in the nation.

From this point of view, it must be recognized that the middl class in America is keenly conscious of the threat of lower-clas encroachments. As was pointed out above this has long been a national characteristic, perhaps an inevitable consequence of a socially mobile people who are status-conscious. During the las quarter of a century, it has become more acute. This leads to th

[27] "It is not clear why economically heterogeneous neighborhoods are innatel; superior to the homogeneous. We do not really know whether economically di verse groups truly mix or merely live side by side. And casual observation indi cates that many exclusively high-income or middle-income neighbors seem t have withstood neighborhood decline extremely well while many economically mixed neighborhoods have proven quite vulnerable. The social gains of mixtur and the social losses from homogeneity have yet to be demonstrated." Loui Winnick, *Facts and Fictions in Urban Renewal*, p. 12. Mimeographed: a speecl delivered before the Forum of the Philadelphia Housing Association (Janu ary 28, 1960). Most planners, however, believe that there are such social gains A recent forum composed of citizens and professionals who met to conside: what neighborhoods should be like "pleaded for variety—variety of housin; types . . . available at a variety of prices and rentals so that a varied neigh borhood population could result, all races, young and old, rich and poor, an people falling between these extremes." Ironically enough, zoning as cur rently practiced was considered a chief deterrent to such mixture. Howard W Hallman, "Citizens and Professionals Reconsider the Neighborhood," *Journa of the American Institute of Planners*, p. 123 (August, 1959). For a somewha similar point of view, see Arthur L. Grey, Jr., "Los Angeles: Urban Proto type," *Land Economics*, pp. 237–238 (August, 1959).

onclusion that many middle-class families will not long voluntarily emain in an area which they believe threatened by lower-class ngulfment; few will migrate to such areas. The second fact that ias to be recognized is that the white middle class fears neighbor-ood deterioration on the entry of nonwhites—an attitude that has artial roots in the history of decline in city services, lax enforce-nent of housing codes, and overcrowding in areas inhabited by ionwhites. Actually, the degree of this fear is often a function of he speed and intensity of nonwhite penetration, although it is oday an almost immediate reaction upon the first evidence of non-vhite entry.[28] Most white middle-class families will not long 'emain in a neighborhood where they are a racial minority. Should hey fear this eventuality, they usually act so as to assure its frui-ion. On the other hand, there are many evidences of whites' ccepting a few Negro neighbors, particularly if they are of com-arable economic and social status.[29]

The Impact of Urban Renewal

Jrban renewal activity concerned with attracting and holding mid-lle-class households in the central city must be geared to creating leighborhoods which offer good schools, a reasonable degree of leanliness, protection from violence, and physical attractiveness.

[28] This is a most complex phenomenon. Its manifestation varies from city to ity, from time to time, and from area to area within a given city. For example, n the color-conscious Washington, D.C., of the present writer's youth, whites lid not hesitate to enter Brookland (a suburb of the central city) despite the oresence of a few middle-class Negro families. R. C. Weaver, The Negro Ghetto, pp. 290–291. As Negro incomes rose in the District of Columbia, an ncreasing number of middle-class colored families moved into Brookland but, untiI World War II, it remained a racially mixed area. By 1952, non-whites had oenetrated adjoining Woodridge and Michigan Park, areas of white middle-lass occupancy. The official organ of the Rhode Island Avenue Citizen's Asso-ciation exhorted whites to remain in Woodridge. Weaver, "Relative Status of the Housing of Negroes in the United States," Journal of Negro Education, op. 351–352 (Summer 1953). But the combined force of the pent-up non-white demand for good housing and the lure of the suburbs in surrounding Maryland and Virginia for whites was too much. Today Brookland is largely Negro, Woodridge and Michigan Park house many non-white families, and Brookland's Negroes are no longer almost exclusively middle-class. The new prestige area for Washington's middle-class Negro families is in the far Northwest, where a relatively few reside among white neighbors.
[29] See Gus Turbeville, "The Negro Population of Duluth, Minnesota, 1950," Sociology and Social Research, pp. 231–238 (March-April, 1952); Arnold M. Rose, Frank J. Atelsek and Laurence R. MacDonald, "Neighborhood Reactions to Isolated Negro Residents; An Alternative to Invasion and Succession," American Sociological Review (October, 1953); Davis McEntire, "A Study of Racial Attitudes in Neighborhoods Infiltrated by Non-Whites," Bay Area Real Estate Report, pp. 126–129 (San Francisco, Second Quarter 1955).

They need not be single-class neighborhoods,[30] but there is
limit—a class tipping point—to which they can at the present b
heterogeneous from a class point of view. Similarly, they can absor
some minority group families of middle-class attributes as well a
some of lower incomes.[31] The class and racial mix will vary fro
new urban redevelopment sites, partial redevelopment and rehabil
tation efforts, and conservation areas. The greatest flexibility is i
the newly reconstructed redevelopment areas—if for no othe
reason, because new areas and new houses have a snob appeal i
themselves.

Proximity to an established blighted nonwhite slum compl
cates or deters white occupancy in redevelopment projects. Eithe
large-scale demolition, or extra value for the housing dollar, or bot
are required to offset this circumstance. Chicago illustrates we
this situation. The New York Life Insurance Company finance
and constructed Lake Meadows, a large redevelopment, medium
cost rental project in the heart of what had been some of the wors
of the city's Negro slums. Although it announced open occupanc
from the start and, despite the scope of the redevelopment and it
inherent desirable location in relation to downtown and in proxim
ity to city-wide health and educational institutions, the attractiv
new facilities failed to appeal to a large number of white tenants.[32]
Intensive efforts and tangible evidences of a new neighborhoo
achieved 20 percent white occupancy and, currently, 25 percent o
the tenants are white.

Prairie Shores was subsequently constructed on the site of a
former Negro slum and on the edge of the Negro ghetto. But it wa
adjacent to Lake Meadows and the upgrading of the neighborhoo
was well under way. Indeed, the promotion of Prairie Shore
describes it as "an entirely new community immediately adjacen
to the Michael Reese Hospital campus." In the words of it
developer—who incidentally evidenced his commitment to the proj
ect by selling his house in the suburbs and moving into Prairi
Shores—"people just recognized a hell of a good buy when they sav
it." The nature of this buy is indicated by the fact that apartment

[30] Those who insist on this will probably move to the suburbs anyway.
[31] For an analysis of the experience of builders of interracial private develop
ments during the last decade, see Eunice and George Grier, *Privately De
veloped Interracial Housing* (Berkeley, California: University of Californi
Press, 1960).
[32] Lake Meadows is located on a 100-acre site and rented initially from $3
per room per month—about a quarter less than comparable accommodation
elsewhere in the city. The first building of slightly less than 600 units at
tracted only about three percent white tenants. Subsequent special effort
appreciably increased white participation. Eunice and George Grier, *op. cit.*
pp. 106–107.

ented for an average of $33 a room as against $45 to $65 for com-
arable new accommodations elsewhere in the city. And the first
42 units in the initial structure of this five-building development
ented quickly. Seventy-seven percent of the occupants were white
ut most households were childless and none had children of high
chool age.[33] As of May 1960, two buildings in Prairie Shores had
een completed. Both were fully rented and leases were being
igned on a third which will be ready for occupancy in late
ummer. The racial mix remained about 80 percent white and,
vhile few families with school-age children were in occupancy,
here were many with pre-school children.

   With rare exceptions a small island of medium-cost redevelop-
nent housing in a sea of nonwhite slums will not attract whites.
This was the experience of the attractive—but not relatively com-
petitively-priced—Longwood Redevelopment in Cleveland. An
exception was the reasonably priced (single-family, sales house)
and slow moving redevelopment project in Richmond, California.[34]
On the other hand, redevelopment in an area which is fairly large
and marked for total treatment can attract middle-class whites
vhen a minority of nonwhites are housed in it. This has been demonstrated in architecturally attractive Capitol Park Apartments of
he Southwest Redevelopment in Washington, D. C. and in the Gra-
iot Redevelopment in Detroit. Both of these are fairly high-rent
and that fact alone has greatly limited nonwhite participation.

   Partial redevelopment and rehabilitation present more difficult
problems. In the first place, frequently the old neighborhood which
s the symbol of the threat of lower-class and minority families is
not destroyed. Even if a new type of area is planned the physical
evidences of the old remain. Where, as in the area around the University of Chicago, there is a sizeable amount of good housing, and
an enduring institutional base, the possibilities of success are
enhanced. The urban renewal plan for the West Side of New
York,[35] which also involved spot clearance and a great amount of
rehabilitation, is also favorably located. On the north is a large
middle-income redevelopment project partially occupied and near-
ing completion, on the east an attractive predominantly upper middle-class residential strip on Central Park West, on the south a
middle-class strip on 86th Street, and on the west a traffic artery.

   In the Chicago and New York projects there has been great

[33] "Open Occupancy Builder Lands 77% White Tenants," *House and Home*,
p. 76 (March, 1959).
[34] "Pilot Project Survives FHA Red Tape, Starts Blighted Area on Road Back,"
House and Home, p. 59 (February, 1959).
[35] *Urban Renewal* (New York: New York City Planning Commission, undated)
and *West Side Urban Renewal Area* (New York: Urban Renewal Board, 1959).

controversy as to how much public housing will be provided. I
both instances the amount has been limited so that low-income fan
ilies will be a definite minority of those in the areas. New York
West Side will also have a sizeable amount of lower medium-rer
facilities or reasonably priced cooperatives, but most of the shelte
will be priced so as to attract middle-income households. There i
no question that both the New York and the Chicago neighborhood
will be predominantly middle class. Both will have some nonwhit
low-income families and some nonwhite, middle-income household
But they will be predominantly middle- and upper-income whit
communities.

Since conservation areas are subjected to the least amount o
physical change, they share characteristics with most of the stand
ard areas of existing housing. While the structures in such areas c
the old city may be imposing in size and appearance, frequentl
they are architecturally obsolete. This may occasion new propert
uses—rooming houses, conversions to apartments of varyin
degrees of adequacy, or other forms of multi-family occupancy
Seldom are they suited for small families, and their utilization b
low-income households usually involves undesirable economic an
social consequences.

In some instances the location of conversion areas (in terms o
proximity to present concentrations of nonwhite families) inspire
acute fear of minority inundation on the part of present residents
Thus, the possibility of panic selling is real and immediate upon th
entrance of nonwhites. There is another complicating factor. Pres
ent residents of these areas have not elected to live with nonwhit
neighbors. The latter have come in after the neighborhood has beer
established as a racially homogeneous one. Thus there may be
feeling on the part of old residents that they had lost the opportun
ity to exercise freedom of choice in selecting nonwhite neighbors
In this regard they differ from those who move into a new or exist
ing biracial community.[36] The physical attributes of conservatior
areas and the process of change involved in establishing racial mix
ture complicate the process in such neighborhoods.

Thus conservation areas present perplexing problems to thos

[36] Henry G. Stetler, *Racial Integration in Private Residential Neighborhoods i*
Connecticut, pp. 72–75 (Hartford, Connecticut: Connecticut Commission o
Civil Rights, 1957). Of course, as has been observed, when one buys or rent
in any neighborhood, one has no vested right in its composition. This wa
emphatically delineated by the 1948 decision of the Supreme Court which
outlawed judicial enforcement of race-restrictive housing covenants and in th
rise of nondiscrimination housing legislation. As a practical matter, however
many people do react to what they consider their freedom of choice in thi
regard and nothing in the law prevents families from moving away fron
neighbors they do not like.

who would attract and hold middle-class whites in the central city. At the outset it must be recognized that many parts of the core city are destined to be occupied by nonwhites. Under present conditions they will provide the almost sole supply of housing for Negroes and other nonwhites who seek better shelter and are achieving or have achieved sufficiently high earnings to pay for it. In addition, if the past is any indication of the future, many areas of this type will, should they lie in the path of the geographic expansion of existing racial ghettos, be occupied by house-hungry lower-income nonwhites.

The degree to which low-income minority families enter these areas depends upon several things. If there is an alternative supply of good housing which better fits the family needs and pocketbooks of nonwhites, the process will be delayed. If housing and occupancy standards are enforced—a thing that is unlikely unless there is an alternative supply[37]—this too will slow up racial displacement. And of course the extent to which the central city becomes more attractive to whites will lessen the availability of such housing to nonwhites. At the same time, however, the volume of migration of nonwhites to urban centers will be a major factor in determining the demand for housing on their part. Finally, in proportion as we continue to concentrate upon clearing slums inhabited by nonwhites the process of racial displacement will take place elsewhere in the city.

In recent years there has been a series of attempts on the part of middle-class neighborhoods to stay the departure of whites with the arrival of colored residents. To date, most, if not all, of these have been delaying tactics at best.[38] Perhaps if such efforts were a part of an over-all program involving new open-occupancy construction, action for spreading the nonwhite demand over a larger area of the central city, prevention of the engineering of panic selling by real estate operators, better enforcement of housing and

[37] "For many years a high-class residential enclave around the University of Chicago, Hyde Park-Kenwood, began developing pockets of slums, then found itself turning from a white to a Negro neighborhood. Concerted community action, with citizen participation on a scale perhaps unmatched in the nation, has done much to slow the drift toward blight. Moreover, the neighborhoods set out to do so on a deliberate interracial basis. . . . Leaders of the effort found out how to make the city government help them enforce decent living standards. But continuing Negro pressure for more housing raised doubts as to whether this unique and pioneering effort could succeed in the face of overwhelming odds. . . . By the end of 1955 physical conversion of apartments into cell-like slum structures . . . had been stopped cold. . . . But conversion by use—moving three or four families into one apartment—had not been stopped." Martin Millspaugh and Gurney Breckenfeld, *The Human Side of Urban Renewal*, pp. 91, 105–106 (Baltimore, Maryland: Flight-Blight Inc., 1958).

[38] *Loc. cit.* See also Mayer, *op. cit.*

occupancy codes and effective action to open the suburbs to non
whites, such programs might succeed in maintaining the bi-racia
character of some well-located and attractive neighborhoods.[39]

■ ■ ■

THE CLASS AND RACE MIX OF THE CITY TOMORROW

This analysis suggests that in northern and border cities there ca
be a degree of class and racial mixture compatible with attractin
and holding middle-class whites. In the expensive and upper medi
um-rental apartments and sales houses this presents few problem
of planning. The income structure assures only token participatio
by nonwhites and of course eliminates the low-income group. If th
desirable mix (from the point of view of maintaining large num
bers of medium-income families) involves limited participation o
low-income households, this too can be achieved by redeveloping o
renewing areas large enough to establish their own identity an
limiting the amount of low-cost housing. This, however, implies th
responsibility for providing in attractive locations an adequat
supply of low-cost units and cessation of such widespread disloca
tion of families as has typified urban renewal to date.

It is at the level of medium-cost housing that real problem
arise. The nonwhite and particularly the Negro housing marke
includes a growing number of families ready, willing, and able t
purchase or rent such shelter. If the market is open to them in onl
a few locations at any one time the "tipping point" may soon b
reached in any one or two developments. As was indicated above
opening the suburbs to nonwhites is one of the necessary prices fo
attracting and holding middle-income whites in the central city.[4]

[39] The same analysis applies to the use of quotas as a means of effecting an
perpetuating interracial neighborhoods. Aside from the troublesome question
of their violation of fair-housing laws, they do not offer permanent barrier
against the economic pressure of a concentration of nonwhite demand on on
or a few locations. For a description of the case for quotas, see Oscar Cohen
"The Benign Quotas in Housing," *Phylon*, pp. 20–29 (First Quarter [Spring
1960). My analysis suggests that benign housing quotas are as temporary
means of stabilizing bi-racial areas as race-restrictive housing covenants wer
to do the opposite. For a discussion of the latter point, see Weaver, *The Negr
Ghetto*, Ch. XIII.

[40] This is a complex matter. It would operate as suggested above by (1
siphoning off some of the middle income demand for housing among nonwhite
from the central city (2) removing the attraction of racial homogeneity fron
the suburbs; (3) reducing the snob appeal of racial exclusiveness since n
area could assure it; (4) reducing the threat of "tipping" in any one raciall
open neighborhood.

Cessation of widespread dislocation of low-income families vas suggested in the earlier discussion of high and upper-medium-cost housing. It was proposed there from the point of view of political expediency and equity. It is pertinent to the discussion of medium-cost housing for another reason. As long as large numbers of low-income families are uprooted by slum clearance they are a potential source for the displacement of middle-income families elsewhere in the community. This is especially true when they are colored and limited to a racially restricted market.

A final approach, applicable chiefly to conservation areas, is to perfect techniques for stabilizing racially transitional neighborhoods. To be effective they must be an element in a comprehensive program for expanding the supply of housing available to non-whites at all price levels. Also, it must be realized that there are some neighborhoods which, because of location in relation to the growth of areas of nonwhite concentration, will not respond to this treatment. This only illustrates that cities are not static institutions. Their physical facilities change and their people move. The problems of class and color can never be solved in any one neighborhood. Today they cannot be solved in the central city. They are problems of metropolitan areas.

If this analysis is valid, it has significance for the kind of cities we may expect in the next generation. While the size and squalor of slums may be decreased we shall not clear all of them. Poverty, rejection, and a certain amount of individual choice[41] will dictate their perpetuation. Through better schools—in terms of plant, quality of teaching and effective programs to reach low-income families—the economic and social status of many slum residents can be raised. If we perfect and apply techniques to give the newcomers a feeling of belonging and provide meaningful assistance to the normal as opposed to the problem family, there can be greater occupational, edccational and residential mobility among this group. For these approaches to work, our urban populations will have to be less color-conscious; and anti-discrimination housing legislation affecting the suburbs as well as central cities will be required. We need also to develop more tolerance to variations from established middle-class values and behavior.[42] American urban centers will not soon, if ever, become a total of class and racial heterogeneous neighborhoods. Realistic and courageous planning, constant progress toward open occupancy, con-

[41] John R. Seeley, "The Slum: Its Nature, Use, and Users," *Journal of the American Institute of Planners*, pp. 7–14 (February, 1959).

[42] R. C. Weaver, "Human Values of Urban Life," *Proceedings of the Academy of Political Science* (June, 1960).

tinued economic advancement on the part of the disadvantaged progress in dealing with transitional neighborhoods, an expanding supply of housing suited to the family needs and pocketbooks of low-income and lower-medium-income households, good schools and the development of techniques to upgrade at a reasonable cost much of the existing housing supply will enable our cities to develop and maintain neighborhoods with varying degrees of class and color heterogeneity. But most of these will be predominantly of one income level; some will be almost exclusively nonwhite; a few will have a small number of medium-income nonwhites; and others will be integrated in varying degrees.

What of the central cities? They will survive. Indeed, their demise, largely on the same grounds cited as threatening them today, has been foretold many times in the past.[43] Of course, they will be different. For years to come they will have trouble attracting and holding middle-income white families with children. As long as there are private and parochial schools, some such households will remain. To the degree that redevelopment, renewal, and conserved neighborhoods, as well as areas which are left alone become or continue to be identified as middle class, there will be middle-income whites with children in the central cities. Good public schools and other satisfactory public facilities will augment the number. Almost equally important will be the success we have in utilizing housing codes and other tools to raise the general level of housing, in developing realistic school programs to raise motivation and achievement in all schools, and in applying effective techniques for accelerating the occupational, residential, and social mobility of the growing number of newcomers who are entering and will continue to enter our cities.

[43] Louis Winnick, *Facts and Fictions in Urban Renewal*, p. 18.

The School as an Instrument in Planning

NATHAN GLAZER
University of California, Berkeley

Some decades ago, when Clarence Perry was developing his ideas about the neighborhood as an appropriate form for urban living and as an elementary building block for the expansion of urban areas, he seized upon the public school as an important element in planning. Perry had to consider how large this elementary community, the neighborhood, should be, and the public school determined for him the appropriate size of a neighborhood. He took the views of the educational authorities of his day on the appropriate size of an efficient public school, multiplied this by the ratio that the whole population generally bears to the school population, and this gave him the whole population of a proper neighborhood. He figured out how far a young child could conveniently walk and estimated in this way the size of a neighborhood.

For Perry, the school became the center of the neighborhood. As an institution to which every family, or almost every family, was vitally attached, it helped transform the physical neighborhood into a real community, by creating a common interest. It would also be the center, as the largest physical structure in the neighborhood, of a variety of community activities.[1]

From the *Journal of the American Institute of Planners*, Vol. 25, No. 4, pp. 191–196 (November, 1959). Reprinted by permission of the author and of the *Journal of the American Institute of Planners*.
[1] Clarence Arthur Perry, *Housing for the Machine Age*, pp. 52–55, 243 (New York: Russell Sage Foundation, 1939). The hazards of depending on educational authorities is evidenced when we compare Perry with G. Holmes Perkins' essay in Coleman Woodbury (ed.), *The Future of Cities and Urban Redevelopment* (Chicago: University of Chicago Press, 1953). Perry, p. 52: "According to authorities in school administration, a public school properly equipped should have a capacity of from 1,000 to 1,600 pupils." Perkins, p. 33: "Today, largely for economic reasons, there is a tendency to build elementary schools of six grades for 500–700 children." Had Perry used the latter figure, his neighborhood unit would have been one third the size of the one he favored, and naturally quite different in many other ways.

403

DEPENDENT OR INDEPENDENT VARIABLE?

The school thus played a central role in the development of one of the most important ideas in the history of planning. Once the idea of the neighborhood was developed, however, the school pretty much disappeared as an important element from planning literature and planning discussion. The school is today treated mostly as a service, and the main job of the planner in relation to a service is to determine how much is needed and where it is best located. The planner's problem in relation to the school is generally seen as one of forecasting the school population, by taking into account such factors as the movement of populations, its composition by family size and age groups, the possible effect of parochial and other nonpublic schools. The estimates become less and less secure as one moves from larger to smaller areas; by the time one comes, in considering big cities, to the relatively small areas that are served by a single elementary school, this forecasting procedure is very risky indeed.[2]

In this approach, the school is the dependent variable; the independent variable is the movement of population, itself unfortunately determined by such a host of factors as changing incomes; changing tastes; race prejudice; the decisions of builders and large employers; the decisions of local public bodies such as housing authorities, urban renewal bodies, and even planning commissions; the decisions of federal housing and finance agencies, and even of federal immigration authorities.

It is convenient to think in terms of independent and dependent variables, even though we are all aware of the risks involved. In an ever more complex urban environment, one cannot work out the major effects of every action simultaneously, and instead one must take certain elements as given and deduce from them which other elements are needed. But convenient as this way of thinking may be, it is also important to see that it may be deceptive, that, depending on time and circumstance, the "dependent variable" may become an "independent" variable. Thus, in transportation, for example, it is obvious that to think of roads and other facilities only in terms of serving "needs" leaves aside the very significant fact that they themselves play a most active role in determining the growth and character of an area and thus create "needs" at least as much as they satisfy them.

[2] Fred Rosenberg, "Intra-Regional Failures in School Planning," *Journal of the American Institute of Planners,* Vol. 23, No. 1, pp. 49–56.

'HE SCHOOL IN NEIGHBORHOOD DECLINE

believe that the school in our large cities now plays a similar role.
The school is so closely involved in the decisions people make as to
where to live that we cannot view it simply as a "service" depend-
nt on an estimate of "need"; we must realize that this "service"
has become so important as to itself determine factors which the
analysis of school needs takes as determinative. The problem of
how the school affects the urban area is as subtle and complex as
any in planning; but if we can solve it, the school may become as
powerful an instrument in creating good small urban areas as the
placement of major roads is in determining the overall form of a
ity.

At the moment we are far more aware of the negative effects
of the school on urban areas than of any possible positive effects.
For the schools are playing an important role in that vast process
whereby the centers of the major American cities are being transformed into the dwelling places of lower-income groups—generally
Negro and, in New York, Puerto Rican—and of childless upper-
ncome groups. Many factors operate in this process: race prejudice, fear of property losses, the aging of housing, and many
others. But in certain places the schooling of children has been a
most important factor in this population movement.

In New York, for example, almost everyone in the inner city
lives in apartment houses, and so fear of property losses is rarely
significant in the individual family's decision to move. Regardless
of the existence of prejudice—and it is probably less extensive than
n most other cities—one finds little tendency there for an upper-
ncome population to be rapidly dispersed by the movement of lower-income groups into the vicinity, or indeed right next door. The
kind of situation portrayed years ago in *Dead End* is not untypical
of a renting city, even without the peculiarly distorting effects of
rent control, which tends to make this kind of close mixing of
upper-income and lower-income groups even more common. And
this situation may be quite stable—as in Greenwich Village, on the
borders of the high-income areas of the East Side, and as it is
coming to be in many areas of the West Side. Neither the status
nor the way of life of lower-income groups need affect in any serious way the status or way of life of the upper-income groups. Contact is likely to occur in only a few places—casually on the streets
(but the upper-income groups do not spend much time there) and
casually in stores (but the two income levels are likely to use
different ones).

INCOME LEVELS AND ATTITUDES ON EDUCATION

There is one place, however, where the contact is not casual but i likely to be sustained for long periods of time—and this is the public school, zoned geographically and including indiscriminately within its zones the children of any families that happen to live there. This is not an area of casual contact, which may lead to some grumbling but no action. While we still know all too little about the different styles of life of different income and occupational groups, of different classes and ethnic and racial groups, we do know that there are marked variations in what these groups expect from education for their children, and in the importance they ascribe to education in general. At one extreme, there are groups in which it is common to regard school as a caretaking institution for children, as a necessary legal requirement, as an obstacle to be overcome before the young people can get to work. At the other extreme, there are groups in which the greatest sacrifices are made to get the best possible education for children, in which the qualifications of different schools are carefully weighed, in which the psychological advantages of one approach to education is balanced against its possible disadvantages in preparing children for higher education, in which parents keep in close touch with teachers and principals.

Families and groups vary not only in their attitudes to education but also in their capacity to support their attitudes, whatever they may be. Thus, one family may have highly educated parents, a room for each child, books and records, an atmosphere which encourages the development of the child's intellectual and aesthetic capacities; another family may be quite the opposite. Thus certain attitudes and circumstances support and supplement the school, and, indeed, push it to do more than it ordinarily would; others make it difficult for the school to carry out even the minimal functions of maintaining discipline and teaching elementary skills. And there is little question that there is a high correlation between these attitudes and circumstances relevant to education, on the one hand, and income, occupation, and membership in certain racial and ethnic groups, on the other.

When, then, the school becomes extremely heterogeneous, with children who are ready for and need widely varied educational experiences, its ability to serve one very specialized need, the need of upper-income parents to have their children prepared for advanced education, declines.[3] These parents may respond, at first,

[3] We know all too little about the effects of increasing heterogeneity on education. The upper-income parents are sure this is the effect of the school's

with an increased interest in the public school, increased activity in the Parent Teachers Association, a strong effort to "keep up standards." These efforts become more and more difficult before the influx of children who have little interest in going on to college and who require a relatively elementary education—English, simple reading and writing, and polite manners. Finally the upper-income parents despair and withdraw their children, sending them to private schools or to special public schools for the gifted or talented, if these are available. If the strain of maintaining children in private schools becomes too great, the parents withdraw from the inner city areas, with its high proportion of Negro and Puerto Rican children, to outlying parts of the city or suburbs.

In other areas, the question of race is not involved, nor is even any large-scale population transition to lower-income groups. Certain declining industrial towns in the Northeast have school systems which the upper-income groups consider poor. A combination of aging school plants, low tax revenues, conservative city administrations (and, in some cities, a lack of strong interest in the public school system by important political elements who are committed to the parochial schools), all tend to lead upper-income groups to leave the city for surrounding villages when their children reach school age.

THE HOLDING POWER OF A SCHOOL

But if the decline in the quality of schooling in the eyes of upper-income parents has a powerful effect in leading them to leave the inner city, the existence of schools which do not apparently decline will, on the other hand, have a powerful effect in keeping them from moving.

The school potentially has the power to attract and retain families as well as to repel them. This possibility has, I believe, as yet played little part in the thinking and planning about the problem of retaining upper-income families in the inner city, or of drawing them back. To my knowledge no urban renewal plan, regardless of its extent, has yet seen fit to deliberately use schools

---

having to service larger and larger numbers of children from lower-income homes. I think they are right; but whether they are or not, they *act* on the basis of such a perception. There is no question that their action is also motivated in part by prejudice, in part by the desire to have their children attend high-status schools, with other children from high-status families. However, there is little question that they are also motivated by the real or perceived change in the character of the education their children receive.

as a tool for reshaping residential neighborhoods; and it is significant that most of these plans are concerned only with bringing the
childless well-to-do back into the city, on the assumption that it is
most unlikely that any with children of school age will return.

But how can the school play an independent role in affecting
the population movements into and out of neighborhoods? Does it
not simply *reflect* these movements? For the most part this is at
present true. But if the school were able to maintain its standards
and its character independent of changes in the social composition
of the immediate neighborhood, it could play an independent role,
to some extent, as a brake on these changes. Let us again consider
New York, which of all cities is probably most successful in holding
large numbers of upper-income families with children in the inner
city. In New York this success is in a measure based on the presence of a large number of private schools and some special public
schools, which are unaffected by the change of population around
them. It is these schools that make it possible for many families to
live next to Negroes and Puerto Ricans and nevertheless get in the
city the kind of education they want for their children.

In effect: *the maintenance of residential heterogeneity in New
York City*—and despite the rapid spread of large housing projects
serving one income group, there does still exist great heterogeneity
in residential areas of New York—*depends on the fact that a central need of the family is met by an institution that does not reflect
the composition of the neighborhood.* The heterogeneous neighborhood in New York exists because the upper-income family is not
dependent for education on a school that serves a delimited physical
area. Insofar as it is not limited to a given small geographic area,
the school takes on some of the freedom of the place of work, which
draws its employees from a wide area and which in so doing also
gives freedom to the employee to choose from a wide number of
places of work.

But the New York situation is a very special one indeed, and
even so this special character we have described affects relatively
few families. For the most part, families must depend on the public
schools; these serve given geographic areas; the freedom that the
father expects in choosing a place to work and that the mother
expects in choosing a place to shop is not ordinarily granted in
choosing a place to educate their child. It isn't, that is, unless they
are willing and able to add the cost of private schooling to the
burden of public school taxes they already pay.

HETEROGENEOUS SCHOOLS AND HOMOGENEOUS NEIGHBORHOODS

Under present social circumstances, then, the effect of the geographically limited school, serving a specific area, is to help create a homogeneous residential area and to contribute to patterns of rapid change-over. For, as the arrival of lower-income groups begins to affect the neighborhood school, the tendency to flight is accentuated; or else the effort to maintain the school as it was leads to a more intense resistance to the entry of lower-income groups into residential areas.

We would then suggest a hypothesis that in large urban areas there is an inverse relationship between the degree to which the schools can serve special and differentiated populations and the heterogeneity of residential areas.[4]

This relationship holds of course only in areas with a relatively large number of schools; the school in a small town or village which has only one school is indeed capable of fulfilling the ideal of the neighborhood theorist—serving as an important center for the heterogeneous population of a single community. For in such a town, moving from one section to another does not affect the nature of the schooling available. Education can only be affected by some general communal action to raise the level of the school standards. But where there is a choice between a number of schools, and this choice can be expressed by moving to the area that a school serves, then the hypothesis we have suggested comes into play and a process of segregation of groups (whether defined by income or race) will be reinforced. We are not saying that the undifferentiated school is the only or even the chief cause of residential segregation; but it is one factor in this process—it is associated with it.

Up to this point our examples have come mostly from New York, but the relationship between school segregation in Southern cities will also support our hypothesis. There is no question, for example, that the progress of desegregation in the South will be accompanied by a stricter and stricter residential segregation, just as the unsegregated schools of the North have been associated with a rather stricter residential segregation than has been typical in the South. I do not wish to suggest that the character of the schools

[4] The relationship between the neighborhood, as a reality and idea, and segregation, has already been effectively argued by Reginald Isaacs, *Journal of Housing*, Vol. 5, No. 8, pp. 215–219 (August, 1948).

has been the only factor affecting the degree of residential segrega
tion in North and South; far from it. But it has been one factor
The Southern white was often willing to live closer to the Southern
Negro because he knew that in the crucial area of schooling (as
well as in others) there would be no contact.

One of the reasons that the school has an important role in
speeding the rapid turnover of population is that it often tends to
reflect the beginning of a change more sharply than do other insti
tutions of neighborhood living. The new incoming families are
likely to have many children of school age; the older population
may also be literally "older" and with relatively few children of
school age. While the change in the streets and the stores is small
and there is no change at all in the churches and organizations, the
change in the public school may be startling. The school then contributes to the cycle of events leading to a rapid turnover of population.

WHAT KIND OF URBAN NEIGHBORHOODS?

If this relationship between the undifferentiated school and the segregated neighborhood tends to operate in our cities, is there any
way in which we can make use of it in the planning of urban residential areas? To begin with, we must first be clear as to what we
want in a small urban residential area. I have tended in this discussion to use rather clumsy circumlocutions to refer to what we generally call "neighborhoods." As a matter of fact, as is well known,
the urban residential area may or may not be a neighborhood in
Perry's sense of a place in which significant social relationships are
created by the mere fact of physical proximity and as a place that
is bounded physically by borders. While our cities contain many
neighborhoods of this sort, they also contain good residential areas
which are not really neighborhoods in this sense; and these areas
are particularly typical of the inner city. There the neighborhood
or the community consists rather of a variety of social neighborhoods or communities occupying the same physical space. For, just
as the city makes possible a wide choice of places to work, spread
over a large physical area, it also makes possible a wide choice of
neighbors or social "communities" spread over a large physical
area.

What then do we seek in small urban residential areas? Traditionally we have sought stability of population, on the assumption
(often but not always reasonable) that a stable population indi-

ates a satisfied and happy one. The physical plan, with its standards for housing and traffic and its provision of amenities, has
argely been justified as a contributor to stability. Recently, however, we have added another goal for small urban residential
areas—heterogeneity. In part this goal reflects our aims for society
n general; in part it reflects our feeling that a homogeneous neigh-
porhood is an uninteresting one and deprives us of some of the possible advantages of living in a large and varied city.

I have suggested that there is a relationship between the stability and heterogeneity of small urban residential areas and the
nature of the schools that serve them, and that the typical relationship of the public school to a fixed geographical area tends to reinforce homogeneity and, in times of population transition, to under-
mine stability. This relationship suggests the desirability of special
schools, serving different needs and perhaps different groups—in
effect, it suggests the desirability of making part of the schooling
of children independent of fixed geographical residence. Obviously
the goal of stable and social neighborhoods is only one social goal;
it may conflict with others; and on occasion it may have to be sur-
rendered for higher values.

Concretely, I would urge the extension of the partial pattern
that exists in New York, in which special high schools exist for science, for music and art, and for a large variety of special kinds of
training. It is this pattern which leads many parents to remain in
New York who might otherwise move out to educate their children
at the good comprehensive high schools of the suburbs. The special
advantage a big city has in being able to support a specialized high
school counteracts its special disadvantages as a place to raise
children.

THE SPECIALIZED SCHOOL IN
NEIGHBORHOOD FORMATION

I believe this pattern could be generalized downward with larger
geographic areas being served by junior high schools and the
higher grades of elementary schools. Parents who were not particularly interested in the content of their children's education could
send them to the nearest school. Those who had special interests—in
college-preparatory programs, in special music and arts programs,
in a somewhat more progressive or more traditional education—
would seek those they preferred among the array of schools made
possible by a process of differentiation or specialization in a large
system.

There are incidental advantages in this type of relationship between school and residence that are considerable. The terrible battles over zoning that today take place in Northern cities and the unhealthy concern with the percentages of Negroes and Puerto Ricans and whites might be replaced with a real concern for what is at issue—the quality of education. Just as the upper-income parent with a concern for certain special values in education could send his child out of his "district" to find a "better school," so could the lower-income parent. An enormously fertile source for civic conflict would be obviated by replacing the concern for proportions of Negroes and whites with concern for the quality of education.

Yet another consequence of this approach to the school should be pointed out. As our cities get larger and larger, as greater and greater numbers of people must be accommodated in urban areas, our tendency to seek mass solutions to the problems of residence, schooling, and the like becomes greater and greater. By a mass solution I mean the design of an area using a single repeated unit to house 10,000 people of one income level, or the construction of twenty or a hundred schools to a single model. The mass solution is not only architectural, it is also administrative. Every school in the system is handled like every other school, it is supposed to have exactly the same curriculum, and it handles its students in exactly the same way. The virtues of a big city should mean that some schools may be very different from others; their differences might help to create a somewhat different quality in the residential area around them, as some people chose the area just for the school (and as this happened these areas would indeed become, in some measure, communities). The distinctive school might help to define or name or give character to an otherwise anonymous residential area rather more effectively than a school which differs from other schools only in name. The largest communal building that is visible in any residential area is usually the school. If it had a distinctive character in its building and its functioning, it might have many effects, both direct and subtle, on its surrounding area, in the same way, though on a smaller scale, that a college may have a beneficial effect on its neighborhood, even though its students and its faculty are drawn from distant areas.

PLANNERS AND EDUCATORS

These suggestions that derive from an analysis of the relation of the school to neighborhood change lie outside the normal administrative province of the professional planner. He may be consulted

n the number of schools needed or on their localities, but he has
othing to do with the administrative setup of the school system or
/ith its curricular content. To say that the building up of a good
ieighborhood depends in part on a good school may be true enough,
ut what can the planner do about it?

I have no imperialistic scheme for planners to take over the
rovince of education. However, we must distinguish between the
lanner as the analyst of the urban environment, who traces
hrough consequences of certain actions and developments, and the
lanner in his administrative capacity, with fixed and delimited
unctions. The planner, as analyst, may and should analyze every-
hing that contributes to the specific qualities of the urban envi-
onment and to its characteristic developmental processes. In this
apacity, for example, he cannot ignore the effect of the private
schools of New York on the composition of its population and on
ertain characteristics of its residential areas. He cannot ignore the
 potential impact of a change from the present system of a fixed
geographic zone for each elementary school. When these effects are
identified it becomes a matter of general public concern which goals
are to be sought, which sacrificed.

The ideal of the "neighborhood school" is a strong one in
American life and it has many values. To design a neighborhood in
relation to a school is a piece of elementary wisdom—elementary
wisdom which is not to be found in the design of most residential
areas, single-family or multiple-dwelling, in this country. And yet
one must also see that the values of the neighborhood school are
considerably diluted in a large city and may serve there only to
reinforce a pattern of segregation, itself susceptible to rapid
change if relatively minor changes occur. When the urban residential area is no longer a real community, then the neighborhood
school at best only leads strangers with different aspirations to rub
shoulders, often to their mutual disadvantage. I say "at best"
because, as a matter of fact, the different social elements will tend
rapidly to separate, either by the physical movement away of certain groups or by attempts to solve their schooling problems outside
the public education system.

Once this principle is accepted, the fairly subtle use of the
instrument of the school in planning becomes possible. If one is
interested, as New York is, in "conserving" certain neighborhoods
—which means maintaining the proportion of upper-income people in them—then a relatively simple means to assist this end is
the provision of special schools. Thus, if the West Side had had two
or three special schools, such as the Hunter elementary school,
the elaborate clearance and rebuilding and rehabilitation operations

now proceeding there, which will involve in the end hundreds of millions of dollars, might well have been quite unnecessary. Certainly one such school in the Columbia University neighborhood would have helped greatly to preserve it as it was in 1945.[5]

Admittedly many questions of public policy are involved in such proposals, and it would be fruitless to argue them all here. The purpose of this article is to suggest that a more active place for the school in the design and preservation of urban residential areas might be considered. The school plays such a role in any case; with more intense analysis, it might play it better.

[5] The suggestion of such a school in the University of Chicago neighborhood for purposes of retaining upper-income and faculty groups was made many years ago by Martin Meyerson; that suggestion was the kernel of the present comment.

INDEX

Migration
of Negroes, 320, 375, 376, 388-389, 405
during World War I, 385
during World War II, 386
poverty and, 22
in underdeveloped countries, 5, 22
urbanization through, 96
Miller, Delbert C., 188
"Industry and Community Power Structure: A Comparative Study of an American and English City," 202-212
Mills, C. Wright, 199, 240*n*
Millspaugh, Martin, 399*n*
Milwaukee, Wis.
extended families in, 255*n*, 256
psychosis in, 319, 321
Miner, H., 111, 119
Minneapolis, Minn., 176
urban renewal in, 376
Minneapolis-Honeywell, 169
Minor civil divisions, 69
Mobility
extended family cohesion and, 239-252
implications for urban life of, 102
psychosis and, 324
residential, 230
suburban, 154-155
Moide, Germany, 271
Monterrey, Mexico, 36
Montevideo, Uruguay, 28, 29, 31
Montgomery, Ala., 63
Morris, R. N., 91
Moscow, U.S.S.R., 21
Mowrer, Ernest W., 322
Mumford, Lewis, 63, 94, 181*n*, 359, 365
My Brother's Keeper (Baker), 277*n*
Myrdal, Gunnar, 85, 189, 224, 228, 232-233, 234

Nashville, Tenn., 63
National Advisory Commission on Civil Disorders, 308
"Conditions of Life in the Racial Ghetto," 345-358
National integration, 81
National Opinion Research Center, 224
Nazis, 271
Negro Ghetto, The (Weaver), 395
Negroes
church membership of, 235
extended families of, 251
living conditions in ghettoes of 345-358
middle class, 361, 393, 395, 395
housing for, 391-392, 399
migration to urban areas of 320, 375, 376, 388-389, 405
during World War I, 385
during World War II, 386
movement out of cities of, 392
in public schools, 407, 408, 412
rate of schizophrenia among 320-321, 323-324
Southern, 409-410
urban renewal and, 372
relocation, 372
voluntary associations of, 223-23
extent of membership, 227-22
friendship and, 230-231
home ownership and, 230
marital status and, 229-230
religious affiliation and, 230
residential mobility and, 230
social class background and 228-229
in Watts riot
McCone Commission views or 330-331
racial conditions in U.S. and 342-343, 344
relation between police and 329, 336-338
unemployment among, 335-33
Neighborhood relations, 295-303
emergency help in, 297-300
friendliness as factor in, 296-29
normative element in, 268-285
hostility and conflict, 282-28
law and, 283-284
in rural communities, 269-27
vs. the sentimental, 280-282
in towns and cities, 274-280
preservation of privacy in 300-303
suburban, 286-294
meaning of homogeneity in 289-290
role of propinquity in, 292-29

variations in homogeneity in, 290-292

New Haven, Conn., 322

New Orleans, La., 62, 63, 133
annexation by, 391

New York, N.Y., 6, 13, 21, 46, 145n, 172, 385
education in, 175
functional specialization of, 63
growth of, 13, 53
low-income families in, 354-355, 357
national influence of, 48, 49
outward movement from, 376
residential heterogeneity in, 405, 408
sanitation in, 353
urban renewal in, 373, 397-398

Nigeria, indigenous urbanization in, 92, 111-122

Non-bureaucratic careers, 246-249

Norfolk, Va., 62

Nuclear family, 100-101, 127

Oakland, Calif., 133

Oberschall, Anthony, 308
"The Los Angeles Riot of August, 1965," 327-344

Octopus Towns (Verhaeren), 80

Oedobo, kingdom of, 115

Ogane (King of Ife), 115

Ogbomosho, Nigeria, 114-121

Oklahoma City, Okla., 59

Oktyabrskiy, U.S.S.R., 19

Omaha, Neb., 62
delinquency in, 317
psychosis in, 319

Ondo, Nigeria, 112

Organization Man, The (Whyte), 136, 157

Oroya, Peru, 35

Overcrowding, harmful effects of, 84-87

Oyo, Nigeria, 114-115,121

Panama, 21

Panama City, Panama, 28, 31

Paotow, China, 19

Parasocial intimacy, 175

Paris, France, 49
during Renaissance, 9

Park, Robert E., 314n

Park Forest, Ill., 150-156, 161, 162, 164, 166, 172, 291, 293
communal controls in, 183
companionship in, 175

Park Merced, Calif., 150

Parker, William, 330, 344

Parsons, Talcott, 189, 237-238, 240n, 242, 252

Patricelli, Robert, 353n

Pasadena, Calif., 63

Pasteur, Louis, 10

Paterson, N.J., 63

Paz del Rio, Colombia, 36

Peasants, in third world countries, 81
standard of living of, 82

Pellegrin, Roland J., 188
Coates and, "Absentee-Owned Corporations and Community Power Structure," 191-201

Peoria, Ill., 319

Pereira, D. P., 115

Perry, Clarence, 403

Personality of urban dweller, 126

Peru, pre-Columbian, 2

Petersen, William, 359, 360
"On the Concept of Urbanization Planning," 362-368

Philadelphia, Pa., 13, 53, 145n, 156
decline of central city in, 371
delinquency in, 316
racial transition of neighborhoods in, 390
urban renewal in, 374, 376

Philadelphia Commission on Human Relations, 390n

Philippines, 363

Phoenix, Ariz., 63

Pike, James, 337

Pittsburgh, Pa., 62

Place, Francis, 11

Planning
city, 362-364
deductive, 365-366
ideological, 364-365
inductive, 367-368
schools as instrument in, 403-414
heterogenous schools and homogenous neighborhoods, 409-410